CORN Publication Series 17

All authors publishing in the CORN Series have been invited by the editors. All articles are intensively discussed at preparatory meetings, reviewed by the book editors and double blind peer reviewed by external reviewers.

ISBN 978-2-503-58509-3

E-ISBN 978-2-503-58510-9

DOI 10.1484/M.CORN-EB.5.117649

ISSN 1780-3225

E-ISSN 2565-9413

Printed in the EU on acid-free paper.

D/2019/0095/180

Stocks, seasons and sales

Food supply, storage and markets in Europe and the New World, *c.* 1600-2000

Edited by

Wouter Ronsijn, Niccolò Mignemi and Laurent Herment

BREPOLS

CONTENTS

LIST OF FIGURES

Chapter 5

Chapter 6

LIST OF TABLES

Preface

Most of the chapters presented in this volume are the result of three meetings organised by the editors in 2014 and 2015: the session *Rhythm and Evolution of Staple Food Markets, 1650-1950*, at the European Social Science History Conference in Vienna, April 2014; the session *Storage of Staple Food and Commercial Networks from the late Middle Ages to the Twentieth Century* at the Rural History Conference in Girona, September 2015, and the conference *Gérer la pénurie, gouverner l'abondance: dynamiques du stockage et de l'approvisionnement dans le secteur agroalimentaire (XVIIIe-XXe siècles)* held at the École française de Rome in October 2015.

These meetings would not have been possible without the financial support of the GDRI-CRICEC CNRS and the CORN research network funded by the FWO. The workshop in Rome (29th-30th October 2015) would not have been possible without the financial and logistical support of the École française de Rome, the Institut français Italia, the Université Franco Italienne/Università Italo Francese, the Permanent Representation of France to FAO, WFP, IFAD, and the UNESCO Chair in World Food Systems at Montpellier SupAgro. The GDRI-AAA CNRS kindly provided funding for several chapters in the volume. All of the chapters have gone through the procedure of double-blind peer review.

We, the editors, especially wish to thank the authors of all the chapters. Without their hard work this book would not have been possible.

Wouter Ronsijn

Niccolò Mignemi

Laurent Herment

Introduction: stocks, seasons and sales

Wouter Ronsijn, History Department, Ghent University, and Dondena Centre for Research on Social Dynamics and Public Policy, Bocconi University Milan

Niccolò Mignemi, Équipe de recherches pour l'histoire du monde rural, CRH-CNRS-EHESS (Paris)

I. Introduction

Food is back on the international agenda. With more than half of the global population living in cities and no longer involved in producing food, the global population expected to reach 10 billion people in a few decades, increasing stress on the agricultural and ecological systems upon which we rely for our food, and the adverse effects of market liberalisation, the threat of widespread food insecurity again looms. To many, the global food crisis of 2007-08 announced the end of cheap food and the beginning of a structural crisis in the global food system (Holt-Giménez and Patel, 2009; Vanhaute, 2011; McMichael, 2013; Moore, 2016).

The creation and management of food stocks, either by producers, consumers, traders, households, governments or NGOs is considered a crucial indicator for the risk of food insecurity. The four dimensions of food security, as defined at the 1996 World Food Summit are the physical *availability* of food (through production, stocks and trade), economic and physical *access* to food (among others through purchasing power), efficient *utilisation* of food (through dietary practices, adequate preparation, intra-household distribution) and finally the *stability* of the three previous dimensions *over time* (EC – FAO Food Security Programme, 2008). Food storage has a role to play in all four dimensions, as it has the potential to make diverse types of food physically available in places where or at times when it is not produced, to keep its price levels within reach of consumers, and to moderate inter-seasonal and inter-annual price swings.

Storage and distribution of food bridge the gap between the point where food is available and the point where it is consumed. This gap can be geographical, temporal or social: food needs to be transported from the place of production to the place of consumption, it needs to be preserved from the moment it is harvested or mature to the moment it becomes a meal, and it needs to be distributed from the producers to the consumers. Hence there is need for transportation, storage and reallocation. This book is about these activities, without which, according the Giovanni Arrighi, "[a]lmost no trade activity can be undertaken". In his own words:

> The reshuffling of goods in space and time, which is what trade is all about, can involve as much human effort and can add as much use-value ("utility") to the goods so reshuffled as does extracting them from nature and changing their form and substance, which is what we understand by production in the narrow sense. As Abbé Galiani once wrote,

Stocks, seasons and sales: Food supply, storage and markets in Europe and the New World, c. 1600-2000, ed. by Wouter Ronsijn, Niccolò Mignemi and Laurent Herment, CORN 17 (Turnhout, 2019), pp. 1-17.

 DOI: 10.1484/M.CORN-EB.5.118251

> "[t]ransport … is a kind of manufacture" […] But so is storage and all other trade-related activities that require human effort and make the goods reshuffled in space and time more useful to potential buyers than they would have been otherwise. (Arrighi, 1994: 177)

This description clearly brings out the value and usefulness of the "reshuffling of goods in space and time", but focuses strongly on the commercial function of storage. Food is not always stored merely to sell it at a profit, but also to have food reserves that are not in the first place meant to be sold, but merely to be eaten. Although the latter can also have obvious economic advantages, adequate food stores and supplies are a factor in ensuring nutritional as well as social and political stability (Bruegel, 2009). Control over stocks, whether private or public, is a source of power over people. This makes food storage and distribution into a conflict area where private interests have always coexisted with public concerns over the organisation and regulation of agro-food issues, a laboratory for different forms of regulation and management of the food trade, and a place where the professional world and administrative bodies can meet, collide or collude.

The contributions to this volume all question how actors in the past – producers, consumers, processors, merchants, governments – dealt with these issues. They focus on how people with stocks monitored market prices to decide whether to sell or not, on the enormous challenges large urban areas faced to ensure its inhabitants are properly fed, and on the attempts by central governments to use storage as a means to offer stability for both consumers and producers. Ten chapters present case-studies from Austria, Belgium, France, Germany, Great Britain, Italy and Mexico, ranging from the seventeenth to the twentieth century. Together, they highlight the many aspects involved in the reshuffling of goods in space and time, and provide new answers to old and new questions.

II. Stocks, seasons and sales in historiography: measuring storage costs and carry-over

As storage is connected to a vast array of fields – economic, political, social – so it is intimately connected to many topics in historiography (even though more often than not it is limited to grain). Historians have thought and written about storage when considering the inner workings of agricultural holdings and their ties to markets and intermediaries (e.g. Meuvret, 1977; 1987; 1988); the long-distance trade in farm products (e.g. van Tielhof, 2002); the economic relations between town and countryside (e.g. Galloway, 2000; Revel, 1975; Grantham, 1997); the "politics of provisions" and maintenance of social and political tranquillity (e.g. Thompson, 1971; Kaplan, 1982; Bohstedt, 2010); the threat of famine (e.g. Alfani and Ó Gráda, 2017; Collet and Schuh, 2018); as well as the connection between the socio-economic environment and the material history of rural and agricultural life (e.g. Gast and Sigaut, 1979-1985).

There is no room here to discuss the wide array of topics in which storage is a crucial element. Instead, we will focus on the extensive debate on grain storage strictly speaking. The influence on this debate of McCloskey and Nash' 1984 article on storage in medieval England still looms large. McCloskey and Nash (1984) reacted against Stefano Fenoaltea's (1976) claim that medieval peasants protected themselves against the risk of harvest failure by storing grain from the previous harvest, rather than by scattering fields as McCloskey (1972) had claimed before. In reply to Fenoaltea, McCloskey and Nash argued that the level of storage was only small and sporadic, due to its high cost. These storage costs consisted of barn costs, grain spoilt, a possible drop in grain prices, but were mainly determined by high interest rates. High interest rates created high opportunity costs for grain storage: the foregone interest on the capital tied up in the grain was substantial. After the Middle Ages, storage costs dropped significantly, primarily due to a drop in interest rates.

Two aspects of McCloskey and Nash' contribution warrant further discussion: the method they used to estimate storage costs, and their concept of man as *homo œconomicus*. First, McCloskey and Nash derived storage costs from seasonal patterns in grain prices. Earlier, Paul Samuelson (1957) had discussed the idea behind this. In the model he formulated, the price of a crop harvested once per year, such as grain, in autumn, will increase steadily throughout the year, reaching its maximum just before the next harvest in the following autumn. When the new harvest comes in, prices will drop to their initial level. The seasonal price increase equals storage costs, the cost it takes to "transport" the grain from one point in time to another. Samuelson understood that this was a simplified model, and that uncertainty in the real world interfered with it. However, all things being equal, seasonal patterns in grain prices will display a sawtooth pattern: year after year, prices will rise after the harvest in accordance with storage costs, and collapse with the next harvest.

Before Samuelson, a sawtooth pattern in grain prices was already described by Ernest Labrousse (1932: 160-162) in his doctoral dissertation on eighteenth-century French price history. Labrousse found that grain prices were low during and shortly after harvest, and high in the months preceding the next harvest, from May to July. However, instead of referring to storage costs, Labrousse pointed to changes in supply and demand to explain this seasonal pattern. Smallholders sold most of their grain in the months immediately following the harvest, either because they needed money or lacked the infrastructure to store the grain adequately. These sales glutted the market and depressed prices. Later in the agricultural year, during the *soudure* when supplies from the last harvest were running out and the new harvest was still standing in the fields, prices rose. At that time, smallholders were in need of extra supplies and bought them, at elevated prices, from those who had been able to store grain, such as large landowners or tithe collectors. As Labrousse admitted, this seasonal cycle was much more outspoken during crisis years than during years with low prices.

Assuming the sawtooth-model of seasonal price development to be correct and to reflect storage costs, McCloskey and Nash (1984: 180) estimated the annual cost to store wheat at about 30 to 40 per cent of its value. This was close to being prohibitively high, and supports their claim that not much more than about five per cent of the harvest was carried over into the next harvest year (McCloskey and Nash, 1984: 178).

After McCloskey and Nash, others have also looked at whether grain prices exhibited a recognisable seasonal pattern, and whether it conforms to the model outlined above. Gregory Clark (2015: 275-279), in one of the most recent contributions to the debate, found a seasonal pattern in grain prices in medieval England which largely followed the sawtooth pattern: low grain prices around harvest, rising prices until February, declining prices after May. However, the amplitude of this cycle was much lower, with an annual rise of about 12 per cent. This implies that storage costs were much lower than McCloskey and Nash estimated, and hence that storage was more extensive.

Others, working on continental Europe during a later period, did not find such a seasonal pattern. In Nuremberg (1498-1855) (Bauernfeind, Reutter et al., 2001: 287-290), Saxony (1763-1874) (Uebele, Grünebaum et al., 2013: 8-9) and Chartres (1748-1790) (Béaur, 2007: 95-99), grain prices did not follow the sawtooth pattern very closely. Rather, grain prices tended to be high (not low), around and/or shortly after harvest time, and to drop (not rise), during winter and spring. A similar pattern is implied in Persson's (1996: 700) figures for expected returns in Cologne, Siena and Pisa (1550-1700). Moreover, these seasonal patterns were very weak. The r^2-values reported by Bauernfeind et al., as well as by McCloskey and Nash were very low (0.07 and below), indicating the time expired since harvest is a very weak predictor of the price increase since harvest. Likewise, Persson (1996: 700-701) emphasised that the standard deviations of the expected gross returns from storage by month (reflecting price increases) were very high. All of this means that seasonal patterns were quite erratic, and that market participants faced enormous uncertainty about the prices that would prevail in the course of the harvest year.

Can it be that some of the assumptions behind the sawtooth-model are wrong, if seasonal patterns in grain prices deviated from it, or did not follow it at all? One crucial assumption, the validity of which has come under severe attack, is that of the profit-maximising individual. The sawtooth-model assumes that historical actors stored grain, i.e. postponed its sale, only if the cost of storage was covered by a higher price at the time of sale. If storage costs exceeded the seasonal price difference, economic actors had no incentive to do so, and little or no grain was stored. On average, market prices could not decrease before the next harvest arrives. If they did, it would imply that too much grain had been put in store, glutting the market before the next harvest. Because of uncertainty about future harvest results, this might occasionally happen before an above-average harvest, but on average market participants, if they are rational and profit-maximising, should "get it right". If on the contrary prices were to decrease systematically before the next harvest, it would imply that the size of the next harvest was consistently underestimated, and that market participants who stored grain throughout the harvest year systematically did so at a loss (Bauernfeind, Reutter et al., 2001: 283-284, 294; Uebele, Grünebaum et al., 2013: 6).

John Komlos and Richard Landes (1991: 42) have called McCloskey and Nash' approach ahistorical by "collaps[ing] the distinction between medieval and modern economic behaviour" and "believ[ing] that the atomized, self-interested, and calculating individual was as typical of the Middle Ages as of our own time." Other scholars have suggested that pre-modern peasants and farming families may have had other motivations besides balancing their account books. In this regard, Nicholas Poynder (1999: 14-17) speaks of the "convenience yield" of storage: preserving grain may have had other benefits beside financial gain. Storing grain entailed risks, but could mitigate others. Among such other risks, hunger was primordial. As Komlos and Landes (1991: 37) emphasised, as staple food "grain stocks are not quite like any other form of investment." Robert Fogel (1989: 26) believed that demand for grain stocks was highly price inelastic, i.e. grain was stored with little regard to its price. Jean Meuvret (1988: 19) concluded that "we should interpret stocks formed by food producers as a guarantee of food security, and not as a means of commercial speculation." He pointed out that even during dearth, family stocks were not consumed, out of fear that one year of dearth might be followed by another. It seems safe to assume that peasants did not find the grain from last harvest less nourishing if its market value had fallen below the hypothetical storage cost.

Because the evidence for continental Europe does not match the sawtooth-model, either due to the timing or the erratic character of the seasonal cycle, several scholars have recognised that there is probably more at play than merely profit-maximising strategies. Bauernfeind et al. (2001: 294) concluded that the pattern in rye prices points towards a "cautionary savings motive": peasants held on to supplies before winter, only to release them when information on the next harvest became available. Persson's (1996: 701-702) finding that seasonal patterns in grain prices were highly uncertain brought him to the conclusion that "inventories were held primarily as a sort of insurance against unexpected events, to cover private consumption in the current harvest year, and for short-term speculation." Long-term storage, beyond the harvest year, would instead be confined to actors operating on a larger scale, with access to more and better information, and with substantial financial reserves to cover for potential losses that they were bound to incur frequently.

While the motivations for intra-year storage remain unclear, several scholars have been able to show that grain was indeed frequently carried over into the next harvest year. While seasonal patterns are used to estimate the *cost* of storage *within* the harvest year, autocorrelation in annual grain prices is used to estimate whether there *is* storage *between* harvest years. If the price of one year is found to influence the price of the next year, i.e. if annual prices are autocorrelated, then this is believed to be the result of carry-over storage. Without any carry-over, prices will rise and fall according to harvest outcomes, whereas storage for longer than one harvest year will smooth prices. An abundant harvest will depress prices and enable a relatively large carry-over, which will depress prices also the next year, even if the next harvest is less than abundant. In contrast, harvest failure will raise prices and reduce the carry-over, and prices will tend to remain relatively high the next harvest year. Autocorrelation in grain prices has been attested for England from the Middle Ages throughout the pre-industrial period by Nielsen (1997: 16-17), Poynder (1999: 18-19) and Clark (2015: 279-280). While admitting that grain storage between harvests may have been smaller before 1350 than afterwards, Clark (2015: 268-269) concludes that carry-over storage had an impact on market prices since at least the twelfth century. For the whole preindustrial period the carry-over could comprise about 40 per cent of the harvest in years with very low prices (Clark, 2015: 281). This is close to Davenant's 1699 figure, cited by Fogel (1989: 14), of about 30-40 per cent of the harvest in normal circumstances being carried over into the next year.

Another method to identify storage is to look at the effect of harvest outcomes on annual prices. McCloskey and Nash (1984: 178) found medieval English grain prices to be strongly determined by harvest results from the same year, and only occasionally by the previous years' harvest, when the latter had been considerably above average. This is in accordance with their claim of low levels of storage, later refuted by Clark (2015). Using data on Swedish harvest results from 1666 to 1870, Edvinsson (2012: 10) found that grain prices in the current year were influenced by the previous year's harvest and that this effect became stronger over time. Furthermore, for the nineteenth century, current prices were also influenced by harvest results from two years previous. This indicates the existence and growing impact of carry-over. It remains unclear, however, how much grain was carried over. For Saxony from 1790 to 1830 Uebele et al. (2013: 13, 24-25) have data on the actual volume of carry-over storage and found that it comprised only two per cent of the harvest.

Also in the study of carry-over storage, scholars argue back and forth on the motivations behind it. Nielsen used his finding that grain prices were autocorrelated against Fogels' claim that grain was stored regardless of prices. According to Nielsen (1997: 21), his results supported the profit-maximising model of storage. To this, Ejrnaes and Persson (1999: 768-769) replied that autocorrelation in grain prices does not prove market participants aimed at maximising profits. Instead, it is also consistent with cultivators following thumb rules, rather than price signals, to smooth their own consumption. Uebele et al. (2013: 26), testing the actual volume of carry-over storage against price and harvest fluctuations, found that storage responded both to harvest results and price signals independently. More grain was stored when prices were low, but also when harvests were large regardless of prices. This, according to them "supports a view of precautionary saving and consumption smoothing independent of market signals"; in the end, they adhered to the reconciliatory view that "[s]torage decisions were a mix of commercial and precautionary behaviour."

III. Stocks, seasons and sales in historiography: social, political and technical aspects of grain storage

In order for the debate to move further, it is necessary to address several questions that have been raised, whether or not explicit. The first among these is which actors did the actual storing of grain, and how their behaviour might have affected the market. For instance, Brunt and Cannon (1999: 14) reject Komlos and Landes' view that most grain was stored by peasants. Instead, they claim medieval agriculture was "dominated by religious institutions", and point out that the data they used was taken from manors owned by Oxford colleges "supervised by the most educated minority in the country", i.e. people who were likely "capable of recognising and exploiting seasonal patterns in grain prices." According to Persson, long-term grain conservation was mainly the domain of large-scale merchants (cfr. supra). Meuvret (1988: 13-38) claimed that the largest stocks were found at the intermediate level of *fermiers* and large urban *amodiateurs* (landlords receiving rents in kind). The majority of food producers below this level rarely had stocks exceeding household needs. Above this level, there were people and institutions collecting dues in kind such as tithes, feudal dues, rents in kind or sharecropping rents. Yet the latter stocks, while substantial, were not always physically centralised, and often redistributed: religious institutions or hospitals needed them for their own members, the sick and the poor, while rural elites used them to support their labourers, servants or other fellow villagers. Meuvret (1988: 22) pointed out that these were stocks not compiled for commercial purposes but rather as a result of a social arrangement, and that trade could do nothing but adjust itself to this situation.

Indeed, two institutions in the premodern period at times amassed stocks that they could use to act against the market: religious institutions and public authorities. Large supplies of grain amassed as tithes by religious institutions or as rents by lords could be used to feed the poor or to bring down market prices in times of dearth (Fenoaltea, 1976: 133;

Zylbergeld, 1973: 281-284; Eiden and Irsigler, 2000: 46-47). During the French Revolution, in the discussion on the abolition of tithes, those in favour of preserving them underlined their importance as a possible palliative against dearth. Considering this charitable role of tithes, Mathieu Arnoux (2010: 156-157 and 2012: 250-255) argued that in principle holders of tithe grain did not fully possess it (i.e. could not sell it) until it was carried over into the next harvest year, and the threat of dearth during the previous harvest year was averted. Jessica Dijkman (2017: 22-30), in a comparative study of three regions in the North Sea Area, found that urban authorities started making emergency grain purchases in the fifteenth and sixteenth centuries. They did so during food crises, with the intent of selling the grain (or bread) at below-market prices. In contrast, attempts to establish more permanent public granaries, buying grain when it was cheap and selling it cheap when market prices were high, were rarer in this region, and usually did not last long (see also Kaplan, 1977 and 1984). Conversely, further to the east and south of Europe permanent public granaries were more prevalent (Aymard, 1966; Collet, 2010; Bauernfeind, Reutter et al., 2001: 284-286; Warde, 2007: 476-479; Corritore, 2012).

Since Antiquity, the Mediterranean was peculiar, as public and private provisioning systems normally coexisted to ensure the food supply of cities and towns. Public and municipal forms of storage were widespread and intended to regulate prices and prevent subsistence crises, as shown by detailed local studies such as those on Rome (Revel, 1972 and 1975; Strangio, 1999; Martinat, 2004), Venice (Faugeron, 2014; Vertecchi, 2009 and 2012), Lyon (Martinat, 2008 and 2012), Madrid and other Spanish cities (Bernardos Sanz, 2008; Mateos Royo, 2008 and 2011; Muñoz Navarro, 2012), and the Mediterranean seaports such as Ragusa (Dubrovnik) and Naples (D'Atri, 2008 and 2012; Marin, 2012) in the medieval and early modern periods. Following geographical and chronological contexts, these systems varied both in terms of purposes and actors involved. However, their long-term resilience has to be interpreted more as the sign of their efficacy and adaptability, than of the Mediterranean decline in changing world-economies, as suggested by the collective book edited by Brigitte Marin and Catherine Virlouvet (2004) on food provisioning, trade circuits and urban markets. The economic rationale for these and other public interventions in food markets, as discussed for instance by Persson (1996), is found among other reasons in the highly uncertain character of seasonal price fluctuations, as well as the drop back to initial price levels after harvest, which precludes any gain to be made from carry-over storage. It also suggests a moral economy of the *giusto prezzo* ("just price") as observed in the Roman case (Martinat, 2004, see also Fogel, 1989; Nielsen, 1997).

What this brief overview shows is that grain was obtained and stored by diverse actors operating under very diverse circumstances. While some obtained it by working the land, whether or not paying rent and wages, others merely collected it, or paid it with public funds. Therefore, a market price that would constitute a loss for one might for another more than cover for storage costs. The problem with using market prices is that the behaviour of all these different actors is aggregated. That makes it extremely difficult for scholars to read actors' motivations from price patterns. Furthermore, as market integration advances, the behaviour of local actors has ever less influence on market prices.

Another issue that is mostly absent from econometric studies of grain storage, is the technical aspect. The importance of this factor has been mentioned several times, but it certainly needs further study. Bart Taub (1987: 1051) suggested that storage costs could decline in the course of the harvest year, as grain would be taken first from those locations where it was most likely to get spoilt. Poynder (1999: 9) indicated that larger farmers may have faced higher storage costs than others, because they tended to store grain in barns, possibly as protection against theft, while others mostly stored grain in ricks in the open air. Finally, there is the issue of how storage costs evolved through time. McCloskey and Nash (1984: 182) claimed that "[n]o changes occurred in the character and cost of barns that would explain the fall in total costs from medieval to early modern times", a claim which Komlos and Landes (1991: 41-42) contested (see also Poynder, 1999: 10).

Current insight into the technical aspects of grain storage owes much to the efforts of François Sigaut (Sigaut, 1978; Gast and Sigaut, 1979-1985). Within Europe in the premodern period, Sigaut (1988: 21-24) distinguished three different systems. In the *Mediterranean system*, the entire grain harvest is threshed and winnowed at once, and the grain is stored in bulk, usually in underground silos, but also in granaries. The *Atlantic Coast system* was a variation of the Mediterranean, with the chief difference that, while grain was threshed in the Mediterranean system by animals treading on the stalks, in the Atlantic Coast system men threshed the grain using flails. The *North European system* differed substantially from both other systems in that grain was stored in sheaves which were not threshed immediately but only later, during winter and spring. Whereas grain in the Mediterranean and Atlantic Coast systems became available immediately after harvest, in the North European system the grain was released only piecemeal, as it was gradually threshed in the months following harvest. In the latter system, sheaves were stored either in barns or in open-air stacks or ricks. Sigaut (1988: 16) believed such open-air ricks "were first an occasional addition to the barn for exceptionally plentiful harvests" and became "a regular mode of storage in modern times only", i.e. possibly from the seventeenth century onwards.

Surely we can expect these regional differences in the timing of threshing to influence seasonal price patterns. That much of the grain in the North European system was made ready for the market only months after the harvest goes against the assumption of almost instantly available harvests in the sawtooth-model. Despite high interest rates and storage costs, grain was stored for at least part of the year because labour needed to be available to thresh it (see also Herment and Ronsijn, 2015: 71-75). This being the case, we can expect seasonal patterns in grain prices to be determined not only by interest rates and storage costs (McCloskey and Nash, Taub), by seasonal patterns in demand and supply (Labrousse) and transportation costs (Komlos and Landes), but perhaps also by seasonally variable labour costs.

Lacking preliminary studies, Sigaut could only speculate on how the three systems originated and developed. However, McCloskey and Nash' claim of virtually constant costs for the construction of barns from medieval to early modern times is, if not incorrect, beside the point. Barn space was used for other purposes beside storage, barns were not the only storage technology, and the efficiency of storage and cleaning technologies developed over time, reducing grain loss (Michel, 2015). Part of the barn was reserved for threshing, while some open space between walls and sheaves was required for ventilation. Large harvests could therefore bring with them a more than proportionately larger need for storage space, though the construction of larger barns might also come with economies of scale. Furthermore, the required amount of storage space depended not only on the amount of grain harvested, but even more the amount of straw. In Normandy, the shift in the nineteenth century from the sickle to the scythe to harvest grain, by cutting it closer to the ground, increased the size of the sheaves by thirty to forty per cent. Due to the resulting lack of space, more grain was stored outside the barns in stacks (Brunet, 1982; Bourdon, 1996). This change in harvest technology shifted the proportion between grain and straw to be stored, and hence affected storage costs per unit of grain and the choice of storage technology. This change took place in different regions at different times: the scythe was introduced in Flanders as early as the fourteenth century (Thoen, 1996: 81). Finally, the straw to which the unthreshed grain remained attached was important as well, to feed farm animals and to make manure, and also entered into the decision how to store and for how long. In the Yorkshire Wolds starting from the late eighteenth century, the design of the so-called "high barn" developed in tandem with winter feeding cattle, to convert straw into manure and thus to improve the fertility of the soil (Hayfield, 1991).

Recently, a number of studies have appeared in history and archaeology that focus specifically on storage in the Middle Ages. These have shed light on the development of storage techniques, but have also broadened the picture, focusing not only on storage by grain producers before sale, as is often the case in the econometric studies. In the northern half of France, Edith Peytremann (2013) found that silos were the main form of grain storage in the Early and High Middle Ages, with granaries and pits for pottery becoming more prevalent. The number and capacity of these facilities grew. Her findings indicate a shift from more private, family-based storage to more centralised facilities. Jean-Michel Poisson (2018) believes the reverse happened in the course of the High and Late Middle Ages. Based on a survey of archaeological research on continental Europe, he showed that individual, private stocks were kept within collective structures (often silos, granaries or cellars near churches, or sacks and pottery within churches), as well as in domestic areas (such as cellars or attics, wooden chests or pottery, sometimes silos and pits). He tentatively concludes that silos became less prominent, whereas small-scale domestic storage facilities appeared more numerously. Mark Gardiner (2013) argued that in Britain before 1200, grain was generally stored unthreshed in ricks, or threshed in wooden chests and pottery. Barns and granaries were rare, until their numbers started growing after 1200, and they became widespread. Jordan Claridge and John Langdon (2011: 1260) showed that, besides this "large-scale end through the prevalence of barns in the countryside", there was also a "small-scale end, particularly in an urban setting." The latter end was informal, private, and not much different from household stocks.

Diverse reasons are cited for these developments. In Britain, barns and granaries, as well as the small-scale informal storage solutions, are associated with the rise of markets for agricultural output. Claridge and Langdon (2011: 1261) describe the development of a "'storage world' […] in tune with the developing commercialisation", a merchant infrastructure allowing grain to be kept safe along rivers or near sea while it was held up during transport from one place to another. Likewise, barns and granaries were a substantial investment in storage infrastructure, which Gardiner (2013: 34-35) suggests aimed at waste reduction and higher gains from market involvement. Yet Niall Brady (1997: 93), in an earlier study, was not convinced that the benefits of barns covered their costs. As he pointed out, "[i]f lords indeed watched their pennies with respect to grain storage, they could have found satisfaction in the far cheaper and quite practical method of outdoor storage in ricks." Rather than cost-benefit analysis, Brady (1997: 78) found a reason for the construction of barns "at least partly in the role [they] played as symbols of prestige and authority."

Peytremann and Poisson came up with other explanations for changes in storage infrastructure. According to Peytremann (2013: 39, 49-52), the expansion of storage facilities in the High Middle Ages responded to economic developments in connection with the growth of towns and military settlements, but also to larger harvests and to the centralisation of harvests by religious institutions (tithes) and elites. Similarly, Poisson (2018: 207-208) connected the shift towards more small-scale, private storage to a decline in yields and possibly higher levies. Yet the latter would at the same time imply more centralised storage by elites. As Gardiner (2013: 34) emphasised, we need to find out "precisely who was investing in the construction of barns and granaries". The same is true for storage infrastructure in general, as this might provide us with clues as to the motivation for their construction, whether commercial, political, social, military or prestigious. This brings us back to the question of who stored grain, and for what reasons.

Since the mid-2000s, several research programs have focused their attention on warehouses and their provisioning networks to analyse the ways storage was organised and connected to trade networks and local food policies, namely in the Mediterranean region since the ancient to early modern period. This long-term perspective has produced rich scientific output and opened new insights in both archaeological and historiographical debates that we can only mention here (Marin and Virlouvet, 2008 and 2016; Chankowski, Lafon and Virlouvet, 2018; Martin, 2019). Thus, drawing up a typology of storage buildings in Ancient Rome, Catherine Virlouvet has particularly underlined the importance of looking at these machines in terms of their functions, organisation, property rights and funding (Bernardos Sanz and Virlouvet, 2016).

Architecture was an important point also in the study of the contemporary silos that transformed the rural landscapes in the nineteenth and twentieth century (Vaquero Piñeiro, 2011; Dorel-Ferré, 2014). However, studying Chicago's interactions with its surrounding western rural frontier, William Cronon (1991) demonstrated that grain elevators were a crucial piece in the process of commodification of agricultural and natural products. Thus, this technical innovation contributed to changing equilibria in the international agricultural markets. At the same time, centralising and storing the agricultural production became a key issue in national political agendas for two reasons: war provisions and market regulation. If the First and the Second World War were of course periods when food storing had priority in government concerns and led to special legislation and innovative solutions for feeding both soldiers and populations, few studies explored in fact this question in wartime circumstances (Dentoni, 1995; Trentmann and Just, 2006; Brassley, Segers and Van Molle, 2012). On the contrary, the interwar period and the consequences of the economic crisis attracted much more the attention of historians. During this period, policies and places devoted to grain storing developed in different geographical and political contexts.

The interwar storing policies have been analysed as laboratories for state regulation and mixed forms of market governance, associating public authorities and farmers' organisations. We can just mention here some examples: farmers' unions and cooperatives confronted to state attempts to regulate the agricultural markets in France (Chatriot,

Leblanc and Lynch, 2012; Chatriot, 2016), the Italian *ammassi* created by the fascist regime but able to persist in the post-war period (Strangio, 2012; Vaquero Piñeiro, 2012), the development of the Canadian pool movement as a global reference (McCollom, 2018). If the regulation of the agricultural markets was a major issue of the emerging forms of transnational cooperation since the second half of the nineteenth century (Nützenadel, 2008: 160-163), important changes took place in Europe and North America during the 1920s-1930s: together with the battle for feeding consumers, the new political and social concern was the protection of prices for local farmers against both overproduction and market fluctuations. On the technical side too, new preservation technologies had emerged, while statistical and information systems were gaining central place because "[c]omplete facts about the fluctuations in total stocks would be of great value in handling the trade-cycle" (Keynes, 1938: 454).

IV. Stocks, seasons and sales in this volume

The contributions gathered for this volume reflect the many challenges and actors involved in food storage and trade from the seventeenth to the twentieth century, in Europe and the New World. Chapters are thematically brought together in three groups, successively focusing on people possessing stocks of food, on urban areas, and on governments. The first three chapters take the point of view of actors possessing grain stocks, either as producers, tithe collectors, or manorial lords, and their storage behaviour. Friederike Scholten considers two noble manors in the Rhineland area between 1650 and 1850, and indicates how uncertainty over future price developments and the state of roads influence storage decisions. Richard Hoyle exploits a late-seventeenth-century dataset to uncover seasonal patterns in four English markets, and the threshing books from the same period of a farmer and tithe gatherer, to investigate to what extent the latter's sales respond to price signals. Finally, using the corn book of a Cambridgeshire farmer in the first half of the nineteenth century, Liam Brunt and Edmund Cannon are able to measure exactly how much grain was stored for how long, and to whom it was sold.

The next four chapters focus on how different ways of food provisioning could shape economic activities, power relations and social conflicts in urban areas. Pablo Luna takes us to the 1692 *Tumulto* in Mexico City, a large food riot illuminating the ambiguous nature of an ethnically stratified food market and supply network in times of crisis. Jonas Albrecht explores how Vienna's demographic expansion and changing dietary preferences went hand in hand with the agricultural and infrastructural transformation of the surrounding landscape. Laurent Herment's contribution on nineteenth-century Paris reminds us that not only peasants, farmers and merchants potentially held grain stocks, but also millers and bakers, and details the economic ties between them. In a chapter on urban agriculture in nineteenth-century Belgium, Pieter De Graef uses municipal-level agricultural census data to measure to what extent towns and cities were able to feed themselves.

The last three chapters deal with public regulation and semi-public management of supplies and resources. They show that, since a very long time, food and environmental issues are recognised as social issues where governmental and professional actors justify their commitment for the common good and welfare. Solène Rivoal widens the range of the foodstuffs to be stocked. She analyses the rules and practices regarding fishing in the Venetian lagoon, a "living stock" of food for the city's inhabitants. Gérard Béaur discusses the attempts by the French government in the eighteenth century to set up so-called *granaries of abundance* in the towns, and why their efforts ultimately failed. Finally, Alain Chatriot's chapter brings us into the twentieth century. He reveals how the government had to find a balance between agricultural and commercial interest groups when supporting the development of storage facilities by the agricultural cooperative movement.

This book is not meant as a synthesis, but rather as an exploration of the issues involved. Many of the contributions gathered here are made by young researchers, a sign of a renewal in scholarly interest in this topic. For the new generation of scholars, many issues remain to be explored. To name but a few venues for further study: the labour and workforce involved in the conservation of food and the everyday management of silos; the ecological and dietary aspects of food storage; food other than cereals, which have dominated research so far, this introduction not excluded; and the international agreements and knowledge networks observing food stocks and market dynamics.[1] With this book we also want to make a call for further action to broaden and deepen our understanding of food storage, seasonal patterns and food trade. All the contributions in this volume are a valuable step in that direction.

References

Alfani, G. and Ó Gráda, C. (eds) (2017) *Famine in European History*, Cambridge.

Arnoux, M. (2010) 'Pour une économie historique de la dîme', Viader, R. (ed.), *La dîme dans l'Europe médiévale et moderne: Actes des XXXes Journées Internationales d'Histoire de l'Abbaye de Flaran 3 et 4 octobre 2008*, Toulouse, pp. 145-160.

Arnoux, M. (2012) *Le temps des laboureurs: Travail, ordre social et croissance en Europe (XIe-XIVe siècle)*, Paris.

Arrighi, G. (1994) *The Long Twentieth Century: Money, Power and the Origins of our Times*, London.

Aymard, M. (1966) *Venise, Raguse et le commerce du blé pendant la seconde moitié du XVIe siècle*, Paris.

Bauernfeind, W., Reutter, M. et al. (2001) 'Rational investment behaviour and seasonality in early modern grain prices', *European Review of Economic History*, 5, 2, pp. 281-298.

[1] During the 2015 conference that we organised in Rome, Philippe Paquotte (FranceAgrimer) presented, for example, the Agricultural Market Information System (AMIS) whose secretariat is hosted in FAO headquarters. AMIS is an inter-agency platform launched in 2011 by the G20 members – inviting seven other major exporting and importing countries of agricultural commodities (Egypt, Kazakhstan, Nigeria, the Philippines, Thailand, Ukraine, and Vietnam) – to improve information on the global food supply and demand situation, focusing on wheat, maize, rice and soybeans.

Béaur, G. (2007) 'La "soudure" n'est plus ce qu'elle était. Contribution à l'étude du mouvement saisonnier du marché du blé et du marché de la terre d'après le cas de la région de Chartres au XVIIIe siècle', Chauvard, J.-F. and Laboulais, I. (eds), *Les fruits de la récolte*, Strasbourg, pp. 93-107.

Bernardos Sanz, J. U. (2008) 'Territorio e infraestructura de almacenamiento en el abastecimiento de pan a Madrid (siglos XVI-XVIII)', *Mélanges de l'École française de Rome. Italie et Méditerranée*, 120, 2, pp. 541-554.

Bernardos Sanz, J. U. and Virlouvet, C. (2016), 'Formes et fonctions: essai de typologie', Marin, B. and Virlouvet, C. (eds) *Entrepôts et trafics annonaires en Méditerranée: Antiquité-Temps modernes*, Rome, pp. 59-82.

Bohstedt, J. (2010) *The politics of provisions: food riots, moral economy, and market transition in England, c. 1550-1850*, Farnham.

Bourdon, J.-P. (1996) 'Des faux, des granges et des étables en Normandie sous le Second Empire', *Annales de Normandie*, 46, 3, pp. 355-366.

Brady, N. (1997) 'The Gothic barn of England: icon of prestige and authority', Smith, E. B. and Wolfe, M. (eds), *Technology and resource use in medieval Europe: cathedrals, mills, and mines*, Aldershot, pp. 76-105.

Brassley, P., Segers, Y. and Van Molle, L. (eds) (2012) *War, Agriculture and Food: Rural Europe from the 1930s to the 1950s*, London.

Bruegel, M. (ed.) (2009) *Profusion et pénurie: les hommes face à leurs besoins alimentaires*, Rennes.

Brunet, P. (1982) 'Les granges de Normandie. Essai d'architecture et d'économie rurale', *Hors-série des Annales de Normandie. Recueil d'études offert en hommage au doyen Michel de Boüard*, 1, 1, pp. 115-128.

Brunt, L. and Cannon, E. (1999) 'A Grain of Truth in Medieval Interest Rates? Re-examining the McCloskey-Nash Hypothesis', University of Bristol Working Paper.

Chankowski, V., Lafon, X. and Virlouvet, C. (eds) (2018) *Entrepôts et circuits de distribution en Méditerranée antique*, Athens.

Chatriot, A. (2016) *La politique du blé. Crises et régulations d'un marché dans la France de l'entre-deux-guerres*, Paris.

Chatriot, A., Leblanc, E. and Lynch, É. (eds) (2012) *Organiser les marchés agricoles. Le temps des fondateurs, des années 1930 aux années 1950*, Paris.

Claridge, J. and Langdon, J. (2011) 'Storage in medieval England: the evidence from purveyance accounts, 1295-1349', *Economic History Review*, 64, 4, pp. 1242-1265.

Clark, G. (2015) 'Markets before economic growth: the grain market of medieval England', *Cliometrica*, 9, 3, pp. 265-287.

Collet, D. (2010) 'Storage and starvation: public granaries as agents of "food security" in early modern Europe', *Historical Social Research*, 35, 4, pp. 234-252.

Collet, D. and Schuh, M. (eds) (2018) *Famines During the 'Little Ice Age' (1300-1800): Socionatural Entanglements in Premodern Societies*, Cham.

Corritore, R. P. (2012) 'Horrea: un'istituzione che "va e viene" nella politica annonaria delle città di Antico Regime', *Storia Urbana*, 35, 134, pp. 11-29.

Cronon, W. (1991) *Nature's metropolis: Chicago and the Great West*, New York.

D'Atri, S. (2008) '*Adi 2 di marzo 1590 porta fornita*: Rupe, il granaio di Ragusa (Dubrovnik)', *Mélanges de l'École française de Rome. Italie et Méditerranée*, 120, 2, pp. 569-580.

D'Atri, S. (2012) '"Le navi e il mar, invece di campi e d'oliveti, tengono la città abbondante d'ogni bene". Il sistema annonario di Ragusa (Dubrovnik) in età moderna', *Storia Urbana*, 35, 134, pp. 31-56.

Dentoni, M. C. (1995) *Annona e consenso in Italia, 1914-1919*, Milan.

Dijkman, J. (2017) 'Coping with Scarcity: a Comparison of Dearth Policies in Three Regions in Northwestern Europe in the Fifteenth and Sixteenth Centuries', *Tijdschrift voor Sociale en Economische Geschiedenis*, 14, 3, pp. 5-30.

Dorel-Ferré, G. (ed.) (2014) *Les silos, un patrimoine à inventer: Actes de la 3e Rencontre internationale de la Section Patrimoine agroalimentaire du TICCIH, International Committee for the Conservation of the Industrial Heritage, Nogent-sur-Seine, 20-22 octobre 2011*, Chambéry.

EC – FAO Food Security Programme (2008) *An Introduction to the Basic Concepts of Food Security*.

Edvinsson, R. (2012) 'Harvests and grain prices in Sweden, 1665-1870', *Agricultural History Review*, 60, 1, pp. 1-18.

Eiden, H. and Irsigler, F. (2000) 'Environs and hinterland: Cologne and Nuremberg in the later middle ages', Galloway, J. A. (ed.), *Trade, Urban Hinterlands and Market Integration c.1300-1600*, London, pp. 43-57.

Ejrnaes, M. and Persson, K. G. (1999) 'Grain Storage in Early Modern Europe', *The Journal of Economic History*, 59, 3, pp. 762-772.

Faugeron, F. (2014) *Nourrir la ville. Ravitaillement, marchés et métiers de l'alimentation à Venise dans les derniers siècles du Moyen Âge*, Rome.

Fenoaltea, S. (1976) 'Risk, transaction costs, and the organization of medieval agriculture', *Explorations in Economic History*, 13, 2, pp. 129-151.

Fogel, R. W. (1989) 'Second Thoughts on the European Escape from Hunger: Famines, Price Elasticities, Entitlements, Chronic Malnutrition, and Mortality Rates', *NBER Historical Working Paper No. 1*.

Galloway, J. A. (ed.) (2000) *Trade, Urban Hinterlands and Market Integration c.1300-1600*, London.

Gardiner, M. (2013) 'Stacks, Barns and Granaries in Early and High Medieval England: Crop Storage and its Implications', Vigil-Escalera Guirado, A., Bianchi, G. and Quirós Castillo, J. A. (eds), *Horrea, barns and silos. Storage and incomes in Early Medieval Europe*, Bilbao, pp. 23-38.

Gast, M. and Sigaut, F. (eds) (1979-1985) *Les Techniques de conservation des grains à long terme: leur rôle dans la dynamique des systèmes de cultures et des sociétés*, Paris.

Grantham, G. W. (1997) 'Espaces privilégiés: productivité agraire et zones d'approvisionnement des villes dans l'Europe préindustrielle', *Annales. Histoire, Sciences Sociales*, 52, 3, pp. 695-725.

Hayfield, C. (1991) 'Manure Factories? The post-enclosure high barns of the Yorkshire Wolds', *Landscape History*, 13, 1, pp. 33-45.

Herment, L. and Ronsijn, W. (2015) 'Seasonal patterns in food markets in north-west Europe in the second quarter of the nineteenth century: the evidence of periodic markets in France, England, and Belgium, 1820 to 1850', *Agricultural History Review*, 63, 1, pp. 60-80.

Holt-Giménez, E. and Patel, R. (2009) *Food Rebellions: Crisis and the Hunger for Justice. The real story behind the world food crisis and what we can do about it*, Oxford.

Kaplan, S. L. (1977) 'Lean years, fat years: the "community" granary system and the search for abundance in eighteenth century Paris', *French Historical Studies*, 10, 2, pp. 197-230.

Kaplan, S. L. (1982) *The Famine Plot Persuasion in Eighteenth-Century France*, Philadelphia.

Kaplan, S. L. (1984) *Provisioning Paris: Merchants and Millers in the Grain and Flour Trade during the Eighteenth Century*, Ithaca, London.

Keynes, J. M. (1938) 'The Policy of Government Storage of Foodstuffs and Raw Materials', *Economic Journal*, 48, 191, pp. 449-460.

Komlos, J. and Landes, R. (1991) 'Anachronistic Economics: Grain Storage in Medieval England', *Economic History Review*, 44, 1, pp. 36-45.

Labrousse, C. E. (1932) *Esquisse du mouvement des prix et des revenus en France au XVIIIe siècle*, Paris.

Marin, B. (2012) 'La "Conservazione de' grani". Strutture di stoccaggio cerealicolo a Napoli in età moderna', Colletta, T. (ed.) *Città portuali del Mediterraneo. Luoghi dello scambio commerciale e colonie di mercanti stranieri tra Medioevo ed età moderna*, Milan, pp. 179-192.

Marin, B. and Virlouvet, C. (eds) (2004) *Nourrir les cités de Méditerranée. Antiquité, Temps modernes*, Paris, Aix-en-Provence, Madrid.

Marin, B. and Virlouvet, C. (eds) (2008) *Entrepôts et trafics annonaires en Méditerranée*, in: *Mélanges de l'École française de Rome. Antiquité*, 120, 1, pp. 109-138 and 2, pp. 275-336; *Mélanges de l'École française de Rome. Moyen-Âge*, 120, 1, pp. 5-72; *Mélanges de l'École française de Rome. Italie et Méditerranée*, 120, 2, pp. 473-606.

Marin, B. and Virlouvet, C. (eds) (2016) *Entrepôts et trafics annonaires en Méditerranée: Antiquité-Temps modernes*, Rome.

Martin, S. (ed.) (2019) *Rural Granaries in Northern Gaul (Sixth Century BCE – Fourth Century CE). From Archaeology to Economic History*, Leiden.

Martinat, M. (2004) *Le juste marché. Le système annonaire romain aux XVIe et XVIIe siècles*, Rome.

Martinat, M. (2008) 'L'organisation des entrepôts de l'Abondance à Lyon au XVIIe siècle', *Mélanges de l'École française de Rome. Italie et Méditerranée*, 120, 2, pp. 581-593.

Martinat, M. (2012) 'Il Consolato e l'Annona. La gestione dell'approvvigionamento alimentare a Lione in età moderna: tra interessi particolari e pubblica utilità', *Storia Urbana*, 35, 134, pp. 95-113.

Mateos Royo, J. A. (2008) 'Control estatal, gestión municipal y abasto público de grano: las reformas borbónicas del pósito de Zaragoza (1707-1808)', *Mélanges de l'École française de Rome. Italie et Méditerranée*, 120, 2, pp. 555-567.

Mateos Royo, J. A. (2011) 'In search of wheat: municipal politics, urban markets and the grain supply in Aragon in the sixteenth and seventeenth centuries', *Urban History*, 38, 2, pp. 211-233.

McCloskey, D. N. (1972) 'The Enclosure of Open Fields: Preface to a Study of Its Impact on the Efficiency of English Agriculture in the Eighteenth Century', *The Journal of Economic History*, 32, 1, pp. 15-35.

McCloskey, D. N. and Nash, J. (1984) 'Corn at Interest: The Extent and Cost of Grain Storage in Medieval England', *The American Economic Review*, 74, 1, pp. 174-187.

McCollom, J. (2018) '"We Love You People Better than We Like Ourselves": Canada, the United States, Australia, the Soviet Union, and the International Wheat Pool Movement of the 1920s', *Agricultural History*, 92, 3, pp. 404-428.

McMichael, P. (2013) *Food Regimes and Agrarian Questions*, Halifax and Winnipeg.

Meuvret, J. (1977) *Le problème des subsistances à l'époque Louis XIV. 1: La production des céréales dans la France du XVIIe et du XVIIIe siècle*, Paris.

Meuvret, J. (1987) *Le problème des subsistances à l'époque Louis XIV. 2: La production des céréales et la société rurale*, Paris.

Meuvret, J. (1988) *Le problème des subsistances à l'époque Louis XIV. 3: Le commerce des grains et la conjoncture*, Paris.

Michel T. (2015) *La Conservation des grains en France au XVIIIe siècle. Ruptures, continuités et limites*, PhD thesis in History (EHESS, Paris).

Moore, J. W. (ed.) (2016) *Anthropocene or Capitalocene? Nature, History, and the Crisis of Capitalism*, Oakland.

Muñoz Navarro, D. (2012) 'L'approvvigionamento di Valencia (1650-1763). Consumi, mercato e istituzioni', *Storia Urbana*, 35, 134, pp. 115-131.

Nielsen, R. (1997) 'Storage and English Government Intervention in Early Modern Grain Markets', *The Journal of Economic History*, 57, 1, pp. 1-33.

Nützenadel, A. (2008), 'A Green International? Food Markets and Transnational Politics, c. 1850-1914', Nützenadel, A. and Trentmann, F. (eds), *Food and Globalization. Consumption, Markets and Politics in the Modern World*, Oxford-New York, pp. 153-172.

Persson, K. G. (1996) 'The Seven Lean Years, Elasticity Traps, and Intervention in Grain Markets in Pre-Industrial Europe', *The Economic History Review*, 49, 4, pp. 692-714.

Peytremann, E. (2013) 'Structures et espaces de stockage dans les villages alto-médiévaux (6e-12e s.) de la moitié septentrionale de la Gaule: un apport à l'étude socio-économique du monde rural', Vigil-Escalera Guirado, A., Bianchi, G. and Quirós Castillo, J. A. (eds), *Horrea, barns and silos. Storage and incomes in Early Medieval Europe*, Bilbao, pp. 39-56.

Poisson, J.-M. (2018) 'Espaces et modes de stockage des denrées alimentaires dans les maisons villageoises médiévales', Journot, F. (ed.), *Pour une archéologie indisciplinée: Réflexions croisées autour de Joëlle Burnouf*, Drémil-Lafage.

Poynder, N. (1999) 'Grain storage in theory and history', Paper presented at the Third Conference of the European Historical Economics Society, Lisbon, October 29th and 30th, 1999.

Revel, J. (1972) 'Le grain de Rome et la crise de l'Annone dans la seconde moitié du XVIIIe siècle', *Mélanges de l'École française de Rome. Moyen Âge-Temps Modernes*, 84, 1, pp. 201-281.

Revel, J. (1975) 'Les privilèges d'une capitale: l'approvisionnement de Rome à l'époque moderne', *Mélanges de l'École française de Rome. Moyen Âge-Temps Modernes*, 87, 2, pp. 461-493.

Samuelson, P. A. (1957) 'Intertemporal price equilibrium: a prologue to the theory of speculation', *Weltwirtshaftliches Archiv*, 79, pp. 181-221.

Sigaut, F. (1978) *Les Réserves de grains à long terme. Techniques de conservation et fonctions sociales dans l'histoire*, Paris, Lille.

Sigaut, F. (1988) 'A method for identifying grain storage techniques and its application for European agricultural history', *Tools & Tillage*, 6, 1, pp. 3-32.

Strangio, D. (1999) *Crisi alimentari e politica annonaria a Roma nel Settecento*, Rome.

Strangio, D. (2012) 'La politica degli ammassi del grano e la sistemazione degli oneri a carico dello Stato italiano nel secondo dopoguerra', *Rivista di storia economica*, 28, 3, pp. 453-486.

Taub, B. (1987) 'A Model of Medieval Grain Prices: Comment', *The American Economic Review*, 77, 5, pp. 1048-1053.

Thoen, E. (1996) 'The birth of "the Flemish husbandry": agricultural technology in medieval Flanders', Langdon, J. and Astill, G. (eds), *Medieval Farming and Technology. The Impact of Agricultural Change in Northwest Europe*, Leiden, pp. 69-88.

Thompson, E. P. (1971) 'The Moral Economy of the English Crowd in the Eighteenth Century', *Past and Present*, 50, pp. 76-136.

Trentmann, F. and Just, F. (2006) *Food and Conflict in Europe in the Age of the Two World Wars*, Basingstoke-New York, 2006.

Uebele, M., Grünebaum, T., et al. (2013) 'King's law and food storage in Saxony, *c.* 1790-1830', Paper presented at the European Historical Economics Society Conference, London, September 6th and 7th, 2013.

van Tielhof, M. (2002) *The 'Mother of All Trades': The Baltic Grain Trade in Amsterdam from the Late Sixteenth to the Early Nineteenth Century*, Leiden.

Vanhaute, E. (2011) 'From famine to food crisis: what history can teach us about local and global subsistence crises', *Journal of Peasant Studies*, 38, 1, pp. 47-65.

Vaquero Piñeiro, M. (2011) 'I silos granari in Italia negli anni Trenta: fra architettura e autarchia economica', *Patrimonio industriale*, 5, 7, 2011, pp. 56-68.

Vaquero Piñeiro, M. (2012) 'Wheat-storage in Fascist Italy: evolution and policies', Lorenzetti, L., Barbot, M. and Mocarelli, L. (eds) *Property rights and their violations. Expropriations and confiscations, 16th-20th century / La propriété violée. Expropriations et confiscations, XVIe-XXe siècles*, Bern, pp. 263-280.

Vertecchi G. (2009) *Il "Masser ai formenti in Terra Nova". Il ruolo delle scorte granarie a Venezia nel XVIII secolo*, Rome.

Vertecchi G. (2012) 'Dal grano al biscotto. Elementi per una storia della politica annonaria di Venezia fra XVII e XVIII secolo', *Storia Urbana*, 35, 134, pp. 57-74.

Warde, P. (2007) 'The origins and development of institutional welfare support in early modern Württemberg, *c.* 1500-1700', *Continuity and Change*, 22, 3, pp. 459-487.

Zylbergeld, L. (1973) 'Le prix des céréales et du pain à Liège dans la première moitié du XIIIe siècle (1re partie)', *Belgisch Tijdschrift voor Filologie en Geschiedenis*, 51, 2, pp. 271-332.

1 Landlords as rational investors? Grain storage on noble manors in the Rhineland area, 1650-1850

Friederike SCHOLTEN, University of Münster

I. Two manors in the Rhineland area

This survey is mainly based on the information of two Rhenish manors (see figure 1). The manor of (1) Heltorf located in the region of Düsseldorf (in the district Angermund), on the right bank of the Rhine, belongs to the noble family von Spee. The castle is the ancestral seat of the family since the middle of the seventeenth century. In the course of time, the family could successfully extend its property. Simultaneously, the respective landowners gained high offices in the provincial administrations or in the German military. The manorial territory comprised about 4000 hectares, of which approximately 1500 hectares were used agriculturally.

The manor of (2) Dyck, owned by the family von Salm-Reifferscheidt, is located in the Lower Rhine Bay, between Jüchen and Neuss, on the left bank of the Rhine (see figure 1). The family inherited the property at the end of the fourteenth century. At the beginning of the nineteenth century, the Salm-Reifferscheidts received the "Reichsfürstenstand" and later the Prussian principality (Bremer, 1959: 192 ff.). Today the whole property is administered by a foundation. In the early modern period, its landholdings comprised around 500 hectares, which were presumably nearly all used agriculturally (Bremer, 1959: 259).

Both manors have a dense tradition of account books (time span covered here: Heltorf: 1680-1850; Dyck: 1808-1851). These include all relevant aspects of the early modern estate administration: total and detailed monetary and in-kind revenues as well as expenses (Wunder, 2016: 195-200), traded quantities and prices and the above-mentioned volumes of grain stocks within the year and from one year to the next.[1] This empirical information is combined with various administrative correspondence between the landlord on the one hand and the local administrator (so called "Rentmeister"[2]) on the other. Especially these letters have a significant historical value as they make economic decisions and interrelations visible and contextualize the empirical data.

---

1 McCloskey and Nash discuss the rareness of these data, 1984: 175.

2 As he administers the "Rentei" of the manor, meaning he has the control over the manorial economy and was mainly responsible for the collection of the revenues, cf. Schütte, 2007: 540, more information on the multiple responsibilities of an administrator on an estate cf. Linnemeier, 1992: 261-281.

Stocks, seasons and sales: Food supply, storage and markets in Europe and the New World, c. 1600-2000, ed. by Wouter RONSIJN, Niccolò MIGNEMI and Laurent HERMENT, CORN 17 (Turnhout, 2019), pp. 19-36.

 DOI: 10.1484/M.CORN-EB.5.118252

Figure 1 Section of the Rhineland with the two chosen manors Dyck and Heltorf

Source: Own design

II. Thematical introduction

II.1 The agrarian system and noble manors

The manorial system, the so-called "Grundherrschaft"[3], was established in the High Middle Ages in the German region west of the river Elbe. As a feudal system with the noble manor in the centre, it comprised a multitude of duties, fees and payments (Henning, 1969: 70 ff.; Lütge, 1957: 102, 112 ff., 166 ff.). These yearly revenues of money and natural products (grain, cattle etc.) were the financial backbone of the landed estates as well as its owners (Feinendegen, 1961: 124-133; Linnemeier, 1992: 483 f.; Wunder, 2016: chapter 3).[4] As a result, manors in the early modern period were complex households, important land lessors (Bracht/Pfister 2018) and centres of a self-reliant economy, as well as of a huge grain and cattle sector and numerous offshoots (grain- and oil-mills, brewery, distillery, brickyard etc.) (Reif, 1979: 64).

[3] The "Grundherrschaft", also called as "lordship over land and people", mainly means that the peasants were legally subordinate to a landowner. The peasants did not own the land they farmed and were dependent on the landlord in their life cycle. Until the middle of the nineteenth century the "Grundherrschaft" was a decisive system of the agriculture as it sustained the cultivation of the fields: Normally the landlord leased out his plots to the peasants. In return, the tenants were subject to the local jurisdiction of the landlord and were liable to pay levies. However research shows that there were regionally substantial differences in the concrete form of the system, cf. Prass, 2016: 46 ff.; Sikora, 2009: 7 f., 32 ff.; Münch, 1998: 77-78.

[4] Besides, some landlords also earned money by holding high offices in politics but income from these offices varied extremely, cf. Reif, 1979: 67 ff; Richarz, 1971: 53-66.

The corresponding property owner was not simply the head of this household[5]; he always found himself in a conflict between his multiple roles and functions in the parish. First, he was also the chair of a large agricultural enterprise (= the manorial estate) (Wunder, 2016: 181-188; Bieberstein, 1998: 14 f.). Second, he had to fulfil the role of a nobleman and in the meantime, as being a paternalistic property owner, he was more or less a caretaker for his dependents (Polanyi 1978; Berdahl 1980; Thompson 1978; Bracht and Pfister 2018: 107-108; Wunder, 2016: 96; Wunder, 2010: 423 ff.). Thus, the manor itself with its complex system of revenues and expenses secured not only a suitable standard of living for the noble family but also for the people living under the lordship. Therefore, the resources available here had to be handled in such a manner that they served all of these purposes.

II.2 The noble grain sector

The central task for the administration (= "Rentei") of these manors was to organize the yearly fluctuating revenues and expenditures. Here, the grain sector turns out to have had a decisive role. At the basis were the annually varying quantities of grain[6], mainly paid by dependents and tenants. The amount and number of payments and fees determined the exact amount of incoming grain. However, harvest outcomes only had little or respectively no influence on volumes as most of the payments were fixed on a long-term level.

Thus within the grain sector, these volumes had to be administered according to the individual requirements of the manor. It turns out that first, a high proportion of this grain was consumed by the manorial household itself (i.e. the manorial family, including servants and the associated livestock, mainly horses). On the two manors portrayed in the present study, the share of rye used for the entire household annually ranged from 31 per cent (Heltorf) to 41 per cent (Dyck).[7] But since the lord was often only temporarily present[8], the number of people and livestock on the castle varied substantially in the

[5] In the sense of Otto Brunner's idea of "the entire house", Brunner, 1966. In this context, the so-called "Hausväterliteratur" has to be mentioned. These guidebooks, mainly written for landlords, contained pedagogical, medical, agro-technical and economical doctrines – understanding the "house" merely as the connection of household and business (including agriculture and the unity of production and consumption, Sikora 2009, 78-79; Bauer, 1997; Münch, 1998: 168-178).

[6] In these regions mainly rye and barley (as consumption grain) and oats (as fodder, only for consumption in times of crisis), wheat was less important (at least until the middle of the 19th century, Kopsidis, 1996: 156-160, 176 ff.

[7] Jakob Bremer points out that in the eighteenth and nineteenth century approximately around seventy persons belonged to the holding of the court at Dyck, including gardeners, kitchen staff, administration, servants and stable staff. This number varied of course over time, cf. Bremer, 1959: 174; Wunder assumes that at least fifteen to twenty persons were needed to maintain the manor, Wunder, 2016: 187; for more information about the size of manorial households Richarz, 1971: 41-52.

[8] Many landlords in the early modern period held more than one political ministry which led to constant journeys. Next to the management of the manor, these princely services were the only possibility to gain further income. Presumably only few lords were able to live only on the monetary levies, duties and fees, cf. Sikora, 2009: 39. Besides, they often had more than one residence: at least one in the countryside and one in a town where they had to fulfill their political functions, cf. Wunder, 2016: 179, 186.

course of the year and therefore also the domestic requirements fluctuated. Besides, grain was also needed for the production in the bakery, brewery and distillery connected to the castle. These products (such as bread, beer and brandy) were mainly sold or donated. Partly, servants were also paid in kind (share of rye for wage: Dyck: 2 per cent, Heltorf: 5.7 per cent). Furthermore, within the conception of the "Grundherrschaft", the landlord also had to take care of poor people. Donations of grain were one of many approved forms of welfare, but generally, the amount varied a lot. Whereas in Dyck 14 per cent of all rye revenues were given to the poor annually, in Heltorf this share was rather small (0.4 per cent).[9]

Apparently, since the seventeenth century, noble manors expanded their economic activities as they realized the possible additional financial benefits (Harnisch, 1991: 83). Many landlords even developed a genuine interest in making at least a small profit before the end of a harvest year[10] by monetizing their available natural products, especially grain: they started selling grain several times in a year.[11] This was also driven by the fact that the yearly incoming quantities of grain[12] exceeded the domestic demand substantially and a further benefit of these surpluses via sales was lucrative (although their effective gain was strongly correlated with the development of the local prices as well as the available market volume (Richarz, 1971: 95)).

In the long run, grain sales had a relatively long tradition on the manors. Whereas they happened quite unsystematically in the beginning, at the latest since the middle of the eighteenth century, sales were increasingly formalized and followed a strict catalogue of rules (Scholten 2019: chapter 8). Also in the observed Rhineland area, many manors established their own local grain sale in the castle courtyard where they offered their yearly surpluses. This local grain market seasonally focused on the third quarter of the harvest year (April, May, June) and took place in the castle courtyard with the landlord as the sole supplier.[13] In Dyck around 41 per cent of all annual rye revenues were sold, in Heltorf 23 per cent. Interestingly, the greatest demand came from the manor's surroundings (Scholten 2019: chapter 8). It was found that in Heltorf, 95 per cent of all buyers were locals and came from neighbouring villages. These people generally had no or only a small patch of land (day labourers, servants) and therefore limited financial means.

---

9 This does not mean for Heltorf that the manor did not support poor people at all. Presumably, support was mainly monetary, not in kind. In general, landlords also built up the almshouse and supported it financially. The amount of the natural and financial donations can be reproduced for a long period (as they were recorded in the account books) for nearly every manor.

10 please note that for the period of observation, years are harvest years, starting in October and ending in September.

11 Other important sales were spirits, beer, bread, cattle and hay. Since the beginning of the 19th century, the selling of wood was extremely important as grain fees decreased because of the liberation of the peasants. In this context the landlords von Spee established an own paper factory in Ratingen, cf. Budde, 2003.

12 Partly from own cultivation but mainly as levies by the dependents.

13 This grain sale probably competed with a peasant market. But for these regions no information on this trade is available, even Kopisidis, 1996 portrays peasant markets in Westphalia.

Thus, they always needed minimal grain quantities, which totally made up around 70 per cent of the available grain sold by the manor. The second important group of buyers were urban merchants. Although they constituted only 3 per cent of all the buyers, they purchased the rest of the grain surpluses, i.e. nearly 30 per cent. Here it appears that the small distance to Düsseldorf led to a certain urban demand for noble grain, although its share was apparently moderate and could have certainly been higher. However, the high share of the local population among the buyers indicates that the noble grain sale had a social relevance in the parish.

Nevertheless, in the end, this grain sale offered the property owner further profit which he could dispose of freely. All grain, which was not consumed or sold, was finally carried over into the next year (carry-over). Consequently, the building-up of grain stocks was an integral part of the manorial grain sector. As grain was only available once a year but was needed during the whole year, every manor had to store grain, inevitably during the year and possibly also from one year to the other. The extent and motives of these long-term stocks will be examined in the following sections.

To begin with, it is important to consider, what motivated a landlord, respectively an administrator, to store (large or small quantities of) grain over a longer period. Until now, current research often stresses the (1) profit maximization idea behind the storage behaviour (Clark, 2001; Persson, 1996 & 1999; Uebele, Grünebaum and Kopsidis, 2013). In this perspective, the landlord as a profit-driven investor only stored large grain quantities when current grain prices are low. Subsequently this storage pays off when prices are high and stored quantities are sold. However, he only builds up his granary when the expected revenues meet the costs of the barn, the depreciation and the opportunity costs (McCloskey and Nash, 1984: 174). This idea assumes a transparent market for grain in which the participant can have a precise idea of future price developments in the interplay with harvest yields.[14]

As an alternative to this idea, the landlord, when deciding on the carry-over volumes, can also act as an (2) investor with little or no solid knowledge about future developments. Here, storage decisions are made on the basis of a thumb rule[15], as a realistic idea about current price developments is missing.

In contrast, the build-up of grain storage can also follow (3) non-profit motives. Considering the landlord and his self-conception as a nobleman (Sikora, 2009: 8-12; Reif, 2016: 324-325), he always took care of his dependents, parallel to being the head of a big agrarian enterprise (Schlenkrich, 2011: 40). According to the traditional feudal idea of protection of his dependants[16], his grain stocks guaranteed food sufficiency for the

---

[14] In terms of "rational expectations", meaning that expectations are forward looking (=standard methodology for modeling expectations in economics). Here all available and relevant information is used (in order to eliminate systematic forecasting errors) to make the best forecast.

[15] In terms of "adaptive expectations", meaning that expectations are solely based on past experience (backward-looking manner).

[16] Stressing that the "Grundherrschaft" was more than an agrarian system. It meant a system of rule and ownership including subservience, patronage, judicial authority and tithing, Sikora, 2009: 32-41; Reif, 1979: 58-59.

parish, mainly in times of crisis (poor harvest, war etc.). Paternalistic welfare therefore secured his position of power in the long run (Schlenkrich, 2011: 50).

In the end, also due to the high uncertainty in the manorial grain administration in early modern times, storage can also be totally (4) unsystematic and happen without any motive at all. Here, the build-up of a grain stock is mainly driven by chance and external conditions, such as personal need.

III. Storage behaviour on Heltorf and Dyck

III.1 Relevance of grain stocks in the manorial grain sector

The idea of storing grain from year to year to even out fluctuations in supplies is thousands of years old. Until the nineteenth century, grain storage was an integral part of every household economy. This is provoked by the fact that during the year grain is a rare good and its production level changed greatly from season to season. Thus, grain always had to be stored, from year to year and at least within the year. Besides, demand for grain was highly inelastic (Uebele, Grünebaum and Kopsidis, 2013: 14; Richarz, 1971: 81)[17] until the cultivation of the potato as an adequate substitute came up (not until the first or second third of the nineteenth century, e.g. for Saxony see Uebele, Grünebaum and Kopsidis, 2013: 5). At this time, the effect of grain stocks in securing sufficient food from the periods of seasonally high production to the periods of low production was highly appreciated. So far, historical research is not completely aware of the extent of private stocks in the rural society. At least for small farm holdings it is assumed that carry-overs were rather limited by space capacities, harvest outcome and organization.

In contrast to that, manorial granaries must have often been utilized to capacity as every year huge amounts came in as payments and fees. Stock books document that every month varying amounts of grain[18] were stored and removed from the barn and the local storage manager[19] was busy with its maintenance. The challenge was that in contrast to grain revenues, which were regulated seasonally by the manorial levy system[20], removals happened according to demand. Only the grain which was not spent could be stored into the next year(s). Consequently, carry-over is apparently a calculation of annual grain revenues minus annual removals (plus storage costs, see below).

[17] Meaning that when harvests are bad, people were willing to spend almost all their income on grain and prices increase in consequence.

[18] Threshed as well as un-threshed grain can be stored, but according to the account books it was common to store threshed grain on the manors (unclear about the state in private peasant stocks), Brunt and Cannon, 2013: 5.

[19] Many but not all manors had a storage manager. He had to take care of the stored grain in form of restoring and measuring the volumes.

[20] Meaning that grain is delivered by the dependents from 11th of November (in the liturgical calendar "Martini") until the 2nd of February (in the liturgical calendar "Maria Lichtmeß (Candlemas)").

Figure 2 Carry-over rate of rye (in per cent) 1680-1850 on the manor of Heltorf

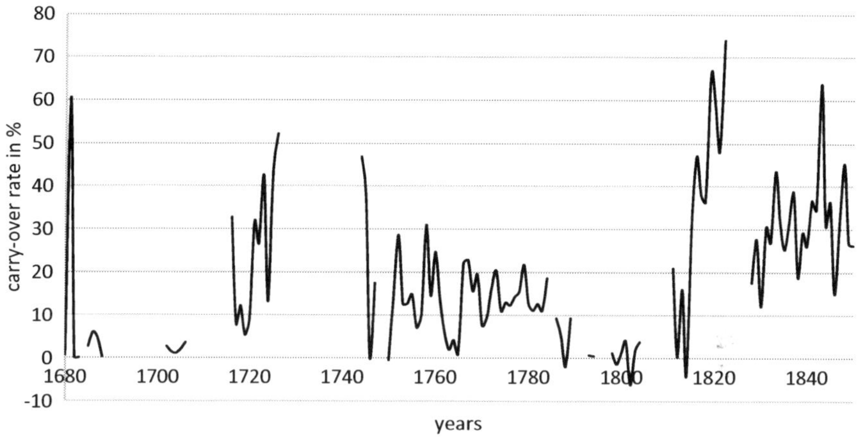

Source: Own calculation from database

Figure 2 shows the development of the storage rate of rye (i.e. the amount of grain stored from one year to the next, expressed as a percentage of the total annual grain revenue) from 1680 to 1850 on the manor of Heltorf. Despite missing data, mainly in the late seventeenth century and in the first half of the eighteenth century[21], it is more than obvious that rye stocks were highly volatile in Heltorf. They vary between maximum values of around 60 per cent of all revenues (1681, 1819, 1824 and 1843) and minimum values in the one-digit minus range (1625, 1750, 1788, 1799, 1802 and 1814). Relatively moderate storage volumes of 18 per cent (nearly meeting the average rate of 19 per cent of the whole period) are characteristic for the first period (beginning of the eighteenth century until the beginning of the Seven Years' War (1756-1763)[22]). Afterwards storage volumes initially decrease moderately until 1785 when they drop rapidly (average: 10 per cent). In contrast to that, the first third of the nineteenth century, a time of political instability (French time) and crop failures, is characterized by strong fluctuations (peaks in 1816 and 1819-22, average rate: 28 per cent). Finally, in the 1830s and '40s, carry-over volumes of rye are less volatile than in the previous period and range around 30 per cent of all revenues.

In contrast to this long observation period, there is only storage data for the manor of Dyck for the first half of the nineteenth century. Comparing figure 2 and figure 3, the difference in the level of the carry-over rate is striking. On average, in Dyck only 4.6 per cent of all rye revenues were stored into the next year. In addition, this rate remains

[21] This has multiple reasons, mainly a lack of tradition or rather documentation.

[22] A conflict between Prussia and Great Britain/Kurhannover on the one hand and the imperial Austrian Habsburg monarchy, France, Russia and the Holy Roman Empire on the other hand about the geopolitical and power-political equilibrium in Europe and the belonging colonies.

Figure 3 Carry-over rate of rye (in per cent) from 1808-1851 on the manor of Dyck

Source: Own calculation from database

relatively constant in contrast to the very volatile rate of Heltorf. According to this it looks like storage in Dyck must have had a different function than in Heltorf.

III.2 Facing the challenge of grain stocks

Before discussing the motives behind the above presented storage behaviour, the challenges of storage have to be considered. Generally spoken, no matter which incentives drive storing, it always meant a capital investment with a relatively high yield-risk.

Research so far discussed the (1) costs of storing grain (McCloskey and Nash, 1984: 178[23]). Although manors were generally remarkable buildings, it cannot be assumed that storage capacities were unlimited. First, these manors were built to represent the dominion and wealth of the family. Their function as the centre of an economy was not taken into account during construction. It remains relatively unclear where exactly grain was stored on a manor; though a barn or a shed are relatively plausible.[24] According to contemporary statements, in England un-threshed grain was mainly stored outside, sometimes even in the ear (cf. Brunt and Cannon, 2013: 5-7). For the Rhenish manors, concrete information is missing on where grain was put after the

[23] "The cost of storing a bushel of wheat is the cost of the barn per bushel plus the percentage rotting in storage plus the expected percentage loss of capital value due to falls in the price per bushel plus the opportunity cost of the interest forgone on the sum expended on the bushel".

[24] On a Westphalian manor (Nordkirchen, between Dortmund and Münster), grain was stored on the attic of the castle as well as of the stable Cf. LWL Archivamt (Münster) Nor A 981b "Abschätzung der zur Oeconomie des Herrn Verwalters Morsbach gehörenden Ackergeräthe, Pferdegeschirre, Hausgeräthe, Fässer, altes Eisen, Kupfer etc."; LWL Archivamt (Münster) Nor. A 2938, A 2943, A 2961, A 3099.

harvest but it is likely that the grain was stored under a roof, in order to reduce the risk of high losses. Losses mainly happened because of a high humidity level in the grain, which accelerated mould and fungus. Besides, also mice were a severe threat to the grain stocks. To counteract this, contemporaries soon developed certain strategies to dry and vent the grain before as well as during the storage process. In addition, stocks always had to be turned by shovelling. In combination with the employment of a storage manager[25] and regarding the capital costs of an appropriate granary and its maintenance, stockpiling must have been expensive for the administration (Brunt and Cannon, 2013: 21-22).

In addition to storage costs, two further challenges appear when planning grain stocks. As stated above, the amount of grain, which could be stored, was highly volatile and strongly controlled by the extent of the annual removals. The main component of the removals was the sale of grain on the local market. Therefore, stocks and sales were presumably correlated and the (2) information on current grain prices as well as (3) market access were additional factors that could affect the level of grain stocks.

IV. What drives grain stocks on Heltorf and Dyck?

The property owner, respectively his administrator, had a limited range of information that could have helped him in making decisions in the grain administration and ergo on the amount of carry-over. It turned out that storage behaviour in Heltorf and Dyck appeared to be radically different from each other (in scale and presumably also in the motivation behind it). However, as grain revenues and thus stocks on manors were not directly linked to harvest outcomes, it is striking what information was relevant for the build-up of granaries.

Coming back to the idea of the "rational investor", rational storing requires a high correlation between prices and quantities carried-over, i.e. when prices are low, stocks are high and the other way around. This will be analysed by the following method. First, an annual rye price based on urban market records from three cities close to the manors (Düsseldorf, Xanten (further up north) and Cologne (south)) is formed. In a second step, the correlation between this price and the local storage rate is tested. A negative correlation with the carry-over rate would support the "rational investor" idea by saying that the contemporaries stored in times of low prices. In turn, a positive correlation means that despite low prices, the landlord sells his stocks in spite of a low return as he might expect prices to decrease further.

When bringing together these two parameters (average annual rye price in Düsseldorf/Xanten/Cologne and (1) carry-over rate in Heltorf (1680-1850) or (2) carry-over rate in Dyck (1806-1851), only a weak negative correlation is visible for Heltorf (Pearson = -0.38). When looking at the corresponding scatter plot (cf. figure 4), the correlation is mainly

[25] For Dyck the employment of a granary master as well as a granary servant is documented, however they are not always employed for the same time span. An annual wage for a master as well as a servant was around 24 Reichstaler.

Figure 4 Scatterplot of annual rye prices (Xanten/Düsseldorf/Köln) in grams of silver (x-Axis) and carry-over rate in Heltorf (y-Axis)

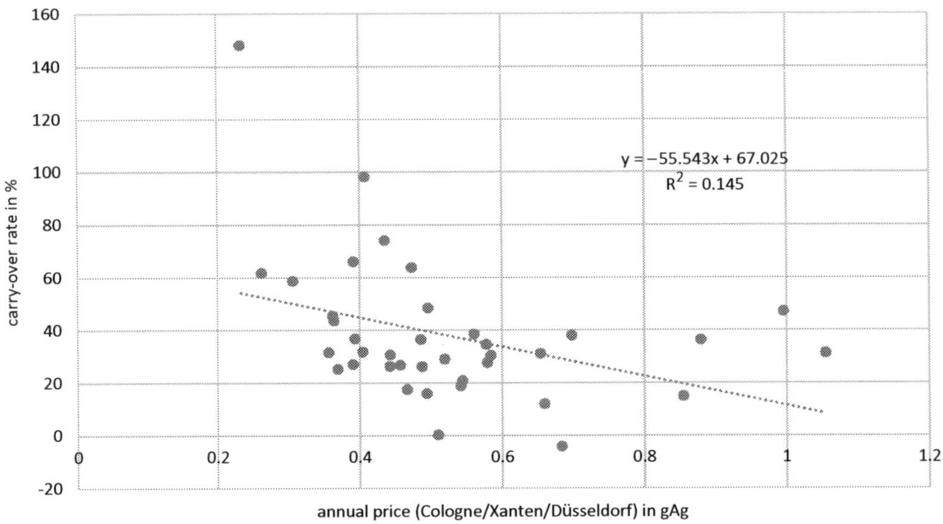

Source: Own calculation from database

driven by individual outliers and therefore has to be treated with caution. For Dyck no correlation at all is verifiable.

This result is surprising and suggests there was no rational investment behaviour on both manors. Besides, it shows that stocks were also not linked to local or national crises (which are visible in prices). But why do prices only have little or no influence on storage decisions? An explanation of this finding might be the obstacles to building up a granary, which were discussed above. It is highly plausible that especially the planning and the administration of these stocks were too difficult and pricy for the contemporaries to use them efficiently.

However, these challenges were no substantial hurdle for the Rhenish manors. In Dyck e.g., physical losses of grain stocks were estimated to be generally around 1 per cent (of the value of rye revenues per year) over the whole time span, which is rather low. Besides, costs for the storage manager were around 9 per cent (of the value of rye revenues per year). Combining these two, storage costs on noble manors were relatively low with only 10 per cent[26], which stands in contrast to the findings of McCloskey and Nash. Storage costs were thus no big issue in the area under investigation.

Furthermore, prices were indeed considered on the manors, at least when planning the grain sector in general. Account books and correspondences prove that information on

[26] The cost of storage is difficult to calculate as data is often missing. Claridge and Langdon, 2011: 1265 compute approximately 10 per cent of the value of wheat for medieval England, which is consistent with the findings here (although the barn costs are missing here).

current grain prices in nearby urban markets were sufficiently available and utilized. This is also supported by the positive correlation between rye prices in Heltorf and Cologne[27] (Pearson = 0.7) and Dyck and Cologne (Pearson = 0.67). Cologne seemed to work as a leading market to the noble grain trade. The contemporaries used these prices when forming their own prices for the local sale.

However, it appears that it was merely the formation of realistic expectations about the future local market developments that made storage difficult to plan. In 1820, the administrator of Dyck writes to his landlord about the difficulties when forming concrete expectations on upcoming prices:

> Your Highness and Count! Gracious Prince! All the field crops of Ramersdorf[28] were usually sold in January or February, but as the current price until now was so low, I was afraid of carrying out the sale. Right now the prices of the field crops increase and I guess that at least rye will catch 5 [Reichstaler] or even higher in the sale of the highest bidder.[29] But as nobody is able to predict a further increase or decrease of the prices, I ask Your Serene Highness to sell the crops right now. (Bonn, 23rd March 1820)[30]

He states that commonly field crops were sold at the beginning of the new year. But as he observes price developments, he abandons the regular cycle and waits for higher prices. This conduct stresses the profitmaking-orientation of the administration when selling grain. But only to a certain extent: As "nobody is able to predict a further increase or decrease of the prices", a longer waiting would be economically too risky and is therefore excluded. As soon as there are signs of increasing prices, a fast sale is recommended.

Within the idea of the "rational investor", a basic prerequisite is always a realistic assessment of future (price) developments, as storage only pays off when a price rise exceeds its costs. The quote above and a positive correlation between removals for sales and the carry-over rate (meaning when they sell much, they also store much grain) proves that expectation formation was problematic and hindered the realization of rational investment behaviour. This is supported by the fact that futures markets only emerged in the 1840s, which could have allowed the rational investor to have concrete ideas about future prices (Bass, 1991: 59).

---

27 Geographically rye prices from Düsseldorf would make more sense but unfortunately, monthly and annual prices in Düsseldorf are only available from 1820 onwards. Therefore Cologne is chosen, as in the nineteenth century prices of Cologne and Düsseldorf correlate well.

28 Ramersdorf was the place of a so called "Deutschordenskommende" (or Commandry of the Teutonic knights). After the secularization at the beginning of the nineteenth century the property was bought by Joseph zu Salm-Reifferscheidt-Dyck. Yet the prince always lived in Dyck, only an administrator took care of the property. They might have stored their grain there.

29 The sale to the highest bidder is a normal way of selling on early modern manorial grain markets. For more information see Scholten 2019: chapter 8.

30 Bestand Dyck A 513, #97: "Durchlauchtiger Fürst und Altgraf! Gnädiger Fürst und Herr! Die Früchte zu Ramersdorf sind sonnst gewöhnlich alle Jahr im Januar oder Februar verkauft worden, allein da der Preiß in diesem Jahr bis hierhin so gering war, fürchtete ich den Verkauf vorzunehmen. Dermalen fangen die Früchten etwas an im Preiß zu steigen, und ich glaube daß das Korn im meistbietenden Verkauf auf 5 oder etwas höher kommen wird. Da also keiner über das fernere Steigen, oder Fallen des Preißes etwas bestimmtes sagen kann, so wollte Euer Durchlaucht gehorsamst anfragen, ob ich die Früchte dermalen verkauffen solle." Bonn am 23. Mertz 1820.

Additionally, grain sales were highly difficult to plan as well. In February 1867 the Lord of Hatzfeldt (castle of Schönstein, Wildenburg and Crottorf in Wissen on the river Sieg, close to the boarder of Rhineland Palantine) wrote his administrator the following letter:

> The present high grain price makes it advisable to start with the sale of the grain stocks from the granaries very soon. With this highest order we draw your attention on that and induce you to let us know within the following four days when you want to carry out the first sale and which underlying price you want to propose.
>
> Count's department Hatzfeldt

To which came the answer:

> Due to continuing bad weather, all paths and roads are unusable and the tenants are behind schedule with their grain delivery. The sale cannot be started earlier than the end of February and my price suggestion is the following:
>
> 1 Prussian bushel rye = 25 silver pennies
>
> 1 Prussian bushel oats = 28 silver pennies
>
> Administrator Janssen[31]

Although the landlord wishes an early grain sale, the administrator points out the problematic infrastructure and therefore cannot carry out his request. The delay in fees and leases stresses the problematic calculability of the grain administration and in consequence of grain sales. And as grain sales were a decisive factor for the level of carry-over, carry-over was difficult to plan as well.

But contemporaries were aware of that problem. In the correspondence, which deals with the planning of grain sales and the volume of carry-overs, they reflect the situation properly. As it can be seen above, the administrator knows the uncertainties of harvests, prices and the receipt of payments by the dependents. As a consequence, the development of a thumb rule was one solution to the problem.

On the castle of Crottorf in 1832 the administrator checked the monthly prices of four grain types (rye, barley, buckwheat, oats) in Coblenz (58 km distance from the castle) from the last year. He highlighted maximum prices (for rye, Heidloh and oats in July, barley in April) with a pen – probably for the planning of their own grain sale.

[31] "Der gegenwärtig ziemlich hohe Stand der Fruchtpreise läßt es rathsam erscheinen als bald mit dem Verkaufe der Fruchtvorräthe auf den Rentheispeichern zu beginnen. Indem wir Sie in höchstem Special-Auftrage hierauf aufmerksam machen, veranlassen wir Sie, uns binnen 4 Tagen anzuzeigen, wann Sie den ersten Verkauf dort abzuhalten beabsichtigen und die demselben zu unterliegenden Taxpreise gleichzeitig in Vorschlag zu bringen." Calcum den 5. Febr. 1867. Gräflich Hatzfeldsche Dom. Direction Antwort: "Durch das anhaltend schlechte Wetter sind hier die Wege ganz unfahrbar geworden und die Pächter bis jetzt mit der Fruchtlieferung in Rückstand geblieben. Es wird hier nicht eher mit dem Verkauf begonnen werden können bis Ende Februar und bringe ich als Taxe ganz gehorsamst in Vorschlag: Pr Scheffel Korn zu 25 Sgr; Pr Scheffel Hafer zu 28 Sgr."

Figure 5 Average prices of field crops (1831) in Coblenz in Reichsthaler/Silbergroschen

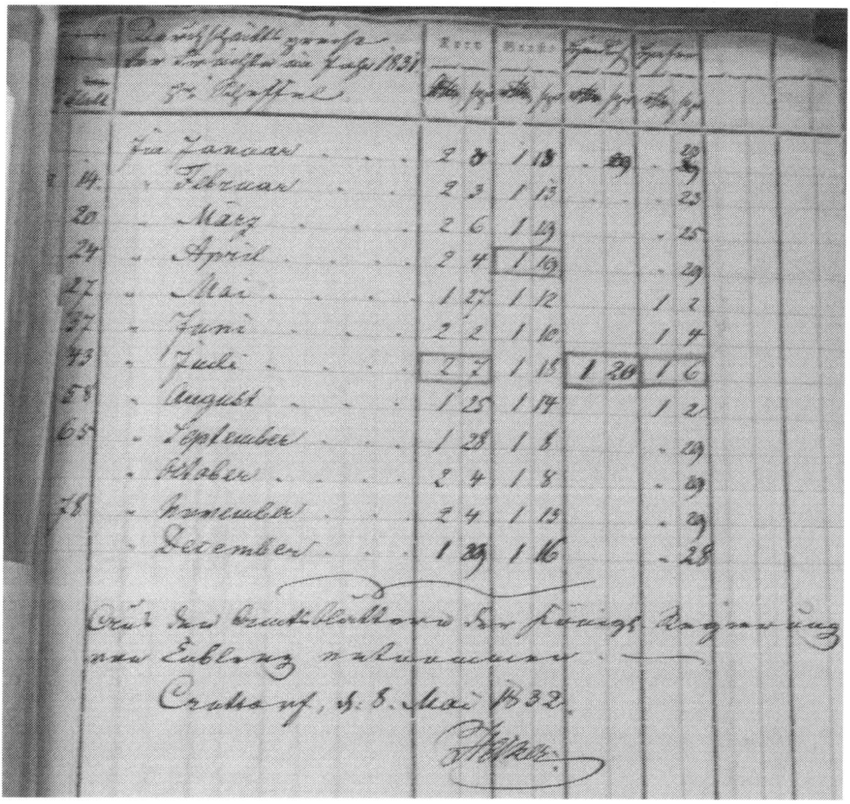

Source: Archiv Schloss Schönstein, A. 6995 (Bestand Crottorf) (title of the source: "Crottorf Früchten Verkauf vom Jahre 1831 und 1832, Abschnitt VII Nro 18"

This means that high grain prices in Coblenz functioned as an indicator for the manor to sell its grain at the same time, hoping to achieve similar prices. The relevance of these prices is supported by the fact that information on their own prices was not available to the contemporaries as the accounting system on the manors regularly needed multiple years for the composition of an account book.

But how reasonable was the orientation towards the urban market? In figure 6 the heydays of the grain trade in Heltorf are visible. In August (with an average quantity of 11,000 litre) and November (average quantity of 8,300 litre) most rye was sold. As stated before, rye prices in Heltorf and Cologne have a high correlation. Therefore, assuming that in Heltorf grain was sold according to a thumb rule, a price orientation of the contemporaries towards a bigger city like Cologne was very plausible. When looking at the

Figure 6 Traded volumes per month (rye) in litre on the manor of Heltorf (1690-1830)

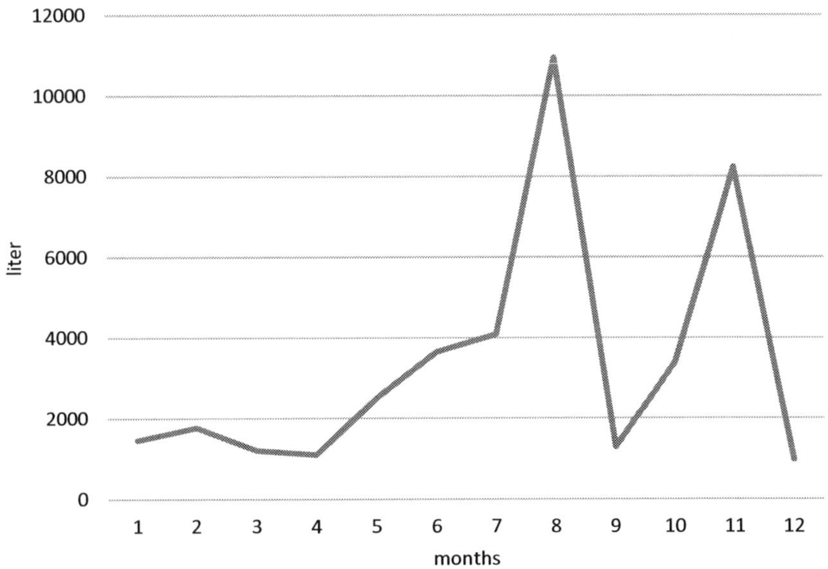

Source: Own calculation from database

monthly progress of rye prices in Cologne (1700-1860) peaks are visible in December and June (see figure 7). To a certain extent, this supports the rule-of-thumb-idea behind the selling-method in Heltorf: according to the urban price signals, the manor usually tried to sell most of its rye when prices in Cologne were high – in the winter and in the summer.

However, comparing monthly prices of Cologne (see figure 7) to those of Heltorf (see figure 8), it is obvious that (1) rye was cheaper in the castle courtyard and (2) local prices were far more volatile than those in the city.[32] Interestingly price peaks are postponed: rye in Heltorf is most expensive in February and July (cheaper in December and June, when it is dearest in Cologne). Therefore, when contemporaries were planning their grain administration (including the carry-over quantity), the best time for selling rye would have been February and July.

So, an orientation towards Cologne was at least partially useful, although it is clear that the local market contained a different dynamic than the urban market. But as their own prices were not available, the development of a rule of thumb according to urban prices is rational. Thereby, contemporaries knew that a sale in December (when prices in Cologne were high) was little reasonable as the wintry conditions would prevent a strong demand.

[32] Due to the lack of market integration of the local prices, a higher volatility was expectable.

Figure 7 Monthly rye price Cologne (1700-1860) in grams of silver per litre

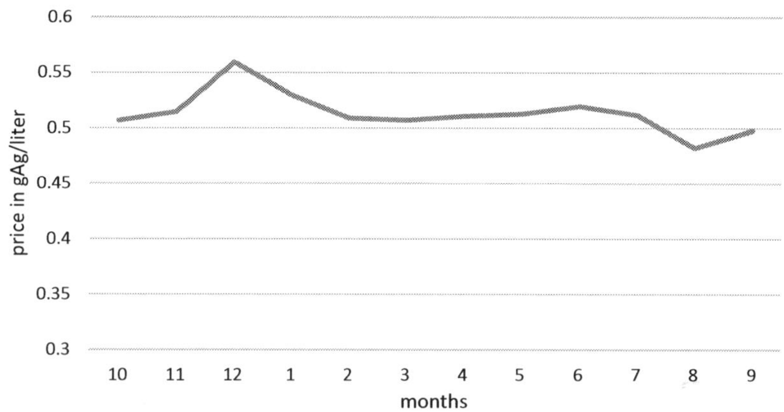

Source: Own calculation from database

Figure 8 Monthly rye price Heltorf (1690-1830) in grams of silver per litre

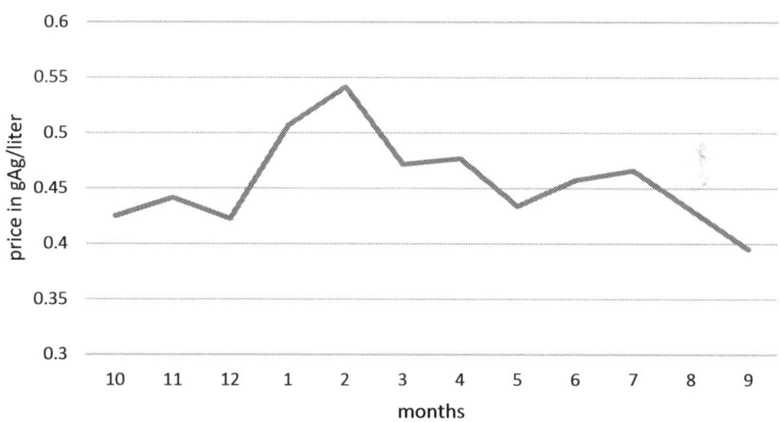

Source: Own calculation from database

V. Results

For the first time the economic history research is able to examine the phenomenon of carry-over on a microhistoric level with respect to concrete information on storage quantities, prices and consumer behaviour. Thanks to the combination of empirical and contextual data, it was possible to reproduce the complex decision-making processes of contemporaries in the administration of noble estates.

It turns out that grain was always stored on a noble manor, but especially the quantity of carry-overs was partly highly volatile and heavily dependent on numerous aspects. Whereas literature stresses the rational profit-maximization idea behind the year-to-year stocks, it appears that the specific motives behind the carry-over stocks on manors were far more sophisticated. Concrete expectations about future harvests and prices, which were vital for rational investment behaviour, were nearly impossible until the middle of the nineteenth century. Moreover, the local infrastructure and the manorial delivery system complicated planning on a large scale.

High (on average 19 per cent), but partly very volatile carry-over-rates are visible on the manor of Heltorf. As a consequence of the planning obstacles, it seems that the landlord and his administrator in Heltorf developed their own heuristic for planning grain sales and therefore carry-over stocks. Based on experience, they always sold grain when prices in Cologne were expected to be high. But as urban markets had a different dynamic from rural markets, this method was only reasonable to a limited extent.

In contrast to this, on the manor of Dyck far less rye was carried over (on average 4.6 per cent). This either hints at the perception of a low risk of running out of food at the end of the harvest year (therefore stocks were emptied) or proves that, in contrast to Heltorf, there was no motive behind it at all. Here, year-to-year stocks were probably constituted by chance and were a simple result of coincidence.

Sources

Manor of Nordkirchen

LWL Archivamt Westfalen (Münster)

Nor A 981b; Nor. A 2938; Nor. A 2943; Nor. A 2961; Nor. A 3099

Manor of Dyck

LVR Adelsarchiv Rheinland (Schloss Ehreshoven, Engelskirchen)

account books 1800-1860

A 513

Manor of Heltorf

Privatarchiv Schloss Heltorf, Düsseldorf-Angermund

Account books 1680-1850

Manor of Schönstein, Crottorf and Wildenburg (Hatzfeldt)

Privatarchiv Schloss Schönstein, Schönstein (Sieg)

A 6995 (Bestand Crottorf)

Bibliography

Bieberstein, J. R. von (1998) *Adelsherrschaft und Adelskultur in Deutschland*, Limburg.

Bauer, V. (1997) *Hofökonomie. Der Diskurs über den Fürstenhof in Zeremonialwissenschaft, Hausväterliteratur und Kameralismus*, Wien.

Bass, H.-H. (1991) *Hungerkrisen in Preussen* während der ersten Hälfte des 19. *Jahrhunderts*, St Katharinen.

Bauernfeind, W., Woitek, U. and Reutter, U. (2001) 'Rational investment behaviour and seasonality in early modern grain prices', *European Review of Economic History*, 5, 2, pp. 281-298.

Berdahl, R. M. (1980) 'Preußischer Adel. Paternalismus als Herrschaftssystem', Puhle H.-J. and Wehler H.-U. (eds) *Preußen im Rückblick*, Göttingen, pp. 123-145.

Bracht, J. and Pfister, U. (2018) *Landpacht, Marktgesellschaft und agrarische Entwicklung. Fünf Adelsgüter zwischen Rhein und Weser, 16. bis 19. Jahrhundert* (manuscript: Münster).

Bremer, J. (1959) *Die reichsunmittelbare Herrschaft Dyck. Der Grafen jetzigen Fürsten zu Salm-Reifferscheidt*, Grevenbroich.

Brunt, L. and Cannon E. (2013) 'The economics of grain storage in England 1663-1846', Working paper.

Brunner, O. (1966) 'Das "ganze Haus" und alteuropäische Ökonomik', Oetter F. (ed.) *Familie und Gesellschaft*, pp. 23-56.

Budde, H. (2003) 'Die Papierfabriken der Grafen von Spee', Soénius U. S. (ed.), *Bewegen – Verbinden – Gestalten. Unternehmer vom 17. bis zum 20. Jahrhundert*, Köln, pp. 207-223.

Claridge, J. and Langdon, J. (2011) 'Storage in medieval England: the evidence from purveyance accounts, 1295-1349', *The Economic History Review*, 64, 4, pp. 1242-1265.

Clark, G. (2001) 'Markets and economic growth: The grain market of medieval England', mimeograph, Department of Economics, University of California at Davis.

Dülmen, R. (1990) *Kultur und Alltag in der Frühen Neuzeit. Erster Band: Das Haus und seine Menschen 16. – 18. Jahrhundert*, München.

Ejrnaes, M. and Persson, K. (1999) 'Grain storage in early modern Europe', *Journal of Economic History* 59, 3, pp. 762-772.

Feinendegen, R. (1961) *Der niederrheinische Adel der Neuzeit und sein Grundbesitz. Eine Untersuchung über die Moerser Drostenfamilie von Pelden gen. Cloudt*, Bonn.

Henning, F.-W. (1969) *Dienste und Abgaben der Bauern im 18. Jahrhundert*, Stuttgart.

Harnisch, H. (1991) 'Grundherrschaft oder Gutsherrschaft. Zu den wirtschaftlichen Grundlagen des niederen Adels in Norddeutschland zwischen spätmittelalterlicher Agrarkrise und Deißigjährigem Krieg', Endres R. (ed.), *Adel in der Frühneuzeit. Ein regionaler Vergleich*, Köln/Wien, pp. 73-98.

Klueting, H. (1991) 'Reichgrafen – Stiftsadel – Landadel. Adel und Adelsgruppen im niederrheinisch-westfälischen Raum im 17. und 18. Jahrhundert', Endres R. (ed.), *Adel in der Frühneuzeit. Ein regionaler Vergleich* (Köln/Wien), pp. 17-54.

Kopsidis, M. (1996) *Marktintegration und Entwicklung der westfälischen Landwirtschaft 1780-1880*, Münster.

Linnemeier, B-W (1992) *Ein Gut und sin Alltag. Neuhof an der Weser*, Münster.

Lütge, F (1957) *Die mitteldeutsche Grundherrschaft und ihre Auflösung*, Stuttgart.

McCloskey, D. N. and Nash, J. (1984) 'Corn at Interest: The Extent and Cost of Grain Storage in Medieval England', *The American Economic Review*, 74, 1, pp. 174-187.

Münch, P. (1998) *Lebensformen in der Frühen Neuzeit. 1500 bis 1800*, Frankfurt am Main.

Persson, K. (1996) 'The seven lean years, elasticity traps, and intervention in grain markets in pre-industrial Europe', *Economic History Review*, 49, 4, pp. 692-714.

Persson, K. (1999) *Grain Markets in Europe, 1500-1900: Integration and Deregulation*, Cambridge.

Polanyi, K. (1978) *The Great Transformation. Politische und ökonomische Ursprünge von Gesellschaften und Wirtschaftssystemen*, Frankfurt am Main.

Poynder, N. (1999) 'Grain storage in theory and history', Conference paper, European Historical Economics Society, Lisbon.

Prass, R. (2016) *Grundzüge der Agrargeschichte. Vom Dreißigjährigen Krieg bis zum Beginn der Moderne (1650 – 1880)*, Köln, Wien, Weimar.

Reif, H. (1979) *Westfälischer Adel 1770-1860. Vom Herrschaftsstand zur regionalen Elite,* Göttingen.

Reif, H. (2016) *Adel, Aristokratie, Elite. Sozialgeschichte von Oben*, Oldenbourg.

Richarz, I. (1971) *Herrschaftliche Haushalte in vorindustrieller Zeit im Weserraum*, Berlin.

Schlenkrich, E. (2011) 'Paternalismus aus Kalkül? Adlige Fürsorgepraxis in ländlichen Gesellschaften Sachsens und der Oberlausitz (18 und 19. Jahrhundert)', *Zeitschrift für Agrargeschichte und Agrarsoziologie*, 59, 1, pp. 35-50.

Sikora, M. (2009) *Der Adel in der frühen Neuzeit*, Darmstadt.

Scholten, F. (2019) *Marktkontakte adeliger Güter in Rheinland und Westfalen, 1650 – 1850* (finishing phd-thesis, published in 2020).

Schütte, L. (2007) *Wörter und Sachen aus Westfalen*, Münster.

Thompson, E. P. (1978) 'Eighteenth-Century English Society: Class-Struggle without Class?', *Social History*, 3, 2, pp. 133-165.

Uebele, M., Grünebaum, T. and Kopsidis, M. (2013) 'King's law and food storage in Saxony, *c.* 1790-1830', *CQE Working Paper*.

Wunder, D. (2016) *Der Adel im Hessen des 18. Jahrhunderts – Herrenstand und Fürstendienst*, Marburg.

Wunder, D. (2010) 'Ökonomie des Niederadels in der Landgrafschaft Hessen-Kassel und im Kanton Rhön-Werra am Beispiel der Greyso und Verschuer (1650-1800)', Eckart Conze Alexander Jendorff und Heide Wunder (eds), *Der Adel im Hessen des 18. Jahrhunderts – Herrenstand und Fürstendienst*, Marburg, pp. 403-434.

2 Prices and seasons in late seventeenth-century England

Richard W. HOYLE, University of Reading

I. Introduction

It would be hard to exaggerate just how important commodity price data is to the study of economic history. It is one of the key statistics that we use to describe the past. One might go so far as to say that without price data there would be no economic history, at least not in the way we practice it, and for that reason alone it is entirely reasonable that much effort has been put into collecting prices and producing price series.

Rural historians have been especially interested in prices. Prices in year two are often used as a guide to the size of the harvest in year one. As real wages they are exploited for the light they shed on living standards. And there has been much interest in relating price to the future behaviour of farmers to establish their economic rationality or at least their receptiveness to price signals.

The truth is that good historical price data is not easy to find but once assimilated into tables is terribly easy to use without much thought. It is recognised in England that much of the available data, which underpins the familiar price series, is based on the bulk purchase of foodstuffs by institutional buyers. The exact relationship between the price at which an Oxford college, or a school like Eton or Winchester, or even a large aristocratic household bought foodstuffs and the price paid by a household for individual consumption is problematic (Thirsk, 1983). This not simply a question of bulk, but also one of quality. Catering tins of baked beans cost less per 100 grams than single tins: but not even baked beans are all the same, with different qualities of beans. The poorest consumers may not eat Heinz beans, but the very richest (if, of course, baked beans feature in their diet at all) may not eat Heinz baked beans either, but for completely different reasons: Heinz beans, in the hierarchy of beans are relatively expensive, but not the most expensive.

There is another problem with which economic historians are familiar. Much of the data we have gives us the price of grain sold in local markets. Some of this grain was sold direct by the farmer to the people who ate it, but much more, and one may suspect an increasing proportion, was sold to merchants, middlemen and factors, who shipped the grain into the larger towns and metropolitan area to be sold at markets there. Of course, when it was sold a second time, the price of this grain had to accommodate the costs of transport, warehousing and the merchant's other costs and still give him a margin for profit. So much of our data comes from two points in the distributive process: farm gate prices secured by manorial bailiffs and latterly farmers in local markets, and purchases made, perhaps out of those same markets, but also out of markets distant from the first point of sale. It is out of this rather rough and ready data that price indices have been constructed.

Stocks, seasons and sales: Food supply, storage and markets in Europe and the New World, c. 1600-2000, ed. by Wouter RONSIJN, Niccolò MIGNEMI and Laurent HERMENT, CORN 17 (Turnhout, 2019), pp. 37-60.

 DOI: 10.1484/M.CORN-EB.5.118253

Table 1 English wheat prices in the thirteenth and fourteenth centuries, percentage rates of change per month

From	Oct.	Nov.	Dec.	Jan.	Feb.	Mar.	Apr.	May	June	July	Aug
Sept	7.5	8.5	2.8	2.3	1.6	2.0	3.4	4.8	2.0	2.4	1.7
Oct		3.8	1.4	0.1	0.3	-0.4	1.6	1.6	0.6	3.9	0.6

Source: simplified from McCloskey and Nash 1984: 179, Table 2.

And one may go on identifying the problems with these indices. They include the fact that the data often comes from quite geographically-scattered locations even though it would be accepted that the grain market is far from integrated before the nineteenth century (Chartres, 1985: 459-465). There is the danger that purportedly "national" prices based largely on southern English sources may misrepresent the movement of prices in the north and west. But more seriously, from our point of view, the data is often taken indiscriminately from across over the year. Yet historians are well accustomed to believing that the price of grain is lowest in the weeks following the harvest and then rises over the following ten or eleven months until the next harvest. This has been empirically verified by McCloskey and Nash (1984) in a now venerable but still influential paper using manorial account data drawn from before 1400 (Table 1). Now the character of the data used by McCloskey and Nash has to be explained. It is paired sets of prices from the same manors which allow a comparison of price at different times of year. It is quite different to the data presented here for the late seventeenth century. By their estimates, the price of barley increased by 10 per cent per month and the prices of small grains by about 4 per cent per month (so about 60 per cent over the course of the year).

McCloskey and Nash only collected data to 1400. Is it the case that prices increased over the course of a year with a steady tread in the early modern period? And if they did so, did they have the effect of pricing people out of the market in the months before the new harvest? Or was there a countervailing tendency for farmers to hold back grain to the latter part of the annual cycle to secure the best price for their produce? If it is pertinent to ask whether farmers played the grain market for their own advantage, it is equally pertinent to ask whether in practice they could play the grain market given that any price signals would have been received by a lot of people at the same moment. If prices rose sharply, suggesting that it would be a good time to sell, the entry of a great many farmers into the market at the same moment might result in all of them selling grain at less than the premium price they expected to receive.

We actually know very little about how early modern farmers connected to their markets. Much recent work has not been farm-centred but market-centred, tracing the trajectory that grain took into the metropolitan market in particular, and has left key questions, including how farmers knew what to grow, and how far they had the information they needed to exercise informed discretion over the timing of their sales, unexplored (Hipkin, 2008; 2012; 2013).

And so the questions to be posed in a tentative sort of way in this paper are whether farmers were capable of playing the market, releasing their produce when prices were high and holding it back when prices were low.[1] Or did they pace the sale of their produce over the year? And, from the point of view of the consumer, did prices vary over the year, and, in particular, were there shortages attended by high prices at the end of the year? Were the weeks before the new harvest hungry weeks?

This paper introduces two new datasets. The first comes from a familiar source, John Houghton's *A collection for improvement of husbandry and trade* which appeared between 1692 and 1703.[2] Houghton's was the first financial newspaper, supplying its readers with the price of commodities in a large number of English markets, together with other fiscal information. The paper carried essays on good practice in a wide range of trades. It also found space for small advertisements from those offering and seeking employment, estate agency-type notices and publishers' notices. It lacks, however, much in the way of comment on market conditions, restricting itself to price data.

To take an issue at random, Houghton's *Collection* for 5 April 1695 gave prices for thirteen commodities in forty-eight markets. The commodities were essentially agrarian products: wheat, rye, barley, malt, oats, horse beans and others, hay, hops, wool and tallow, but also coal. Not every cell in the matrix had a price, so coal was given a price in only twenty out of the forty-eight markets. Most of the markets were in southern England. At this time Houghton had correspondents in Brecon and Pembroke and remarkably, Edinburgh. But he had no market information from Newcastle upon Tyne although he had prices from both Hull and Liverpool. Inevitably, he was very reliant on people sending him price data. He attempted to recruit Dr Thoresby of Leeds into his circle of correspondents but Thoresby did not bite and Leeds never featured in the weekly price table (Glaisyer, 2000: 244). The problem, as became apparent when this data was keyboarded, was that his contacts were not always reliable correspondents. When Houghton had no new data to hand, he tended to carry forwards the previous weeks'. In the case of Appleby in Westmorland the *Collection* carried plausible-looking price data for a period, but it never changed after August 1696 and the Appleby entry was dropped in May 1697. One must therefore expect some stickiness in the data with the reported prices trailing actual prices by a week or two, but it is also necessary to be vigilant for data which was merely being carried forwards from the last report Houghton had received. On the other hand, the four market centres selected for discussion here are very much within the orbit of London (Norwich perhaps less so than the others) and one would expect that Houghton could have easily discovered from London merchants attending the markets there what prices were current. (That said, Royston comes to exhibit the same characteristics as Appleby and is eventually deleted from the weekly returns.) The volatility of the data, and the tendency for it to move in parallel, suggests that for most

[1] Of course, farmers were often accused of hoarding grain to take advantage of the expectation of rising prices, but we need not take this social criticism as evidence of their intention.

[2] 583 issues appeared, the first on 30 March 1692 and the last one on 24 September 1703. Publication was suspended in the second half of 1692, starting again on 20 January 1693. They were reprinted in 1796 in nine volumes and in facsimile in 1969 (in four volumes). For an account of the *Collections*, see Glaisyer, 2000.

of the period it is essentially sound. On the other hand, Houghton's *Collections* do cover one of the most troubled periods of the seventeenth century, with widespread difficulties caused by poor weather, periods of high prices and further afield in Scotland and northern France, successive years of severe famine and dislocation (Cullen, 2010; Hoyle, 2017; Beaur and Chevet, 2017).

Houghton was drawn on by Andrew Appleby in his discussion of the 1690s and I subsequently re-analysed some of the same data (Appleby, 1979; Hoyle 2013). The second source employed in this paper is less familiar. This is price data taken from the "harvest" or, more exactly, the threshing books of the Reverend John Crakanthorp of Fowlmere in Cambridgeshire (d. 1719). Part of his surviving archive is in print: a further portion of the same archive was identified some years ago (Brassley, Lambert and Saunders, 1988; Hoyle, 2013).[3] Crakanthorp was a cleric and a farmer, but the majority of the produce passing through his barns came from his activities as a tithe owner. It is impossible to separate his farming from his tithe-gathering activities but it is not necessary for us to do so for our purposes here. Crackanthorp's archive gives us important data on both the price of grain and the seasonality of its disposal over a period of twenty-two years between 1680 and 1702.

II. The yearly dynamic of grain markets

Why should the price of grain have increased over the year? In terms of the laws of supply and demand, whilst consumption may well have remained constant from month to month, the stock was obviously shrinking and it is not impossible that supplies were very low at the end of the year. Consequently it should not surprise us if the price of what little remained for purchase moved upwards towards the year end. This diminishing supply would be further put under pressure by the entry into the market of people who could achieve a partial self-sufficiency in grain but who, in the final few months of the year, needed to purchase foodstuffs. The idea of the *soudure*, a period of shortage and perhaps hunger in the months before the new harvest, is common in the French historiography but has never been current in the English.[4]

An upward movement in prices is perhaps no more than we might expect when we consider the grain market in these terms. And yet the price behaviour of the market has been over-intellectualised by a succession of economists, of whom the best known are McCloskey and Nash. For them the increase in prices was a reflection of the fact that without such an increase, farmers would have been better off selling their produce at the beginning of the year and investing their income. Added to this, farmers had other costs to carry, including those of housing the crop and insuring it, but also watching it shrink in quantity and deteriorate in quality as it grew damp and succumbed to vermin. Hence,

---

[3] The dataset is that used in Hoyle (2013) based on the threshing books published by Brassley, Lambert and Saunders (1988) and two further books located subsequently which in sum give continuous data from 1680 to 1702. Crakanthorp's one surviving book of household/farm accounts is the last in a series and starts after the end of the extant threshing books.

[4] The *soudure* has been reconsidered by Beaur (2007).

the price had to rise to cover the costs the farmer incurred whilst holding stocks of grain, which had to be included in the profit he would otherwise have made on his investment (McCloskey and Nash, 1984).

This makes perfect sense in its own terms but not in terms of the agrarian society to which it relates. Here a digression into how grain was stored is necessary. Grain was brought in from the fields on the stalk and held in barns or in stacks until it was needed. Whilst stacks were outside, it seems likely that a well-thatched stack could keep grain dry and in good condition for a year or more until it was needed. The grain needed to be threshed from the straw: it might then be stored in chests or "arks" until it was needed for consumption or it could be loaded into sacks for conveyance to market. Threshed grain was vulnerable to damp, to insect and rodent damage where a stack might remain water tight and too tightly packed for insects to damage it until it was broken open, when decay might set in. There were therefore good reasons why it made no sense to thresh grain before it was needed for sale. Moreover, threshing was a physically demanding job. It had to be fitted in amongst the other demands of the farming calendar. This alone made it impossible for the whole harvest to be threshed in the weeks following the close of harvest.

That said, there is slightly later comment by Charles Smith that poorer farmers sought quick sales to raise their Michaelmas rent and settle their shop debts: all their grain might have gone by Christmas. Farmers with their rent in hand or a better line of credit may have avoided selling in September and October whilst the market was glutted (Smith, 1756: 11-12).[5] If a farmer had that financial freedom, then it seems unlikely that he would have seen any advantage in getting his grain off the farm and into the hands of a purchaser at the beginning of the new year. Moreover, he might not have seen the point in selling his crop when the price was at its seasonal lowest: indeed, every farmer bringing his total produce to market at the same moment would surely have been fatal to prices and so farm incomes. A farmer might sell his crop on harvest and arrange to deliver it to his purchaser at agreed times throughout the year, but this carried the risk that one or other party would lose money on the transaction and regret entering into it. Purchases made over the year at a current price may well have been an answer to seasonal price volatility.

If there were good reasons why farmers would have preferred not to thresh all their grain in the weeks following the harvest, it made equally little sense for merchants trading in grain to buy (and take receipt of) a year's supply in September. Grain is perishable. They did not want to buy threshed grain in September for use the following August *even* if they had the money to lay out, *even* if it might have been a good investment, because the risk of its loss or impairment by rodents, insects and damp was too great. Nor did they want to carry the costs of warehousing and there was always the danger that prices would fall and purchases made in September or October would look foolish months later. And whilst they would doubtless have purchased on credit, there was surely a danger that a merchant who guessed wrongly could well be bankrupted by his miscalculation.

What is certain is that the medieval peasant (and probably the early modern farmer too) did not think of the seasonal increment of prices in terms of income lost on money

[5] Smith distinguishes four categories of farmers each with different approaches to the market: we discuss this below.

which might have been out at interest: it seems barely plausible that they could have secured interest rates anything like as large as McCloskey and Nash infer underpinned the logic of holding stocks.

So we can explain the price behaviour identified by McCloskey and Nash in terms of risk being avoided by some elements within the supply chain and passed back to the farmer. But what this price behaviour also suggests is that there was actually a shortage of produce in circulation: that by the summer there was less rather than more in the market, and the market increasingly became a seller's market rather than a buyer's market. Hence this behaviour in medieval England may suggest that the *soudure* applied: but did it in the early modern period?

It seems reasonable to suppose that grain prices will be at the highest in the weeks before the next harvest but as we shall see, in a late seventeenth-century context, this seems not to be so. Now there are a number of reasons why prices should rise over the period of a harvest year. There could, of course, be short term runs in high prices if farmers found it difficult to get their grain to market because of flooding, or even if the cold made it hard to thresh grain. Price rises could follow upon quantity factors: the quantity could remain the same, but of course higher prices elsewhere could encourage an outflow in grain to distant markets encouraging local prices to rise. Conversely, the arrival of imports into those same distant markets could result in falls in prices at a distance (Hoyle, 2017: 145; Holt, 2013: 52-54, the last describing speculative voyages taking grain from the north-west to the south-west of England in the 1670s). But what we want to suggest here is that the price of grain is also determined by the prospect for the next harvest. McCloskey and Nash allowed for this in an important concession which seems to undercut their prevailing logic (McCloskey and Nash, 1984: 179).

If the harvest looks as though it will be good, then it plainly makes sense to offload the remaining stocks of threshed grain onto the market and restock granaries with new corn in the autumn. We might expect a good harvest to be anticipated by a degree of discounting. If the prospects were poor however, then it is more likely that the price would rise as it would be assumed that some of this year's grain would be needed to support the market in the following year. We can therefore suppose that in some years there might be a deliberate carry-over of grain: in others the retention of a reserve of the previous year's produce might be seen as far from desirable.

III. Patterns of prices and future supply

Having laid out some of the questions, we can employ some of the data from Houghton to try and answer them. The price data from four towns will be drawn upon: Norwich, itself a big urban centre, Hitchen and Royston, both towns about forty miles north of London (and about sixteen miles apart), both strongly engaged in the supply of the capital and Reading, thirty miles west of London in the Thames valley, and a town from which grain was shipped down river to the metropolis. Regrettably the Royston data ends in January 1697 but that for Hitchin is complete.

The pattern of prices for the four markets over the period when Houghton was collecting and gathering data is strongly synchronous, probably more so for wheat than barley

Figure 1 Wheat prices (*s.* per quarter), 1693-1702 from Houghton (monthly averages)

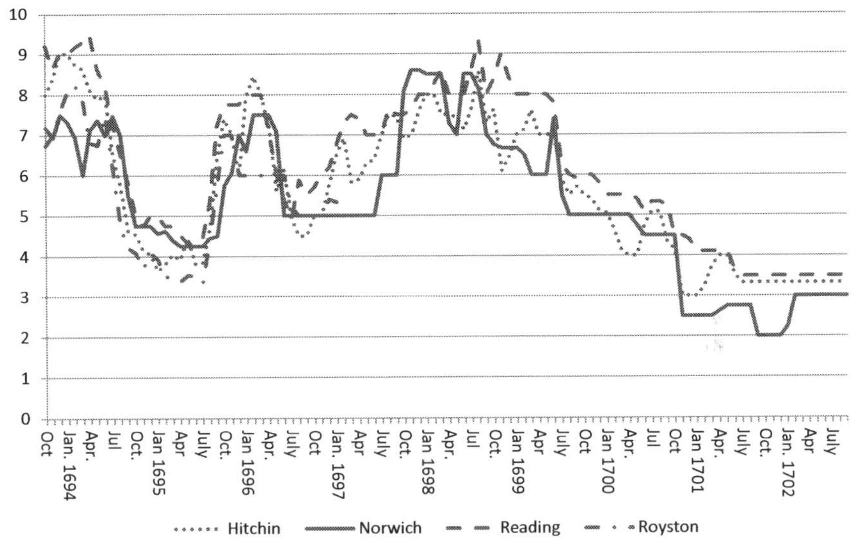

Source: calculated from the data in John Houghton, *A collection for improvement of husbandry and trade* (1692-1703).

(Figures 1 and 2).[6] Particularly for wheat, we can see the volatility of prices over the 1690s, with the high prices following the harvest of 1693, the good harvest of 1694, the poor harvest of 1695 which launched a turbulent period brought to an end by the harvest of 1698, after which prices fell to very low levels, The pattern for barley is less clear cut, partly because of breaks in the price data (a point to which we will return) but the same essential pattern is visible.

If we look at the record of monthly grain prices for Reading taken from Houghton for the same years, then we do indeed find instances in which the price of grain is higher at the end of the year than at the beginning (Figures 3 and 4). But this is very much an occasional occurrence as Table 2 shows. In the case of wheat, then there are only three instances, 1694-95, 1696-97 and 1697-98, of this pattern of behaviour. The record of 1694-95 is especially interesting: the price followed a long slow downward curve until May but after July it turned sharply upwards. Something similar happened the following year when a long downward curve was suddenly replaced by a sharp upwards movement in July, but on this occasion there was a degree of falling back on August. In 1696-97 an upward curve was pretty consistent throughout the year, so prices opened at 5.7*s.* in October but closed at 7.5*s.* in the following September. Inevitably the following year opened at a very high level of 7*s.* odd, reached a peak in March (9.3*s.*), then sagged a

[6] Figures in the next paragraphs are monthly means of the weekly data.

Figure 2 Barley prices (*s.* per quarter), 1693-1702 from Houghton (monthly averages)

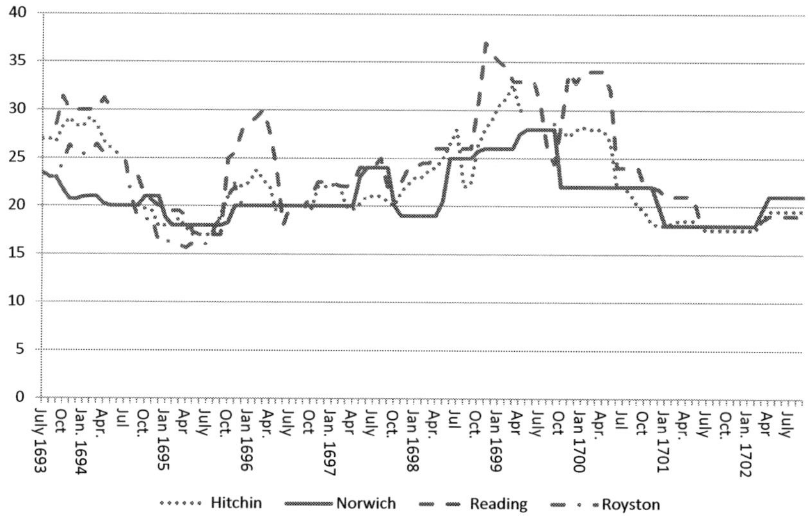

Source: calculated from the data in John Houghton, *A collection for improvement of husbandry and trade* (1692-1703).

Figure 3 Reading wheat prices (*s.* per quarter), 1692-3 to 1701-2, from Houghton (monthly averages)

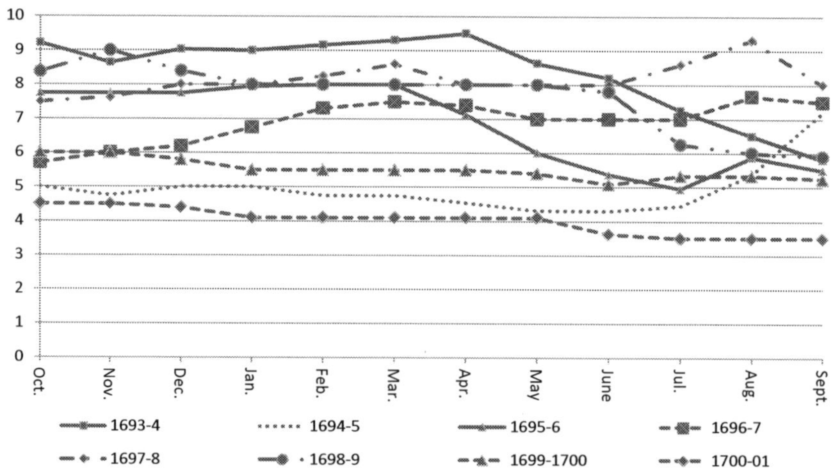

Source: calculated from the data in John Houghton, *A collection for improvement of husbandry and trade* (1692-1703).

Figure 4 Reading barley prices (*s.* per quarter), 1693-4 to 1700-1, from Houghton (monthly averages)

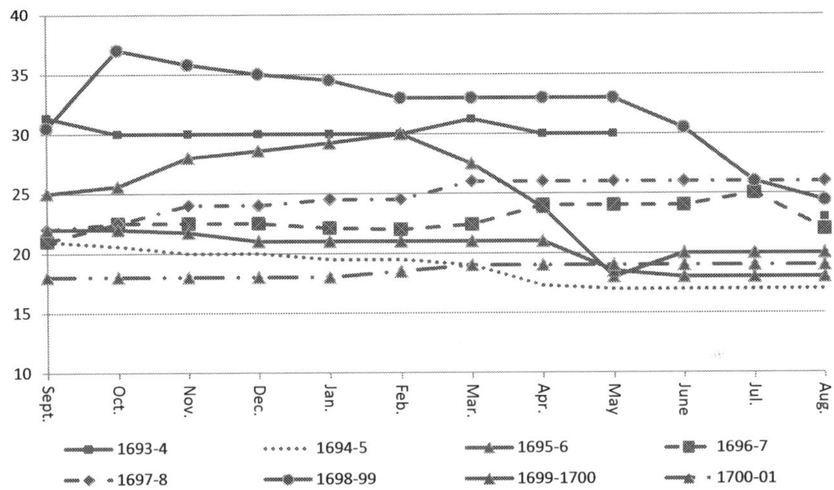

Source: calculated from the data in John Houghton, *A collection for improvement of husbandry and trade* (1692-1703).

little before achieving a new peak in August of 8.6*s*., after which they fell back a little to a September mean price of 8*s*. Inevitably the following year opened at a high price of 8.375*s*. The price stayed at around 8*s*. until June after which it fell sharply, so that by September 1699 it stood at 5.9*s*.

In the case of Barley (Table 2), in two years, the price at the year end was higher than that at the opening. In 1696-97 the price opened at about 21*s*., slowly climbed to 25*s*. in August and closed at 22*s*. In 1697-98 it opened at much the same level but for the last six months stood at a monthly average of 26*s*. It is possible to point to three years, 1695-96, 1698-99 and 1699-1700 in which the price was higher at some point mid-year than the closing price.

Figures 3 and 4 for wheat and barley respectively show no regular pattern in the movement of prices over the year. But they do show a number of breakpoints in the pattern in which the direction of travel of the price of grain was either reversed or accelerated. In most years we see an autumn adjustment – probably starting before the harvest is gathered in – as prospects for the harvest and predictions of its quantity bring about a transition from the previous year's price to the new year's price. This then establishes a sort of base price against which all other movements need to be considered.

For wheat, November forms a breakpoint in four years: we may take this to be the moment at which information about the success of the sowing of winter wheat could filter into the system. There is a similar breakpoint in March and April reflecting the sowing of spring wheat. In three years, 1693-94, 1695-96 and 1697-98, the price of wheat begins

Table 2 Reading grain prices at the beginning and end of the year

	Wheat mean prices (*s.*)		**Barley mean prices (*s.*)**	
	First three months	**Last three months**	**First three months**	**Last three months**
1693-4	8.96	6.52	30.5	23.0
1694-5	4.91	5.67	20.53	17
1695-6	7.75	5.44	26.2	20.0
1696-7	5.96	7.39	22.0	23.66
1697-8	7.71	8.6	22.83	26.0
1698-9	8.6	6.05	34.43	26.97
1699-1700	5.93	5.30	31.77	24.0
1700-01	4.46	3.5	21.92	18

Source: calculated from the data in John Houghton, *A collection for improvement of husbandry and trade* (1692-1703).

to fall from the mid-year point. There then follows a succession of years with breakpoints in the summer. In 1697-98, the price began to rise after June and did so for two months before falling back. In June 1693-94 however, the price, having fallen a little from a November peak, fell sharply from June as there was plainly confidence in the prospects for the forthcoming harvest. On three other occasions, a lack of confidence in July forced the price up: in 1694-95, after the price had been fairly stagnant over the year, 1695-96, after the price had fallen substantially and 1696-97. On three occasions, nervousness in June or July, which had set prices rising, was replaced by optimism in August which set prices falling.

The pattern of barley prices had obvious breakpoints in November. On three occasions prices rose after this month (1695-96, 1698-99 and 1699-1700): in 1693-94 a falling market was stopped. Breakpoints in the spring are less obvious, except in 1695-96 where a rising market was reversed once it became clear that the sowing of spring barley had proceeded satisfactorily. Something similar happened in April 1699-1700 where a market which had remained largely unaltered since the previous November fell sharply. June forms a more obvious breakpoint: in 1698-99 prices fell sharply after June. The following year a fall was brought to an end, as it had been in 1695-96.

Now the implication of this analysis is not that the price was solely set by the quality of the previous harvest, but that the price was sensitive to the prospects for future supply. The rises and falls in price have to be related to the reports reaching the mercantile community of the likely quality of the next harvest: if good, prices tended to fall. If it looked poor, then they rose. In some cases alarms proved to be short lived and prices fell back when a particular episode had passed. Current price then was determined not only by supply, but by a calculation of how long that supply might have to last.

What we are seeing is an indirect reflection of the weather translated through reports of sowing and growing conditions. Figures 5 and 6 show the movement of wheat and barley

Figure 5 Hitchin, Norwich, Reading and Royston wheat prices, June 1693-December 1695, from Houghton (weekly prices)

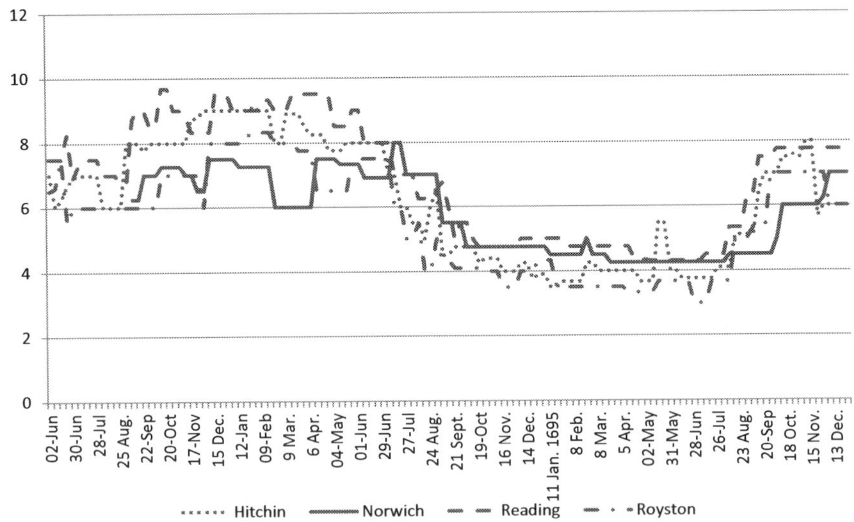

Source: calculated from the data in John Houghton, *A collection for improvement of husbandry and trade* (1692-1703).

Figure 6 Hitchin, Norwich, Reading and Royston barley prices, June 1693-December 1695, from Houghton (weekly prices)

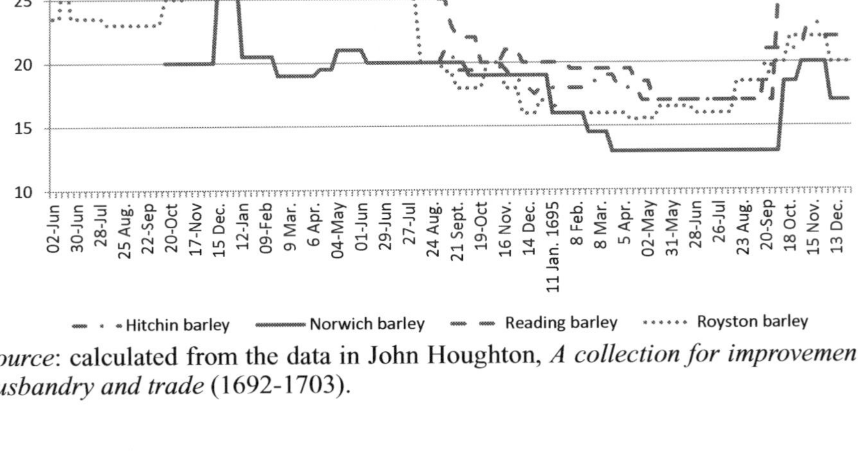

Source: calculated from the data in John Houghton, *A collection for improvement of husbandry and trade* (1692-1703).

Table 3 Excessive gaps in Houghton's price data (grains only)

			Price before	Price after
Reading	Barley	30 June to 1 Sept 1693	25 s.	29 s.
Royston	Barley	27 Mar.-6 Apr. 1694	25.9 s.	25.5 s.
Hitchin	Barley	18 May-24 Aug. 1694	26 s.	20 s.
Reading	Barley	8 June-24 Aug 1694	30 s.	25 s.
Hitchin	Barley	29 May-17 July 1696	18.5 s.	20 s.
Hitchin	Barley	22 July-19 Aug. 1698	28 s.	22 s.
Hitchin	Barley	26 May-25 Aug. 1699	30 s.	28 s.

Note: Malt not included.
Source: calculated from the data in John Houghton, *A collection for improvement of husbandry and trade* (1692-1703).

prices in the four markets for a period of eighteen months in 1693-95. Even over quite extended distances, it is plain that breakpoints occur at much the same moments. The wheat data is more complete than that for barley. It shows how in the ten weeks following the beginning of July there is a seasonal correction which starts before the harvest is declared and continues for a few weeks after it but that the prices continued to be adjusted over the year. For instance, when compared to the 1694 harvest, it is plain enough that the 1693 harvest finds it hard to find a stable price: in both Reading and Norwich there are short moments of price reduction in November and again in March. The price in Reading and Hitchin falls from the end of May: there is some anxiety about the harvest in Norwich and the prices rises in July. The fall to 1694 prices is delayed until August. The price is never quite static because the market is looking not only backwards to the supply of grain from the previous market, but forwards to the likely supply of grain from the next market. As the forward prospects look poor, prices rise to enforce a system of rationing to make the product last longer. Hence we can envisage a constant dialogue between the corn factors and their suppliers, the farmers: how does the crop look? Has an adequate area been sown? Has it been damaged by frost, flooding, too little rain/too much rain?

So the price of grain was sensitive not only to stocks but also to future supply. The price could go up as well as down in the months before a new harvest was declared. What we do not see though is any regular pattern of high year end prices which indicate a shortage in the markets. This then raises a question: how were the markets supplied to ensure that there was no end of year shortage?

In turn, this raises another question. When Houghton fails to give prices for a commodity in the midst of much longer series, what is he trying to tell us? That he had no information or that no produce was presented for sale? The number of occasions on which this happens for more than two consecutive weeks is small and the examples in the dataset under discussion all come from Reading or Hitchin. They are summarised in Table 3. What is striking is that they all concern barley and all save one come at the end of the year, precisely when we might expect there to be little grain available for sale. The intervals without dates are all associated with high prices, in two cases with substantial falls in prices. The possibility needs to be taken seriously that the supply of barley dried up in some summers in some markets. But barley is a brewing and not a bread grain: the shortfall might impact on the supply of beer, but not bread.

IV. Farmers' approaches to the market

Other than short term fluctuations caused by breaks in supply (problems of transportation, snow, floods and the like), price is therefore the outcome of the market weighing three factors. The first is the size of the previous harvest then being sold. The second is confidence in the following harvest. The first is fixed: the second could introduce volatility into the price as farmers reported on how well sowing had gone, how the grain was filling out and the likely yield of the harvest. A third factor which could bear on the price is the possibility of inter-regional transfers or even international flows. Markets could anticipate the arrival of supplies attracted by high prices which would bring down prices: perhaps less easy to anticipate is the outflow of grain from districts where the price was low to those where it was higher. It was the sight of this happening which produced public discontent.

How far was farmer's behaviour coloured by this sort of consideration? Before turning to Crakanthorp, it is worth looking a little further at Smith's discussion of farmers if only to make the point that farmers were not a homogenous group who all responded in the same way to price signals (Smith, 1756: 11-14). Smith identified four categories. The first were the poor farmers who sold their grain quickly to satisfy their landlord and creditors. "[T] heir crops are generally all threshed, sold and gone before Christmas, or by the time their lands are in order and the seed put into the ground for the next year's crop". The "farmers in moderate circumstances" needed to sell to cover immediate costs, "and if they have any corn left in May, they think themselves well off". The "farmers in good circumstances" "generally have it in their power, after seeding their lands, paying rent, purchasing live stock and paying all other expenses through the year to reserve a few loads of wheat to sell in, or after, harvest in order to bear the expense thereof, and in expectation, if the season should prove bad, to make a better price than before harvest". In a small way they had the capacity of playing the market. The "rich farmers" were able to "keep the whole, or the greatest part of their crops, the year over, speculate on the markets, thresh out and sell when they like the price". Now this may suggest that they were speculating in the market: but Smith read their behaviour a different way. They acted as granaries and, whilst acting in their own interest, released their grain into the market when the price was dear and by doing so stopped it going higher. There were too few of them to cause distress to the poor, and the cost to them of holding back grain was high ("the waste made by vermin makes their expense in keeping it very great, and frequently forces them to market sooner than they might otherwise intend to go"). They therefore fulfilled a social role as well as playing the market.

V. Crakanthorp's rhythm of threshings and sales

Crakanthorp's threshing book allows us to see in detail the behaviour of one farmer/tithe gatherer. In the light of Smith's comments we cannot take a single farmer as representative of all farmers. How well does Crakanthorp fit into the classification Smith suggests?

The Crakanthorp data is a series of accounts kept year by year from 1680 to 1702 of the threshing ("dressing") of Crakanthorp's grain and its disposal. Where the grain was sold, we normally have a note of the purchaser and where he came from, the quantity and the price secured. Crakanthorp generally sold wheat and barley in large units to corn merchants at Royston and other neighbouring towns. Rye he tended to sell locally, one assumes at the farm gate. Unfortunately the threshing books do not give the date of sale, but their implication is that the grain was sold quickly after threshing, especially in the case of barley when Crackanthorp was threshing every week or ten days. On one occasion we have a note that wheat threshed in May 1688 was sold the following Michaelmas, but this is an exceptional occurrence and there is no second example to cite. Crakanthorp also had small quantities of oats, but sold little of this, and so it is not considered further here. In terms of the volume, most of the grain passing through Crakanthorp's hands was barley and this was almost entirely sold in large units and, one supposes, malted locally or conveyed to London to be malted there. Wheat was threshed for household consumption but was also sold to corn merchants. The number of wheat threshings though is insufficient to allow any great conclusions to be drawn over price. Crackanthorp also sent barley to be malted on his own account, but in very variable quantities, and we have no further evidence of how this was disposed of.

In Tables 4-6 we give the dates of the first and last threshings for the three grains under consideration. For both wheat and rye the first threshing was often to produce grain for sowing and household consumption or local sale. For this reason the tables give the dates of the first threshing and the first threshing for sale (by which we mean sale to a corn factor in large volumes rather than farmgate sales of small parcels). Of course, threshing dates are variable because the date of the harvest was variable. Summary data by month is presented in Table 7. This gives the average number of threshings per calendar month over the whole twenty-three years. An average of 1.0 implies that Crakanthorp threshed on average once in that month: a figure of 4.0 that he threshed weekly.

The first threshing of wheat was generally in September, occasionally the last days of August or the first week of October (Table 4). The first threshing for sale could be at any time between late September or the first months of the new year: the last threshing for sale was generally in May or at latest the first weeks of June. (The last threshing of 1701 on 29 June is wholly exceptional.) Wheat threshed in September and October was usually for seed for sowing. Crakanthorp only occasionally threshed wheat in the five consecutive months November-March: he threshed in these winter months only forty-two times over twenty-three years. The chief period for threshing wheat was April and May, in a few years continuing into early June. The general pattern was that he threshed for grain to sow and household consumption in late August-early October, then threshed no more than twice in an average year between November and April, and threshed his remaining wheat for sale in April, May and early June (Table 7). He therefore contributed little to the trade in wheat between harvest and April.

The pattern for rye is similar (Table 5). Crakanthorp generally threshed nine or ten times over the year. Generally he threshed twice for seed and the consumption of his household in late August-early October, but he sold rather more rye (albeit locally) through the

Table 4 Crakanthorp: number of threshings of wheat each year and first and last dates of threshings for sale

Harvest	Number of threshings	Date of first threshing	Date of first threshing for sale	Date of last threshing for sale
1680	6	1 September	6 September	4 June
1681	10	17 September	17 September	9 May
1682	7	2 October	3 November	31 May
1683	8	17 October	22 December	7 June
1684	6	26 August	26 August	28 April
1685	8	8 October	8 October[a]	10 May
1686	6	2 September	20 September	24 May
1687	6	6 September	18 October	19 May[b]
1688	6	8 September	18 January	17 May
1689	7	17 September	2 January	26 May
1690	9	16 September	9 October	20 June
1691	8	7 September	28 September	14 June
1692	9	26 September	18 October	8 May
1693	8	29 September	17 October	16 May
1694	9	20 August	6 October	6 June
1695	5	4 October	25 February	10 April
1696	6	18 September	21 November	1 May
1697	5	8 September	13 October	10 May
1698	7	7 September	20 December	13 May
1699	8	23 September	7 December	3 May (17 May)
1700	7	31 August	28 December	6 June
1701	7	30 September	6 October	29 June
1702	7	22 September	12 October	4 May

Note: 'Date of first threshing for sale' excludes earlier threshings where small volumes are sold locally.
[a] In this year Crakanthorpe only sold wheat 'at home'.
[b] Five quarters sold at Michaelmas following.
Source: Author's spreadsheet of the Crakanthorp threshing books, Brassley, Lambert and Saunders, 1988, pp. 35-119; University of Reading, Museum of English Rural Life, D60/18-19.

Table 5 Crakanthorp: number of threshings of rye each year and first and last dates of threshings for sale

Harvest	Number of threshings	Date of first threshing	Date of first threshing for sale	Date of last threshing for sale
1680	9	24 September	24 September	16 June
1681	9	22 September	30 September	24 June
1682	10	18 September	26 October	27 April
1683	11	14 September	7 December	30 June
1684	10	30 August	18 October	10 June
1685	12	2 September	18 September	22 June
1686	9	9 September	20 November	2 June
1687	12	16 September	22 September	23 June
1688	8	12 September	18 September	22 June
1689	9	12 September	16 September[a]	14 June
1690	12	20 September-1 October	7 October	30 May
1691	9	17 September	25 November	23 May
1692	14	21 September	6 October	1 July
1693	7	20 September	9 December	7 June
1694	13	12-18 September	27 September	28 June
1695	12	17 September	24 September	11 June
1696	8	6 October	12 October	10 June
1697	6	13-29 September	1 March	8 June
1698	11	9 August	5 December	20 June
1699	12	5 September	15 September	14 June
1700	7	6 September	11 October	28 May
1701	10	30 August-9 September	9 September	13 June
1702	9	10 September	20 October	13 May

Note:
[a] But no further threshing to 14 February.
Source: Author's spreadsheet of the Crakanthorp threshing books, Brassley, Lambert and Saunders, 1988, pp. 35-119; University of Reading, Museum of English Rural Life, D60/18-19.

Table 6 Crakanthorpe: number of threshings of barley each year and first and last dates of threshings for sale

Harvest	Number of threshings	Date of first threshing for sale	Date of last threshing for sale
1680	24	18 November	19 April (25 April)
1681	17	9 December	17 April
1682	27	20 November	26 April
1683	26	12 November	12 May
1684	25	12 November	23 April
1685	23	3 November	22 April
1686	23	26 October	28 March
1687	29	1 November	28 April
1688	22	8 November	16 April
1689	25	30 October	18 April
1690	23	3 November	3 April
1691	25	3 November	6 May
1692	25	1 November	16 May (19 May)
1693	24	7 November	11 April (23 April)
1694	25	6 November	8 May
1695	24	2 November	24 April
1696	20	10 November	5 May
1697	21	23 November	12 April (19 April)
1698	17	10 November	7 April
1699	23	25 October	12 April
1700	24	1 November	28 April
1701	23	21 October	30 March
1702	20	23 October	6 April (19 April)

Source: Author's spreadsheet of the Crakanthorp threshing books, Brassley, Lambert and Saunders, 1988, pp. 35-119; University of Reading, Museum of English Rural Life, D60/18-19.

winter. So in an average year he threshed three or four times between November and the end of March but again, most of the threshing was done in April, May and June when he generally threshed four times in ten or eleven weeks (Table 7). As Table 5 shows, his last threshing generally took place in the first half of June. This was generally for household consumption.

Table 7 Crakanthorp: number of threshings by calendar month by grain type, 1680-1702, and average per month

	August	September	October	November	December	January	February	March	April	May	June	July	TOTAL
Wheat													
Number of Threshings	4	22	23	5	10	9	10	8	29	33	9	0	162
Average	0.17	0.96	1.0	0.22	0.43	0.39	0.43	0.35	1.26	1.43	0.39	0	7.04
Rye													
Number of Threshings	2	38	8	6	16	13	19	27	22	41	35	1	228
Average	0.09	1.65	0.35	0.26	0.70	0.57	0.83	1.17	0.96	1.78	1.52	0.04	9.91
Barley													
Number of Threshings	0	0	7	86	93	97	82	91	67	8	0	0	531
Average	0	0	0.30	3.74	4.04	4.22	3.57	3.96	2.91	0.35	0	0	23.1

Source: Author's spreadsheet of the Crakanthorp threshing books, Brassley, Lambert and Saunders, 1988, pp. 35-119; University of Reading, Museum of English Rural Life, D60/18-19.

Barley was quite different. There was no need to thresh in the autumn for seed. Nor was much consumed or sold locally. As Table 6 shows, threshing generally started at the end of October or in the first days of November and was completed in April or at worst early May. In between those dates Crakanthorp threshed on average twenty-three times (Table 7), so roughly weekly (although nothing quite so regular can be detected in the threshing books). We should note however that there is normally a gap in sales in late February or March as the barley threshed was diverted into seed for sowing. This can be seen plainly when the sales for an individual year are plotted: it is less obvious in Figure 7.[7]

In a typical year all the barley was finished in April, all the wheat in May and all the rye in June. Nothing was threshed in July and August in any year and so as far as can be told, Crakanthorp never carried unthreshed grain over into the following year and very rarely had old corn to sell in the new harvest year. He did not use corn from the previous harvest to sow either, but this may have been regarded as bad practice carrying the risk of poor germination.

It is hard to tell whether Crakanthorp responded to short-term price movements. It might be possible to maintain an argument that the holding back of wheat was itself a calculation based on price. On the other hand, this may have been when the corn dealers wanted the grain. It would seem less rather than more likely that Crakanthorp would take large volumes of grain speculatively to market without being assured that a purchaser would be there to receive it, and so decisions on the timing of sales may have been made by his purchasers rather than Crackanthorp himself. Given that the pattern of sales never changes from year to year, there is no sign that Crakanthorp either sold early to take advantage of high winter prices or staggered his sales to take advantage of high summer prices.

This can be seen if we take six years' data starting in 1690 as in Figure 7. These are years which span the beginning of the bad years of the 1690s: they have been chosen in part because we have for part of the period (but not all) Houghton's data for prices at Hitchin and Royston which can be compared with the prices Crakanthorp secured for his grain. This figure also includes the barley sent for malting. In some years no barley was used this way: in others quite large amounts were diverted into malt and we have to assume that Crakanthorp then sold some or all of the malt onto third parties – the volumes concerned seem too large to be used in domestic brewing.

The figure shows graphically just how short a period in the year Crakanthorp was selling grain. He did not obviously curtail or extend the period in the light of the prevailing price. In 1690-91, when barley was selling about 12*s.* a quarter, he sold out at the end of March. In 1693-94 when the prevailing price was about 25*s.*, he sold out in early April. In other years the selling season was extended into May, but it is hard to come to any conclusion that high prices encouraged him to adopt a different strategy.

A closer scrutiny shows how the pattern of prices differs from year to year. In 1690-91 there was very little movement: the opening price in November (11*s.* 0*d.* a quarter) pretty much held good through to the end of March. In 1691-92 uncertain opening prices of between 11*s.* 6*d.* and 12*s.* 6*d.* had moved sharply upwards by the middle of December

[7] The charts for individual years can be obtained from the author.

Figure 7 Christopher Crakanthorp, barley transactions 1690-5 with prices at Hitchin and Royston from Houghton

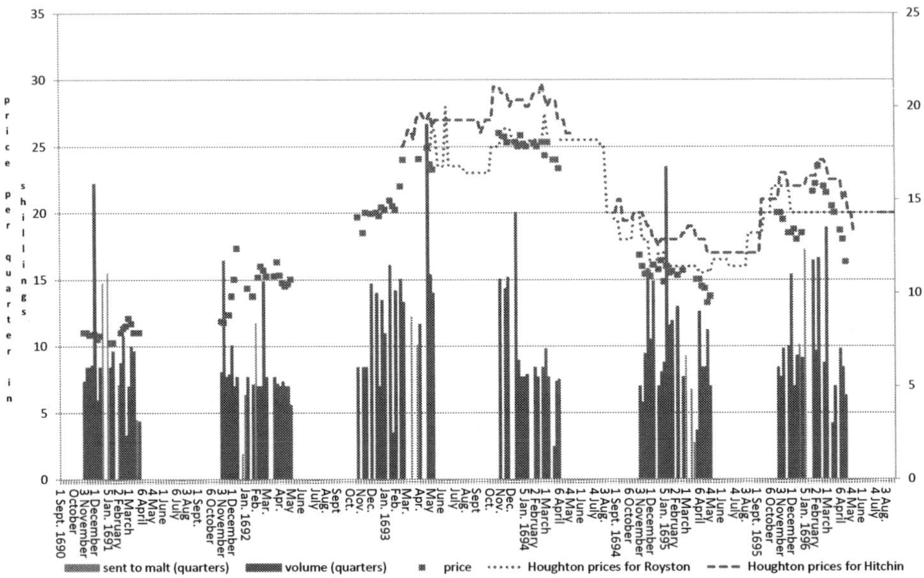

Source: calculated from the data in John Houghton, *A collection for improvement of husbandry and trade (1692-1703)*, and the Crakanthorp threshing books, Brassley, Lambert and Saunders, 1988, pp. 35-119; University of Reading, Museum of English Rural Life, D60/18-19

(17*s*. 4*d*.) and whilst falling back a little, stayed at around 15*s*. for the remainder of the selling season. These movements have to reflect an assessment of future prospects in the winter of 1691-92. In 1692-93 the market opened at a higher price than had been seen in previous years. Crakanthorp's first sale was at 19*s*. 8*d*., his second at 18*s*. 6*d*. and subsequent sales at November and December were at around 19*s*. or 20*s*. This was an unsettled and nervous market without a single price reflecting anxieties about the supply available. In February the price edged up to 24*s*., reaching 25*s*. in April. As this upwards movement coincided with the sowing season for spring grains, it reflects additional nervousness over the following harvest. By May confidence had grown and the price fell back a little. The following year, 1693-94, showed similar features. It opened even higher than 1692-93 at 25*s*. or 26*s*. a quarter and stayed in that general frame through to the last sale in April and fell a little with the sowing of the following crop in March. The harvest of 1694 was much better and prices fell by a third to 15*s*. or 16*s*. a quarter, remaining at that level through the winter and dropping a little as confidence built in the following harvest. In 1695-96 the price opened at 20*s*. but sagged a little between November and the end of the year. The sowing of spring crops was watched with some anxiety and the price moved upwards, touching 23*s*. 6*d*. in February only to fall back over April and May as confidence in the following harvest grew. Crakanthorp's last sale was made at 16*s*. 4*d*. and was the worst price he secured in the year. By this time Houghton's correspondent in Royston had become inactive and it may be seen in Figure 7 how the Royston price is carried forwards without amendment. At Hitchin the price of barley shows a marked decline over the spring, matching the pattern of Crakanthorp prices.

A very close scrutiny of the week-by-week data suggests that there are occasions when prices were high and Crakanthorp brought forwards quite large quantities of barley for sale in the space of a few days. How far this was to take advantage of the price it is hard to tell: given that we are talking of barley, it is difficult to see him bringing forwards large quantities with the social objective of bringing the price down to help poorer purchasers. But overall one feels that Crakanthorp was, if not impervious to the market, not trying to play it either. In the definitions used by Smith, he was somewhere between a farmer in "moderate circumstances": who felt he had done well if he still had grain in hand in May and a farmer in "good circumstances" who was able carry grain forwards into the new season. The fact that he sold everything by the end of June may reflect his own preference and the desire for a certain sort of housekeeping rather than any pressing need to pay rent or settle debts.

VI. Is there any seasonal advantage in grain markets?

It would be wrong to claim that a study of little more than two decades at the end of the seventeenth century, and based largely on the threshing accounts of a single individual, can speak for the whole of England in the early modern period. Of course, despite its faults, there is nothing equivalent to Houghton's weekly data until much later and good farm accounts are not two-a-penny at any time. But this paper surely shows the interest of the issues and the need for additional materials to be examined.

We do not find any steady rise in price over the harvest year in the way detected by McCloskey and Nash. Rather, prices seem to have found their level soon after the harvest and in years without external shocks kept within fairly narrow bands over the year. Where there were shocks, the price tended to rise until confidence in the next harvest grew. In the autumn, there was interest in how the sowing of winter grains had proceeded and in February and March spring-sown grains. The likely quantity and quality of the forthcoming harvest was the subject of discussion over the summer. Ralph Josselin mentions this developing assessment of the harvest in his diary on a number of occasions. Of July 1667 he noted that "grass scarce, corn thin on all dry grounds, but good on many cold and heavy lands, so that it was a good year, confirming that a drought breeds no famine in England". On 1 July 1675 he noted that "The weather gave hopes, for rain and colds a sad time, yet it made no flood God be praised, Corn rose again [in price], rye being gappy and [it is] feared wheat sets ill". Fears for future supply set prices rising (Macfarlane, 1976: 534, 586).

Now if this assessment is right, then there is a question to be asked about whether McCloskey and Nash read the medieval data correctly or whether the dynamics of the medieval market differed from that of the late seventeenth century. The difference between the two may well have lain in the development of a corn factoring business with warehousing facilities which contained buffer stocks. Again Smith offers some useful comments on this although he is talking of a period half a century and more after the data discussed here. The granaries of the corn merchants stood in place of public granaries. They plainly had a role in the regulation of the trade by evening out the supply of grain, buying when supply was plentiful at the beginning of the harvest year. But Smith does not see the merchants as holding grain over long periods, but holding individual parcels of corn for no more than a matter of months so that the corn remained "sweet". Hence the contents of a granary turned over as rapidly as once a month and never less than three times a year (Smith, 1756: 13-15).

So we find no indication of higher summer prices but a little evidence for the market in barley not being active in the summer and perhaps even drying up in some years. This focuses us back on seasonality. Smith shows that the strategies that farmers employed were not all the same, and some had a greater freedom to choose when they sold than others for whom a quick sale at the beginning of the year was necessary. Crakanthorp can only be read as representing Crakanthorp, but it is plain enough that he did not rush into the market immediately after the harvest but bided his time until November. Thereafter his strategy varied from grain to grain, but he seems to have made no attempt to exploit summer prices. Indeed, it is far from clear that he ever tried to play the market for advantage. He may have felt that as a clergyman he was under a degree of public scrutiny and could not been seen acting to his private advantage. He may have been less of a capitalist than some others, or he may simply have seen little advantage in holding onto grain. It may not be irrelevant here that he generally sold within a fairly narrow group of merchants. Occasionally he sold to people whose names he barely seemed to know, but it may be that he sought to protect long-standing relationships with factors, to fall out with whom would limit his capacity to sell (or the ease with which he could sell) and therefore he had to bring grain forwards when they called for it.

The pattern of sales suggests that the opportunities for large farmers to hold back grain to take advantage of seasonal high prices was limited: indeed, it may be queried whether in an ordinary year there were any seasonal high prices. Perhaps farmers had greater opportunities when they were selling wheat. In the same way as Crakanthorp is not representative of all farmers, barley is not representative of all grains.

VII. Conclusion

So, where have we arrived? We find little evidence that prices rise over the year. The normal pattern seems to be that the price was largely set at the beginning of the year. Variations in that level do take place and appear to be connected with fears for – and in some case confidence in – the next harvest. We can therefore identify breakpoints at which the price begins to rise or fall according to the signals being received from farmers about the state of the next year's grain in the fields and the promise of the harvest. The price was a compound based on the quality of the previous year's harvest and the predicted quality of the following harvest. It would not be unreasonable to suppose that the former gave a base price and the anticipated harvest caused the price to rise and fall around that base price. The result however was that there was no regular pattern of the price rising over the year: we showed examples of the price being lower at the end of the year than at its beginning as confidence in the following harvest grew.

This surely impacted on the behaviour of farmers bringing their grain to market. The logic adduced by McCloskey and Nash seems to be inapplicable to early modern England and it may be questioned whether it applied any better in the late middle ages. There were a variety of logics that might have persuaded some farmers to bring their corn to market late in the year, but this may be more a case of personal preference than profiteering. Indeed, Smith saw farmers who held their grain until late in the year as fulfilling a public service by entering the market when smaller suppliers were running low on stocks. There is no sign that farmers who were late entrants into the market withheld stocks because they believed that prices would be higher.

With Crakanthorp we can begin to penetrate into the world of the individual farmer. He is not quick into the market after the harvest, and he rarely sold grain in the summer: and in between his sales of barley in particular, if not entirely regular, were sufficiently frequent to suggest that he had no interest in playing the market for advantage. That he seems to have sold little between the end of May and the end of September in most years suggests an element of the *soudure*: grain markets may have been quiet over the summer. As Smith suggests, some farmers may have been compelled to rush into the market to raise their Michaelmas rents (21 September), but there is no suggestion in Houghton's weekly reports that summer prices were habitually higher. In a few years though it is possible that the trade in barley came to a halt.

Whilst Houghton's prices can be taken to be representative of the markets to the north and west of London that supplied the metropolis, Crakanthorp, as a clerical small farmer and tithe proprietor, is an unusual figure. On the other hand, it is hard to see how his connection to the market would have differed from that of many other farmers. Whilst Crakanthorp's archive directs a shaft of light into an area which has been obscure, the search is surely on for other accounts which can shed equal light and offer the comparative element which we need to understand properly these questions of seasons and prices.

Bibliography

Appleby, A. (1979) 'Grain prices and subsistence crises in England and France, 1590-1740', *The Journal of Economic History*, 39, 4, pp. 865-887.

Béaur, G. (2007) 'La "soudure" n'est plus ce qu'elle était. Contribution à l'étude du mouvement saisonnier du marché du blé et du marché de la terre d'après le cas de la région de Chartres au XVIIIe siècle', Chauvard, J.-F. and Laboulais, I. (eds), *Les fruits de la récolte. Études offertes à Jean-Michel Boehler*, Strasbourg, pp. 93-107.

Béaur, G. and Chevet, J.-M. (2017) 'France', Alfani, G. and Ó'Gráda, C. (eds), *Famine in European History*, Cambridge, pp. 73-100.

Brassley, P., Lambert, A. and Saunders, P. (eds) (1988) *Accounts of the Reverend John Crakanthorp of Fowlmere, 1682-1710*, Cambridge.

Chartres, J. A. (1985) 'The Marketing of Agricultural Produce', Thirsk, J. (ed.), *The Agrarian History of England and Wales. Vol. V 1640-1750. II Agrarian Change*, Cambridge, pp. 406-502.

Cullen, K. (2010) *Famine in Scotland: the 'ill years' of the 1690s*, Edinburgh.

Glaisyer, N. (2000) 'Readers, correspondents and communities: John Houghton's *A collection for improvement of husbandry and trade* (1692-1703)', Shepard, A. and Withington, P. (eds), *Communities in early modern England*, Manchester-London, pp. 235-251.

Hipkin, S. (2008) 'The structure, development, and politics of the Kent grain trade, 1552-1647', *The Economic History Review, 61, s1 (Feeding the masses: plenty, want and the distribution of food and drink in historical perspective)*, pp. 99-139.

Hipkin, S. (2012) 'The coastal metropolitan corn trade in later seventeenth-century England', *The Economic History Review*, 65, 1, pp. 220-255.

Hipkin, S. (2013) 'The conduct of the coastal metropolitan corn trade during the later seventeenth century: an analysis of the evidence of the Exchequer port books', *Agricultural History Review*, 61, 2, pp. 206-243.

Holt, J. S. (2013) 'A new view of the Fells: Sarah Fell of Swarthmoor and her cashbook', Hoyle, R. W. (ed.), *The Farmer in England, 1650-1980*, Farnham, pp. 43-68.

Houghton, J. (1692-1703) *A collection for the improvement of husbandry and trade* (repr., 1796, facs. in four volumes, 1969).

Hoyle, R. W. (2013) 'Why was there no crisis in England in the 1690s?', Hoyle, R. W. (ed.), *The Farmer in England, 1650-1980*, Farnham, pp. 69-100.

Hoyle, R. W. (2017) 'Britain', Alfani, G. and Ó'Gráda, C. (eds), *Famine in European History*, Cambridge, pp. 141-165.

McCloskey, D. N. and Nash, J. (1984) 'Corn at interest: the extent and cost of grain storage in medieval England', *American Economic Review*, 74, 1, pp. 174-187.

Macfarlane A. (ed.) (1976) *The Diary of Ralph Josselin, 1616-1683*, London.

[Smith, C.] (1756) *Three tracts on the corn trade and corn laws* (sec. edn).

Thirsk, J. (1983) 'The Horticultural Revolution: A Cautionary Note on Prices', *The Journal of Interdisciplinary History* 14, 2, pp. 299-302.

3 A case study of corn sales: Harston Manor's corn book 1823-1842

Liam BRUNT, Department of Economics, Norwegian School of Economics, Bergen

Edmund CANNON, Department of Economics, University of Bristol

I. Introduction

In this short paper we analyse the Corn Book of a medium-sized farm, Harston Manor, in Cambridgeshire for the harvest years 1823-42. The available information is sufficient to provide detailed answers to a series of important questions about how this farm marketed grain: the seasonal pattern of sales and prices; the importance of intra-year and inter-year storage; the relationship between the farmer and the purchasers of grain. As far as we know, there are relatively few analyses of this nature: Hoyle's analysis of Crakanthorp's accounts in this volume is a rare exception. Until a much larger set of such accounts have been analysed, we cannot know with certainty whether Harston Manor is representative or unusual, but this analysis provides a preliminary perspective on the way that an English farm marketed its produce before the repeal of the Corn Laws in 1846.

To provide context, it is useful to consider what is currently known about grain markets at this time. The widespread availability of historical prices has resulted in a huge number of statistical analyses of price behaviour in grain markets, evidenced by the hundred or so papers using this approach cited in Federico's (2012) survey. Unfortunately, many of these papers rely almost solely on price data, sometimes supplemented with information on transport costs, and this means that they can address only a limited range of questions.

The most common approach is to consider a set of markets that might plausibly trade with each other and then see if the prices in the two markets tend to equality (i.e. they look for the action of the law of one price, or LOOP). If data are measured at a relatively high frequency then it is also possible to analyse the dynamics of prices (e.g. if prices move apart, then how quickly – or "efficiently" – do they move back together again?). Unfortunately, in historical studies it is rare for the price data to be clearly associated with grain of a given quality and therefore some of the variation in price is almost certainly due to variations in the quality of grain rather than behaviour of the grain market. Brunt and Cannon (2015) provide contemporary evidence on the quality of wheat and show that tests of both LOOP and market efficiency may be significantly contaminated by the presence of quality variation.

However, a more obvious criticism is that such studies really tell us only about the ability of market actors to arbitrage price differences between markets; they provide virtually no information about anything else. For example, McCloskey and Nash (1984) have suggested the Middle Ages were characterised by minimal carryover of grain from one harvest year to the next (that is, inter-year storage). But price data alone do not allow us to confirm or

Stocks, seasons and sales: Food supply, storage and markets in Europe and the New World, c. 1600-2000, ed. by Wouter RONSIJN, Niccolò MIGNEMI and Laurent HERMENT, CORN 17 (Turnhout, 2019), pp. 61-75.

 DOI: 10.1484/M.CORN-EB.5.118254

reject this hypothesis with confidence, either for the Middle Ages or later periods, and there are very few (direct) data on inter-year storage from other sources. In the presence of production shocks (i.e. bad harvests), an economy can smooth consumption either by arbitrage across regions (trade) or by arbitrage across time (inter-year storage). But it is clearly difficult to measure market efficiency when data on one of these possibilities (i.e. inter-year storage) is virtually absent (Persson, 1999). Another question relates to how market actors engaged with each other. Clearly, a supply chain had farmers at one end and consumers at the other end, with intermediate productive steps of millers and bakers. But we do not know to what extent farmers traded directly with millers or relied upon middlemen, such as corn factors.

One way to address some of these issues is to look at very detailed data from individual farmers' accounts. Farmers' account books have already been used to address issues such as the seasonality of different types of farm work (Burnette, 2013) and gender inequality in wages (Burnette, 2008). Brunt and Cannon (2017) have also used farm account books to infer the intra-year pattern of wheat storage, using the date at which wheat was threshed to place a time limit on when it might have been brought to market. Most of these sources were either general account books or explicit diaries of labour payments.

But within the archives there is a third type of account book – albeit much rarer – namely a Corn Book. Typically, a Corn Book would note the produce of a given harvest and when it was threshed or sold (or possibly both). In this study we analyse the particularly detailed Corn Book of Harston Manor. Harston is a small village about six miles south of Cambridge and eight miles north-east of Royston (in the neighbouring county of Hertfordshire), both of which we know to have grain markets because the markets were monitored by the British government: the prices and quantities traded each week in both of those towns were published in the London Gazette.

II. The Harston Manor Corn book and sales of wheat

The Harston Manor Corn Book is a hardbound tome about 21½ cm by 17½ cm (reference R51/17/35 in the Cambridgeshire Archives). For each harvest from 1823 to 1842 it records the quantities of grain sold, when they were sold, to whom, and for what price.

We do not know the precise date of wheat harvesting on Harston Manor: in the absence of such information, our descriptive analysis is based on a "harvest year", which we define as the twelve-month period starting on 1 August and ending on 31 July. This dating is consistent with the contemporary records suggesting that, in this historical period, the harvest in the south of England usually started in early August (Lawes and Gilbert, 1864). On this definition, inter-year storage (carryover) is any wheat sold in or after the August in the following year. In our analysis we also consider a slightly more conservative definition of carryover – being any wheat sold in or after the September in the following year – to make sure that we are not overestimating inter-year storage by choosing an incorrect terminal date.

An example of the entries in the Corn Book is given in Figure 1, which shows the harvest of 1827. The total sales revenue from this harvest comes to £738/1/0 (i.e. £738, 1 shilling and 0 pence). The quantity sold was 386 Loads and 2 Bushels, i.e. 1,932 Bushels

Figure 1 Example pages from the Harston Manor Corn Book

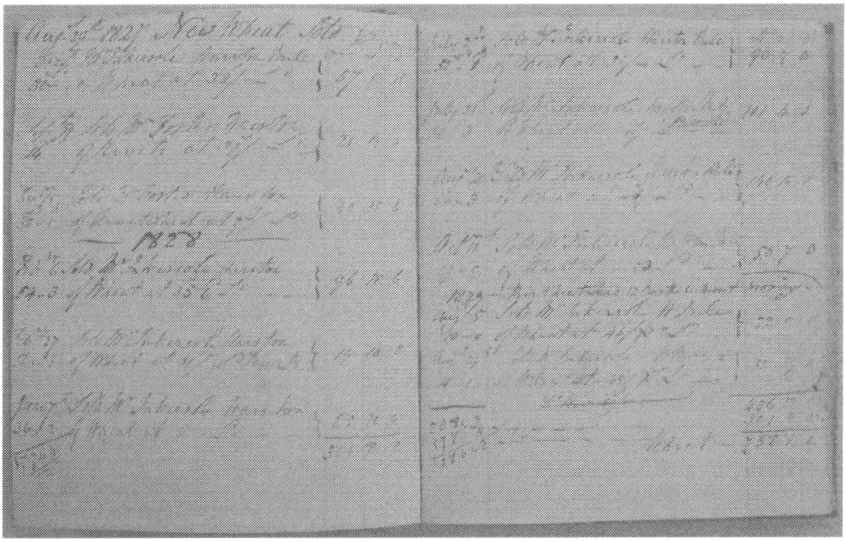

Source: Cambs Archives R51/17/35

or 241½ Quarters. Unfortunately, we cannot be sure what form of Bushel is being used: England moved from using the Winchester Bushel to the Imperial Bushel in 1826, but no mention is made of a change of unit in this corn book. It is probable that the measures are Winchester Bushels, since this measure continued to be widely used, and we make this assumption throughout the paper.[1] A quantity of 1,932 Winchester Bushels is 681 Hectolitres. Not all of the wheat from the harvest of 1827 was sold in the harvest year 1827-28 and the final sale of did not take place until 29 August 1829. Figure 2 illustrates the annual totals harvested and sold in each year and we shall consider the issue of inter-year storage more carefully in the next section.

Assuming yields of around 25 Bushels per acre, we can infer that Harston Manor was harvesting around 70 Acres (30 Hectares) of wheat per annum. This suggests that the farm must have been well over a hundred acres: on a four-field rotation with two seasons of wheat, one of barley and one of roots or fallow, this would be at least 140 acres.

[1] There was only incomplete standardisation of units at this time. According to the "Returns from corn inspectors of the customs or practices of selling corn in their districts" (British Parliamentary Papers, 1834) in 1833 both Cambridge and Royston used a measure of a Load equalling five Bushels for sales of wheat. The Cambridge corn inspector makes no comment on the Winchester versus Imperial issue. The Royston corn inspector noted that "the Imperial bushel … is much detested in this neighbourhood, although submitted to …", but that only applies to transactions made in the market place and, as we shall see, most sales from Harston Manor were directly to millers. Many corn inspectors from other parts of the country noted that farmers preferred to continue using the Winchester bushel. The difference is anyway small, with the Winchester Bushel being 31/32 of an Imperial Bushel.

Figure 2 Annual totals of wheat harvested and wheat sold

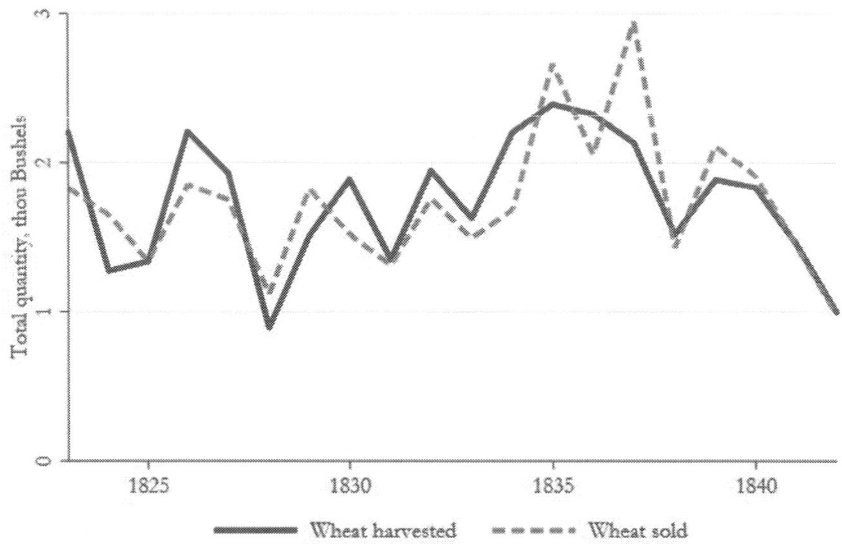

Source: data from Cambs Archives R51/17/35 and authors' calculations.

This is consistent with the entry in the 1873 Return of the Owners of Land, which gives an area of 162 acres for Harston. Usefully, this is close to the mean farm size for Cambridgeshire in 1851 reported by Shaw-Taylor (2012: 34), suggesting that our farm may be fairly representative of farms in the area.

Looking more carefully at the individual transactions, the first sale from the 1827 harvest was that of 30 Loads sold on 29 August to Mr. Inkersole of Harston Mill for 38 shillings per Load. This was quite a large transaction: over the entire period 1823-42, the modal transaction was just under 20 Loads and the mean transaction was 23½ Loads (i.e. 117½ Bushels). From Harston to Cambridge is 9.7 miles; and from Harston to Royston is 8.1 miles; each of these would have been a round trip from Harston in one full day. But there was considerable variation, as illustrated in Figure 2, which summarises data for all transactions in our data set.

The harvest of 1827 was sold in twelve transactions in total, of which ten were to Mr. Inkersole of Harston Mill and two were to Mr. Foster of Hauxton. The Corn Book is not consistent in its references to Mr. Inkersole – some refer to "Harston Mill" and some merely to "Harston" – but we assume that these are synonyms. Similarly, Mr. Foster is often referred to as being of "Hauxton Mill", so the entire harvest of 1827 was sold direct to millers. The full list of buyers for the entire Corn Book is shown in Table 1, which shows that most of the wheat (59 per cent) was sold to Harston Mill and 87 per cent went to the five largest buyers. The first reference to Mr. Inkersole is in June 1826 and up until then the biggest buyer was Mr. Wallis, also of Harston: one possible conjecture

Figure 3 Distribution of size of transactions

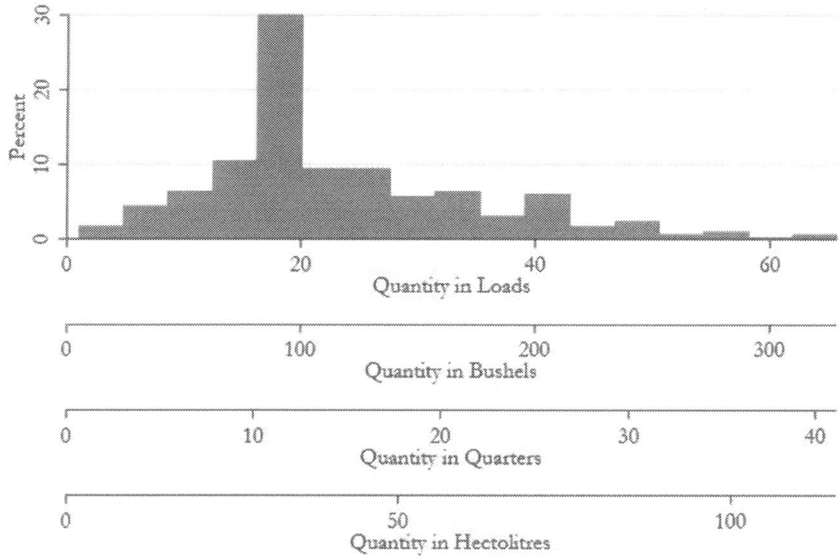

Source: data from Cambs Archives R51/17/35 and authors' calculations.

is that Mr. Wallis was the miller in Harston until Mr. Inkersole took over. But Harston Manor also sold wheat to mills in Danford, Shelford, Shepreth and Barrington: Figure 4 shows that most wheat was sold to buyers that we can clearly identify as millers. This is consistent with other studies that found grain was sold direct to millers (Tann, 1980), as well as with contemporary accounts from the 1826 Parliamentary Enquiry.[2] It is also consistent with the fact that only a quarter of the wheat grown in England passed through the most important grain markets monitored by the British government for this period (Fairlie, 1969: 96, Appendix 2).

III. Grain prices for wheat sold by Harston Manor

We have a total of 295 observations from the Corn Book and, in each case, we observe the quantity sold, the total value of the transaction and the unit price. Obviously these three variables should obey the requirement that *price* × *quantity* = *value* but there are a few cases where we do not observe this. Sometimes this is because of small rounding

[2] For example: "A great proportion of the supply that feeds the population of London consists of flour, which is brought from above [London] Bridge, and does not appear in the market at all; that flour is generally sold by the flour factors, without ever being brought to market at all. One great object of building the new market [the rebuilding of Mark Lane in 1827] was to afford the flour factors an opportunity of exhibiting their flour in the market." Evidence of Thomas Dimsdale, corn factor, in British Parliamentary Papers (1826-27: 674).

Table 1 Buyers of wheat

Buyer	Number of transactions	Total purchased (Bushels, %)	Average size of purchase (Bushels)
Mr. Inkersole, Harston Mill	166	20580 (59%)	124
Mr. Foster, Hauxton Mill	33	4220 (12%)	128
Mr. Wallis, Harston	20	2910 (8%)	146
Mr. Nutter, Danford Mill	11	1383 (4%)	126
Mr. Thurnale, Duxford	13	1372 (4%)	106
Mr. Smith, Royston	9	945	105
Mr. Nutter, Shelford Mill	5	609	122
Mr. Thurnale, Whittlesford	6	537	90
Mr. Moule, Kneesworth	6	477	80
Mr. Wallis, Shepreth	5	397	79
Mr. Shaw, Cambridge	2	238	119
Mr. Lawrence, Royston	1	180	180
Mr. Dickerson, Bassingbourn	2	150	75
Mr. Swannell, Royston	1	114	114
Mr. Pearce, Shepreth Mill	2	105	53
Mr. Heaver, Kneesworth	1	100	100
Mr. Flitton, Morden	1	100	100
Mr. Sutton, Bassingbourn	1	90	90
Mr. Titchmarsh, Royston	1	86	86
Mr. Smith, Barrington Mill	1	85	85
Mr. Fordham, Barrington	1	47	47
Mr. Northfield, Harston	2	44	22
Mr. Sergent, Haslingfold	1	30	30
Mr. Whitechurch	1	25	25
Mr. Oakey, Sandon	1	25	25
Mr. Wallis, Haslingfield	1	20	20
Mr. Watson, Harston	1	15	15
Mr. Pate	1	15	15

Sources: Cambs Archives R51/17/35 and authors' calculations.

Figure 4 Wheat sold to millers and others

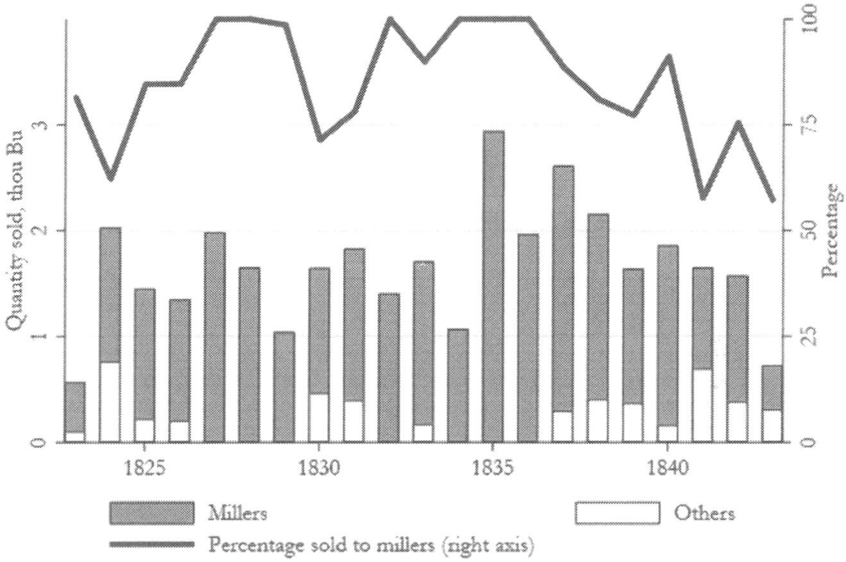

Source: data from Cambs Archives R51/17/35 and authors' calculations.

errors, but in ten cases the discrepancy is more than 5 per cent and we discard these observations.[3] We have already seen that Harston Manor was selling wheat from different harvests in the same year and an obvious question to ask is whether older wheat traded at a different price. There are only eight days where Harston Manor sold wheat from both the most recent harvest and from an earlier harvest: if we compare the prices of these simultaneous transactions then we find that new wheat sells for 2 per cent less but – unsurprisingly – this is statistically insignificant. To expand our sample size, we look at each month where we observe transactions of both new and old wheats: this means that we now have twenty observations, but the comparisons are imperfect, because they are asynchronous and prices could have changed within the month. Our calculations are illustrated in Figure 5 and show very large differences in absolute size (almost certainly more than would result from price changes over such short periods of time). But, again, there is no systematic price premium for new wheat. This is interesting because it suggests that any fall in the value of wheat parcels held in storage arises from physical losses (such as being eaten by rats) rather than a diminution of quality of the overall parcel (such as being due to mould).

Based on this analysis we now compare the Harston Manor prices against the prices in Cambridge and Royston, where the latter is the weekly official weighted-average price

[3] These observations sometimes have additional notes in the Corn Book, suggesting that the transaction involved other crops. We have also dropped a single observation of tail wheat (i.e. the lower quality kernels that drop out at the very end of the threshing process).

Figure 5 Price comparison of new and old wheat

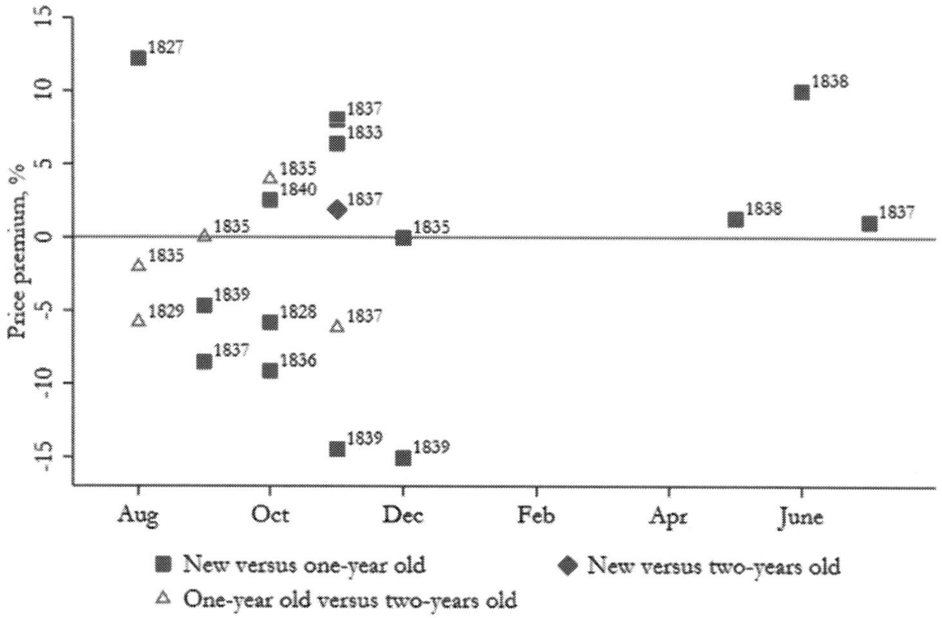

Source: data from Cambs Archives R51/17/35 and authors' calculations.

reported in the London Gazette (Brunt and Cannon, 2013), where we have converted the official price into Winchester Bushels. Figure 6 plots the Harston Manor and Cambridge prices (the Royston prices are available only from 1828 onwards, when they are almost indistinguishable from the Cambridge prices on a graph of this size). We do not observe the Harston Manor price every week but, in weeks when it is observed, it averages 4 per cent higher than the corresponding end-of-week price in Cambridge and 5 per cent higher than in Royston.[4] One possible reason for this is that the data in the Corn Book are actually in Imperial Bushels rather than Winchester Bushels, since the Imperial Bushel is approximately 3 per cent larger, but this is at variance with the evidence that farmers preferred Winchester measure and it does not explain all of the price difference, especially with Royston. Instead, it might be the case that the Harston Manor wheat is slightly higher quality than the average in the market; or it could be that the Manor and the miller save the cost of freight (to and from the market) and split the saving between them.

Finally, we look at the determinants of price, using a series of regressions of the logarithm of the price on possible explanatory variables: we are interested whether the price depends upon the size of the transaction, whether the price is different for millers and whether the price varies systematically through the year. Our regression results are reported in Table 2.

[4] In both cases, this difference is statistically significant: the standard errors of the mean price differences are 0.47 and 0.58 respectively.

Figure 6 Comparison of price in Harston Manor and Cambridge

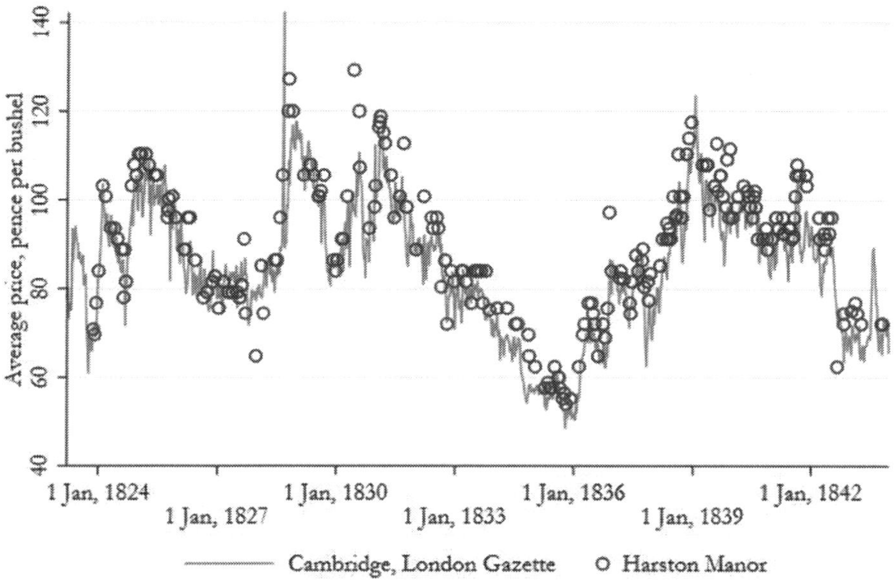

Source: data from Cambs Archives R51/17/35 and the London Gazette.

Our first regression includes only the variables of interest, where the seasonal pattern in prices is modelled by eleven dummy variables for months of the year. Our measure of the size of the transaction is the logarithm of quantity, so the coefficient on this variable can be interpreted as an elasticity. It appears from the first specification that larger transactions have lower prices, with an elasticity of about 4 per cent (but marginally statistically significant); and that millers pay 6 per cent less (statistically significant). An F-test for the joint significance of the monthly dummy variables suggests that the seasonal pattern is not statistically significant.

These results could be misleading because they ignore the year-to-year variation in prices, leading to both omitted variable bias and incorrect standard errors, so we include dummy variables for each harvest year in the second specification. This has much smaller parameter estimates and suggests that there is no relationship between price and any of the explanatory variables and that the seasonal pattern is still statistically insignificant. The parameter estimates of the month-dummy variables increase approximately linearly through the harvest year, consistent with the saw-tooth pattern noted by McCloskey and Nash (1984), so we estimate a final specification with a linear trend within the harvest year (i.e. starting in August and finishing in July). The parameter on this trend is statistically significant and suggests that prices rise on average by 0.46 per cent per month, which is 5.7 per cent when expressed at an annual rate. This is a much smaller seasonal variation than the 12 per cent found by Brunt and Cannon (1999) when they re-analysed the medieval data used by McCloskey and Nash (1984). It suggests that the fall in grain prices at the end of the harvest year was relatively small, and thus the costs to the farmer of inter-year storage (arising from the price decline) were correspondingly small. We turn to the issue of storage in the next section.

Table 2 Determinants of wheat price

Dependent variable: ln(Price)	Specification 1	Specification 2	Specification 3
ln(Quantity)	-0.0408+	0.00922	0.0117
	(0.0215)	(0.0120)	(0.0118)
Mill dummy variable	-0.0619**	-0.0184	-0.0207
	(0.0238)	(0.0151)	(0.0149)
Harvest-year Month			0.00463**
			(0.0017)
Month dummy variables	✓	✓	
Test for joint significance of month dummy variables	F(11, 269) = 0.80 [p = 0.64]	F(11, 233) = 1.41 [p = 0.17]	
Year dummy variables		✓	✓
Sample size	283	283	283

Robust standard errors in parentheses; in specifications 2 and 3 these are clustered by week.
$+p<0.10$, $^{**}p<0.01$. Source: Cambs Archives R51/17/35 and authors' calculations.

IV. Intra-year and inter-year storage

One of the longest-standing gaps in our understanding of grain markets is about both intra-year and inter-year storage of grain, due to a lack of direct evidence on what was being held in store. For this reason, many analyses have relied upon indirect tests of storage by looking at price behaviour (McCloskey and Nash, 1984; Nielsen, 1997) or possible grain storage capacity (Fenoaltea, 1976: 138-139). All of these studies are for the medieval or early-modern period. In this section we answer the question directly by looking at when wheat from each harvest was sold.

Our analysis is summarised in Figure 7, which illustrates both the seasonal pattern of sales and the delay between harvest and sale. The top left-hand graph shows the quantities of wheat sold in each month over the entire twenty-year period. To check whether this pattern is due to the seasonality in years with particularly high sales, we also calculate the proportion of wheat sold within a harvest year and report the mean and inter-quartile range for the proportions in each month: this is illustrated in the bottom left hand graph. This confirms the pattern in the bar chart, but also shows that there was considerable variation in seasonality from year to year.

The two graphs in the left-hand column of Figure 7 show when grain was sold, but conflate grain from different harvest years. The two graphs in the right-hand column show the quantities sold from each harvest in months after the harvest (assumed always to be in August, since we do not have more precise information on the harvest date). For clarity of exposition, the top right-hand graph distinguishes wheat sold within the harvest

Figure 7 Timing of wheat sales

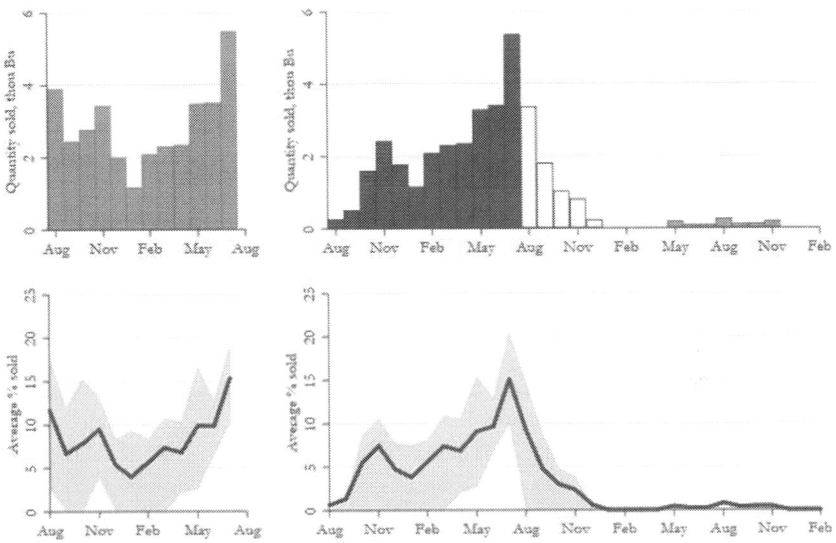

Source: data from Cambs Archives R51/17/35 and authors' calculations.

year (bars coloured black), wheat sold the following autumn (bars coloured white) and wheat sold in the succeeding calendar year (bars coloured grey). The two most striking features of these data are the extent of carryover and the peak in sales in July. We find both of these elements quite surprising.

In terms of carryover, 21 per cent of the harvest was sold in the period from August to December one year after the harvest and a further 3 per cent was sold in the following calendar year: the total carryover on the farm was just under a quarter of the whole harvested crop. Even if we use our more conservative definition of carryover to include only wheat sold from September onwards, it still constitutes 17 per cent of the crop. There is a verbal hint in the Harston Manor Corn Book that selling wheat shortly after the following harvest was usual, since only wheat sold in the following calendar year (i.e. the grey bars in the figure) was referred to as "Old", whereas wheat sold within sixteen months of the harvest was still considered "New". Indeed, of all the wheat sold in the period August-December, only 38 per cent was from the most recent harvest with the remainder from one or two years earlier.

We also remark upon the high level of sales in July. One possible reason for this would be for the farm to create space for the next harvest, but this raises the question of why so much wheat was carried over. Another possible reason is that farmers were getting short of cash at that time, given the extra labour payments for haymaking and harvesting. A separate issue, which we cannot answer here, is when and how the wheat was threshed – and hence in what form it was stored. It is conventional to assume that labour was in relatively short supply while it was needed for the harvest, suggesting that a farmer would not wish to thresh at this point in the harvest cycle. Yet the sale of wheat in August and September from the most recent harvest suggests that there actually was little or no labour constraint.

Figure 8 Carryover of wheat

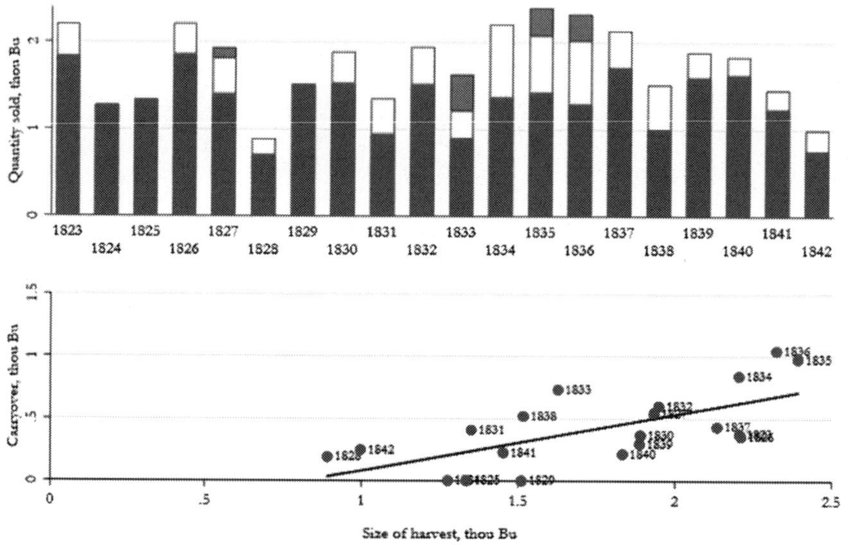

Source: data from Cambs Archives R51/17/35 and authors' calculations.

Our result here is strikingly different from the theory of McCloskey and Nash (1984), which assumed a minimal grain carryover for society as a whole. Of course, their model of minimal carryover also assumed a large seasonal pattern to grain prices (to compensate people for holding the grain through the year) whereas we showed in the previous section that the seasonal increase in grain prices was small.[5] Clearly, by the nineteenth century carryover could take place on a substantial scale. But the real issue is why there was so much inter-year storage on the farm or, indeed, why this farm was selling wheat at all in the period from August to October (given that the wheat from the previous harvest could have been sold earlier, and the wheat from the most recent harvest would have to be threshed at a time of high labour demand).

We finish this section by discussing the frequency of carryover in more detail. The top panel of Figure 8 shows sales from each harvest: black again denotes sales between August and July, white denotes sales from the following August to December and grey shows sales in the following calendar year. Only three harvests out of twenty saw no carryover whatsoever.[6] The bottom panel shows the relationship between the total size of the harvest and the quantity carried over, together with an OLS line of best fit: above the threshold of 818 Bushels (2,880 Hectolitres) every extra Bushel of wheat harvested

[5] Note that our data are only for carryover on the farm: some grain was stored as part of the supply chain by millers (or by bakers in the form of flour), and there was presumably also some inter-year storage by corn merchants.

[6] Using the more conservative definition of carryover of sales from September onwards would increase this to seven years with no carryover.

is expected to result in 0.45 Bushels of carryover (standard error of 0.12, statistically significant with a p-value of 0.002). Since there is a small amount of left censoring, we could also estimate this with Tobit, but the results are almost identical; similarly, using the more conservative definition of carryover makes little difference to the results.

The fact that the farm nearly always sold wheat in the autumn following the harvest suggests that the farmer was not relying upon prices being at their highest just before the harvest, contrary to the McCloskey and Nash story of the seasonality of wheat prices. A significant determinant of carryover was the size of harvest, consistent with the farmer selling regularly and thus having more to carry over when the harvest was larger but, at the margin, only about a half of each extra bushel of harvest was carried over, suggesting that the farmer partly smoothed fluctuations in output. One possible reason for this behaviour is that the farmer was cash constrained and needed to sell wheat in the autumn to get specie.

V. Summary and discussion

The Harston Manor accounts offer a fascinating and tantalizing insight into some key issues surrounding grain production and storage in the early nineteenth century, and probably earlier as well. Historians have asked the question: how much carryover was there from one harvest year to the next? Was the carryover grain stored in barns or granaries? Was it held by merchants or farmers, in town or country? Was there a labour constraint in threshing (i.e. to what extent did farmers face a trade-off in September between threshing the newly harvested grain and planting the crop for the next season)? How did this affect the adoption of threshing machinery? Historians have tackled these questions using several different approaches – such as looking for patterns in the price data, or estimating the storage capacity of barns. But these methods are indirect – and thereby open to challenge – whereas the Harston Manor records are direct and straightforward to interpret.

The key patterns of behaviour revealed by the Harston Manor records are as follows. First, the farm always stored wheat throughout the harvest year, usually stored wheat from one harvest year into the following autumn, and sometimes stored wheat into the following calendar year. Second, the farmer overwhelmingly sold direct to millers (not to merchants). These two results contradict the McCloskey-Nash characterization of grain production and also explain why we see such a low proportion of output being traded in the markets monitored by the government (i.e. most grain never passed through those markets).

The other striking fact is that, over the whole period, 59 per cent of wheat was sold to a single buyer: the prices paid were consistent with the spot market prices paid in nearby Cambridge, but it would be inappropriate to characterise such a relationship between Harston Manor and Harston Mill as a spot market. Rather, it suggests that there must have been an ongoing relationship between seller and buyer.

This kind of micro-study offers data and results that are rich and precise. The disadvantage is that it is based on only one farm: although it is an average size farm, we suspect that wheat brought to market disproportionately came from large farms. The challenge is then to collate Corn Books for more farms, preferably from different parts of the country and including much larger farms than Harston, in order to paint a fuller picture that can be taken as generally representative of England in the nineteenth century. We should then like to extend the evidential basis, and the analysis, backwards in time to the early modern period. This is our next line of research.

References

British Parliamentary Papers (1826-27) 'Report from the Select Committee of the House of Lords appointed to inquire into the price at which foreign grain may be shipped in foreign ports; the quantity of such grain; and the price at which such grain can be imported into this country; and to report to the House together with the minutes of evidence taken before the said committee', BPP 1826-27, vol. 6, pp. 633-848.

British Parliamentary Papers (1834) 'Returns from corn inspectors of the customs or practices of selling corn in their districts', vol. 49, pp. 251-317.

Brunt, L., and Cannon E. S. (1999) 'A Grain of Truth in Medieval Interest Rates? Re-examining the McCloskey-Nash Hypothesis', University of Bristol, Department of Economics Working Paper, 98/462.

Brunt, L., and Cannon E. S. (2013) 'The truth, the whole truth, and nothing but the truth: The English Corn Returns as a data source in economic history, 1770-1914', *European Review of Economic History, 17, 3*, pp. 318-339.

Brunt, L., and Cannon E. S. (2015) 'Variations in the price and quality of grain, 1750-1914: quantitative evidence and empirical implications', *Explorations in Economic History, 58,* pp. 74-92.

Brunt, L., and Cannon E. S. (2017) 'The economics of grain storage in England, 1663-1846', mimeo, University of Bristol.

Burnette, J. (2008) *Gender, Work and Wages in Industrial Revolution Britain*, Cambridge.

Burnette, J. (2013) 'The Seasonality of English Agricultural Employment: Evidence from Farm Accounts, 1740-1850', Hoyle, R. W. (ed.), *The Farmer in England, 1650-1980*, Farnham, pp. 135-164.

Fairlie, S. (1969) 'The Corn Laws and British wheat production, 1829-76', *Economic History Review*, 22, 1, pp. 88-116.

Federico, G. (2012) 'How much do we know about market integration in Europe?', *Economic History Review*, 65, 2, pp. 470-497.

Fenoaltea, S. (1976) 'Risk, transaction costs and the organization of medieval agriculture', *Explorations in Economic History, 13, 2*, pp. 129-151.

Gras, N. S. B. (1967) *The evolution of the English Corn Market*, New York.

Lawes, J. B., and Gilbert, J. H. (1864) 'Report of experiments on the growth of wheat for 20 years in succession on the same land', *Journal of the Royal Agricultural Society of England*, vol. 25, pp. 93-185.

McCloskey, D. N., and Nash, J. (1984) 'Corn at interest: the extent and cost of grain storage in medieval England', *American Economic Review*, 74, 1, pp. 174-187.

Nielsen, R. (1997) 'Storage and English Government intervention in early modern grain markets', *Journal of Economic History*, 57, 1, pp. 1-33.

Persson, K. G. (1999) *Grain markets in Europe, 1500-1900*, Cambridge.

Shaw-Taylor, L. (2012) 'The rise of agrarian capitalism and the decline of family farming in England', *Economic History Review,* 65, 1, pp. 26-60.

Tann, J. (1980) 'Cooperative corn milling: self-help during the grain crises of the Napoleonic Wars', *Agricultural History Review, 28, 1*, pp. 45-57.

4 Production and provisioning: the *Tumulto* of 1692 in Mexico City*

Pablo F. Luna, Sorbonne University & EHESS CRH – Erhimor

I. Introduction

On 8 June 1692, a subsistence crisis touched off a series of disturbances in Mexico City, turning the city centre of the Spanish town into a rallying point for the malcontents. These events have often been characterised as a typical Old Regime "disturbance and uproar" (*tumulto y alboroto*). These were short-lived, one-off, ephemeral events, but were nevertheless a tangible manifestation of a power struggle in an emerging colonial society. It may indeed have been this society's first real power struggle, which would explain why the year 1692 was long remembered by contemporaries as the year of the *tumulto*.

The Mexican Indians were the main protagonists in the rebellion, but they were joined by mixed-race groups in both town and country, even by some groups of poor Spaniards, and, even less likely, by some students, though assuredly few in number. In fact, this was a moment in which a solid opposition bloc formed in the capital of New Spain. Had this reaction been building up over preceding years of resentment and rancour? Was there a latent and muted "political" or psychological discontent, or repressed bitterness over real or imaginary humiliations inflicted by the vice-regal authorities, or by the Spanish in general? Coming as it did more than a century and a half after the arrival of the Europeans, this may indeed have been the case. However, it was when hunger, or the fear of hunger, made its appearance – depending on circumstances, one could matter as much as the other – that revolt became possible, revealing, at one stroke, all the grievances of the lowest classes against the powerful in the city and in society.

This was not the first revolt against the colonists or against the Spanish authorities in Mexico or in New Spain.[1] But it was perhaps the first time in the history of the viceroyalty of New Spain since the initial conquest and Iberian colonisation that a relatively broad reaction spread through several levels of society, aimed at the entire power structure and colonial presence, striking at the heart of the Spanish establishment. The aim of this article

* My thanks to several colleagues whose stimulating comments and suggestions have helped shape and improve this text from its earliest version onward: Laurent Herment, Gérard Béaur, Thomas Calvo, Natalia Silva P., Florence Gauthier, Laure Guillebot, and the anonymous readers who examined the manuscript for publication. Needless to say, any faults are mine alone.

[1] In 1624, there had already been an outcry and resistance at Mexico City against the corruption of the administrative personnel and the Spanish vice-regal authorities, though in that case it had reflected the rivalry of civil and religious authorities (Feijóo, 1964; Israel, 1975; Gruzinski, 2005; Bautista, 2010). And this was not the only example of many different sorts of movements against various Spanish authorities that broke out within the immense viceroyalty of New Spain during the sixteenth and seventeenth centuries.

Stocks, seasons and sales: Food supply, storage and markets in Europe and the New World, c. 1600-2000, ed. by Wouter Ronsijn, Niccolò Mignemi and Laurent Herment, CORN 17 (Turnhout, 2019), pp. 77-101.

 DOI: 10.1484/M.CORN-EB.5.118255

is mainly historiographical, to reassess this uprising and the documentation concerning it, to ask how the crisis of production and food shortages occurred, and to re-examine its consequences for the Spanish-American colonial society of the Old Regime.[2]

II. General approach

The Viceroyalty of New Spain was a Spanish colony in America where mining, mainly of silver, had been the principal economic activity since the sixteenth century. It was also a place where European agriculture had gained a foothold, often spearheaded, from its very start, by the uncontrolled expansion of stock-rearing, which destroyed and laid waste indigenous agriculture and gradually depopulated the space it occupied (Florescano, 1990: 99-101; Sempat, 1999: 33). In this, the colony followed other examples of recent Castilian implantation, on the American continent and elsewhere. This replacement of people by livestock lasted about a hundred years, beyond the first third of the seventeenth century, impervious to the resistance of indigenous peoples and evidently ineffective legal barriers.

Subsequently, the object was to develop the elements of an alternative food system along with a suitable trading network; at the same time stock-rearing, hitherto unknown, was systematically introduced, along with all the other products it generated (Castaño, 2017). This was aimed at victualling the mining centres and Spanish colonial towns as well as the missionary establishments which had gradually spread across the viceroyalty of New Spain (Galindo, 2014). The vice-regal authorities clearly encouraged this sort of agriculture (except for stock-rearing) from the second half of the sixteenth century onwards (Florescano, 1965). Land seizures, whether by usurpation or by "legal" methods (often simultaneously) cleared the way for commercial agriculture; they had been common practice ever since the first occupation and increased considerably after 1570.[3] Along with this went the depopulation of occupied spaces and the cyclical epidemics that decimated the indigenous population (Chevalier, 1952; Séjourné, 1971).

By the end of the seventeenth century a "mixed" form of agriculture had taken shape, growing maize to feed the Indians but adding the food products of the European colonisers, particularly wheat and sugar, which spread both in competition with local products and as a complement to them. The hybridization of Indian and Iberian food systems was thus well underway (Suárez, 1985; Hidalgo, 2016; Meza, 2016). Cereal and flour could be produced abundantly, and they generated large surpluses, some of them already used for export. But in the process an agricultural mixing took place that reflected the nature of colonial society itself. Though we may speak of "two agricultures" it was clear that

[2] See the bibliography. Since 2007 the essential reference work on the 1692 Mexico City uprising has been Natalia Silva P.'s study, a massive synthesis based on previous research that appeared in her doctoral thesis and several articles. Among other works that directly examine the disturbances of 1692 at Mexico City are De Sigüenza, (1692) 1932; Leonard, 1932; Guthrie, 1938; De Robles, (1692) 1946; Feijóo, 1965; Cope, 1994; Muriel, 1998; Calvo, 2004; Pazos, 2005; Gonzalbo, 2008; Hidalgo, 2016.

[3] This had been the real royal policy, both in Andean America since the rationalisation of the mining enterprises by the Viceroy Toledo, and in New Spain, after the discovery of silver deposits at Zacatecas and subsequent lodes of the precious metal to the north of Mexico City.

one of them subordinated and subjected the other. The gradual consolidation of the existing hacienda system and the expansion of *latifundia*, which were to continue in the countryside of New Spain, played an important role in this process.

It should be remembered that this took place in a colonial space where the conquering group mixed biologically with the conquered group, the "Indians", a generic term that included a variety of peoples on the high plateaus of Anahuac and beyond. But this indigenous group, or its surviving members, still retained a good number of its essential cultural characteristics in the second half of the seventeenth century, agricultural practices and ways of exchanging and distributing produce, including the use of collective labour. This process of assimilation was not harmonious or peaceful; far from it.

In addition, this racial mixing took place amidst and despite the "demographic catastrophe" which struck the whole continent of America during the sixteenth and seventeenth centuries, after the arrival of the Iberian *conquistadores*. As we now know, this process had among other things, many epidemiological, military and psychological aspects. According to known estimates, it is thought that, for different reasons, the original population of about twenty-five million inhabitants in 1519[4] for the territories in the former Aztec Confederation, may have fallen to around two million at the end of the seventeenth century in the entire viceroyalty of New Spain. Territorially, this area had been built up over the 150-odd years since the first third of the fifteenth century, on the remains of land previously conquered by the Mexican Triple Alliance plus other Mesoamerican spaces before the Castilians finally conquered and incorporated it into the viceroyalty.

The Indians made up the largest "demographic stock", that is the most important source of labour, but many black slaves[5] were increasingly brought in to work the mines and fields from the second half of the sixteenth century onwards; there were also other immigrant groups of European origin. In addition, there were Asians such as Filipinos and Chinese, living in Mexico City, who very often came as stowaways in Chinese ships (*naos*) by way of Acapulco. Generally speaking, despite the legal barriers that Spanish authorities erected to strengthen their hold over the population, racial mixing gradually spread through society and through the viceroyalty and its capital city.

Little by little the number of salaried workers in Mexico City – acculturated Indians, métis and poor Spaniards – increased. As a result, this created various hybrid forms of paid work that existed side by side with other kinds of labour, more or less forced, or partly unpaid. The number of urban artisans also went up; among them were many of Indian or mixed race (Von Wobeser, 1988: 290-293; Araya, 2004: 63, 71-72; Gruzinski, 2005: 12-13) who had learnt Spanish trades, or adapted to them, very quickly. The immediate Iberian presence and the sovereignty exercised by the Spanish monarchy and its Spanish American administration over the more than five million square kilometres of continental *Septentrional Mexicana* remained as vague

4 Some estimates suggest 10-15 million, and others more than 25-30 million. But it is now held certain that there was a demographic collapse in the conquest period and during the first stages of Castilian colonialism.

5 During the seventeenth century, which was also marked by the struggle for available labour between mining and agricultural producers.

and indefinite as its vast and ill-delimited boundaries. This article focuses on the situation in Mexico City, the capital of the viceroyalty and its near hinterland, an area of rivers, lakes and countryside.

III. Mexico City and its countryside

By the second half of the seventeenth century, Mexico City was the most important market in the viceroyalty of New Spain. Its food supply came from the agricultural haciendas of the Mexico valley, created by Spanish colonists from land appropriated in various ways, and also from agricultural holdings in the valleys and other regions close to hand (mainly Puebla-Tlaxcala, Toluca and *Bajío*[6]). The town had been built on an island which, despite the progress of drainage works, was constantly in danger from floods (Cruz, 1991: 102). Men and goods traded in and out of the town in all directions across fifty wooden or stone bridges, several roads or paths, lakes, rivers and streams and old Aztec ways and footpaths (Gibson, 1967; Rubial, 1998, 2008). These exchanges were local but they were supplemented by others from farther abroad: with Western Europe and South America by way of Veracruz, the Caribbean and the Atlantic; with the Orient, including China and the Philippines, through Acapulco and across the Pacific; and with South America. The two biggest ports in the American viceroyalty, Veracruz and Acapulco, had gradually become crucial for the Spanish monarchy and its world-wide trade.[7] The city and the vice-regal authorities found controlling these circuits to be no easy task.

There had been some changes, but at that time, the Spanish area of residence and occupation was still the *traza*, that is, the exclusively Spanish thirteen to fourteen blocks which the conquistadores had set aside in the centre of town. By then it had become the Spanish parish of *Sagrario Metropolitano*. The centre of the *traza*, the great square (*Plaza Mayor*), constituted the real heart of the Spanish establishment, situated on an esplanade which, significantly, had been the site of the Aztec sovereign's palace. There were to be found the main buildings of the civil and religious powers, most notably the Viceroy's palace, alongside the royal *Audiencia* and the cathedral church of Mexico City.[8]

It was also the site of the central city market, dominated by perhaps three hundred fixed trading stalls (*cajones*), authorised by the municipality and reserved for Spanish merchants. But in and around these fixed sites was a second market: a myriad of mobile stalls, strolling vendors and various spots where goods could be exchanged at lower prices. These were kept by indigenous people or members of the lowest urban classes. Though they were theoretically restricted to trade in second-hand (*segunda mano*) goods, they in fact did all kinds of business. This whole mercantile conglomeration was designated by an unusual term, the *Baratillo*, the "cheap little market", a name that should have applied only to the "second" market, but which gradually came to be used for everything,

[6] In that order, corresponding to the amounts supplied and chronology of settlement.

[7] The important role of New Spain in the trade by the Spanish monarchy to Asia is well known. Money from the royal coffers of New Spain was fundamental in upholding the Spanish presence in the Philippines and Asia (Klein and TePaske, 1981: 133).

[8] For a chronological approach to the importance of the Plaza Mayor (including the merchants' point of view) see Rubial, 2008 and Exbalin, 2015: 219.

even the fixed stalls. In reality, the central market of Mexico City was host to all kinds of exchange, open or underground, authorised or illegal.[9] Of this, the municipal and vice-regal authorities were perfectly aware.

The *Baratillo* brought together merchants, including some second-hand sellers and receivers of stolen goods, with buyers and direct consumers (Olvera, 2007: 73-99) in a joyous and dynamic informality. The fixed stalls mainly supplied the Spanish population with products imported from Europe – the so-called *productos de Castilla* – or from other places as far away as China; these were mainly manufactured goods, cloth and textiles.[10] They also supplied *productos de la tierra*, local products, as did the movable stalls and strolling traders. But a range of traffickers and their accomplices also brought stolen goods to the *Baratillo*, petty artisans sold their own products, and the English and Dutch contraband trade contributed small manufactured metal goods. Again, the authorities were well aware of all these dealings.

Around the *traza*, and in the rest of the island and branching out into the gradually widening space outside the city, were seven Indian *doctrines*, that is, seven Catholic parishes of hybrid form, seven areas of religious syncretism and various degrees of blending. The clergy, mostly members of religious orders, were theoretically responsible for the religious needs of seven districts or areas inhabited by Indians. The same seven zones also possessed civil administrations, generally named by the indigenous people. By the middle of the seventeenth century, these *doctrines* had become proper parishes. The two most important ones were the successors of the two previous Aztec cities: Santiago Tlatelolco[11] and San Juan de Tenochtitlán. Then came Santa Maria la Redonda, San Pablo, San Sebastián, Santa Cruz and Santo Domingo. Since the sixteenth century, the surviving heirs of Tenochtitlán, the former Aztec capital, had lived in a world of movement and constant change, where new neighbourhoods were created in a partly orderly disorder encompassing overlapping jurisdictions and local authorities (Sánchez, 2004: 68-69).

In fact, the whole of late seventeenth-century Mexico City looked much like the *Baratillo*: a Spanish world surrounded and shot through by indigenous institutions and by the mixed-race poor or *castas*, as the administration called them. Indeed, Spaniards

---

[9] There were several attempts to get rid of this market during the seventeenth century. The last came in November 1689, two and a half years before the *tumulto* of 1692 (Martin, 1985: 107; Olvera, 2007: 77-79). Count De Galve, the new Viceroy, soon came to realise that the interests involved in the *Baratillo* constituted an almost insurmountable obstacle. It was not until the royal Brevet of 30 January 1694 was issued in response to the disturbances of 1692, that construction could begin on a market (*El Parián*) built in stone, and no longer in wood, with stalls leased to the merchants by the city in emphyteusis (Suárez, 2009: 444). The new building was completed in April 1703. The first merchants to set up there were the most prosperous in the city; they who had made their fortunes in trading with the Philippines and Asia.

[10] The rural and urban artisans and the *obrajes* (manufactures with Indian labour and Spanish owners and managers which produced rough cloth) met the demand for textiles from the Indian and mixed-race communities, who were too poor to buy European fabrics.

[11] Many of the Indians taking part in the uprising came from this *doctrine*: they were called the *santiagueños*. Showing pride in belonging to this group and bearing its name played a very big part in the disturbances; the repression after the revolt was very severe.

themselves sometimes settled in neighbourhoods set aside for the Indians, even though the authorities themselves considered such behaviour as unusual or illegal (Cruz, 1991: 97; Sánchez, 2004: 68). In the real world, that was how the city was organized.[12] Despite religious and legal notions, and despite the official settlement plan calling for two separate "republics", with the Spanish on one side and the Indians on the other, there was a big gap between the theory and its application. As so often, reality got the better of legal and mental representation, as we shall soon see in the troubles of June 1692.

To be sure, the more aware of the Vice-regal civil and ecclesiastical authorities did actually see the city as excessively fluid, disorderly and uncontrolled (Silva, 2007: 168-169). The situation was a constant source of fear, particularly among the Spanish living in the *traza*. It generated a literature, a vocabulary and a mentality which constantly referred to the danger represented by the Indians and the poor in the city (Gonzalbo, 2008: 11). And with the fear there developed also an ambivalent feeling of contempt, among the authorities and vice-regal administrative personnel, from the second half of the sixteenth century on (Cope, 1994; Calvo, 2005).

In 1673, for Mexico City alone, the Viceroy estimated the combined number of mixed-race people (the *castas*) and poor at *doscientas mil almas* (200,000 persons) (Calvo, 2005). But they must certainly have been much less than this as the most recent estimates, based on various sources such as travellers' accounts, now only reckon the whole city population at the end of the seventeenth century at about 50,000 to 70,000 inhabitants.[13]

After the mid-seventeenth century, when declining silver mines reduced the population of Potosí in upper Peru, the town of Mexico seems to have become the biggest city in the American New World (Béligand, 2007: 76). The number of Indians in Mexico City (the *macehuales* or common Indians) has been reckoned at about 26,000 in the middle of the century, though estimates vary greatly (Cope, 1994: 20) – some would have it twice as high, one putting it at 40,000 by the end of the century.[14] And the Indians were not the biggest group among the working people of Mexico City: most were people of mixed race (*castas*) living inside the town.

Ever since the Aztec period, as we have seen, the river and water transport of goods to Mexico City had been carried out over a system of canals, in small boats, generally managed by Indians. Land transport was handled by a network of muleteers and wagon drivers, and also by Indians and people of mixed race. Alongside these, a colourful band of small businesses called *regatonería*, made up of local merchants, many of mixed race, worked through varied and frequently changing trading routes. The vice-regal and municipal authorities of the city looked askance at this hodge-podge and blamed it for

[12] Because both the European Spanish in the city, and the *criollos* (Spaniards born on the American continent) needed Indian labour.

[13] The difficulty is to determine the boundaries of the zone in question, and whether the episcopal jurisdiction corresponded to the surface of the city. See Gemelli, 1968; De la Maza, 1968: 18-20. Some estimates give 110,000 to 120,000 inhabitants for the capital of the viceroyalty of New Spain (Béligand, 2007; Calvo, 2005).

[14] The number of Indians "foreign" to the city (*extravagantes*) living there, has been estimated at 25,000 (Silva, 2001: 84-85).

the rising cost of essential products and the volatility in their supply. They had been struggling against the operations of these small merchants, or *regatones*, ever since the second half of the sixteenth century, but with very little success.

Indians living in the town, who maintained regular contact with their home village and with their clan chiefs, their friends and their relations in the countryside, could act as intermediaries between the townsfolk and the country people living around Mexico City or in its more distant hinterland. This took various forms: in economic and commercial exchanges, in migratory movements, by providing contacts for new arrivals; and in communications, by keeping open cultural and linguistic ties to their origins. Whether on their own initiative or under compulsion, they had been doing this ever since the sixteenth century (Florescano, 1965; Jalpa, 2010: 80), and it would not be surprising to learn that these kinds of contacts and practices went back even further, as they had in the Andean environment, to roots in the pre-Hispanic period.

These Indians not only transported goods and products but also mastered the geography of the roads and paths which they chose to move the shipments that they loaded and unloaded. As they did this, they also transmitted information and rumours, through the formal and informal networks that they built up. In effect, they moulded a public opinion shaped outside of any visible official control: they alone created and made use of images and stereotypes from their own mental universe and from the information they received or imagined. In this way they moulded a public opinion that accommodated all sorts of material interests and different loyalties.

For example at the start of the food crisis to be examined below, when the Viceroy brought in food, particularly maize, from other parts of the viceroyalty, these Indians quickly learned that the quantities arriving in the city were not exactly the same as those which had been bought and loaded in its places of origin.[15] Had these foodstuffs been diverted into clandestine trade or were they being substituted for other cereals by "declassed" consumers? We shall return to this question in a moment.

The Indians could also detect harvest "leakages" during times of acute speculation and, themselves, take part in what were considered fraudulent transactions on their own account. The great merchants could easily build their speculations on the activity of the small operators (the *regatonería*), and even turn it to their own ends – or it might work the other way around. In short, these Indian transporters occupied an important intermediate, strategic position in all sorts of activities and not just speculation: a crucial point for the analysis of these risings.

IV. The crisis of production and provisioning

As is well known, the price of basic foodstuffs entered a long upward trend starting in the middle of the sixteenth century, which extended, as far as we can tell, to the whole of the viceroyalty of New Spain, even though prices of specific agricultural or mining

[15] See Silva's review (Silva, 2007:112) for the months preceding the mutinies.

products did sometimes tend to move in contrary directions (Klein and TePaske, 1981).[16] This was related both to climate change and the crises it produced, and also to growing demand from urban and mining populations.[17] The economy of New Spain[18] seems to have entered a period of general long-term growth from the mid-1670s until the beginning of the nineteenth century (Klein, 1985: 562; Romano, 1993: 25), interrupted only by occasional short crises stemming from the powerful and ever-present short-term agricultural cycle (Florescano, 1968: 519). Silver production was apparently the main source of this growth; it kept on improving by recycling previously-mined ore in the old mining areas and prospecting for new lodes.[19]

From the 1670s to around 1697, the whole viceroyalty apparently enjoyed a medium-term period of fairly vigorous production growth (Garavaglia and Grosso, 1986: 551; Klein and TePaske, 1982). If this is the case, the production crisis of 1691-1692 under consideration here may have been a mere blip in the curve of a relatively prosperous final phase in the last, inter-decennial, cycle of the seventeenth century, though of course it was significant for other reasons.

But when short-term events intersect with middle-term trends, the result can often be surprising. In this case, the geography of the subsistence and provisioning crises cut across the interaction of social groups and their psychological reactions. The resulting complexity needs careful and thorough examination, taking into account other analyses of similar events in early modern times (Labrousse, 1933; Vilar, 1982, (1972) 1994; Béaur, 2000, 2016). This is particularly true of Spanish America, where whole sectors of Indian production, and even the output of items like maize, cannot be studied because there are no tithe records (Garavaglia and Grosso, 1986: 553-554); and because local authorities and tax farmers applied and collected consumption taxes in very different ways (Klein and TePaske, 1981: 129).

There were several elements in the critical fluctuations of 1691-1692. The first was abnormally high rainfall in the summer of 1691, because the over-abundant water seriously damaged crops in the countryside near the capital.[20] On top of this came a disease proper

[16] A rise in salaries following from rural depopulation and the decline of the Indian population might also explain rising food prices. It seems that the middle of the seventeenth century was the lowest point of the demographic curve (Araya, 2004: 69), though there were signs of improvement, for instance in Mexico City and its hinterland; this is a much-debated question.

[17] Much remains to be done on short-term economic crises in New Spain in the seventeenth century, e.g. in sugar production, which employed a great deal of labour.

[18] Taking into account all the difficulties inherent in treating such a vast area as a single economy.

[19] Scholarship on mid-term economic tendencies in the viceroyalty of New Spain seem to confirm the picture of a seventeenth century where all the productive and fiscal indicators grew only modestly, if at all, before the last third of the century, and then a more dynamic eighteenth century. After 1680 the gap between the two "historic" viceroyalties of Hispanic America (New Spain and Peru) became definite and irreversible (Klein and TePaske, 1981:120). This illustrates two different sorts of linkage between the European and the emerging American economies, which not only evolved in contrary directions, but involved still further contrary movements at the regional level within the American continent itself.

[20] There had already been heavy rainfalls in 1689. They returned in 1691, a year before the uprising. This provoked fears of further flooding, as had occurred in 1629.

to maize, caused by a grub that fed on the stalks. Not surprisingly, the cereal harvest – mainly maize and wheat – was poor; this was evident by the second half of 1691 and had predictable effects on stocks of available grain. As a result maize prices rose considerably between June and December 1691. And this was only the start of the price increase.[21]

Then, the heavy rains of 1691 were followed by cold and hailstorms. To complete the list of climate disasters, there was drought from the beginning of 1692.[22] The hail also killed off draught animals, making it all the harder to get supplies to the capital. From April of that year, worries began about whether the city could be supplied. Indeed, the difficulty of getting in cereal and meat supplies was common to the central region of the viceroyalty (Feijóo, 1965: 657). This was in reality a typical crisis cycle, familiar to students of the emerging Mexican economy (Florescano, 1968, 1969).

The Viceroy worked together with a committee set up specially to study the situation, which included the chief civil and ecclesiastical authorities of the viceroyalty. Although initially tempted by the idea of imposing an official maximum price (*tasa*) on cereals and seizing crops, he opted for the opposite policy, proclaiming the grain trade and its price to be free (Calvo, 2005: 89).[23] It is hard to believe that the central authorities, who had had plenty of administrative experience in the Iberian Peninsula, did not realize that such a measure would push up prices in a time of failing production. These authorities would have been aware of similar experiments during the second half of the sixteenth century and throughout the seventeenth century, and not just in the Spanish American viceroyalty; they must have known that such a temporary, one-time "liberalisation" could not lower, or even stabilize, consumer prices.

In fact, the explicit aim of this "liberalisation" was to stimulate and encourage people to bring into town the grain that was visibly moving around through informal networks or being kept in storage, and to get it out of the hiding-places. Such a measure was taken even though, at first, grain was allowed to be sold at prices above the official or usual prices. It is extremely likely that the viceroy's people were perfectly well aware that available grain was being hoarded. Forced to choose between two dangerous alternatives, a further price rise, or the breakdown of provisioning, the authorities apparently adopted the first course, while believing, perhaps not entirely ingenuously, that they could avoid the second. In the event, they got both outcomes simultaneously.

It may be that this measure was supported, or even desired and promoted, by pressure groups in the special consultative committee that had been set up – landowners, stock-raisers and traders, both laymen and clergy chosen among the outstanding members of municipal and vice-regal institutions. They knew from past experience the positive, if temporary, impact that free price-setting could have on their own commercial profits, in

[21] In addition, several outbreaks of measles were recorded at that time, mainly among the Indians (De Robles, 1945: 111, 223-236).
[22] The people may have attributed this to the total solar eclipse of 23 August 1691 (Feijóo, 1965: 677). This was not a negligible matter in the psychological makeup of the crisis. As Ernest Labrousse pointed out, the "concomitance" of events quite possibly independent of each another — in this case, natural catastrophes and crises of production — can set off powerful reactions in the minds of people living during a critical time (Labrousse, 1948).
[23] The measure was taken on 26 April 1692 (Feijóo, 1965: 659; Silva 2007: 112).

a situation where production and circulation had declined.[24] They could also count on their own ability to stockpile and preserve grain. Contrary to naïve or disingenuous liberal doctrine, freedom of pricing during crises of climate and production very often favours speculators rather than consumers.

The Viceroy's personal efforts to mobilize shippers and administrative personnel to buy in grain from outside and bring it to Mexico City[25] dated back to the second half of 1691, when, as we have seen, poor harvests and the victualling crisis had already become inevitable. However, the population and consumers, prodded by some clergymen who disliked the Viceroy, may have regarded his attempt to get additional supplies, particularly of maize, from places like Chalco and Celaya, as speculative manoeuvres on his own part (Silva, 2003: 33; Calvo, 2005: 89). This was the more so as the then Viceroy, who was close to some of the town merchants, had a bad reputation for making profits for himself and his friends on irregular or even illegal trading (Taiano, 2013: 628-629) linked to smuggling networks, including imports and exports (Gutiérrez, 1993: 87; Silva, 2004: 371; Pazos, 2005: 767, 772).[26]

When the Count De Galve arrived as the new viceroy at Mexico City, it was a clear sign that certain officials in the city council and in the vice-regal administration were going to be bypassed in favour of several relatively new personalities, and a few older ones, close to the Viceroy. These came mostly from among stockbreeders and merchants who exported cereals, particularly wheat (Pazos, 2005: 767-768). This shift probably corresponded to a momentary convergence of several interests with tendencies in the mid-range or long-term economic trends in New Spain, in the context of the Viceroyalty's trade relations with Europe, the Philippines and China, and with the rest of Spanish America.[27]

In this situation, caught between rumours and certainties, the Viceroy, his government and officials came to be seen as "responsible" for the difficulties of victualling, the production crisis and the bad weather, or even guilty of profiting from them. This reduction of events to politics shielded or concealed expressed disagreements and conflicts between both civil and ecclesiastical authorities themselves.[28] People were all the readier to react this way because, as we have seen, the maize stopped arriving in town at a particular moment, having probably been diverted to places where it could be sold at greater profit. This event may also have stimulated the speculative operations of hacienda owners and

---

[24] Pierre Vilar has often raised this question. Researchers need to examine more closely the appropriateness of remedies advertised as "favourable to the consumer", such as the free price-setting proposed during the crisis periods of the Old Regime (Vilar, (1962) 1987: II. 393-394, 406). The clumsiness of the administrative personnel, their unawareness of popular reaction or contempt for it, and also the timing of such measures, could rapidly spark revolt (Vilar, (1972) 1994).

[25] A policy which nevertheless ran the risk of creating extra local supply problems when the production crisis occurred within a relatively small area. When the authorities became involved in trade the "positive" risks of speculation were often tempered by the "negative" risk of disturbances.

[26] For the discontent with the Count De Galve, and the people he annoyed, see also Hidalgo, 2016.

[27] In a way, the Viceroyalty was witnessing a sort of readjustment of economic activity. Increased silver production for local needs was perhaps a sign — both a consequence and perhaps a cause — of this (Klein and TePaske, 1981: 135).

[28] Accompanied in this case moreover by the discrediting of administrative policies and the suspected corruption of public authorities.

wholesale merchants who were close to the municipal administration, or belonged to it. Not to mention that the Indians and the *castas*, anticipating yet more shortages or perhaps even higher prices, may have increased their stocks by hiding or burying their maize, as some accounts claimed (Feijóo, 1965: 658).

Of course, the wholesale price of wheat and maize may have risen less than it did at other critical moments. Thus for example, the price of maize had increased by as much as 550 per cent in other seventeenth-century crises (Sempat, 1999: 47).[29] Nevertheless, its rise on this occasion was remarkable and also revealing.[30] In comparison with the average price during periods considered normal, wheat rose by about 45-50 per cent at the crisis peak, while maize rose by 350 per cent. Even though there were not many salaried workers and they could be hired, organized and paid in many different ways, it is worthwhile trying to make a few prudent estimates to pin down the effect of such price rises quantitatively, without of course claiming any universal validity for them. An Indian family with four or five members would need about two *fanegas* of maize a month (Giordano, 2010:114).[31] This could use up the whole monthly family earnings of 6 to 7 pesos (of 8 reals each), and not all families made that much. In sugar production, the highest monthly salary, earned by a "team captain" working full time, was less than 7 pesos (Araya, 2004: 83) at that time.[32] Moreover, the production crisis inevitably threw more people onto the labour market and thereby brought pay rates down. Finally, it should be remembered that when Indian families could afford to buy their food, they could do so only on a day-to-day basis, from the *regatonería*, the segment of the market that specialized in "petty speculation".

There were several reasons why the price of maize rose much more than that of wheat. First, of all, the crisis in wheat had come earlier and hit production harder (Calvo, 2004: 88). Necessarily, when there was no more grain there could be no more purchases. But the maize crisis, coming after the bad weather and the disease that worsened its effect, probably touched off powerful fears among the Indians, as it was "their" cereal. There is perhaps a second reason, related to those mentioned above: this price increase may possibly be explained by speculation, even carried out by Indians themselves. These price rises might have been an automatic response, but they could also have been calculated to "generate discontent" an expression used in several accounts compiled after the disturbances (Feíjóo, 1965: 658).

However, the discrepancy between price rises that were greater for maize than for wheat may also be explained by product substitution during the crisis by consumers, as those accustomed to eating one cereal turned to an alternative that was worse, or

[29] Taking the example of the seventeenth-century price rises for maize in the whole of the Viceroyalty of New Spain, the critical periods 1615-1616, 1620-1625 and 1641-1644 seem just as violent as that of 1691-1692 if not more so (Soria, 1988: 125-126).

[30] At the height of the crisis, the wholesale price of wheat could have reached 76 *reales* f.o.b. (as against 52 in normal times, a rise of about 50 per cent), and that of the *fanega* (about 50 litres) of maize, 28 *reales* (against 8 in normal times, a rise of 350 per cent) (Silva, 2007: 80-81). And this is without taking into account the volatility of the amounts consumers paid at the retail level.

[31] Giordano uses Arij Oweneel's estimates for eighteenth-century central Mexico.

[32] This is only an approximation, as there are no statistical registers for the period.

considered worse, than what they would normally eat (Feijóo, 1965: 657). On this occasion the Spanish and mixed-race consumers of wheat and wheat bread may have chosen to eat "below their class" (Labrousse, 1933) thus pushing up maize prices, if only momentarily and involuntarily.[33] All this could be true even without the activities of Spanish and mixed-race speculators in maize, who may have occasionally tried to fish in troubled waters.

The system of supplying cereal foodstuffs to the city had been re-organised between 1579 and 1584 by adding a Castilian set of rules[34] to the previously-existing distribution networks which the Castilians had at first used to subject the Indians to their tax system (*tributo*) (Florescano, 1965; Vasquez de W., 1968; Hernandez, 2013). The proposed aim of this composite system was to guarantee and regulate urban consumption[35] without abandoning country people to their fate. It had been placed under municipal control, but in addition it directly involved the vice-regal authorities, who also lived in the capital, with all the institutions of administrative power that they possessed.[36] Moreover, by the second half of the seventeenth century, despite legislation to the contrary, the aldermen (*regidores*) in the city council were already recruited among the principal landowners, the most powerful stockbreeders and the owners of the mills surrounding the town. Most of them had got these positions because they had grown rich and thereby could take advantage of the system of venal office purchase that the Habsburgs had set up under the pretext of building up an administration,[37] an arrangement that spread to all Castilian possessions in America.

In this reorganization of supply, two municipally-run institutions of Castilian origin played a fundamental role: the public municipal storehouses (*pósito*) and the Grain Market (*alhóndiga*), both inspired by European and Iberian namesakes, but adapted to the peculiar conditions of the viceroyalty and the city of Mexico.[38] The responsibility for running these institutions forced local authorities to work together like a proper town government, mainly to avoid price rises (Vásquez de W., 1968: 395). Their dual function sometimes makes it difficult for us to distinguish the specific roles of each institution. The municipal storehouses were supposed to buy grain from farmers and store it as a permanent reserve

---

[33] The "declassment" of consumption, a phenomenon of subsistence crises in the Old Regime, which Labrousse studied in great detail for eighteenth-century France, seems to have affected the poorest members of the European and mixed-race population of Mexico City who, lacking wheat and bread, began to consume more maize: this increased demand put pressure on prices (Feijóo, 1965: 657).

[34] The same was true of meat, regulated earlier, in the first half of the sixteenth century (Galindo, 2014: 57).

[35] It came in response to a series of provisioning failures and recurrent price rises in the second half of the sixteenth century, provoked, it was said, by the action of plebeian speculators (*regatoneros*) (Florescano, 1965).

[36] For a broader treatment of relations between authorities and the storehouses, see Hernández, 2013.

[37] Jimenez's recent study (2012) provides a more general treatment of venal office-holding under the old regime Spanish monarchy.

[38] For the situation in Spanish cities, particularly seventeenth-century Madrid, see, among others, Andres and Lanza, 2012. For the Muslim origins of the *alhóndiga* and the more obscure antecedents of the *pósito*, see Hernández, 2013: 22 ff.

for consumers, guaranteeing them against the hazards of production, prices, or anything else. The Grain Market was conceived as a great warehouse and shopping place where one could buy products – mainly cereals – arriving in town, at prices set and regulated by town authorities, with particular attention to the relative prices, weights and measures of grain, flour and bread.

The object was to concentrate and centralise provisioning in order to cut out speculators, particularly those of the petty sort. But the producers and traders, particularly the biggest ones, could see that the two institutions might possibly limit their profits and put their own production under surveillance, principally by implementing price controls. Needless to say, the landowners, who also owned the products of the soil, kept a close eye on the price that the public grain market paid for them.[39] And they viewed the public storehouse as a potential competitor, when it had the means to carry out its task. They could not fail to react and try to defend their interests. In other words, neither town provisioning nor municipal price controls could be carried out without taking into account the interests of those who owned the grain and who wanted to get a good price for it.

Thus these two institutions were put under much greater tension, and their interests ran up against each other more, in times of bad weather and production crises than in so-called normal times. They were torn: on the one hand was the consumers' interest, which they were supposed to protect, and which was theoretically represented by the town authorities and the Viceroy; on the other were the interests of producers' and traders. It was a hard balance to maintain, particularly if the members of the two institutions themselves had their own interest to defend as well. That was exactly the problem, as it occurred in the crisis.

V. The Revolt of June 1692

During the three days before the mutinies of Sunday 8 June, the Grain Market, which also happened to be situated on the Plaza Mayor, had no grain to sell and so closed its doors. It was then besieged by consumers, mainly Indians and mixed race, most of them women. This was the prelude to demonstrations of open discontent which broke out on the same Plaza Mayor. They were followed, on Saturday 7 June, by harsh treatment inflicted on the Indian women calling for maize, including a pregnant woman who was said to have lost her baby during the clashes.[40] Then the demonstrators simply burned down the Grain Market (*alhóndiga*). As for the public Municipal Storehouse (*pósito*), it too had no grain on hand for consumers. Once provisioning was no longer assured, panic took hold of consumers and pushed them to protest and counterattack.

---

[39] They paid representatives or attorneys (*encomenderos*) to defend high prices for their products in the *alhóndiga*. The presence of these *encomenderos* was however forbidden by law. Regular and frequent reiterations of this legislation were no doubt a sign that in reality it was not applied (Vásquez de W., 1968: 426), as was also the case in other areas under colonial and vice-regal government.

[40] Other accounts refer to the death of a small child, suffocated during the women's demonstrations (Gonzalbo, 2008: 15).

Likewise, the chief city officials were visibly incapable of meeting the protestors' demands, either by symbolic acts or by holding discussions. First, the archbishop of Mexico, the highest Church authority, could not manage to offer even a word or gesture of sympathy to the Indian women when they went to ask him to intercede with the Viceroy; instead, doorkeepers and junior vicars firmly turned them away (Calvo, 2004: 90-91); he then tried, unsuccessfully, to flee from his palace. But the archbishop's lack of Christian charity no more than replicated the actions of the local judicial authority, the *corregidor*, who, on several occasions, demonstrated his own inability and unwillingness to meet the rebels.[41] After that, it was the turn of the Viceroy himself to disappoint the demonstrators (see below). The requests by the Indians and poor of the city and its surrounding area for cereal supplies were at first peaceful, but the authorities neither heard nor satisfied them. The lack of maize and of grain to make bread, and the fear of a lasting famine which laid hold of the demonstrators naturally fed the fires of mutiny, but so did the behaviour of the authorities.

After the market and Sunday Mass, two social occasions that allowed news and gossip to flow freely, the movement broke out openly on the afternoon of Sunday 8 June, lasting five or six hours, until nightfall. An angry and gradually swelling crowd of women and men from the Indian neighbourhoods massed in front of the Viceroy's palace. The mutineers openly targeted "government people", giving voice to several variants of an all-purpose watchword, "Long live the King! Down with bad government!" that exonerated faraway supreme authorities such as the King, the saints, God and the Virgin Mary.[42] This did not deter them from simultaneously proffering a wide range of rebel cries in which raillery accompanied insult and even attacks on public authority, just as occurred in early modern European revolts against "bad rulers" and in the 1624 Mexico City rebellion. Initially, the demonstrators targeted the Viceroy, the Count De Galve.[43] But they also targeted the local colonial authorities, including churchmen, and, noticeably, the very presence of Spaniards, whom they mocked as *gachupines* – pretentious metropolitans. All this demonstrated the heterogeneous, complex mental universe of the rebels and also a real social merging of discontents of many and varied origins.

Townspeople, or at least many members of the lowest social classes of the city, "the rabble of this country" (*gentualla de este país*)[44] seem to have taken part in the uprising,

[41] To get a hearing, the demonstrators may have pretended that an Indian woman had died. But that also was in vain.

[42] Eric Hobsbawm's classic analysis of social revolts situated in the dichotomy between a government close to hand and a distant ruler, seems particularly apposite (Hobsbawm, 1959: 111-112). Far from acting irrationally or in pure anger, the protagonists in this movement had a clear social idea of their targets. There are some obvious parallels, in the mutinies at Madrid in the second half of the seventeenth century (Castroviejo, 2013), and also in the Neapolitan revolt of 1647-1648 (Enciso, 2004).

[43] Gaspar Melchor Baltazar de la Cerda Silva Sandoval y Mendoza was the eighth Count De Galve and the thirtieth Viceroy of New Spain. For a biographical study of him and his governorship in New Spain, including its darker aspects, see, among others, Gutiérrez, 1993. Taiano's study (2013) compares criticism and praise of the Viceroy by his contemporaries. For an overall discussion of the content of the demonstrators' watchwords, see Silva, 2003.

[44] In the words of Count De Galve's private secretary, Don Pedro Manuel de Torres (Calvo, 2005: 43).

in all their social variety and all colours of skin, alongside Indians from both town and countryside. This was a display of social reality quite unlike the alternative representation and idea of a colonial society frequently expressed as deeply and irrevocably divided by insurmountable bitterness and hatred between Indians and *castas*.[45] Puzzlingly, and unacceptably, these groups had joined to act together: reality had overtaken the mental and legal vision of the social body. The number of participants has been estimated, both by direct contemporary witnesses and by historians at between 10,000 and 20,000 with Indians largely in the majority.

The demonstrators burned important and symbolic parts of the old Palace of the Viceroys and the royal *Audiencia*: the archives, the prison (after freeing the prisoners), the judges' and notaries' chambers and so on. They also burned the gallows and the pillory, and the houses and buildings belonging to the town council, the diocese, local notables and members of the colonial nobility. Next, they sacked and burned a good many *cajones*[46] on the Plaza Mayor, those fixed booths described above, generally owned by Spanish merchants and serving mainly Spanish customers.

Apart from the tools and rudimentary arms used in the attacks – mostly stones, knives and machetes, some of them stolen, and pre-Hispanic arms dusted off for the occasion – the two weapons of the revolt, which the rebels wielded openly in full daylight, were fire and theft. Fire was an arm for wreaking destruction and total annihilation; it was used against official buildings and symbols of the Spanish presence. Theft was a means to negate or set aright legal property relations, represented in this case by merchandise from abroad or goods looted from official offices – though other objects were also stolen: in a spontaneous revolt there could be, by definition, no respect for existing structures.

People in power appeared to have only fragile and derisory forces to defend their buildings against the rebels' fury; there was no regular army, only a rather small palace guard and the militias belonging to the corporations of merchants and tradesmen (Exbalin, 2013: 16-18). With only a few exceptions, when people close to power put up resistance to the crowd's attacks, the Spanish *vecinos*, that is, the notables, merchants, administrators and volunteers, did not mobilise to defend the official buildings until after the uprising was over. However, the palace guards did fire on the crowd and killed some demonstrators (García, 1907: 240).

Mexico City was at that moment in the middle of the annual Corpus Christi celebrations, which had begun three days earlier, on 5 June. This festival was one of the most important religious events in Spanish life at that time, affirming as it did the validity of transubstantiation in the Eucharist. It was a public festival and a street festival, as the Spanish Church intended, a festival with a part to be played by all the vice-regal authorities and the institutions representing the Spanish presence. The ceremonies and public displays – official festivities, several parades and dressing up, bull fighting, performances of religious plays, games and jousting, official banquets and various drinking parties, in which the ruling groups featured prominently – had no doubt been taken as a real

---

[45] And even within these two generic groups.

[46] Made of wood and perishable materials, they were a ready prey to fire. During the rebellion 280 *cajones*, almost all of them, were burned (Suárez, 2011: 443).

provocation, particularly the most ostentations ones held on 5 June (Muriel, 1998: 111). They were of a kind to offend the sensitivities of anyone, particularly those, including poor Spaniards[47] and mixed-race people, who had to put up with the worst consequences of the agricultural crisis and rising prices.

On the morning of Sunday 8 June, the protests began a little earlier than usual in the markets of the capital, particularly the *Baratillo* on the *Plaza Mayor*.[48] The first rioters, or some of them, went to the neighbourhoods where the Indians and the poor lived, to rouse these people to protest; it is not known if this had been previously planned. The rebels made arms of whatever they could find, mostly stones and flammable material, and went back to the city centre. Though the fear of famine may have touched off their fury and turned it into revolt, its success must surely be explained by underlying vindictiveness, resentment and structural discontent.

To get such a subversive movement going, there must have been at least some organisation and perhaps some premeditation, if only sketchy. This would hardly be surprising; the popular *pulquerías*[49] scattered all around the city were places where the Indian and the poor population met; the Spanish authorities looked on them with suspicion. They might have helped prepare the movement and even give it some structure and leaders. It should also be noted that, perhaps significantly, in the days preceding people noticed an increasing number of Indians, métis and Blacks arriving in the capital: wanderers, migrant workers or people fleeing abusive masters on a hacienda. Some were no doubt fleeing poverty in the countryside and looking for maize, others perhaps came to see the Corpus Christi festival, or for some other reason.[50] Most importantly, however, the rebellion showed very clearly that Indians were permanently present in the Spanish part of town. This was a subterranean, almost informal presence that had gradually and silently swollen (Silva, 2001: 81, 83, 87, 108). This presence had been ignored or tolerated by the Spanish in their neighbourhood, the *traza*, although these Indians were not supposed to live there permanently (Gonzalbo, 2008: 13).

The Viceroy was absent from the government palace when the disturbances broke out; the members of the crowd could not speak with him directly. The Count De Galve had left that morning for a convent in the city, to assist at the Corpus Christi celebrations. Afterwards, when he learned of the string of disorders, the attack on the Viceroy's palace and the extent of the troubles, he decided simply to seek temporary refuge in the convent of San Francisco el Grande, in another part of the city. The Spanish authorities were certainly surprised by the rebellion but they clearly hesitated to take it seriously.[51] Perhaps

---

[47] The *zaramullos*, according to a witness, De Sigüenza y Góngora [(1692) 1984], that is, Spanish *pícaros, chulos y arrebatarropas* (knaves, rascals and thieves who snatch clothing).

[48] The Plaza Mayor had a very large space for gatherings: about 200 m long and 240 m wide (Exbalin, 2013: 15).

[49] The many taverns serving *pulque*, a local alcoholic drink of pre-Hispanic origins.

[50] The Spaniards' fears could have been increased by the arrival of these outside elements in town, as happened in other circumstances, elsewhere and at other critical moments. Such events are well known and have been well analysed (Lefebvre, 1932).

[51] Some witnesses reported that the presence of the demonstrators elicited smiles and laughter from some of the palace guards at first (García, 1907: 238); that did not last long.

they underestimated the level of discontent and the consumers' fear of famine until it was too late (Silva, 2007: 71, 216); this happened at other times, in other circumstances, for example in the Naples revolt of 1647-1648 (Enciso, 2004: 143).

Some authorities or officials may have also thought that the revolt was anti-Spanish treason, or a form of madness, thus proving the ever-unreasoning and barbarous nature of the Mexican Indians who had formed the core of the mutinies (Calvo, 2005: 44). Thus the violent protests in Mexico City on 8 June 1692 brought to light the gap that sometimes appears between the power of popular discontent and the tardy and deficient perception of it by public and political authorities (Labrousse, 1948).

Other mutinies or acts of rebellion happened between 1692 and 1693, or a little later, before the beginning of the eighteenth century, in other parts of the territories of New Spain. Indeed one took place only six days after the Mexico City rising, at Tlaxcala, not far away (Calvo, 2004: 82; Silva, 2007: 68-69; Exbalin, 2013: 1.3). Thus the *tumulto* of 1692 may have been an element in a complex of uprisings and revolts, distinct from meteorological events[52] and extending beyond the strictly Mexican context, which might itself have helped trigger the conflict.

These analyses require further refinement. Was the rising also related to the contradictions caused by a process of enrichment? Or was it a crisis of impoverishment? If so, who was being enriched or impoverished? Was the crisis related to speculation and to the activities of certain social groups that were involved in international exchanges rather than with just Castilian or Iberian merchants? Was there a link between agricultural cycles and the internal consolidation of certain social groups? These are obvious questions, but they need to be asked about the 1692 revolt, and indeed about the whole Hispanic American situation at the end of the seventeenth century.

However, to return to the Mexico City crisis, it is noteworthy that on the day after the revolt, Monday 9 June, grain and bread suddenly reappeared in the city. Did they come from other territories of the viceroyalty, as was claimed,[53] or did the vice-regal authorities force the hoarders, who they knew existed, to bring out the hidden stocks they were keeping back for speculation, and to start making bread that very night? The solution to the crisis had been quickly decided and carried out, after a Sunday of terror and destruction. The Viceroy was even said to have ordered free maize to be distributed that very same day, particularly to the Indian women, "despite their ingratitude, typical of the rabble" (Gonzalbo, 2008: 20), and his order was believed to have been strictly obeyed by both his administrative staff and the shopkeepers.

[52] Calvo (2004: 81) suggests this may have been true on a world-wide scale, citing the work of Emmanuel Le Roy Ladurie. Other similar cases existed, for example the "long summer" of 1692-1694 in New Grenada, the diseases that accompanied it and the dreadful frosts that followed (Castaño, 2017: 104-105); these were related, as we now know, to the recurrent cycles of *El Niño*, and its companion, *La Niña*, several months later. For a general approach to the history of climate in the last decade of the seventeenth century in Europe, see O'Grada, 2007: 9-10.

[53] Such imports had been carried on since the beginning of 1692 but had not until then succeeded in averting a provisioning crisis. This means that imports of this kind were not the only way the crises was resolved, though they may have helped.

Such an outcome may require us to qualify claims about the gravity of the climatic and production crisis of 1691-1692, which we have tried to situate in its context[54] and in the middling term. However, the extent of the provisioning crisis, the degree of speculation and the fear of famine should not be minimised either. The speed with which the authorities responded to the popular protests shows that. But it would be wrong to think that the solution to the crisis was mostly a practical matter or that it simply consisted of improving victualling and distribution. In fact the Viceroy and the "corporation" of Vice-regal authorities, as well as "vital forces" of the capital city, adopted a truly general response, which was put into practice by the administrative personnel. Even without documentary evidence, the process by which decision-making and implementation was concentrated and centralized is clear. By forging a renewed and effective alliance, the dominant forces in Mexican society wanted quickly to turn around an unfavourable power relationship that had briefly knocked them off balance.

They clearly were bent on immediate action, starting the next day, vigorously and openly, sure, no doubt, of their own strength and of the weakness of the rebels, who lacked any known or proclaimed decision-making mechanism and had been weakened by repression and psychological pressure, particularly from the clergy.[55]

Fear of class war, probably increased by the colonisers' guilt-feelings, quickly brought about an integrated, complete, strong and united response, to be carried out immediately. A solid blow had to be stuck at once to turn the situation around. From that moment on fear must suddenly have changed sides; the moment for revenge had come. If the "guilty" were people who had justly revolted and protested against the grain shortages from which they suffered, and not those who had caused them, so much the worse.

About a hundred people were said to have been killed in the rebellion, mostly Indians. Some bodies were found; others may have been retrieved by the victims' relations. The Viceroy had a list of the rebels drawn up; police enquiries and judicial proceedings began on Wednesday 11 June. Extrajudicial reprisals against the rebels, striking particularly at designated leaders – mostly qualified artisans or people working in petty urban trades such as tailors and shoemakers, especially Indians – were dreadful (Exbalin, 2013: 34-35). But this, too, was not unknown, either in New Spain or Spanish America.

Clearly most of the rebels had been Indians and it was they who were initially targeted for reprisals.[56] Yet other sectors of society were also touched by the repression in the wake

---

[54] As we shall see below, the origins of this critical episode should be examined in a more continental context, more Spanish-American and general. For a perspective close to this, see Gutiérrez, 1993: 95. Other refinements of the extent of the productive crisis can be found in Hidalgo, 2016 or Rodríguez, 2005.

[55] The Viceroy and the main civil and ecclesiastical authorities, escorted by the militias, and accompanied by *gremios y oficios* — the trade corporations and all their members — made a victory tour of the Plaza Mayor the day after the crisis in order to reassure the Spanish who lived in the *traza* (and everybody else), but also to show that matters had been taken in hand (Calvo, 2004: 100). This happened before a tour of different parts of the town that took the form of a procession, but whose real significance, influence or actual course is unknown (De Sigüenza y Góngora, 1984; Exbalin 2013).

[56] This included a ban on *pulque*, the alcohol made from agave, of Aztec origins, as some contemporaries claimed that consuming it drove Indians and rebels to commit the most radical actions. Kasiak, 2012 takes up this question, following on from earlier works. But this argument should not be forced too far.

of the revolt. Five Spaniards were hanged.[57] But another point is also worth mentioning. In the measures the authorities took after the revolt, they demonstrated their desire to restore the former state of affairs, before the uprising, a wish to return to the schema of "two republics", which aimed at the separate development of the two worlds, the world of the Spanish on the one hand and that of the indigenous peoples on the other. Here is one example. The revolt had brought to light the numbers of Indians living in the city, and that they had been working there for years. One of the measures was to try to compel these people to go back to their own reserved neighbourhoods, their own *doctrines*, or to their villages in the countryside. The aim was to end "contaminating" contacts (the expression used) between the Indians and the Spanish and mixed-race populations, or stop them from turning into *ladinos*, that is, Spanish-speaking Indians, shrewd and clever, versed in city ways (Sánchez, 2004: 72-73).[58] The same purpose was behind measures seeking to forbid Indians from wearing European clothes or to limit Spaniards' right to have Indian servants living in their houses.

The subsistence crisis was followed in 1692 and after by a notable epidemic and demographic crisis (Béligand, 2004). Certain diseases such as measles wreaked havoc and worsened the existing demographic crisis (Robichaux, 2007). The epidemiological crisis did not affect only Mexico City; it seems to have occurred in other regions too (Morin, 1972; Silva, 2007: 232-233), though this question needs more research. However, the harvest of 1693 was abundant and there was then another "sorting out" of consumers: the European and mixed-race populations could now return to wheat, which in turn drove downward the price of maize, the basic cereal consumed by the Indians. But there was also probably less scope for speculation, at least for the time being, until another chance returned.

VI. Conclusion

The existing literature on the *tumulto y alboroto* in Mexico City illustrates the short-term connection between a production crisis in the countryside and a provisioning crisis in the city, both set off as much by speculation, large and small, as by fear of famine. The Indian revolt, the popular revolt, the practical unity of different social groups for a period of six hours, as well as the initial institutional paralysis in dealing with it were its direct result.

We cannot however document the way the vice-regal power managed, or was obliged, to compel the economic and commercial leadership of Mexico City to accept its short-term solution to the crisis. We cannot know what went on in the discussions and negotiations that must have taken place on the evening of 8 June 1692, and likely that night and the following morning, between the various institutional protagonists, who certainly realized

[57] The Jesuits seem to have played an important role on June 8, by calming the rebels, convincing them to leave the square in front of the Viceroy's palace and putting an end to the revolt (García, 1907: 246). They were also thought to have interceded in favour of the Indians during the legal proceedings after the revolt (De Robles, 1946: I. 246-248; Gonzalbo, 2008: 17).

[58] It should also be noted that this "contamination" represented a net tax loss for the vice-regal authorities, as *ladino* Indians had stopped paying their *tributos*, the taxes they were obliged to pay as vassals of the King of Spain.

the advantages of concertation in the heat of the crisis. Yet this consensus evidently must have been obtained.

These negotiations and discussions were followed by quick and targeted action aimed at transporting and supplying grain and bread, bringing them back out of their hiding-places to the markets and bakeries by the next morning. How did the Viceroy use his authority to impose this solution? Was it he, himself, or the royal *Audiencia*, the legal arm of the Spanish sovereign in America, who forced a solution? What were the terms of the negotiation, if there was one? Were agreements struck whereby positions in the municipal administration were sold at highly advantageous prices, a recurrent request? Or about bringing back to power certain personalities in Mexican society whom the Count De Galve had passed over in favour of his own close associates (*allegados*)?

Beyond the victory of the "vital forces" in the city and Viceroyalty, and the defeat of the rebels, it may well be asked whether this temporary and rather limited reversal of the colonial mechanisms of enrichment, was not a local and momentary forerunner of a more global and general crisis. In that case, this setback would have been rather the sign of a more serious contradiction or limitation in the emerging economic system of New Spain and in the long-term evolution of its colonial mode of accumulation, a contradiction in the relations between internal exchanges and international trade and between the legality and illegality of the operations tolerated in those social and economic conditions. This blockage, this growing tension would have appeared differently in other parts of New Spain. This would require us to look at the systemic power crisis during the Mexican crisis of 1692, in the wider and more general context of Hispanic America,[59] or even in the Asian and European context, where there were blockages to its insertion in the world and its needs that were inherent to the way colonial domination worked in Spanish America. For nothing requires us to assume that this insertion was a basic fact, or taken for granted, at the end of the seventeenth century.

Following on from these conclusions, the revolt of June 1692 also calls into question two representations of life that were shared by the colonial authorities and Spanish contemporaries themselves in the evolving colonial society of New Spain. The first was the idea of the "two republics", co-existing and evolving separately, or at least thought to be doing so. The second was the supposedly insurmountable gap between Indians and *castas*. As we have seen, the rebellion, in a practical fashion, cut across these two representations of society, or these twin stereotypes, and made them look out-of-date, even though the uprising did not really shatter, or even weaken, them for the foreseeable future.

Of course, the actual events of the powerful social movement that crystallized during the crisis lasted only for six hours, but they clearly revealed the true workings of a much more complicated society in the emerging colonial world of the old regime. Put more succinctly, there were not in fact "two republics" in the viceroyalty but rather a many-coloured social conglomeration in the process of formation, surprising because it was so unexpected, and corresponding to interests and affinities that had not been foreseen in the law. There was moreover no impenetrable wall between Indians and the *castas* or

[59] Thomas Calvo suggested this already in 2004, although from a very different perspective than the one outlined here.

the other kinds of inhabitants and recently-formed social groups: rather a web of social relations that were more horizontal than vertical, more open than closed. The threads of a sociological spiders' web had been spun over the fissures in a wall that was already clearly cracked open.

Were the colonial authorities of New Spain ready to face up to the image that this emerging society formed of itself in its practical reality? Were they capable of doing so? Or, with their compulsion to return mentally to the past, were they not trying rather to suppress the new representation of emerging reality by restoring, so to speak, the old imagery? Did the naked reality frighten them? Seen this way, their society was trapped in a conflict between social and legal notions, in which the social world simply could not fit into the garments of the legal world, no matter how carefully they had been tailored to control it.

Bibliography

Andrés, J. I. and Lanza, R. (2012) 'El abasto de pan en el Madrid del siglo XVII', *Studia historica, Historia Moderna*, 34, pp. 61-97.

Antoine, A. and Michon, C. (2006) *Les sociétés au XVII*e *siècle*, Rennes.

Araya, A. (2004) 'Lógicas productivas y empresa colonial desde la historia cultural. El caso del ingenio san Nicolás Tolentino, Nueva España, finales del siglo XVII', *Fronteras de la Historia*, 9, pp. 61-91.

Bautista y Lugo, G. (2010) 'Los indios y la rebelión de 1624 en la ciudad de México', Castro, F. (ed.), *Los indios y las ciudades en Nueva España*. México, pp. 197-216.

Béaur, G. (2000) *Histoire agraire de la France au XVIII*e *siècle*, Paris.

Béaur, G. (2016) 'Tierra, trabajo y relaciones sociales en la Francia de la Edad Moderna y de comienzos de la Epoca Contemporánea, (siglos XVI-XIX)', García G., F., Béaur, G. and Boudjaaba, F. (eds), *La historia rural en España y Francia (siglos XVI-XIX). Contribuciones para una historia comparada y renovada*, Zaragoza, pp. 245-267.

Béligand, N. (2004) 'La mortalidad en una parroquia novohispana del Valle de Toluca: Calimaya en los siglos XVII y XVIII', Hernández P., J. (ed.), *Enfermedad y muerte en América y Andalucía, siglos XVI-XX*, Sevilla, pp. 145-200.

Béligand, N. (2007) 'La mort dans la ville de Mexico, au XVIIIe siècle', *Annales de Bretagne et des Pays de l'Ouest*, 114, 4, pp. 73-95.

Calvo, Th. (2004) 'Mexico-Guadalajara-Tlaxcala, la semaine des pierres, 8-14 juin 1692', Croq, L. (ed.), *Le prince, la ville et le bourgeois,* Paris, pp. 81-107.

Calvo, Th. (2005) 'La plèbe à l'aune des vice-rois américains (XVIe-XVIIIe siècles)', *Caravelle*, 84, pp. 37-63.

Castaño, Y. (2017) 'El consumo y el abasto de la carne y de otras materias primas pecuarias, en la ciudad de Santafé del Nuevo Reino de Granada, 1572-1716', *Fronteras de la Historia*, 22, 2, pp. 76-113.

Castroviejo, A. (2013) 'Las revueltas populares en Madrid, en la segunda mitad del siglo XVII', *Revista Historia Autónoma*, 3, pp. 47-62.

Chevalier, F. (1952) *La formation des grands domaines au Mexique. Terres et sociétés, au XVIe et XVIIe siècle*, Paris.

Cruz R., M. S. (1991) 'La emergencia de una ciudad novohispana. La ciudad de México en el siglo XVII', *Zaloamati, Anuario de Historia y Cultura de México*, 3, pp. 89-115.

Cope, R. D. (1994) *The Limits of Racial Domination. Plebeian society in the Colonial Mexico City, 1660-1720*, Madison.

De la Maza, F. (1968) *La ciudad de México en el siglo XVII*, México.

De Robles, A. [(1692) 1946] *Diario de sucesos notables (1665-1703)*, México.

De Sigüenza y Góngora, C. [(1692) 1984] *Seis Obras*. Caracas ['Alboroto y motín de los Indios de México', 1692, pp. 94-141].

Enciso, I. (2004) 'Revueltas y alzamientos en Napoles. La crisis de 1647-1648 en la historiografía', *Studia historica, Historia Moderna*, 26, pp. 129-153.

Exbalin, A. (2013) *L'ordre urbain à Mexico (1692-1794): Acteurs, règlements et réformes de police*, Unpublished doctoral thesis, Université d'Aix-Marseille.

Exbalin, A. (2015) 'Riot in Mexico City: A challenge to the colonial order?', *Urban History*, 43, 2, pp. 215-231.

Feijóo, R. (1964) 'El tumulto de 1624', *Historia Mexicana*, XIV, 1, 53, pp. 42-70.

Feijóo, R. (1965) 'El tumulto de 1692', *Historia Mexicana*, XIV, 4, 56, pp. 656-679.

Florescano, E. (1965) 'El abasto y la legislación de granos en el siglo XVI', *Historia Mexicana*, XIV, 4, pp. 567-630.

Florescano, E. (1968) 'Meteorología y ciclos agrícolas en las antiguas economías: El caso de México', *Historia Mexicana*, 17, 4, pp. 516-534.

Galindo, M. (2014) 'Los 'señores de la tierra' y los mecanismos del abasto de carne en Tlaxcala en el siglo XVI', *Revista Complutense de Historia de América*, 40, pp. 155-177.

Garavaglia, J.-C. and Grosso, J.-C. (1986) 'La región de Puebla/Tlaxcala y la economía novohispana (1670-1821)', *Historia Mexicana*, 35, 4, pp. 549-600.

Gemelli, G. [(1699) 1968] *Le Mexique à la fin du XVIIe siècle, vu par un voyageur italien*. Paris.

Gibson, C. (1967) *Los Aztecas bajo el dominio español, 1519-1810*, México.

Giordano S.-V., C. A. (2010) 'Agricultura tradicional en la Nueva España', *Revista de História Regional*, 15, 1, pp. 108-130.

Gonzalbo, P. (2008) 'El nacimiento del miedo, 1692. Indios y españoles en la ciudad de México', *Revista de Indias*, 68, 244, pp. 9-34.

Gruzinski, S. (2005) 'Genèse des plèbes urbaines coloniales: Mexico au 16e et 17e siècle', *Caravelle*, 84, pp. 11-35.

Gutiérrez L., M. del P. (1993) *De la corte de Castilla al virreinato de México: El Conde de Galve (1653-1697)*, Madrid.

Guthrie, C. L. (1938) *Riots in Seventeenth-Century Mexico: A Study in Social History with Special Emphasis upon the Lower Classes*, Berkeley.

Hernández S., J. A. (2013) *De piedra y maíz. Las alhóndigas y el abastecimiento de granos en San Luis Potosí durante el Virreinato.* San Luis Potosí.

Hidalgo, P. (2016) 'El motín de 1692 revisado: ¿Un golpe de Estado contra el virrey Conde de Galve?', *Librosdelacorte.es Monográfico 4*, 8.

(https://repositorio.uam.es/bitstream/handle/10486/675140/LCM_4_6.pdf?sequence=1&isAllowed=y)

Hobsbawm, E. (1959) *Primitive Rebels. Studies in Archaic Forms of Social Movement in the 19th and 20th centuries*, Manchester.

Hugon, A. (2011) *Naples insurgée. De l'événement à la mémoire, 1647-1648*, Rennes.

Israel, J. (1975) *Race, Class and Politics in Colonial Mexico, 1610-1670.* Oxford.

Jalpa F., T. (2010) 'Migrantes y extravagantes. Indios de la periferia en la ciudad de México, durante los siglos XVI-XVII', Castro G., F. (ed.), *Los Indios y las ciudades de Nueva España*, México, pp. 79-104.

Jimenez, A. (2012) 'Poder, dinero y venta de oficios y honores en la España de Antiguo Régimen: un estado de la cuestión', *Cuadernos de Historia Moderna*, 37, pp. 259-272.

Kasiak, N. R. (2012) *Fermenting Identities: Race and* Pulque *Politics in Mexico City, between 1519 and 1754*, Unpublished MA thesis, Department of History, Eastern Kentucky University, Richmond.

Klein, H. (1985) 'La economía de la Nueva España, 1680-1809: un análisis a partir de las Cajas Reales', *Historia Mexicana*, 34, 4, pp. 561-609.

Klein, H. and TePaske, J. (1981) 'The Seventeenth-Century Crisis in New Spain: Myth or Reality', *Past and Present*, 90, 1, pp. 116-135.

Klein, H. and TePaske, J. (1982) *Royal Treasuries of the Spanish Empire in America*, Durham.

Labrousse, C. E. (1933) *Esquisse du mouvement des prix et des revenus en France au XVIIIe siècle*, Paris.

Labrousse, C. E. (1944) *La crise de l'économie française à la fin de l'Ancien Régime et au début de la Révolution.* Paris.

Labrousse, C. E. (1948) '1848-1830-1789. Comment naissent les révolutions', *Actes du congrès historique du centenaire de la Révolution de 1848*, Paris, pp. 1-20.

Labrousse, C. E. (1973) *Fluctuaciones económicas e historia social*, Madrid.

Lefebvre, G. [(1932) 1973] *The Great Fear of 1789: Rural Panic in Revolutionary France*, London [translation by Joan White of *La Grande Peur de 1789*, Paris].

Leonard, I. (ed.) (1932) *Alboroto y motín de México del 8 de Junio de 1692*, México.

Martin, N. F. (1985) 'Pobres, mendigos y vagabundos en la Nueva España, 1702-1766: antecedentes y soluciones presentadas', *Estudios de Historia Novohispana*, 8, pp. 99-126.

Meza, R. de L. (2016) 'El cultivo de trigo en Nueva Galicia durante el siglo XVII', *Secuencia*, 94, pp. 39-76.

Muriel, J. (1998) 'Una nueva versión del motín del 8 de junio de 1692', *Estudios de Historia Novohispana*, 18, pp. 107-115.

O'Grada, C. (2007) 'Making Famine history', *Journal of Economic Literature*, 45, pp. 5-38.

Olvera, J. (2007) *Los mercados de la Plaza Mayor en la Ciudad de México*, México.

Pazos, M. L. (2005) 'Una ciudad en crisis: El ayuntamiento de México, antes y después del motín de 1692', Gutiérrez A. and Laviana M. L. (eds), *Estudios sobre América, siglos XVI-XX*, Sevilla, pp. 767-774.

Robichaux, D. (2007) 'Mortalidad en el México indígena: Tendencias seculares en dos parroquias (siglos XVII al XX)', Boleda M. and Mercado M. C. (eds), *Seminario Internacional de Población, 2005,* Salta, pp. 99-129.

Rodríguez, M. (2005) *Cádiz en el sistema atlántico. La ciudad, sus comerciantes y la actividad mercantil (1650-1830)*, Madrid.

Romano, R. (1993) *Coyunturas opuestas: Las crisis del siglo XVII en Europa y América*, Mexico.

Romano, R. (2004) *Mecanismos y elementos del sistema económico colonial americano, siglos XVI-XVIII*, México.

Rubial, A. (1998) *La plaza, el palacio y el convento. La ciudad de México en el siglo XVII*, México.

Rubial, A. (2008) 'De la visión retórica a la visión crítica. La plaza mayor en las crónicas virreinales', *Destiempos*, 3, 14, pp. 413-429.

Sánchez, E. (2004) 'El nuevo orden parroquial de la ciudad de México: Población, etnia y territorio (1768-1777)', *Estudios de Historia Novohispana*, 30, pp. 63-92.

Sejourné, L. (1971) *América Latina. I. Antiguas culturas precolombinas*, Madrid.

Sempat A., C. (1989) 'La organización económico-espacial del sistema colonial', Coraggio, J. L., Sabaté, A. and Colman O. (eds), *La cuestión regional en América Latina*, Quito, pp. 417-456.

Sempat, A. C. (1999) 'El movimiento de la producción agraria en Tlaxcala', Menegús, M. and Tortolero, A. (eds), *Agricultura Mexicana: Crecimiento e innovaciones*, México, pp. 33-65.

Silva, P. N. (2001) 'Impacto de la migración urbana en el proceso de "separación de repúblicas". El caso de dos parroquias indígenas de la parcialidad de san Juan Tenochtitlán, 1688-1692', *Estudios de Historia Novohispana*, 24, pp. 77-109.

Silva, P. N. (2003) 'Estrategias culturales en el tumulto de 1692 en la ciudad de México: Aportes para la reconstrucción de la historia de la cultura política antigua', *Historia Mexicana*, 53, 1, pp. 5-63.

Silva, P. N. (2004) 'Violencia en las tensiones del orden colonial: El caso del motín urbano de 1692 en la ciudad de México', Ortega M., Castañeda, J. C. and Lazarín, F. (eds), *Violencia: Estado y sociedad, una perspectiva histórica*, México, pp. 365-393.

Silva, P. N. (2007) *La política de una rebelión. Los indígenas frente al tumulto de 1692 en la Ciudad de México*, México.

Soria, V. M. (1988) *Crecimiento económico, regulación y crisis en la Nueva España, 1521-1810*, México.

Suárez, C. E. (1985) *La política cerealera y la economía novohispana: el caso del trigo*, México.

Suárez, M. T. (2009) 'Los mercados de la ciudad de México y sus pinturas', Long, J. and Attolini, A. (eds), *Caminos y mercados de México*, México, pp. 435-458.

Taiano, L. (2013) 'Críticas, acusaciones, encomios y justificaciones: escritos en contra y a favor del Conde de Galve', Van der Walde, L. and Reinoso, M. (eds), *Virreinatos II*, México, pp. 600-637.

Thompson, E. P. (1971) 'The Moral Economy of the English crowd in the Eighteenth Century', *Past and Present*, 50, pp. 76-136.

Thompson, E. P. (1975) *Whigs and Hunters: The Origin of the Black Act*, London.

Vasquez de W., I. (1968) 'El Pósito y la Alhóndiga en la Nueva España', *Historia Mexicana*, XVII, 3, pp. 395-425.

Vilar, P. (1982) *Une Histoire en construction. Approche marxiste et problématiques conjoncturelles*, Paris.

Vilar, P. [(1962) 1987] *Cataluña en la España Moderna*, Barcelona.

Vilar, P. [(1972) 1994] 'Le "motín" d'Esquilache et les crises d'Ancien régime", Vilar, P., (ed.), *Nations, nationalismes et questions nationales*, Paris, pp. 13-45.

Von Wobeser, G. (1988) *La hacienda azucarera en la época colonial*, México.

5 The need for wheat: the pre-industrial expansion of Vienna's grain supply, 1800-1840*

Jonas M. ALBRECHT, Department of Social and Economic History, Johannes Kepler University Linz, Austria

I. Introduction

The "urban explosion in nineteenth-century Europe" (Bairoch, 1988: 216) presented the continent's cities with historically unprecedented challenges to secure quantitatively and qualitatively satisfying food supplies for their quickly increasing numbers of inhabitants. Making sure enough and healthy food was available at affordable prices year-round was among the main concerns of both municipal and state administrations to prevent social unrest and upheaval, especially after 1789. The increasing amounts of food brought into the cities to sustain the urban dwellers were but the tip of the iceberg, or the result, of vast and complex underlying processes of improvements in agriculture, transportation, food processing and sanitation techniques as well as accelerating interventions in hinterland environments. However, whereas these developments regarding urban food supply have been studied and outlined extensively for both the periods before 1800 and especially after 1850, the early nineteenth century remains surprisingly absent in the international debate. This is also true for Vienna as a case study. Although the Habsburg capital was among the largest cities of the continent by mid-century, its food supply system, particularly during the *Vormärz*, the period before the March Revolution of 1848, remains largely unexplored.

This paper aims to close that gap by investigating the effects and consequences of the wave of urbanisation during the first half of the century on the city's cereal supply structures just before industrialised means of transportation became available. Largely without steamships and railways, how did the exploding population change Vienna's provisioning with basic foods? Furthermore, how did the development of the centre of the Habsburg Monarchy compare to other urban experiences?

Answering these questions, the paper will proceed as follows: at the outset, a rough summary of the state of research regarding Vienna in comparison to other western urban centres is presented, followed by an overview of the demographic development of the city of Vienna before 1850. Then, the main body of the text will develop three key arguments. First, by exploring heretofore disregarded sources and presenting a more comprehensive dataset on urban cereal provision, it will be demonstrated that Vienna experienced a notable shift in the composition of its grain supplies that can be termed as *wheatification*. Second, this shift towards wheat consumption was realised through both a substantial reorganisation and expansion of cereal production in the city's more traditional hinterland and a simultaneous expansion of the supply area into the Hungarian Pannonian Plain already

* I would like to thank the anonymous reviewer as well as Ernst Langthaler, Peter Eigner and Erich Landsteiner for their valuable and helpful comments and suggestions.

Stocks, seasons and sales: Food supply, storage and markets in Europe and the New World, c. 1600-2000, ed. by Wouter RONSIJN, Niccolò MIGNEMI and Laurent HERMENT, CORN 17 (Turnhout, 2019), pp. 103-127.

 DOI: 10.1484/M.CORN-EB.5.118256

before the introduction of industrial means of transportation to address the "energy and resource scarcities in the core area". As this development "deeply influenced massive and growing human-induced environmental change", it will be identified as the expansion of the *Urban Food Frontier* (Richards, 2003: 4; Hoffmann, 2001; Moore, 2000). It will thus be concluded that the pre-industrial expansion of Vienna's grain supply introduced a new quality in the city's relation to its hinterland economies and ecologies. Moreover, it laid important geographic foundations for the implementation of steam-transport technologies.

II. State of research

Despite the very rich literature on urban food provisioning, early nineteenth-century, pre-industrialised grain supply has received much less attention than either the medieval or early modern periods (Charruadas, 2012; Dewilde-Poukens, 2011; Kaplan, 1984, 1996; Keene, 2012; Woolgar, 2013), or the period after 1850 (Blackman, 1963; Cronon, 1992; Fava-Guárdia-Oyón, 2016; Scholliers, 1992). Studies that cover the half century between the French and March revolutions have either concentrated on other goods, especially meat (Baics, 2016; Guárdia et al., 2017; Horowitz-Pilcher-Watts, 2004), milk (Atkins, 1977), water (Graber, 2007; Tello-Ostos, 2012), metals (Lestel, 2012), broader approaches (Kim-Barles, 2012; Scola, 1992), or, increasingly, the retail sector (Alexander, 1970; Alves-Morris, 2017; Blonde, 2009; Bohstedt, 2010; Furnée, 2014; Kelley, 2016; Miller, 2015; Mitchell, 2010; Shaw-Wild, 1979; Smith, 2002; Stobart-van Damme, 2016; Streng, 2017). However, a number of valuable studies allowing for a comparative approach exist for Paris (Barles, 2007; Billen et al., 2009; Billen et al., 2012), Belgian cities (Segers, 2001), Madrid (Ringrose, 1983), and New York City (Swaney et al., 2012).

Regarding Paris, also experiencing a doubling of the population from 550,000 to more than one million urban dwellers, it has been shown that, although "the increase in urban pressure for food was very real during the nineteenth century", total flour supplies doubled between the 1810s and 1850s (Barles, 2007: 52). Before the introduction of railways in the 1840s, this was realised mainly through the development of water transport infrastructure, and more importantly, agricultural specialisation and intensification of grain production in the Paris basin, rather than a spatial expansion of the city's grain hinterland (Billen-Garnier-Barles, 2012). Thereby, relatively stable levels of per capita supplies were ensured throughout the period; average consumption figures rose slightly from the 1780s to the 1820s, and maintained a constant level until the 1850s (Billen et al., 2009).

A somewhat different pattern has been observed for Madrid. There, the increase of the urban population from some 160,000 to 220,000 inhabitants induced a "continued growth of the city's grain supply area" between the end of the eighteenth and the middle of the following century (Ringrose, 1983: 205). In that period, both the "fundamental reality of a politically subsidised market", organised in a complex set of public, commercial and small-producer supply networks, and the expansion of agriculture, especially in Castilia, helped to stabilise Madrid's bread supply, expressed in relatively stable per capita consumption estimates (Ringrose, 1983: 154, 325).

Meanwhile, in New York City, growing much more spectacularly from 30,000 inhabitants in 1790 to 800,000 by 1860 (Baics, 2016: 11), mechanisms of both intensification and extensive expansion of the urban supply chains appeared. The "rapid growth of agricultural production regions in upstate New York" was driven particularly by the construction of the Erie Canal, completed in 1825. Between the early 1800s and 1840, "faster and cheaper transportation [...] lowered the cost of transporting bulky crops within the NYC metropolitan area and from agricultural regions in western New York and beyond. Farmers were aided in meeting demand by technological innovations that improved crop and livestock productivity" (Swaney et al., 2012: 371). However, due to the massive population explosion, "from the 1830s through the Civil War, urban demand for [...] foodstuff in New York and elsewhere outpaced the supplies available. Even as new transportation technologies [...] linked the cities to expanding hinterlands, agricultural output failed to keep up with urbanisation [...] Judged against the favourable conditions of the Early Republican Period, antebellum New Yorkers found it more challenging to sustain their provisioning standards" (Baics, 2016: 201-202).

An even more differentiated picture has been painted with regard to Belgium, where the combined population of eight cities grew from about 270,000 inhabitants in 1800 to 460,000 by 1846 (Segers, 2001: 307). Population growth and urbanisation led to "decreasing grain consumption for Ghent, Bruges, Brussels and Lier", as well as Antwerp and Mechelen because the "Belgian agriculture, which had displayed a 'traditional' character up to 1850, was not in a position to satisfy the growing demand for food. The available land was limited and techniques remained more or less unchanged", causing "a sharp increase in the retail prices of foodstuffs" and a "radical polarisation of the consumption patterns" (Segers, 2001: 320-321, 326, 329). On the one hand, this was expressed in the growing consumption of potatoes by the poorer strata of the urban societies. On the other hand, there was a structural shift towards wheat consumption by those better off, realised by a notable expansion of the Belgian wheat production between 1812 and 1846 when "farmers apparently saw the way the wind was blowing and anticipated the socioeconomic shifts and the growing (urban?) demand for better-quality bread grain" (Segers, 2001: 322). As a result, by mid-century, urban dwellers in Belgium consumed either more potatoes, or overwhelmingly wheat bread (Segers, 2001: 322).

In comparison, Vienna's early nineteenth-century supply system has been studied only in fragments. A number of articles cover the city's hinterland relations (Krausmann, 2013), its food, feed and waste supply and disposal systems (Gierlinger, 2015), or the Danube's importance to urban resource flows from 1830 onwards (Gingrich-Haidvogl-Krausmann, 2012). However, they all rather focus on the latter part of the century, and emphasise the effects of industrialisation on the urban metabolism as "the emergence of the railroad system radically changed the spatial relations between city and hinterland in the mid-19th century" (Krausmann, 2013: 258). Others, focussing on Vienna's urban administration, food policies, small-scale food retail trade, and living standards, have concluded that the early nineteenth-century population growth had devastating effects. Findings on per capita consumption produced by Sandgruber suggest a degradation of average cereal supplies between the 1780s and 1830 (Sandgruber, 1982a: 150). According to Opll,

> although during this period the number of inhabitants of Vienna exploded, the methods of supplying the city were not changed. Instead, they continued in the old, traditional, very inadequate patterns and had to come under decisive pressure in case of the slightest disturbances like harvest failures (Opll, 1981:52).

This has been considered to be due to both the failure of Vienna's municipal and governmental administration to respond to supply challenges posed by population growth and the delayed implementation of supply improvements like railways, steamships, and steam mills. Measures to improve the urban supply system taken after 1839 were "too late to effectively prevent the supply crisis of 1845-1847/48" (Opll, 1981: 53; Weigl, 2014: 134).

Summarising, there are some lessons to be derived from the case studies available. First of all, Paris, Madrid, New York City and the Belgian agglomerations tightened their respective grip on hinterland resources during the pre-industrial population gains of the first decades of the nineteenth century. All of them did so either by intensifying existing patterns of resource extraction from rural areas, by expanding the space from where resources were drawn, or by combining both mechanisms – even before steam-driven transportation was implemented. Second, in all four cases, both more intensive patterns of resource allocation from hinterlands and the incorporation of new productive areas into the urban supply systems were actively driven by urban and national administrations and private interests. Municipalities, governments, investors and even farmers were involved in facilitating urban supplies through market regulations and controls, transportation improvements, and shifts in agricultural practises. In comparison, the research regarding Vienna has dismissed any of those developments for the early half of the century and has firmly argued for the failure of urban and court authorities to respond to challenges posed by population growth before 1850. In the light of the comparative literature cited, this is striking. Was Vienna's supply system that sluggish during a time of dramatic increases in urban inhabitants? Did only steam-transport technology break the chains of pre-modern inertia and stagnation?

III. Population growth

From the last third of the eighteenth century until the 1840s, when steam-powered food transport and production facilities were implemented, the city of Vienna experienced a phase of dramatic population growth. Still within the limits of a pre-industrial energy regime, the expansion during the *Vormärz* represents one of the most dramatic growth scenarios in the city's history. Almost exclusively driven by immigration, the population of the urban area doubled in the decades after 1815, making Vienna one of the hotspots of European population growth (Clark, 1996: 30-31). By 1815, some 230,000 people lived within the urban area, roughly as many as by the turn of the century. Then, the real boom started. During the twenty-five years after the Congress of Vienna, the annual average population increase was about three times as high as it had been in the five decades before (Weigl, 2000: 50-63, 75-86). More than 170,000 people poured into the city, swelling it to just over 400,000 inhabitants by the 1840s. By mid-century, Vienna and its suburbs had surpassed a population of half a million and emerged as the third-largest urban centre of Continental Europe, excluding Russia (Lenger, 2013: 53). Moreover, population growth was not confined to the urban area. Between 1780 and 1850, the total population of the province of Lower Austria surrounding Vienna grew from 760,000 to nearly 1.1 million. Similar to urban population growth, the increase in the rural population occurred largely after the Napoleonic era (Sandgruber, 1982a: 26).

IV. Sources

The development of Vienna's provision with various kinds of foodstuffs, beverages, building materials, and fodder can be quantified in great detail. The information is derived from city and fiscal toll registers spanning the period from the late eighteenth to the early twentieth century.

The importation of a wide range of goods into the urban area was subject to taxes since the late seventeenth and early eighteenth centuries. From 1704, the *Linienwall*, built as a semi-circular first defence line around the city, was used as customs boundary separating city and suburbs from rural surroundings. In the course of the century, the complex system of various simultaneously existing taxes supervised by different authorities was gradually simplified, until in 1811 the *Stadtmauttarif* constituted a first attempt to centralise all fees. After that date, the collection of all taxes was in the hands of the state, executed at checkpoints adjoining the city gates. In 1829, the tax system was again reorganised into the empire-wide *Allgemeine Verzehrungssteuer*, administered by the k.k. Ministry of Finance. Effective from November 1st of that year, 250 different goods were taxable upon crossing the tax limits. Important to both fiscal and municipal budgets, Vienna's *Verzehrungssteuer* represented up to two percent of total state revenues and between seven and twenty-four percent of the city's budget throughout the century. Consequently, only rather minor changes in tax levying and execution were made before the city toll was reformed in the wake of urban expansion in 1892 (Hauer, 2014: 13-35). Both municipal and fiscal authorities created massive collections and publications of data regarding absolute import numbers, tax revenues, and, partly, exports (Hauer et al., 2012).

V. Urban cereal provision, 1780-1847: evidence from the toll registers

Although a complete dataset is not available for the entire period, the interval information for the early and mid-1780s and the Napoleonic Era up to the Congress of Vienna combined with continuous information from 1828 onwards suffice to outline the most important trends of Vienna's food supply up to mid-century. Yet, some hiatuses within the dataset are not avoidable. Most importantly, the supply of potatoes is continuously documented only from 1828 onwards. As potatoes did likely gain importance in the diets of urban dwellers since the late eighteenth century, this leaves a certain share of the urban food supply unaccounted for (Sandgruber, 1982a: 149). Second, barley, registered as individual tax item until 1829, was subsumed into the general category of *Brotfrüchte* – bread grains – thereafter. Furthermore, some individual figures, for example for 1828 and 1829, respectively, need to be interpreted very carefully.

Figure 1 shows the development of Vienna's supply with major food cereals and potatoes, and the city's population during the last decades of the eighteenth and the first half of the nineteenth centuries. Two main patterns appear. First, regarding cereals, Vienna's provision did not keep pace with population growth after 1815. Although the city's grain supply could be drastically enhanced under the terms of the war economy, this expansion was only temporary. By the 1780s, the city was provided with a total of 40,000 to 45,000 tons of flour and grains, plus some 3,000 to 6,000 tons of barley each year. During the period of the Napoleonic Wars, significantly more food was brought into the city, and annual fluctuations

Figure 1 Annual cereal and potato supply 1782-1847 in tons per annum (left), and population (right)

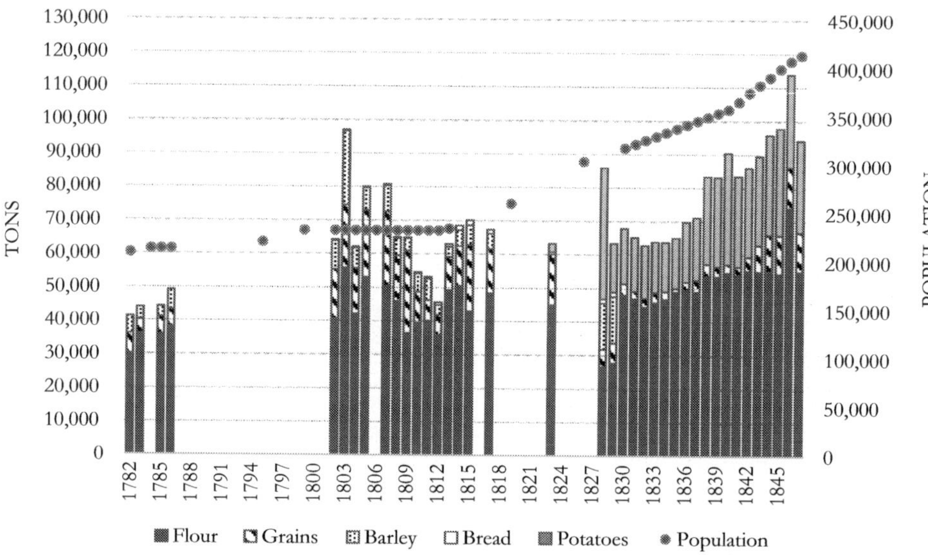

Sources: Luca, 1785: 274-276; Pezzl, 1787, 1805, 1823; Pezzl and Tschichka, 1826: 24-29; Wiener Zeitung 12 April 1806: 1586; Vaterländische Blätter für den österreichischen Kaiserstaat 17 January 1809: 20; 5 January 1810: 239; 9 January 1811: 18; 8 January 1812: 20; 13 January 1813: 24; 5 January 1814: 12; 13 January 1816: 24; *Tafeln zur Statistik der Österreichischen Monarchie*, 1828: §95 ; from 1830: (Hauer *et al.*, 2012). *Note*: Grains expressed in flour weight, assuming an average milling grade of 80%. See Petersen, 1995; Rahlf, 1996.

were much more pronounced. While supplies with flour and grains rose to around 60,000 tons per annum in what appears as rather regular war years, barley provisions remained relatively stable. However, during the war era, both lows and peaks were drastic. In 1802-1808, year-to-year fluctuations in flour and grain imports reached nearly 20,000 tons. In the peak years of 1803, 1805, and 1807, the tax collectors recorded cereal imports nearly twice as high as during peacetime twenty years earlier. The absolute high was reached in 1803, when more than 75,000 tons of flour and grains plus a dubious amount of 22,000 tons of barley inflated the urban cereal supply to almost 100,000 tons. Downward fluctuations were equally pronounced, especially during the inflationary period. Between 1807 and 1812, cereal provisions gradually decreased by 30,000 tons, almost halving. By the time of the Congress of Vienna in 1814 and 1815, as well as in 1817, cereal imports had recovered, again reaching levels of 60,000 tons, while barley imports remained rather average. Unfortunately, except for 1823, there is no data on urban supplies for the next decade. Comparing the single years of 1817, 1823 and 1828/1829 might suggest that at least Vienna's flour supply decreased during the economic recession of the following decade (Komlos, 1983: 90-104). However, there are insufficient data to prove that point satisfactorily. Yet, by the late 1820s, when data is available again, Vienna's flour and grain supplies had certainly withdrawn from the high war levels, although the 1828 and 1829 figures appear somewhat unreliable.

Table 1 Annual average per capita supply of cereals and potatoes, 1782-1847, in kg

Period	5-Year Averages	
	Cereals	Potatoes
1782-1786	213	
1802-1807	333	
1808-1812	247	
1813-1817	281	
1828-1832	157	64
1833-1837	149	48
1838-1842	159	77
1843-1847	174	72

Sources: see Figure 1. Notes: no data 1806 and 1816; 1828 and 1829 omitted due to questionable data. Compare also Sandgruber, 1982a: 150

Thus, despite the large increase in the urban population, quantitatively the city's provision was hardly different from what it had been half a century ago. Around 1830, with less than 50,000 tons transported into Vienna, the city's flour and grain supply almost completely failed to respond to population growth. However, supplies started a continuous upward trend after 1832, when the pan-European cholera epidemic had hit Vienna and depressed urban food provisions to some extent. After 1833, provisions started to improve gradually, rising steadily from some 47,000 tons of flour and grain to around 65,000 tons in the mid-1840s. More precisely, the years around 1840 appear as a first caesura for the supply system. While flour supplies abruptly leaped from 1837 to 1838, when Vienna's first railway line was opened, grain imports grew even more significantly after 1842, when the city's first steam-powered flour mill started production. Nevertheless, until mid-century, the amounts of flour and grain brought into the city, then partly by industrial means, would not surpass the peak levels reached during the Napoleonic Wars.

Second, the stagnation in grain and flour imports was met by increasing supplies of potatoes. Although reliable information is only available from 1828/1829, according to Sandgruber it is relatively safe to assume that potatoes gained importance in the diets of both better-off and poorer strata of the Viennese society from the late eighteenth century, and especially during the Napoleonic Era (Sandgruber, 1982a: 145-153). By the 1830s, they had already assumed a relatively stable and prominent position in the composition of the city's food supply with some 15,000 tons of potatoes being imported annually before 1835. Then, provisions increased, leaping upward to around 26,000 tons in 1838 and approaching 30,000 tons per annum in the years just before the revolution.

These two patterns had far-reaching consequences for the average per capita consumption of urban dwellers. As shown in Table 1, by 1830, average per capita cereal supplies had declined radically from the levels of the 1780s. While urban residents had been supplied with more than 200 kilograms per capita per annum at the start of the period under investigation, only about 150-175 kilograms were available per capita during the *Vormärz*. Average consumption was lowest during the mid-1830s, when cereal availability declined to 150 kilograms, but recovered afterwards and kept rising up to the eve of revolution. Potato consumption showed a comparable trend. After having reached a low point during 1833-1837, per capita supplies were almost twice as high in the following five years, and would more or less maintain this level until 1847. In italics are shown the respective numbers for the years 1800-1817, however, these are rather unsubstantial for the analysis of average consumption due to the large numbers of both Austrian and French troops garrisoning the city in various turns.

Thus, contrary to Paris, Vienna's flour and grain supply did not keep pace with the city's rapid population growth after 1815. Only after the mid-1830s did cereal supplies surpass the levels of the 1780s, though not by large before the mid-1840s. By 1845, compared with 1785, provisions had increased by about half while the population had almost doubled. Meanwhile, potatoes had gained in importance, probably since the previous century, and certainly after 1835. The result was a remarkable decline of average per capita cereal availability. Up to this point, as noted by previous research, the quantitative evidence does suggest anything but an expansion of Vienna's grain supply before the 1840s. However, the most eminent development before mid-century was not a quantitative one – it was quality that mattered.

VI. The need for wheat

As pointed out earlier, throughout the late eighteenth and early nineteenth centuries the lion's share of Vienna's cereal supplies consisted of flour. Although scattered, available evidence hitherto disregarded allows analysing the composition of the city's grain provision in more detail. This much closer look at the capital's supplies reveals the important structural change that occurred before mid-century: the *wheatification* of grain provisions (Otter, 2011:188).

From the 1820s until mid-century, the city's grain provision was restructured decisively, shifting qualitatively towards largely wheat-based supplies in just a few decades. Contrary to Sandgruber's estimates, rye was almost as important as wheat before 1830 (Sandgruber, 1982a: 141). Except for 1808-1812, both wheat and rye flour contributed about one third to the city's total cereal supplies (Table 2). Although wheat imports were permanently higher than rye imports, the difference was not yet very pronounced. The same ratio probably applied to grains imported into the city untreated. In 1803, city authorities estimated grain demand at 250,000 *Metzen* of wheat and 200,000 *Metzen* of rye (Mayr, 1940: 134).[1] After 1830 however, this ratio was unbalanced relatively quickly. Those involved in the trade already noted this development. "The bakers in Vienna," wrote famous geographer and statistician Wenzel Blumenbach in 1835, "strongly prefer flour made of Banat wheat [...]" (Blumenbach, 1835: 40). Just twenty years later, urban demand had largely shifted towards wheaten flour. According to estimates by the Lower Austrian Board of Trade, Vienna's annual wheat consumption had

[1] One Metzen = 61,487 litres.

Table 2 Composition of cereal supplies, 1780-1855.

Period	5-Year Averages/ Estimates				
	Total Supply, in tons			Share of Total Supplies, in %	
	All Cereals	Wheat Flour	Rye Flour	Wheat Flour	Rye Flour
1782-1786	45 137	17 750	14 944	39	33
1802-1807	77 219	25 892	22 228	34	29
1808-1812	57 341	24 116	14 867	43	26
1813-1815/17	54 253	24 464	22 660	36	34
1828-1830/32	50 030	14 273	12 624	28	25
1850-1854	69 847	54 000	15 000	70	20
c. 1870	217 000	108 000	32 000	50	32

Sources: see Figure 1. Notes: no data 1784, 1806, 1816. 1850-1854: Niederösterreichische Handels- und Gewerbekammer, 1855: 19; 1870: estimate for Vienna and surroundings taken from k.k. Handelsministerium, Enquête über die Approvisionirung Wiens, 1871: 40.

risen from some 15,000-25,000 tons to more than 50,000 tons by mid-century, whereas the demand for rye had barely changed (Niederösterreichische Handels- und Gewerbekammer, 1855: 18). By 1870, the President of Vienna's Produce Exchange estimated the agglomeration's wheat demand to be more than three times as high as the need for rye (k.k. Handelsministerium, 1871: 40). Just a few years later, Court Baker and new President of the Produce Exchange Roman Uhl in his retrospect on Vienna's flour and bread industries noted that "in the years 1820-1830, the general demand for white flour increased daily [...]" (Uhl, 1873:176).

VII. The expansion of the urban food frontier

The structural shift in Vienna's grain supplies towards wheat was facilitated by the notable expansion of wheat production in the urban hinterland. This expansion was an integral part of the spatial spread and intensification of land use in the province of Lower Austria during the eighteenth century, as the growing population "put intensifying demands on scarce natural resources – especially food and energy" (Richards, 2003: 11). Just like "population pressures drove the expansion of arable land in Tudor and Stuart England", when "woodlands, forests, moors, heaths, fens, and other lightly inhabited tracts were colonized, reclaimed, and settled" (Richards, 2003: 123), urban and rural population growth induced the expansion of the frontier in Lower Austria after 1750. Between the 1780s and 1850s, the province's "unproductive" land was almost extinguished, declining from about one fifth of Lower Austria's total area to merely four percent (Table 3). By the

Table 3 Land use change in Lower Austria, 1789-1830/50, in 1000 ha

Usage	Year	Area	% of total area	Change, %
Cultivated area, total	1789	1 608	81	19
	1830/50	1 913	96	
Unproductive	1789	374	19	-81
	1830/50	70	4	
Forestry	1789	452	23	40
	1830/50	631	32	
Arable, total	1789	740	37	10
	1830/50	815	41	
of total Arable: Main cereals	1789	379	19	31
	1830/50	497	25	
Meadows and Gardens	1789	219	11	18
	1830/50	258	13	
Pasture	1789	151	8	0,2
	1830/50	152	8	

Sources: Sandgruber, 1978b: 146-153, Tables 79, 80, 81, 83, 84, 85, 93

middle of the nineteenth century, the area under any form of cultivation nearly equalled the province's total surface of 1,982,500 ha. Formerly non-productive soils were turned into areas devoted to either forestry, food, or fodder production.

As the frontier milled its way into the forests, it ploughed its way into the plain. Just like "war against untamed nature was being waged" in Frederician Prussia (Blackbourn, 2007: 46), the Austrian state's settlement policy with regard to agricultural expansion and modernisation, market access and the removal of trade barriers assumed a leading role in frontier expansion from above. While in Russia "the tsarist state had extended its fortified frontier lines to make new areas safe for pioneer settlement and cultivation" during the eighteenth century (Richards, 2003: 272), Emperors Maria Theresa and Joseph II sent out large numbers of settlers to plough the black earth of the Hungarian and the sandy soils of the Lower Austrian frontiers (Bruckmüller, 2008; Feigl, 1982; Gutkas, 1984). With expansion came new settlements, like Theresienfeld (1763) or Oeynhausen (1773) in Lower Austria, and many other new villages in the Banat (Sugar, 1990: 142-143; Fata, 2014). The draining of marshlands, construction of irrigation works and other measures to expand the surface available to agriculture followed these new foundations. Like Golden Age Dutch waterworks engineers accomplished "the land reclamation that literally changed the face and shape of whole regions" (de Vries and van der Woude, 1997: 27), the enlightened Austrian state administration and Austro-Hungarian landlords developed plans and made efforts to gain more control over the empire's rivers and wetlands, especially the Danube, although much less effectively (Glassl, 1970; Hohensinner

Table 4 Average cereal harvests in Lower Austria, 1789-1851

Cereal	Year	Harvest, 1000 t	Change, %
Wheat	1789	25	123
	1851	56	
Rye	1789	149	52
	1851	226	
Barley	1789	20	113
	1851	43	
Oats	1789	97	52
	1851	148	
Total	1789	291	63
	1851	473	

Source: Sandgruber, 1978b: 163-166, Tables 109-112.

et al., 2013; Thiel, 1905-1906). One of the largest attempts at land reclamation was the partial drainage of the Hanság marsh at Lake Neusiedl southeast of Vienna. Begun by Count Esterházy in the 1770s, drainage schemes were developed and partly carried out. Between 1777 and 1780, a road of over three kilometres long with 20 bridges, allowing up to four wagons to drive side by side, was constructed to improve transportation through the swamp. By the 1820s, "huge amounts of hay" grown on soils claimed from the marsh could be transported via the Hegedus Canal, built 1795-1813, to Lower Austria and Vienna (Horváth, 2008: 386-389; 2011: 164).

As a result, the area devoted to the production of basic food and feedstuffs in Lower Austria grew by almost a third in the course of the early nineteenth century. Compared with the late eighteenth century, when cereal production had occupied around one fifth of Lower Austria's total surface, the incorporation of frontier soils lifted this share to about a quarter by the 1850s. Moreover, additional room to grow cereals was not only gained by making land arable but also by giving already cultivated plots over to grain cultivation.[2]

The result of frontier expansion in Lower Austria was a decisive increase in cereal output (Table 4). Compared to the province's total annual grain production of some 300,000 tons around 1790, by the early 1850s yearly harvests approached half a million tons. Although rye and oats remained more important in terms of the actual area under cultivation and total harvest output, wheat and barley became ever more significant to the regional agriculture. Like their Belgian counterparts, Lower Austrian farmers, landowners and agronomists "saw the way the wind was blowing" (Segers, 2001:322). Indeed,

[2] Until mid-century, the area under the four major cereal crops, wheat, rye, barley, and oats, grew by 120,000 ha, whereas the total arable area grew only by 75,000 ha, indicating that 45,000 ha of land already used for other purposed were turned into fields.

Table 5 Lower Austrian average wheat harvests and Vienna's average wheat supplies 1789-1857, in tons.

Year	Wheat Harvest	Vienna Wheat Supply	Period
1789	25 000	17 750	1782-1786
1851	56 000	54 000	1850s

Source: See Tables 1 and 4

wheat cultivation directly replaced rye growing to some extent, just as contemporary observers would have it (Burger, 1833). By the late 1780s, Lower Austria produced some 25,000 tons of wheat and some 150,000 tons of rye per annum. Sixty years later, wheat harvests had more than doubled to about 55,000 tons, while rye crops grew by about half to 225,000 tons annually.

However, between the major grains, output increases were generated quite differently. Wheat was among the main objectives of frontier expansion – and pushing out the boundaries of the wheat frontier was the single most important response to growing demand. Within the Lower Austrian agriculture, gains in wheat harvests were almost exclusively generated through the extension of cultivation before the 1860s. By mid-century, the area under wheat had grown more than twofold compared with the situation around 1790, while little or no gains in area productivity were achieved on the overall provincial level (Bruckmüller, 2001: 209-212; Sandgruber, 1978a: 210).[3] Barley cultivation followed a similar pattern, but the production of both oats and rye exhibited a different behaviour. For the latter types of grain the intensification of production, that is the increase in yields per hectare, was much more important. Whereas the wheat and barley frontiers widened in the course of the first half of the nineteenth century, both the rye and oat frontiers deepened.

Yet, the regional widening of the wheat frontier was not enough to satisfy the growing urban appetite. A comparison of average wheat harvests with average wheat imports into Vienna shows how large the capital's demand loomed (Table 5). The city required nearly 18,000 tons of wheat in flour each year at the eve of the French Revolution. Since wheat delivered in the form of grains and supplies for the royal court are excluded in this figure, the actual demand was probably even higher, maybe over 20,000 tons. On this scale, Vienna's consumption of wheat was almost as high as the total annual wheat output of the entire province of Lower Austria. Despite the great extension of the cultivated area, there was no real change in this ratio before the middle of the following century. Hypothetically, Vienna would still devour almost all wheat grown in the province by the 1850s.

---

[3] To be sure, agricultural modernisation, such as summer stall feeding and increased use of manure, abolition of fallow, and implementation of leguminous crops were essential parts of the physiocratic program during the "transition from traditional to advanced organic farming". Indeed, they were highly important locally, especially on large estates. See e.g. Güldner and Krausmann (2017).

Early nineteenth-century observers were quite aware of Lower Austria's chronic deficit in wheat supplies, as agronomist Johann Burger commented around 1830:

> Considerable amounts of grain need to be imported from Hungary. For the year 1830, the official customs registers document 976,814 Metzen [ca. 45,000 tons] of wheat and 1,741,024 Metzen [ca. 66,000 tons] of oats, rye, maize and barley. [...] We have to be grateful that we are provided with our neighbours' abundance, who themselves would be seriously embarrassed if we were capable to satisfy Vienna's demand ourselves (Burger, 1833: 62).

Thus, the expansion of the Urban Food Frontier across Vienna's traditional hinterland was insufficient to satisfy the capital's ever-growing need for white bread – and beer. As Burger noted, the solution was to be found in the east.

Wheat from the western parts of Hungary had been important for Vienna's provision since the Middle Ages. In contemporary descriptions of the capital, "Hungary" is mentioned regularly as a source of grain supplies (Luca, 1787: 105, 399; N.N., 1803: 181; Pezzl, 1816: 327). According to scattered data on grain transactions in Hungarian markets in 1772/73, the largest amounts of grain changed hands in markets in the western provinces of Hungary, and especially markets distinctly located close to Vienna. Neusiedel, a small border village just 45 kilometres east of Vienna, held the largest grain market in all of Hungary with nearly 1,500 tons of cereals sold in that year (Dányi, 2007: 177-188; Grailich, 1820: 118, 124). Due to the incapability of the Austrian hinterland, population growth and wartime demand during the Seven Years' War and the Napoleonic Wars had been a major incentive for Hungarian landlords to convert waste lands into arable soils, especially in the border districts of Moson and Sopron. Consequently, not only "Esterházy estates close to the Danube and the Austrian border produced grain for the Vienna market" since the eighteenth century (Gates-Coon, 1994: 88, Kállay, 1980), and Moson county was considered "one of the granaries of Vienna and Austria" by 1820 (Grailich, 1820: 108). However, before the turn of the century "profits from [...] estates less favourably situated, further south in Vas and Somogy counties and far down the Danube, were limited by economic handicaps common to most of Hungary: difficult, costly transportation and dependence on a weak local market" (Gates-Coon, 1994: 88; Blum, 1948: 92-95; Orosz, 1971: 6; Szántay, 2014: 269-270; Vári, 2008: 25). Cereal transports from central Hungary remained unprofitable, except for times of dearth like 1771/72, and these districts were much less important for the supply of the Habsburg capital by the late 1700s. With the turn of the century, this would change. Following the rise in grain prices since the late eighteenth century,

> demand for Hungarian grain – in the hereditary provinces and the army – grew steadily from the middle of the century, and especially the final twenty or thirty years. When this could no longer be satisfied by the feudal manors of the Lesser Hungarian Plain, grain started to be transported from the Great Plain (Rácz, 2013: 217).

This expansion of the frontier was greatly facilitated by the state. Settlement programs to colonise the fertile plains of the Banat and Bačka provinces and boost agricultural production had been at the heart of the imperial policies of both Maria Theresa and Joseph II since the middle of the eighteenth century (Fata, 2014). At first, mainly the areas along the Danube and Tisza rivers accessible by ship were incorporated (Pinke, 2014;

Vári, 2008: 25). However, from the 1750s on, it became obvious that it was not enough to colonise only the land – it was also necessary to conquer the water. Simultaneous to the core's settlement endeavours, the navigability of the Danube started to receive serious attention with respect to the natural, technologic, and legal conditions of water transport. The systematic navigation and mapping of the entire river between Engelhartzell and Belgrade was begun under the auspice of a court commission in 1771, resulting in extensive plans to tackle the main obstacles of shipping, particularly ship mills, bridges, overgrown riverbanks, and floods. For that purpose, the *Navigationsdirektion* appointed engineers for certain sections of the river who were to recruit labourers locally in order to chop down trees and other vegetation overgrowing the towpaths, remove obstacles in the current, construct bridges at confluences, build dams, drain swamps, and fill up side arms where necessary (Glass, 1970). At the same time, other frontier waterways also received accelerating attention (Pinke, 2014).

Secondly, the state actively facilitated technological improvements of water transportation. By offering a price of 1,000 fl. to anyone who would "navigate the Danube with the best sailing ship and reduce the present freight rates" (Glass, 1970: 56), Maria Theresa sought to introduce up-to-date shipbuilding technologies to her empire. In 1775, Johannes Matthäus Heppe, shipbuilder from Mainz, was charged with the modernisation of the empire's Danube fleet. Already in 1771, he had been granted to open a shipyard in Karlovac, Croatia, where he was to establish a large-scale production site for his Dutch-inspired "Rhineland ships", followed by another shipyard in Eckhartsau, near Vienna. By the late 1770s, others had picked up the new technology, such as Count Theodor Batthyány, who established a large construction site on his Croatian estates on the Kupa river and secured a royal privilege to build improved ships in 1793 (Slezak, 1974: 77-78). A third public measure concerned the legal circumstances of river transportation. Beginning in 1770, the *Navigationsdirektion* was to elaborate how the complex system of navigation taxes and fees could be simplified to ease trade and transportation. In this context, the state attempted to regulate the trade by creating a shippers' organisation with professional codes and qualification guidelines, as well as wage and tariff regulations for apprentices and drivers (Glass, 1970).

Besides these direct, though in their success somewhat limited state attempts, private encounters also tried to grab a slice of the pie and invested into ventures aiming to generate profits from the increasing amounts of frontier goods that literally flowed westwards. From the 1750s through the 1840s, piecemeal regulation works were carried out in the Tisza Valley where "rises in grain prices in the late eighteenth century led landowners to convert waste lands, pastures, forests and marshes [...] into arable land" (Pinke, 2014: 95). The most prominent, and probably most important of these endeavours was the construction of the *Franzenscanal* by the *k.k. priv. ung. Schifffahrts-Gesellschaft* between 1793 and 1801, which shortened the route from Timisoara to Vienna by 250 kilometres (Petrovic, 1982). In its first year of operation, some 10,000 tons of grain passed through the waterway, largely shipped towards Austria. These numbers reached 40,000 to 60,000 tons at the height of the Napoleonic Wars, declined to about 30,000 tons in the years afterwards and again reached 60,000 to 70,000 tons by the 1820s and 1830s (Benda, 1973: 187-198; Hesperus 59, December 1815: 470; Allgemeine Handlungs-Zeitung, 2 May 1819; Wiener Zeitung 8 June 1824, 26 March 1825, 1 September 1827, 14 December 1833).

Liberalised from trade restrictions in 1817, the supply of frontier wheat, as the prime cereal of choice to Vienna's flour and bread producers, was ensured by vast grain trading networks unfolding eastwards, partly controlled by Jewish wholesale firms that almost all did at least "a little business in grain" (Hanak, 1992: 65-68; Csendes and Opll, 2006: 79). Within these networks, merchant firms in Vienna, Bratislava or Budapest had very close business links with the grain growing regions through a number of intermediaries, such as itinerant merchants, shopkeepers or innkeepers, who were centrally involved in the local and regional grain trade. Bought by agents in the producing regions, the grain was shipped westwards via the Tisza and Danube rivers. Having passed the *Franzenscanal*, the caravans of *Kelheimer* barges mainly used in grain transportation entered the Danube near Bezdan. Up to forty meters long and seven meters wide, the ships had carrying capacities of 300 to 500 tons. Each needed up to eight boatmen, 30 drivers and 40 horses to be hauled upriver as well as pioneers, cooks and other staff to be operated. Usually, a caravan consisted of three to four barges, each with three to four additional steering boats, making these shipments the endeavour of several hundred men and horses (Blumenbach, 1835: 182; Neweklowsky, 1952: 181, 291-330; Promnitzer, 1994: 182). After months of perilous journey and several pit stops in trade ports such as Baja, Dunaföldvár or Pest along the Danube, the caravans would reach the town of Györ situated east of Vienna on a side arm of the Danube (Figure 2). There, the large barges could go no further. Called "bad waters", in this area the main branch of the Danube was fragmented into several shoal, winding arms with unpredictable winds, currents and sandbanks that made the journey onwards dangerous and long (Hauer-Hohensinner-Spitzbart-Glasl, 2016). Consequently, in Györ the cereals bound for Vienna and Lower Austria were reloaded into smaller ships and carried on the river's side arm to Moson. There, water transport finally ended. The ships were unloaded and the grain eventually driven towards Vienna, less than a two-day journey by horse cart (Horváth, 2011: 182; Winkler, 1872: 87-90). Given these circumstances, in the course of the early nineteenth century Moson and Györ became the epicentres bundling the growing streams of frontier wheat. Whereas around 1820 some 300 ships unloaded about 60,000 tons of grains into Moson's granaries, those figures grew to more than 220,000 tons and about 2000 ships by the early 1840s. By that time, most of the town's population were involved in the trade as agents, brokers, drivers, accountants or by simply renting out their basements as grain store facilities (Ditz, 1867: 385-387; Grailich, 1820: 118; N.N., 1845). Moson's position had become so important that only about one tenth of Vienna's grain supplies arrived directly in the city via the Danube waterway (Gingrich-Haidvogl-Krausmann, 2012: 288). Furthermore, the town had developed storage facilities large enough to make separate granaries in Vienna virtually unnecessary and unprofitable, a fact often bemoaned by Viennese merchants and politicians (Heller, 1901: 13-17; k.k. Handelsministerium, 1871: 39-48, 63-74). As traveller-geographer Johann Georg Kohl noted, Moson,

> Raab [Györ] and Timisoara can be called the endpoints of a great shipping line, of which Raab lies near to an area in need (Vienna), whereas Timisoara is located in the centre of a grain-growing country (Kohl, 1842, 205-206).

From the Moson and Györ magazines, merchants and agents would bring grain samples to Vienna, where they met on Wednesdays and Saturdays with millers, brewers and other traders at the *Mehlgrube* and a small number of other distinctive taverns, the business's informal meeting points (Heller, 1901: 13). After sales were agreed upon, instructions were

Figure 2 Grain exportation from Hungary, late eighteenth and early nineteenth centuries

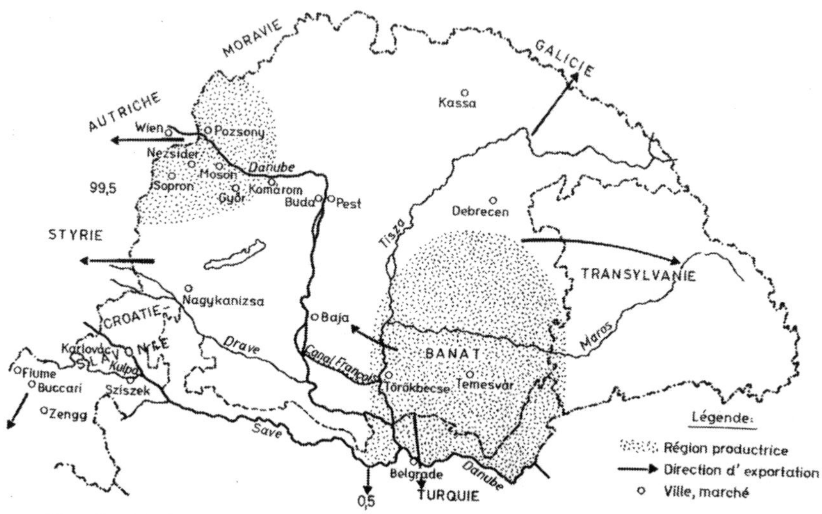

Source: Benda, 1973: 195

sent back to local hauliers contracted to transport the purchases to the mills in Vienna's hinterland or, in the case of international purchases, to Nußdorf north of Vienna, where the cargo would be reloaded on ships bound northwards (N.N., 1845).

Thus triggered, Hungarian grain production grew significantly. Cereal outputs more than doubled in Moson County between 1769 and 1844, grew more than tenfold in the counties of Pest and Bács-Bodrog, and more than fivefold in Békés County (Komlos, 1983: 54). Decisive tendencies towards market integration between Austria and Hungary appeared during the *Vormärz*. Wheat prices in Hungarian and Austrian markets converged rapidly between 1811 and 1826 and there was a significant wheat price correlation between Vienna and Hungarian as well as Banat markets already before 1847 (Cvrcek, 2013: 15; Dányi, 2007: 32-34). As the growth of Hungary's agricultural sector "was contingent on exports to Vienna" (Komlos, 1983: 89), steppe wheat gained importance for the capital's supply system.

When the *Vormärz* era ended, the Urban Food Frontier expanded deep into the Pannonian Plain. Hungarian grain exports towards the Austrian lands had increased from around 90,000 tons by the 1780s to 130,000 tons in the early 1830s and reached more than 300,000 tons before mid-century (Hassinger, 1964: 87; Komlos, 1983: 60, 75-76). In Vienna, the sheer, constantly growing quantities of Pannonian frontier wheat floating *up* the Danube helped to ease the pressures of rising demand after the financial and supply turmoil of the first fifteen years of the century (Figure 3). Following the peak of 1816, when the eruption of Mount Tambora had caused the Year Without a Summer, wheat prices in the Austrian capital essentially declined more or less to pre-war levels and remained relatively steady throughout the 1830s and early 1840s, despite the huge population growth.

Figure 3 Annual wheat prices and bread consumer price index in Vienna, 1786-1847, in grams of silver per litre

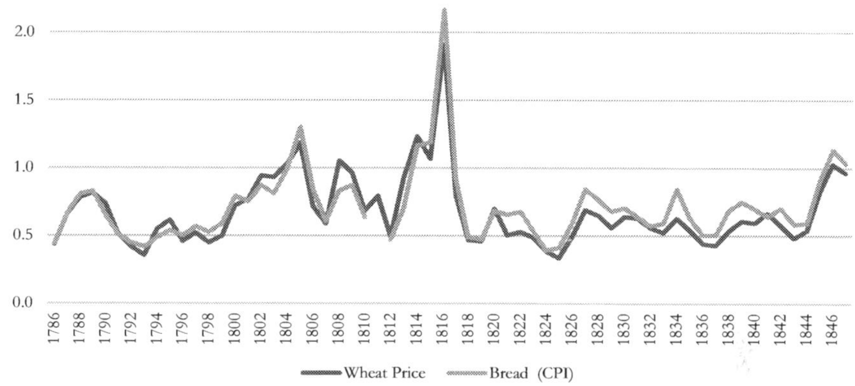

Source: Robert C. Allen, Prices and Wages in Vienna, 1439-1913, Consumer price indices, nominal / real wages and welfare ratios of building craftsmen and labourers, 1260-1913, International Institute of Social History data files, available at http://www.iisg.nl/hpw/data.php#austria, accessed July 25, 2018.

By the 1820s, advertisements for "real, good flour made from famous Banat wheat" produced by local mills appeared in Vienna's major newspapers (e.g. Wiener Zeitung, 18 May 1821: 992, and 11 December 1822, Allgemeines Intelligenzblatt: 1125; 30 December 1833: 726). In 1836, a trade report from Bratislava, an important intermediate market, remarked, "in the last two years local harvests failed, but Hungary's great granary, the Banat, helped out everywhere" (Wiener Zeitung, 3 November 1836: 1399), and by 1848, a petition of Vienna's Bakers Guild argued:

> The four markets [of Vienna, Stockerau, Enzersdorf and Fischamend] together do not supply the twelfth part of rye and wheat needed [...]. Surely, the quality of cereals sold on these markets does not suffice to produce the kind of flour that satisfies the requirements of local authorities and customers. As a matter of fact, Hungarian wheat sold in Wieselburg [Moson] or Raab [Györ], [is] largely covering Vienna's flour demand [...] (Darstellung der gewerblichen Zustände der Wiener Bäcker-Innung, 1848: 3).

As an 1855 evaluation of the city's supply system by the Lower Austrian Board of Trade reads, around mid-century, Vienna's reliance on frontier food was taken for granted:

> Wheat, the major article of Vienna's demand, is mainly delivered from Banat, because, as is generally known, regarding fineness and quality Banat wheat is the most excellent in the entire Monarchy (Niederösterreichische Handels- und Gewerbekammer, 1855: 19).

Finally, in his already mentioned portrayal, Roman Uhl's narration probably provides the best prosaic summary of Vienna's food frontier expansion:

> In the years 1814-1815, Banat wheat was ground in Lower Austrian mills for the first time. The flour samples established the superior quality and the bakers' demand for this sort of flour became more and more urgent. [...] When the '30s began, [...] diligence

> and knowledge had made arable the Hungarian steppes and pusztas, and the rich yields of this blessed soil poured into all mills in Vienna's vicinity. Trading firms were created in Wieselburg [Moson] in order to reload wheat delivered on large ships from the Banat. We see carters with countless wagons bringing Hungary's harvests in mighty caravans to the Lower Austrian mills, and Vienna and her vicinity are flooded with the best grains. Hungary became the granary of Vienna (Uhl, 1873: 176-177).

VIII. Conclusion

In the course of the half-century before 1850, just before the implementation of steam-transport technologies, the city of Vienna experienced a phase of dramatic population growth, doubling in size over only three decades. Contrary to the experience of the French Capital, this pre-industrial increase of urban dwellers went hand in hand with a stagnation of the overall grain supply in quantitative terms, leading to a large decrease of average per capita consumption. However, qualitatively, supplies shifted from a balanced wheat-and-rye ratio before 1830 towards the *wheatification* of provisions until mid-century. Compared with their predecessors half a century earlier, by 1850 the diet of Vienna's population was probably more polarised. Like in Belgium, on average, urbanites ate less bread, and more potatoes. However, bread had changed, too, as it was now wheat bread that dominated the fare. Contrary to earlier findings, this was realised through a decisive expansion of the Urban Food Frontier both across the regional agricultural system, and into the Pannonian Plain. On the one hand, the local agriculture underwent a decisive shift towards the production of wheat and barley, driven by local landowners, intellectuals, and farmers responding to demand. On the other hand, as regional wheat production was insufficient to satisfy the rising urban need for wheat, Hungarian soils much further away from the place of consumption were incorporated into the city's food system. As a result, by 1840 the Austrian capital's grain supplies were largely dominated by wheat grown on the colonised steppe frontiers to the east which helped to keep food prices in the city at bay. In this sense, the case of Vienna adds important insights into the debate on feeding the city. Here, royal authorities, (local) elites and entrepreneurs seeking profits from selling agricultural products to the monarchy's centre came together to develop frontier rivers and wetlands and to cultivate frontier soils. Thus, the Urban Food Frontier expansion, locally and in the Empire's periphery, was an essential driver of intervention in both close and remote environments, ecologies, as well as societies. Further, frontier expansion itself was driven by intense official policies and commercial endeavours. This pre-industrial extension of the city's grain supply was crucial for the relations between city and hinterland – or core and periphery. It were the late eighteenth and early nineteenth centuries that added a new quality to urban-rural relations with regard to basic foodstuffs, even in a location not famously involved in international maritime trade like Amsterdam or London. Thus, the "emergence of the railroad system" *did not* radically "change the spatial relations between city and hinterland" (Krausmann, 2013: 258) in the Austrian case. Rather, mid-century railway construction and steamship traffic only intensified commodity flows that had emerged in the course of the preceding century. Therefore, like Paris or Madrid, the city of Vienna apparently did exercise decisive, nearly empire-wide socio-economic and ecologic influences over the areas within its political control by the late eighteenth century. In contrast to Paris, however, Vienna appears to have drawn much more on the expansion of its hinterland than on the intensification of local grain production, although the Austrian capital was only half the size of the French metropolis by mid-century. In this regard, the Vienna case seems to have more in common with the experiences of Madrid and New York City, where the recourse on external land resources apparently was the readier path to sustaining urbanisation. As a result, this paper illustrates two paths to feeding pre-industrial (western) urbanisation: intensification and expansion of resource allocation. It underlines the historical peculiarities of individual case studies, embedded in their respective social, economic, political, geographical, ecological and technical environments that need to be taken into account. In conclusion, to Vienna's population it was commonplace to regularly consume products of distant origin already well before the introduction of steam transportation, industrialisation, and globalisation. By the first half of the nineteenth century, the urban consumption of bread in Vienna was essentially bound to the fate of distant people and environments.

References

Alexander, D. (1970) *Retailing in England during the Industrial Revolution*, London.

Allgemeine Handlungs-Zeitung, mit den neuesten Erfindungen und Verbesserungen im Fabrikwesen und in der Stadt- und Landwirthschaft (2.5.1819).

Alves, D. and Morris, J. (2017) 'The evolution of the retail trade sector in Iberian cities from the nineteenth century to the Second World War', *History of Retailing and Consumption*, 3, 2, pp. 71-86.

Atkins, P. J. (1977) 'London's Intra-Urban Milk Supply, circa 1790-1914', *Transactions of the Institute of British Geographers*, New Series 2, 3, pp. 383-399.

Baics, G. (2016) *Feeding Gotham: The Political Economy and Geography of Food in New York, 1790-1860*, Princeton.

Bairoch, P. (1988) *Cities and Economic Development. From the Dawn of History to the Present*, Chicago.

Barles, S. (2007) 'Feeding the city: food consumption and flow of nitrogen, Paris, 1801-1914', *The Science of the Total Environment*, 375, 1-3, pp. 48-58.

Benda, G. (1973) 'Production et exportation des céréales en Hongrie (1770-1870)', Köpeczi, B. and Balázs, É. (eds) *Paysannerie française, paysannerie hongroise*, Budapest, pp. 187-197.

Billen, G. et al. (2009) 'The food-print of Paris: Long-term reconstruction of the nitrogen flows imported into the city from its rural hinterland', *Regional Environmental Change*, 9, 1, pp. 13-24.

Billen, G. et al. (2012) 'Grain, meat and vegetables to feed Paris: Where did and do they come from? Localising Paris food supply areas from the eighteenth to the twenty-first century', *Regional Environmental Change*, 12, 2, pp. 325-335.

Billen, G., Garnier, J. and Barles, S. (2012) 'History of the urban environmental imprint: Introduction to a multidisciplinary approach to the long-term relationships between Western cities and their hinterland', *Regional Environmental Change*, 12, 2, pp. 249-253.

Blackbourn, D. (2007) *The conquest of nature: Water, landscape, and the making of modern Germany*. New York.

Blackman, J. (1963) 'The Food Supply of an Industrial Town', *Business History*, 5, 2, pp. 83-97.

Blonde, B. (ed.) (2009) *Fashioning Old and New: Changing Consumer Patterns in Western Europe (1650-1900)*, Turnhout.

Blum, J. (1948) *Noble Landowners and Agriculture in Austria, 1815-1848: A Study in the Origins of the Peasant Emancipation of 1848*, Baltimore.

Blumenbach, W. C. W. (1835) *Neueste Landeskunde von Oesterreich unter der Ens*, Vol. 2, Güns.

Bohstedt, J. (2010) *The politics of provisions: Food riots, moral economy, and market transition in England, c. 1550-1850*, Burlington.

Bruckmüller, E. (2001) *Sozialgeschichte Österreichs*, Vienna.

Bruckmüller, E. (2008) 'Eine "grüne Revolution" (18.-19. Jahrhundert)', Cerman, M., Steffelbauer, I. and Tost, S. (eds) *Agrarrevolutionen: Verhältnisse in der Landwirtschaft vom Neolithikum zur Globalisierung*, Innsbruck and Vienna, pp. 206-226.

Burger, J. (1833) 'Ueber die Vortheile der Vergrößerung der Cultur des Weitzens, und die Anwendung der Schaufelpflüge', k.k. Landwirtschaftsgesellschaft in Wien (ed.) *Verhandlungen der k.k. Landwirtschaftsgesellschaft in Wien, und Aufsätze vermischten ökonomischen Inhaltes*, Vienna, pp. 57-79.

Charruadas, P. (2012) 'The cradle of the city: The environmental imprint of Brussels and its hinterland in the High Middle Ages', *Regional Environmental Change*, 12, 2, pp. 255-262.

Clark, P. (ed.) (1996) *Capital cities and their hinterlands in early modern Europe*, Aldershot.

Cronon, W. (1992) *Nature's metropolis: Chicago and the Great West*, New York.

Csendes, P. and Opll, F. (2006) *Wien: Geschichte einer Stadt*, Vienna.

Cvrcek, T. (2013) 'Wages, Prices, and Living Standards in the Habsburg Empire, 1827-1910', *The Journal of Economic History*, 73, 1, pp. 1-37.

Dányi, D. (2007) *"Az* élet ára*": Gabona* és élelmiszerárak *Magyarországon, 1750-1850*, Budapest.

Darstellung der gewerblichen Zustände der Wiener Bäcker-Innung (1848), Vienna.

Dewilde, B. and Poukens, J. (2011) 'Bread provisioning and retail dynamics in the southern Low Countries: The bakers of Leuven, 1600-1800', *Continuity and Change*, 26, 3, pp. 405-438.

Ditz, H. (1867) *Die ungarische Landwirthschaft*, Leipzig.

Fata, M. (2014) *Migration im kameralistischen Staat Josephs II. Theorie und Praxis der Ansiedlungspolitik in Ungarn, Siebenbürgen, Galizien und der Bukowina von 1768 bis 1790*, Münster.

Fava, N., Guárdia, M. and Oyón, J. L. (2016) 'Barcelona food retailing and public markets, 1876-1936', *Urban History*, 43, 3, pp. 454-475.

Feigl, H. (ed.) (1982) *Die Auswirkungen der theresianisch-josephinischen Reformen auf die Landwirtschaft und die ländliche Sozialstruktur Niederösterreichs: Vorträge und Diskussionen des ersten Symposiums des Niederösterreichischen Institutes für Landeskunde, Geras, 9.-11. Oktober 1980*, Vienna.

Furnée, J. H. (ed.) (2014) *The landscape of consumption: Shopping streets and cultures in Western Europe, 1600-1900*, New York.

Gates-Coon, R. (1994) *The landed estates of the Esterházy princes: Hungary during the reforms of Maria Theresia and Joseph II*, Baltimore.

Gierlinger, S. (2015) 'Food and feed supply and waste disposal in the industrialising city of Vienna (1830–1913): A special focus on urban nitrogen flows', *Regional Environmental Change*, 15, 2, pp. 317-327.

Gingrich, S., Haidvogl, G. and Krausmann, F. (2012) 'The Danube and Vienna: Urban resource use, transport and land use 1800-1910', *Regional Environmental Change*, 12, 2, pp. 283-294.

Glassl, H. (1970) 'Der Ausbau der ungarischen Wasserstraßen in den letzten Regierungsjahren Maria Theresias', *Ungarn-Jahrbuch-Zeitschrift für die Kunde Ungarns und verwandte Gebiete*, 2, 2, pp. 34-66.

Graber, F. (2007) 'Inventing needs: Expertise and water supply in late eighteenth- and early nineteenth-century Paris', *The British Journal for the History of Science*, 40, 3, pp. 315-332.

Grailich, A. (1820) 'Die Wieselburger Gespannschaft in Ungern', *Erneuerte Vaterländische Blätter für den österreichischen Kaiserstaat*, 27, 28, 29, 30, 31, 32, 33, 35, pp. 105-108; 109-111; 115-116; 118-120; 123-124; 127-128; 131-132; 138-140.

Guàrdia, M. et al. (2017) 'Meat consumption and nutrition transition in Barcelona, 1709-1935', *Urban History*, 26, pp. 1-21.

Güldner, D. and Krausmann, F. (2017) 'Nutrient recycling and soil fertility management in the course of the industrial transition of traditional, organic agriculture: The case of Bruck estate, 1787-1906', *Agriculture, Ecosystems & Environment*, 249, pp. 80-90.

Gunst, P. (1991) 'Agrarian Systems of Central and Eastern Europe', in Chirot, D. (ed.) *The origins of backwardness in Eastern Europe: Economics and politics from the Middle Ages until the early twentieth century*, Berkeley, pp. 53-91.

Gutkas, K. (1984) *Geschichte Niederösterreichs*, Vienna.

Hanak, P. (1992) 'Jews and the Modernization of Commerce in Hungary, 1760-1848', Silber, M. K. (ed.) *Jews in the Hungarian economy 1760-1945: studies dedicated to Moshe Carmilly-Weinberger on his eightieth birthday*, Jerusalem, pp. 23-39.

Hassinger, H. (1964) 'Der Aussenhandel der Habsburgermonarchie in der zweiten Hälfte des 18. Jahrhunderts', Lütge, F. (ed.) *Die wirtschaftliche Situation in Deutschland und Österreich um die Wende vom 18. zum 19. Jahrhundert: Bericht über die Erste Arbeitstagung der Gesellschaft für Sozial- und Wirtschaftsgeschichte in Mainz 4.-6. März 1963*, Stuttgart, pp. 61-98.

Hauer, F. (2010) 'Die Verzehrungssteuer 1829-1913 als Grundlage einer umwelthistorischen Untersuchung des Metabolismus der Stadt Wien', *Social Ecology Working Paper 129*, Institute of Social Ecology, IFF-Faculty for Interdisciplinary Studies, Klagenfurt, Graz, Vienna.

Hauer, F. (ed.) (2014) *Die Versorgung Wiens 1829-1913: Neue Forschungsergebnisse auf Grundlage der Wiener Verzehrungssteuer*, Innsbruck.

Hauer, F. et al. (2012) 'Die Wiener Verzehrungssteuer. Auswertung nach einzelnen Steuerposten (1830-1913)', *Social Ecology Working Paper 134*, Institute of Social Ecology, IFF-Faculty for Interdisciplinary Studies, Klagenfurt, Graz, Vienna.

Hauer, F., Hohensinner, S. and Spitzbart-Glasl, C. (2016) 'How water and its use shaped the spatial development of Vienna', *Water History*, 8, 3, pp. 301-328.

Heller, V. (1901) *Der Getreidehandel und seine Technik in Wien*, Tübingen.

Hesperus: ein Nationalblatt für gebildete Leser (December 1815), 59, pp. 469-471.

Hoffmann, R. C. (2001) 'Frontier Foods for Late Medieval Consumers: Culture, Economy, Ecology', *Environment and History*, 7, 2, pp. 131-167.

Hohensinner, S. et al. (2013) 'Two steps back, one step forward: Reconstructing the dynamic Danube riverscape under human influence in Vienna', *Water History*, 5, 2, pp. 121-143.

Horowitz, R., Pilcher, J. M. and Watts, S. (2004) 'Meat for the Multitudes: Market Culture in Paris, New York City, and Mexico City over the Long Nineteenth Century', *The American Historical Review*, 109, 4, pp. 1055-1083.

Horváth, G. K. (2008) 'Rendi autonómia és fiziokratizmus. Kísérlet a Hanság lecsapolására az 1820-30-as években (1. rész)', *Soproni szemle: művelődéstörténelmi folyóirat*, 62, pp. 378-390.

Horváth, G. K. (2011) 'Rahmen des bäuerlichen Handels im Wieselburger Komitat (Ungarn) in der ersten Hälfte des 19. Jahrhunderts. Modell der Kommerzialisierung einer west-ungarischen Region', Konersmann, F. and Lorenzen-Schmidt, K.-J. (eds) *Bauern als Händler: Ökonomische Diversifizierung und soziale Differenzierung bäuerlicher Agrarproduzenten (15.-19. Jahrhundert)*, Berlin and Boston, pp. 163-184.

Horváth, G. K. (2013) 'Grenzgebiet an Alltagen. Das Wieselburger Komitat in der ersten Hälfte des 19. Jahrhunderts', Pejkovska, P. I. and Demeter, G. (eds) *Regions, borders, societies, identities in Central and Southeast Europe, 17th-21st centuries*, Sofia, pp. 77-88.

k.k. Handelsministerium (1871) *Enquête über die Approvisionierung Wiens: II. Teil. Lebensmitttel (ausgenommen Fleisch)*, Vol. 2, Bennholz und Mineralkohle, Vienna.

Kállay, I. (1980) *Management of big estates in Hungary between 1711 and 1848*, Budapest.

Kaplan, S. L. (1984) *Provisioning Paris: Merchants and millers in the grain and flour trade during the eighteenth century*, Ithaca.

Kaplan, S. L. (1996) *The bakers of Paris and the bread question: 1700-1775*, Durham.

Keene, D. (2012) 'Medieval London and its supply hinterlands', *Regional Environmental Change*, 12, 2, pp. 263-281.

Kelley, V. (2016) 'The streets for the people: London's street markets 1850-1939', *Urban History*, 43, 3, pp. 391-411.

Kim, E. and Barles, S. (2012) 'The energy consumption of Paris and its supply areas from the eighteenth century to the present', *Regional Environmental Change*, 12, 2, pp. 295-310.

Kohl, J. G. (1842) *Hundert Tage Reisen in den oesterreichischen Staaten. 4. Teil, Reise in Ungarn, zweite Abtheilung*, Dresden.

Komlos, J. (1983) *The Habsburg monarchy as a customs union: Economic development in Austria-Hungary in the nineteenth century*, Princeton.

Krausmann, F. (2013) 'A City and Its Hinterland: Vienna's Energy Metabolism 1800-2006', Singh, S. J. (ed.) *Long term socio-ecological research: Studies in society-nature interactions across spatial and temporal scales*, Dordrecht, pp. 247-268.

Lenger, F. (2013) *Metropolen der Moderne: Eine europäische Stadtgeschichte seit 1850*, Munich.

Lestel, L. (2012) 'Non-ferrous metals (Pb, Cu, Zn) needs and city development: The Paris example (1815-2009)', *Regional Environmental Change*, 12, 2, pp. 311-323.

Luca, I. de (1787) *Wiens gegenwärtiger Zustand unter Josephs Regierung*, Vienna.

Luca, I. de (ed.) (1785) *Erbländische Staatsanzeigen IV*, Vienna.

Mayr, J. K. (1940) *Wien im Zeitalter Napoleons: Staatsfinanzen, Lebensverhältnisse, Beamte und Militär*, Vienna.

McCagg, W. O. (1989) *A history of Habsburg Jews, 1670-1918*, Bloomington.

Miller, M. (2015) *Feeding Barcelona, 1714-1975: Public market halls, social networks, and consumer culture*, Baton Rouge.

Mitchell, I. (2010) 'Retailing innovation and urban markets *c.* 1800-1850', *Journal of Historical Research in Marketing*, 2, 3, pp. 287-299.

Moore, J. (2000) 'Sugar and the Expansion of the Early Modern World-Economy: Commodity Frontiers, Ecological Transformation, and Industrialization', *Review Fernand Braudel Center*, 23, 3, pp. 409-433.

N. N. (1803) *Beschreibung der Handlung und des Industriefleißes der k.k. Haupt- und Residenzstadt Wien: oder: merkantilischer Wegweiser durch Wien und das Erzherzogth. Oesterreich*, Leipzig.

N. N. (1845) *Der Fruchthandel in Wieselburg, Niederösterreichisches Landwirthschaftliches Wochen=Blatt, Beiblatt 7*, 15 May, p. 87.

Neweklowsky, E. (1952) *Die Schiffahrt und Flößerei im Raume der oberen Donau* (3 vols), Linz.

Niederösterreichische Handels- und Gewerbekammer (ed.) (1855) *Statistische Übersicht der wichtigsten Productionszweige in Oesterreich unter der Ens*, Vienna.

Opll, F. (1981) 'Studien zur Versorgung Wiens mit Gütern des täglichen Bedarfs in der ersten Hälfte des 19. Jahrhunderts', *Jahrbuch des Vereins für Geschichte der Stadt Wien*, 37, pp. 50-87.

Orosz, I. (1971) 'Die landwirtschaftliche Produktion in Ungarn 1790-1849', *Agrártörténeti Szemle*, 13, Supplementum, pp. 1-24

Otter, C. (2011) 'Liberty and Ecology: Resources, Markets, and the British Contribution to the Global Environmental Crisis', Gunn, S. and Vernon, J. (eds) *The Peculiarities of Liberal Modernity in Imperial Britain*, Berkelely, pp. 182-198

Petersen, C. (1995) *Bread and the British economy, c. 1770-1870*, Aldershot.

Pezzl, J. (1787) *Skizze von Wien* (6 vols), 3, Vienna.

Pezzl, J. (1805) *Neue Skizze von Wien* (3 vols), 1, Vienna.

Pezzl, J. (1816) *Beschreibung der Haupt = und Residenz = Stadt Wien*, Vienna.

Pezzl, J. (1823) *Johann Pezzl's Neueste Beschreibung von Wien*, Vienna.

Pezzl, J. and Tschichka, F. (1826) *Johann Pezzl's Beschreibung von Wien*, Vienna.

Pinke, Z. (2014) 'Modernization and decline: An eco-historical perspective on regulation of the Tisza Valley, Hungary', *Journal of Historical Geography*, 45, pp. 92-105.

Promnitzer, W. J. (1994) 'Die historische Ruderschiffahrt und die "Schopperei"', Kulturreferat der OÖ. Landesregierung (ed.) *Die Donau: Facetten eines europäischen Stromes: Katalog zur Oberösterreichischen Landesausstellung 1994 in Engelhartszell*, Linz, pp. 178-189.

Rácz, L. (2013) *The Steppe to Europe: An environmental history of Hungary in the Traditional Age*, Cambridge.

Rahlf, T. (1996) *Getreide in der Sozial- und Wirtschaftsgeschichte vom 16. bis 18. Jahrhundert: Das Beispiel Köln im regionalen Vergleich*, Trier.

Richards, J. F. (2003) *The Unending Frontier: An Environmental History of the Early Modern World*, Berkeley.

Ringrose, D. R. (1983) *Madrid and the Spanish economy: 1560-1850*, Berkeley.

Sandgruber, R. (1978a) 'Die Agrarrevolution in Österreich', Hoffmann, A. (ed.) *Österreich-Ungarn als Agrarstaat: Wirtschaftliches Wachstum und Agrarverhältnisse in Österreich im 19. Jahrhundert*, Vienna, pp. 195-271.

Sandgruber, R. (1978b) *Österreichische Agrarstatistik 1750-1918*, Munich.

Sandgruber, R. (1982a) *Die Anfänge der Konsumgesellschaft: Konsumgüterverbrauch, Lebensstandard und Alltagskultur in Österreich im 18. und 19. Jahrhundert*, Vienna.

Sandgruber, R. (1982b) 'Produktions- und Produktivitätsfortschritte der niederösterreichischen Landwirtschaft im 18. und frühen 19. Jahrhundert', Feigl, H. (ed.) *Die Auswirkungen der theresianisch-josephinischen Reformen auf die Landwirtschaft und die ländliche Sozialstruktur Niederösterreichs: Vorträge und Diskussionen des ersten Symposiums des Niederösterreichischen Institutes für Landeskunde, Geras, 9.-11. Oktober 1980*, Vienna.

Scholliers, P. (1992) 'From the "crisis of Flanders" to Belgium's "social question": Nutritional landmarks of transition in industrializing Europe (1840-1890)', *Food and Foodways*, 5, 2, pp. 151-175.

Scola, R. (1992) *Feeding the Victorian city: The food supply of Manchester, 1770-1870*, Manchester.

Segers, Y. (2001) 'Oysters and rye bread: polarising living standards in Flanders, 1800-1860', *European Review of Economic History*, 5, 3, pp. 301-336.

Shaw, G. and Wild, M. T. (1979) 'Retail Patterns in the Victorian City', *Transactions of the Institute of British Geographers*, 4, 2, p. 278.

Slezak, F. (1974) 'Zur Geschichte der Donauschiffahrt (1765-1829)', *Der Donauraum*, 19, 1-2, pp. 77-81.

Smith, C. (2002) 'The wholesale and retail markets of London, 1660-1840', *The Economic History Review*, 55, 1, pp. 31-50.

Stobart, J. and van Damme, I. (2016) 'Introduction: Markets in modernization: transformations in urban market space and practice, *c.* 1800-*c.* 1970', *Urban History*, 43, 3, pp. 358-371.

Streng, M. (2017) *Subsistenzpolitik im Übergang: Die kommunale Ordnung des Brot- und Fleischmarktes in Frankreich 1846-1914*, Göttingen.

Sugar, P. F. (ed.) (1990) *A history of Hungary*, London.

Swaney, D. P. et al. (2012) 'Historical changes in the food and water supply systems of the New York City Metropolitan Area', *Regional Environmental Change*, 12, 2, pp. 363-380.

Szántay, A. (2014) 'Serfdom in 18th century Hungary', Cavaciocchi, S. (ed.) *Schiavitù e servaggio nell'economia europea, secc. XI-XVIII: Atti della "Quarantacinquesima Settimana di studi", 14-18 aprile 2013*, Florence, pp. 263-279.

Tafeln zur Statistik der Österreichischen Monarchie (1828), Vienna.

Tello, E. and Ostos, J. R. (2012) 'Water consumption in Barcelona and its regional environmental imprint: A long-term history (1717-2008)', *Regional Environmental Change*, 12, 2, pp. 347-361.

Thiel, V. (1905-1906) 'Geschichte der Donauregulierungsarbeiten bei Wien II. Vom Anfange des XVIII. bis zur Mitte des XIX: Jahrhunderts. Von der Mitte des XIX. Jahrhunderts bis zur Gegenwart', *Jahrbuch d. Vereins f. Landeskunde von Niederösterreich*, 4-5, pp. 1-102.

Uhl, R. (1873) 'Mühlen-Industrie', in Exner, W. F. (ed.) *Beiträge zur Geschichte der Gewerbe und Erfindungen Oesterreichs von der Mitte des XVIII Jahrhunderts bis zur Gegenwart*, Vienna, pp. 173-178.

Vaterländische Blätter für den österreichischen Kaiserstaat (17.1.1809, 5.1. 1810, 9.1.1811, 8.1.1812, 13.1.1813, 5.1. 1814, 13.1. 1816).

Vári, A. (2008) *Herren und Landwirte: Ungarische Aristokraten und Agrarier auf dem Weg in die Moderne (1821-1910)*, Wiesbaden.

Vries, J. de and van der Woude, A. M. (1997) *The first modern economy: Success, failure, and perseverance of the Dutch economy, 1500-1815*, Cambridge.

Weigl, A. (2000) *Demographischer Wandel und Modernisierung in Wien*, Vienna.

Weigl, A. (2014) 'Der Einfluss geänderter Ernährungsgewohnheiten auf den "biologischen" Wohlstand der Wiener Bevölkerung im 19. und frühen 20. Jahrhundert', Hauer, F. (ed.) *Die Versorgung Wiens 1829-1913: Neue Forschungsergebnisse auf Grundlage der Wiener Verzehrungssteuer*, Innsbruck.

Wiener Zeitung (12.5.1806, 18.5.1821, 11.12.1822, 8.6.1824, 26.3.1825, 1.9.1827, 14.12.1833, 30.12.1833, 3.11.1836).

Winkler, J. (1872) *Wien und die Entwicklung des Donauhandels*, Mitteilungen der k.k. geographischen Gesellschaft in Wien 15, pp. 72-92.

Woolgar, C. M. (2013) 'Philip Slavin, Bread and Ale for the Brethren: The Provisioning of Norwich Cathedral Priory, 1260-1536', *Rural History*, 24, 2, pp. 220-221.

6 The respiration of Paris' catchment area in the nineteenth century: stocks and flows

Laurent HERMENT, CNRS CRH-CNRS-EHESS, UMR 8558

As Steven Kaplan has shown, during the early modern period, the supply of Paris with wheat and flour was a major concern for the King and the administration of the city (Kaplan, 1988).[1] During and after the *Révolution*, the French administration never ceased to scrutinize the provisioning of Paris for two reasons. On the one hand, the population of Paris wanted to eat the best quality of bread, the so called "pain blanc" (white bread) made with wheat flour.[2] In the middle of the nineteenth century, it was necessary to provide around 120,000 to 150,000 quintals of bread, and the same quantities of flour every month to provision the bakers of Paris. Fearing for a new revolution, the Government constantly worried about a shortage of wheat or flour and an increase in the price of bread.

On the other hand Paris was the biggest continental city in Europe. From about 600,000 inhabitants before the *Révolution*, the population increased to one million in 1850 and two million at the End of the Second Empire in 1870. Unlike London, Istanbul, Naples or Barcelona, but like Vienna, Paris has no access to the sea. Until the building of a railway network from 1840 to 1860, the supply of Paris depended crucially on its "rayon d'approvisionnement" (catchment area) which comprised six neighbouring *départements* (Loiret, Eure-et-Loir, Seine-et-Oise, Seine-et-Marne, Oise et Aisne), a waterway network (Oise, Marne, Seine, Canal de Briare, and later Canal de l'Ourcq), and the network of the main roads in the kingdom (Paris-Orléans, Paris-Pontoise, Paris-Chartres).[3]

Beyond Paris, it was necessary to provision the six *départements* of the *rayon de Paris* with a population of two and a half million people, including several towns: Versailles, Beauvais, Orléans, Chartres, Pontoise, Meaux, Laon, Etampes, etc. Until the middle of the nineteenth century, in case of supply shortages (1816-1817, 1829-1830, 1846-1847, 1853-1857), Paris not only competed for wheat with its own hinterland but also with all the cities of north-west Europe, including Rouen and Antwerp (around 100,000 inhabitants in 1850), Amsterdam (more than 200,000 inhabitants in 1850), and of course London. During these periods the catchment area of Paris expanded to include almost the whole of Europe, and the Baltic grains, sometimes oddly called in France *blé de Hollande* ("Holland grain"), played a role to supply Paris.

---

[1] On the provisioning of Paris during the early modern period see Abad, 2002. On the provisioning of European cities see Grantham, 1997.

[2] Studies on this issue are numerous. For the middle of the nineteenth century see for example the *Journal d'agriculture pratique*, January 1850, p. 21, and *Enquête sur la boulangerie du département de la Seine, ou recueil de dépositions concernant les commerces du blé, de la farine et du pain, faites en 1859*, Imprimerie nationale, Paris, 1859, Paris, pp. 12 and pp. 174-175.

[3] On the *rayon d'approvisionnement* see Bourguinat, 2002: 98 and 109. On the evolution of these networks see Price, 1983: 207-289.

Stocks, seasons and sales: Food supply, storage and markets in Europe and the New World, c. 1600-2000, ed. by Wouter RONSIJN, Niccolò MIGNEMI and Laurent HERMENT, CORN 17 (Turnhout, 2019), pp. 129-146.

 DOI: 10.1484/M.CORN-EB.5.118257

The supply of Paris was then a major political issue (Bourguinat, 2002). Though it might be an exaggeration to say that the cause of the successive revolutions in Paris was the price of bread or the shortage of flour, any political leaders considered the provisioning of Paris a crucial element to prevent revolutionary turmoil. Even Jean-Baptiste Say recognized it was difficult for the state not to intervene.[4]

Beyond the political issue, the provisioning of Paris was also an ecological and an economic issue. For the past fifteen years, specialists of the urban metabolism have studied the problem of the supply of Paris. The work of Sabine Barles, Gilles Billen, Josette Garnier, etc. in the Piren project, considers this issue from a socio-ecologist perspective (Barles: 2007; Billen and al., 2009, 2012; Billen, Barles and Garnier, 2012; Esculier, and al. 2017; Bognon and al., 2018; Le Noé and al., 2018). While these works allow us to question old problems, the historical perspective remains sometimes weak. Regardless of the weakness of the historical material, the Piren Group reminds us that it is necessary to better analyze how the material flows of commodities took place.

The works of Roger Price (Price, 1983) and Judith Miller (Miller, 1998) provide a historical study of the supply of French towns during the nineteenth century. Though this question is not central in the work of the former, Price shows that the development of a railway network is the major element to explain the expansion of the grain catchment area of Paris and the development of French agriculture (Price, 1983: 207-289).[5] Judith Miller stresses the role of the state which became, during the eighteenth and nineteenth centuries, more and more accustomed to the rule of the market, and could progressively undertake the liberalization of the wheat and bread markets. As Judith Miller stressed, if we focus only on the railway or more generally on material infrastructures, it is not possible to understand the specificity of the French case. But, due to the kind of sources she used, her outlook seems disembodied. The movement towards a more liberal system to supply Paris, is due to several factors, and it is necessary to analyze this evolution at the stakeholders' level, including millers and bakers in connection with the development of a railway network, transformations in the milling industry, changes in the commercial and financial relations between millers and bakers, and long lasting but fruitless attempts by the government to implement a system of storage of flour in Paris.

In this chapter we examine first the transformation of the grain catchment area of Paris due firstly to the construction from 1840 onwards of the railway network which linked Paris with Orléans, Chartres, Champagne, Lorraine and Normandy, and secondly to the transformation of the milling industry. The redefinition of the role of the "halles

4 Cited by A. Des Cilleuls, *Histoire de l'administration parisienne au XIXe siècle*, Tome 1, Honoré Champion, 1900, Paris 1900, pp. 264-265.

5 For the history of the French railway network see Caron, 1997. Studies on the impact of the railway networks on the development of French agriculture include Schwartz, 2010; Schwarz, Gregory and Thévenin, 2011; Thévenin, Schwartz and Sapet, 2013. For a very good source see *Carte figurative et approximative des tonnages des marchandises qui ont circulé en 1855 sur les voies d'eau et de fer de l'empire français*, dressée par M. Minard, 1855. Available on https://gallica.bnf.fr. On the growth of agricultural production in nineteenth-century France see for example Hubscher, 1979-1980; Farcy, 1986. For studies in English see Clout, 1980; Grantham, 1992, 1997; Herment, 2015.

aux blé" of Paris, the marketplace for grain and flour in Paris, was also very important. We shall show that these transformations allowed Paris and its suburbs to face up to the demographic growth. In the second part we analyze the transformations of the commercial and financial links between millers and bakers. At the end of the period, thanks to the range of these transformations, the supply of Paris, which initially rested on the storage of a huge amount of flour, more or less overseen by the administration, now rested on a just-in-time management of the flow of flour, and led to a partial liberalisation of the flour market and the baking industry in Paris.[6]

I. Changes in the grain and flour catchment area of Paris

In 1850, Parisian people ate every day an average of 400 to 500 grams of bread. Bakers had to produce around 12,000 to 16,000 metric tons of bread every month, and used the same quantities of flour. Of course infants and children ate less than adult men, and the working class ate more bread than the bourgeoisie, but the bourgeoisie did eat a large range of cakes and pastries. Beyond the diversity of food items, the production of such quantities of bread necessitated an efficient transport network and an efficient milling industry. During the first part of the nineteenth century these two industries experienced major changes.

I.1 Railway networks

Between 1840 and 1860 the railway network could complement the old system of roads and waterways which connected Paris with its traditional supply areas. In 1850, Paris was connected by train with Brie, Beauce, Vexin, Mantois, Valois and Picardie. Two lines were very important: the lines Paris-Chartres and Paris-Orléans connected the city and the millers of the Paris region with the main wheat-basket of Paris, the *Grande Beauce* and the *Petite Beauce*, which had no waterway connections with Paris.[7]

Moreover, the building of new long-distance lines allowed millers from distant regions to operate on the Parisian flour market. The Paris-Strasbourg railway-line allowed millers from Champagne and Lorraine to operate on the Parisian market.[8] The long-distance digressive tariffs for bulk transports implemented by the railway companies (*tarifs de pénétration*) gave a clear advantage to the biggest millers of these regions (Price, 1983: 249-250).

As noted by Aubin in 1859:

> The gradual extension of the supply radius of Paris guarantees the sincerity of the price [of flours] to the public. Indeed, as soon as the prices of flour in Paris increase, the supply radius expands, bids come from distant regions, and millers from Sarthe, Normandy, the North, Lorraine, Champagne and Burgundy, capable of quickly releasing their products by train, hurry themselves to offer them if prices are a bit higher in Paris than in other locations in France.[9]

---

[6] About the regulation of the grain market in nineteenth-century France, see Ronsijn and Herment, 2016.

[7] See for example *Journal d'agriculture pratique*, 1845, seconde série, tome 3, p. 30.

[8] See for example *Journal d'agriculture pratique*, 1850, p. 418, and 1851, p. 269.

[9] *Enquête sur la boulangerie...*, pp. 389-390.

But the millers of the Paris Basin also took advantage of the new transport network to export their products. The opening of the Paris-Rouen line not only allowed millers from Upper-Normandy to transport flour to Paris, but more importantly allowed Parisian millers to export their products to England, Belgium or Ireland, and to import grain from abroad[10]. For example, Darblay's mills at Corbeil were linked to Paris by train and by the Seine River, and hence had a double access to the main railway networks.

If the extension of the railway network played a major role, canals and rivers remained important especially for long-distance transport in some regions. For example, Léger, a miller of Olivet, near Orléans (Loiret), noted that as long as the prices were low, flour could be sent to England if the Loire River remained navigable.[11]

It is then important to underline that the extension of the grain catchment area of Paris is not only due to the demographic growth. There are two kinds of distortions.[12] The first one is the connection of the market of Paris with distant regions. Millers from Champagne, Burgundy, Normandy, etc. could send their flours to Paris when prices increased. But also important is that the biggest millers of the Paris region could export their products. They offered two types of product: they sent the best quality of flour to England, and flours of lower qualities ("petites farines") to Ireland for example.[13]

I.2 A powerful milling industry

The emergence of a powerful milling industry is the second important change which transformed the supply system of Paris. It is first necessary to underline that steam engines did not play a significant role in the modernisation of the milling industry at this date. As the survey of 1851 and the inquiry of 1859 show, only few of the biggest millers of Seine-et-Oise did use steam power.[14]

According to Burat, who testified at the committee of inquiry of 1859 directed by Le Play, the use of steam engines in Paris did not allow millers to obtain better flour at a lower price. Urban consumption taxes (*octroi*) and wages and fuel prices impeded the establishment of steam mills in the Paris region.[15] From this point of view provincial towns were sometimes better equipped. For example, Leclerc-Fleureau, director of the "manutention civile" of Orléans mentioned six mills equipped with steam engines in the region of Orléans. According to Leclerc-Fleureau, to install steam mills it was necessary to choose a location close to the railway and to customers. Yet if a miller had a choice it was always better to choose water power.[16] Moreover, the miller who used water power could choose how many millstones were operating depending on the flow of water. Conversely, Salone, the director of the Central Bakery of the Public Hospital in Paris (*usine*

---

[10] See for example *Enquête sur la boulangerie…*, p. 41, p. 225, p. 404, p. 624, pp. 580-581, p. 583. See also *Journal d'agriculture pratique*, 1850, p. 418, p. 443, p. 605, and p. 634.
[11] Ibid., p. 625.
[12] About the distortion of space due to the railway network see Thévenin, Schwartz and Sapet, 2013.
[13] See *Journal d'agriculture pratique*, 1850, p. 418. See also Ibid., p. 443, p. 605 and p. 634.
[14] Archives départementales des Yvelines, 15 M 26.
[15] *Enquête sur la boulangerie*, p. 180.
[16] Ibid., p. 434.

Scipion), stated that this rule applied only to the biggest plants.[17] According to him, the irregularity of the water flow was the main criticism against water power. And he underlined that M. Darblay had established steam engines in his mill to supply power when the flow of water was insufficient.[18] Then, even for the most powerful miller of France, a steam engine was installed as backup equipment.

In the middle of the nineteenth century the supply of Paris with flour crucially depended on a network of water-powered mills established on the tributaries of the Seine, Oise and Marne Rivers. During periods of drought (usually at the end of summer) and cold weather (January and February) factories stopped working.[19] The interruption of factories could explain two important phenomena. Firstly, the short-term prices of flour could soar temporarily during these periods as noted by Dumas, former Minister of Agriculture and a famous chemist.[20] Yet as I have shown above the threat of competition from Lorraine, Burgundy and Normandy annihilated the effect of water scarcity. Secondly, and more important, fluctuations in the milling industry seem linked primarily with the rhythms of the grain market which was very active from October to March.[21] Millers seemed to receive grain during autumn and spring while the water flow is adequate. Anyway, at no point during this period the supply of Paris with flour was threatened by the level of water flows or frost.

Beyond technology, the rapid process of concentration and consolidation of the milling industry in the Paris region, and more generally in France, is due to the financial and commercial strength of some enterprises. On the one hand the biggest millers imposed high quality standards of flour at low prices on the milling industry. On the other hand they could provide bakers regularly and offered attractive financial terms. I examine here the first point.

Aubin, a miller at Etampes, noted in 1859 that the biggest millers did not want high prices. They wanted first and foremost to prevent competition from ordinary millers. If necessary they could accept a very low trade margin and supported the cost of storage of flour.[22] Moreover, they organised the market to impose their standards with the quality label called "farines quatre marques" and, when Darblay, the most powerful miller joined them in 1861, the label was named "farines six marques".[23] It was thus possible to regularly provide flour of the best quality at a reasonable price.

---

[17] Ibid., p. 29.
[18] Ibid., p. 30.
[19] *Journal d'agriculture pratique*, tome 2, 1854, p. 255. See also Ibid., 1850, p. 634; 1851, p. 306 and 1858, tome 2, p. 391.
[20] *Enquête sur la boulangerie*, pp. 89-90.
[21] See Herment and Ronsijn, 2015.
[22] *Enquête sur la boulangerie…*, p. 394
[23] See A. Blay, *Un mot sur l'opportunité d'admettre les farines fleur supérieure de M. Darblay jeune comme auxiliaires dans les Marchés de farines quatre marques*, Imprimerie N. Chaix, Paris, 1858. The "farines quatre marques" was the label of the flour provided by Aubin-Baron, Rabourdin et Thirouin, E. Morel and Labiche. Finally, Darblay and Truffaut joined the label in 1861. It then became "farines six marques". See *Journal d'agriculture pratique*, 1861, tome 2, p. 108. Later, several others millers joined the label.

Figure 1 Level of production (in francs) for different locations in the *arrondissements* of Corbeil, Etampes, Pontoise and Rambouillet.

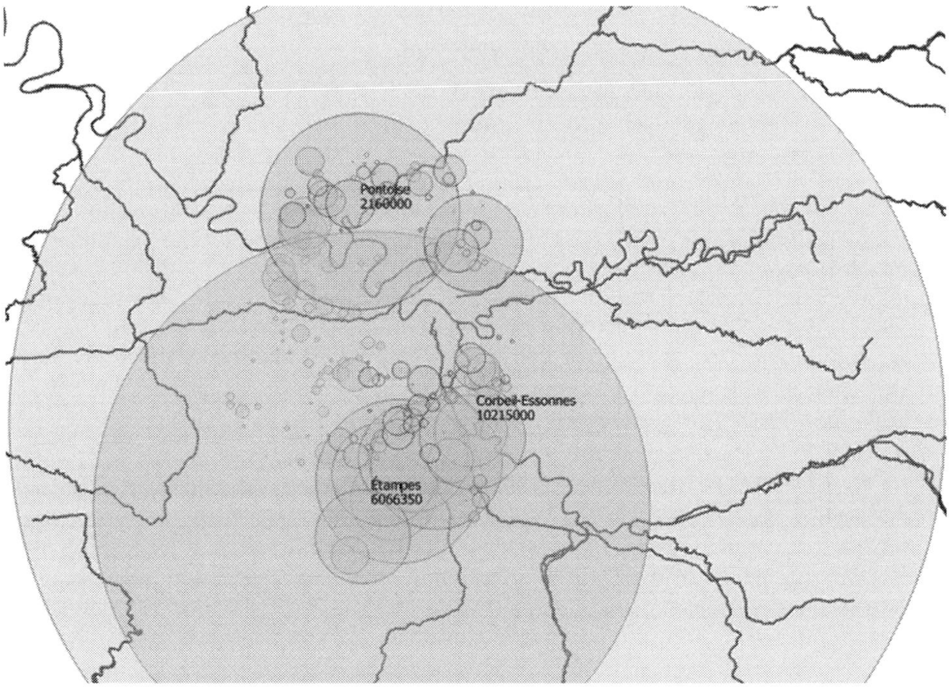

Source: Archives départementales des Yvelines, 15 M 26

The survey of 1851 provides us some insight into the concentration of the milling industry around Paris.[24] It is possible to map the importance of the milling industry in the *département* of Seine-et-Oise which surrounded Paris. The map below shows the importance of three production centres: Corbeil, Etampes and Pontoise. With a turnover of more than ten million francs, Corbeil, the location of Darblay's mill, is by far the most important. These three production centres could provide around 600,000 quintals of flour every year, equivalent to four or five months of the bread intake of Parisian people.

The Darblay brothers were the most important millers of Seine-et-Oise. The turnover of their three big mills in Corbeil can be assessed at around seven to eight million francs, though they owned other mills not taken into account in these statistics. Aubin, another big miller, could produce 230 quintals every day.[25] And Rabourdin who, like Aubin is one of the *quatre marques* producers, provided seventy bakers in Paris.[26]

[24] Archives départementales des Yvelines, 15 M 26. I have information for four *arrondissements*: Versailles, Corbeil, Etampes et Rambouillet. I have no information for Mantes, but this does not affect the global result. In Versailles, Etampes and Rambouillet I have production figures for every mill, in Pontoise I have the number of mills and the global production.

[25] *Commission d'enquête*..., 1859, pp. 391-392.

[26] *Commission d'enquête*..., 1859, p. 585.

II. The supply of bakers

The financial power of big millers allowed them to provide bakers with several types of contracts. The most important is called *marché à cuisson* ("baking contract"). During the July Monarchy and the Second Empire, this contract becomes central for bakers who were obliged to build up a mandatory reserve stock of flour. Nevertheless, if at first glance during the first half of the century, the regularity of the supply of Paris seemed ever more to depend on these mandatory stocks, which were never fully implemented nor completed, the progressive emergence of new links between and millers and bakers, first and foremost the *marché à cuisson*, allowed Paris to be less and less dependent on the mandatory reserve stocks.

II.1 The system of advance deliveries to finance Parisian bakers

As sales on credit, the *marchés à cuisson* reinforced the power of the milling industry. According to Bethmont, the representative of the bakers behind the inquiry commission of 1859, the *marchés à cuisson* accounted for three-fifths of the total consumption of flour in Paris.

To understand the importance of *marchés à cuisson* it is necessary to explain the system of the *taxe du pain* (Assize of Bread). In Paris, as in numerous other cities and towns in France, the price of bread was calculated from the average price of flour to prevent price increases during a period of scarcity. The prices of flour and bread fluctuated in the same way but not perfectly in parallel.[27] The administration added a *prime de cuisson*, i.e. a conventional bonus to compensate the cost of the baking process (baking bonus). With *marchés à cuisson* the miller provided the baker with flour at a certain date (for example 15 March), but the price of the commodity was determined conventionally at the same date or, more often, at a later date (for example 15 June). Moreover the baker paid the miller only later (15 June for example or later on). This is then a sale on credit with the price only determined at a later, fixed date.

Why did millers use this type of contract? To understand this, it is necessary to examine the process of the production of bread. The administration assumed it was possible to produce 204 kilograms of bread with 157 kilograms of flour. According to all sources, the largest millers supplied flour of the best quality which yielded more bread than common flours. Then, millers sold the flour at a higher price than the average price on which the *taxe du pain* was calculated at the date of payment. In the end, a part of the baking bonus went to the miller (hence the term *marché à cuisson* because the bonus for baking is shared).[28] Not only could the largest millers sell their products at a higher price than the average price of flour, they also created captive clients.

---

[27] For a more comprehensive explanation see Ronsijn and Herment, 2016. It is nevertheless important to note that the method to calculate the *taxe du pain* varied from one town to the other.
[28] See Quevy (d'Ouge), *Méthode nouvelle de comptabilité commerciale et spéciale des marchés à terme ou à livrer appliquée au commerce des grains et farines, à la meunerie, à la boulangerie et à la bourse. Contenant le nouveau tarif de taxe et les règles de cuisson*, 1843, p. 10, and *Commission d'enquête...*, p. 58.

Figure 2 Commercial relations between Darblay (miller) and Bernier (baker).

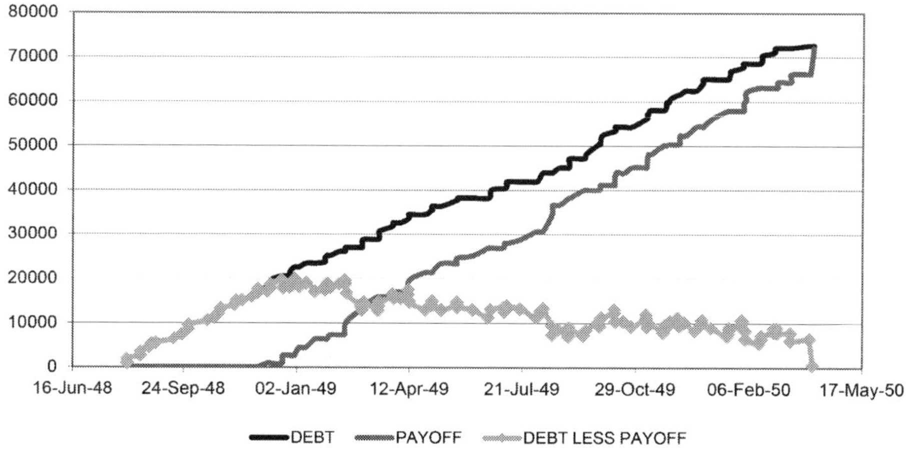

Source: Archives départementale de l'Essonne, J 78.

Bakers also supported this system. The regularity of the supply of flour of good quality was the first advantage for the baker. But the main advantage was financial rather than commercial. Analysis of the relation between the baker Bernier and the miller Darblay offers a clear insight in this issue. All following information came from the accounting book of Darblay between 1848 and 1851.[29]

Bernier was a second class baker in Paris.[30] He was installed at 22, rue aux Ours, in the centre of Paris since 1846.[31] We can follow in the Darblay general ledger the relation between the miller and the baker from 4 August 1848 to 30 January 1850. During this period Darblay sold to Bernier 1,461 sacks of flour, that is 2293.77 quintals,[32] likely more than two-thirds of the flour used by Bernier. As shown in figure 2, Darblay regularly delivered flour to Bernier.

From August 1848 to December 1848, Darblay sold around 20,000 francs of flour on credit. Starting from December 1848, Bernier gradually paid off Darblay. The debt of Bernier declined steadily from 20,000 to around 10,000 francs. Finally during March 1850 Bernier paid off his entire debt. As Bernier, a lot of bakers were enthusiastic about this arrangement. On the one hand they could finance their activity, especially during the first years of activity when they lacked working capital. For

[29] Archives départementale de l'Essonne, J 78.

[30] For the different classes of baker see below.

[31] See *Annuaire de la boulangerie* 1850…, p. 298.

[32] A sack of flour contains 157 kilograms (net weight), 159 kilograms including the sack. Since 13 April 1842, the official price of flour was recorded per 100 kilogram, but bakers and millers continued to use the ancient measure (157 or 159 kilograms). The baking bonus for 100 kilograms is 6 francs against 11 francs for 157 kilograms. Quevy (d'Ouge), *Méthode nouvelle*…, p. 10.

example, during one year and a half Bernier could purchase flour and pay off months later. On the other hand millers provided good quality of flour at an affordable price. For example, in February 1850, Bernier paid the flour purchased 26 December 1849 at 26.75 and 27.39 francs per 100 kilograms. During the first half of February, the price of flour which determined the level of *taxe du pain* were 27.35 and 28.05 (first quality) and 26.15 to 26.75 francs (second quality).[33] This example shows that bakers had no interest to call in question a system that allowed them to purchase regularly flour of good quality at an attractive price, and through which they could overcome their lack of working capital. Moreover they also could purchase flour from others millers if it proved necessary.

Nevertheless, they asked a modification in the determination of the *taxe du pain*, and wanted that the *marchés à cuisson* would become part of the calculation. Obviously, this was not possible because the price of such a deal was determined by the *taxe du pain* itself. They also requested the administration for an augmentation of the baking bonus, but did not obtain this[34]. Indeed such an increase could be shared between the two parts of the contract.

II.2 A mandatory regulation of bakeries in Paris

During the Consulat (November 1799-May 1804), a set of rules had developed to regulate the bakery industry in Paris. In this section we specifically examine the issue of storage of flour. The decree of 19 vendémiaire year X (11 October 1801), obliged bakers to deposit a stock of flour amounting to fifteen sacks of best quality flour at the *magasin Elisabeth* (article 1).[35] At this date, there were three classes of bakers in Paris depending on their level of production. The second article of the same decree indicated that the bakers of the first class had to keep a permanent stock of sixty sacks, and the second and third classes thirty and twenty sacks respectively. Keeping stocks to supply Paris with wheat was therefore a responsibility of the bakers as Judith Miller noted. But indeed, it is not proven that mandatory stocks were always completed.

A royal ordinance of 21 October 1818 increased the level of mandatory flour stocks for bakers. The first class of bakers had to have a stock of 140 sacks of 159 kilograms. The bakers of the second, third and fourth class had to store 110, eighty and thirty sacks respectively. That is almost 130,000 quintals of flour, more than one month of the consumption of flour in Paris at this date (see table 1). Several reasons explain why these provisions were raised. The crisis of 1816-1817 had demonstrated the weakness of the supply of Paris, and the number of bakers dropped from more than 1,000 at the beginning of the century to 600 in 1818.[36] Together with the number of bakers, the volume of mandatory stocks automatically collapsed.

---

[33] *Journal d'agriculture pratique*, February 1850. During this period, prices of the best quality of flour (*farine de choix*) were 28.65 to 29.35 francs.

[34] See for example *Commission d'enquête...*, p. 37.

[35] The *magasin Elisabeth* is the former convent *Sainte-Elisabeth*. I thank Maurizio Gribaudi for this clarification.

[36] See A. Des Cilleuls, *Histoire de l'administration parisienne au XIX*e *siècle*, Honoré Champion, 1900, Paris 1900, p. 284.

Table 1 Quantities of flour (in quintal) theoretically sent to the *grenier d'abondance*

Classification of bakeries		Deposits at the *caisse de la boulangerie* (implemented during the 1853-1857 crisis)		Precautionary supplies (regulations of 1818 and 1836)				Total supplies at the *grenier d'abondance* (sum of (4) and (8))	Total supplies (sum of (4) and (6))
(1)	(2)	(3)	(4)	(5)	(6)	(7)	(8)		
Class	Number of bakeries	Per bakery	Per class	Per bakery	Per class	2/5 at the bakeries	3/5 at the *grenier d'abondance*		
1	218	31.40	6845.20	219.80	47916.40	19166.56	28749.84	35595.04	54761.60
2	275	31.40	8635.00	172.70	47492.50	18997.00	28495.50	37130.50	56127.50
3	105	31.40	3297.00	125.60	13188.00	5275.20	7912.80	11209.80	16485.00
4	3	31.40	94.20	47.10	141.30	56.52	84.78	178.98	235.50
Total	601		18871.40		108738.2	43495.28	65242.92	84114.32	127609.60

Source: *Annuaire de la boulangerie*, 1850.

Figure 3 Map of the *Bassin de l'Arsenal*. The *magasin d'abondance* is the long building with five towers along the *Bassin de l'Arsenal*

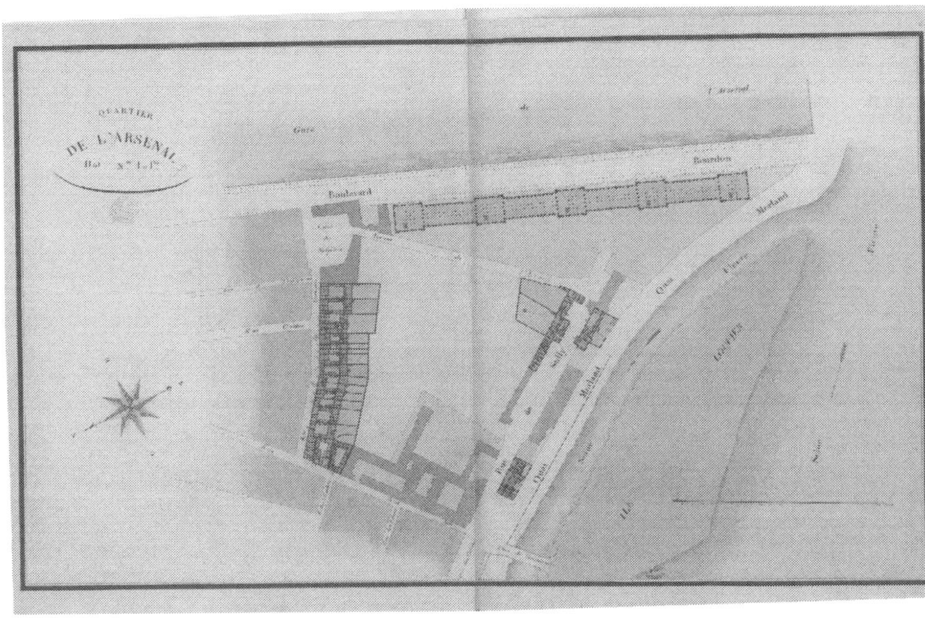

Source: Kindly provided by Maurizio Gribaudi, Laboratoire de Démographie et d'Histoire Sociale, Centre de Recherches Historiques, UMR 8558 EHESS-CNRS.

In 1836, by a special request of the city of Paris, bakers had to store three-fifths of their stock in a storehouse made available for free by the city. In 1837 (21 March 1837), an order (*arrêté*) of the Prefect obliged bakers to send their flour in the *magasin des greniers d'abondance*, near the Arsenal Basin (*Bassin de l'Arsenal*). But the bakers failed to comply with this order. The city of Paris asked the Prefect to issue a new order. On 29 August 1842 the Prefect asked the bakers again to comply with his orders. They had to deposit a third of their stock each month in January, February and March 1843[37]. Table 1 (below) shows the importance of the very theoretical stock. These measures sought to provide a permanent stock to provision Paris.[38]

At the outset of the summer of 1853 a crisis began which lasted until the summer of 1857. Yields dropped not only in France but in a large part of Europe. The price of bread soared for almost four years. To face the problem of the price of bread in Paris and to prevent any turmoil, the government implemented a complex scheme to

[37] The city of Paris asked the Prefect to issue this new order.
[38] Unfortunately this building burnt down during the *Commune of Paris*. There is a picture of the building after the fire in *Ruines des greniers d'abondance après la Commune*, 1871, Paris, available on https://gallica.bnf.fr.

subsidise the price of bread (the *caisse de la boulangerie*). It cost several millions of francs which had to be paid off when the price of wheat and flour decreased.[39]

One of the measures introduced to face such a crisis was an expansion of reserve stocks. The level of the mandatory stock was increased. An Imperial order of 1 November 1854 (article 8) obliged bakers of the city and suburbs of Paris to hold a stock equivalent to three months of consumption. However, because the price of flour was very high at this time, the new rules would be implemented later. At that date, during a period of high prices, it was not possible to ask the bakers to constitute such a huge stock. It was not until the end of 1857 that the Prefect asked the bakers to comply with this rule. Yet they never did. Beyond the problem of buying such a stock is the question of how to store it.

II.3 Level of stock in Paris

While *la halle* was the market for flour in Paris where the prices of wheat and flour were determined, the stock available here was often very low. Sometimes the level of transactions was also virtually zero. For example in March 1853, just before the beginning of the crisis of 1853, the *Journal d'agriculture pratique* noted that purchases at *la halle* formed only a small part of the total demand.[40] Usually bakers bought flour at *la halle* only to complement their transactions with millers (see above). Because of the changes in the flow of trade and the limited available space, *la halle* lost its importance. A large part of the supply of Paris passed through La Villette in the north of Paris and other peripheral storage places. Moreover, as noted above, the government and the Paris administration had built up a *grenier d'abondance*.

The project to build a *grenier d'abondance* near the *Bassin de l'Arsenal* to store the flour dated back from 1812. The original project envisaged a building of 344 meters of length and 25 meters wide with seven floors (figure 3 above). Actually only two floors were built.[41] As already noted the bakers never fully complied with the obligation to store their flour in this building.

Nevertheless it was necessary to store flour which arrived in Paris. In March 1853, the *Journal d'agriculture pratique* provided some details. According to the newspaper one storehouse, able to contain 100,000 quintals, was located at La Villette (in the north). Another storehouse was located near the *gare de Strasbourg* (nowadays *gare de l'est*) able to contain around 20,000 quintals. There was a last storehouse near the *Gare Saint-Lazare* at *Batignolles*.[42] Then, all supplying regions, Picardie, Champagne, Normandy, were connected with Paris by train or by waterways (Oise river, Marne river, Seine river, canal de l'Ourcq and Canal Saint-Martin). It was then not necessary to send the flour to *la halle* located in the centre of Paris. It was possible to store 240,000 to 360,000 quintals of flour in all these storehouses including *la halle*.[43]

---

[39] About this system, see Horii, 1984 and Herment, 2011.
[40] *Journal d'agriculture pratique*, 1853, p. 297.
[41] See Thomas, A., *Mémoire sur les réserves des grains*, Imprimerie Felix Malteste et Cie, 1841, Paris, p. 18 and note 1, p. 18. As noted above this building burnt down during the *Commune de Paris*. After 1863, when a decree liberalised the baking industry in Paris, the building was let to a certain M. Godillot. See A. Des Cilleuls, *Histoire de l'administration...*, tome 2, foot note 1044, p. 628.
[42] *Journal d'agriculture pratique*, 1853, p. 297.
[43] *Journal d'agriculture pratique*, 1850, p. 640.

But far from being filled with flour, the Parisian storehouses were sometimes more or less empty. Graph 2 shows the level of transactions and stocks in *la halle* between 1850 and 1856.[44] In October 1850 the *Journal d'agriculture pratique* signals a great stockpile of flour in Paris due to consignments from regions which previously never sent flour to Paris (see above). There were around 300,000 quintals in the storehouses[45]. The stocks at *la halle* amounted to 80,000 quintals. Could such quantities protect Paris against shortage? The answer is obviously negative: 300,000 quintals represent at best three months of consumption.

Indeed, as soon as prices increased during the year 1852-1853 stocks fell down gradually. During summer 1853, when prices began to soar, stocks went down and reached a minimum during the summer of 1854. Stakeholders predicted an increase of the price of flour and tried to protect themselves. As figure 4 shows, during the period of high prices the volume of transactions could be very important. This is the most interesting aspect of these figures. During the crisis of 1853-1857, far from relying heavily on existing stocks, the bakers and the Parisian people relied on the regularity of deliveries.

But stocks played a very important role in the global equilibrium of the industry. As the graph shows, bakers used their stocks as a means to protect themselves not against the shortage of flour, but against the increase of prices. The mechanism is simple: they used the flour they purchased several months earlier at a low price, and sold bread at the current price. This way, they received more than the baking bonus for their products. Not only did the bakers constitute stocks when prices were low, but the Prefect also allowed them not to reconstitute their mandatory stocks and even to remove mandatory stocks if prices skyrocketed. For example, according Des Cilleuls, in 1847, when prices of flour were at their pinnacle, the Prefect authorised bakers to use flour stored in the *grenier d'abondance*.[46] The same occurred in September 1854.[47] Of course this was not a long-term remedy. These remarks allow us to better understand the two decisions of the prefect in 1854 we have evoked above: to establish a larger mandatory stock, and to postpone the implementation of this until prices fell down again.[48]

Then, at least from the end of the 1840s stocks of flour appeared to have two roles. The first one was to reassure the Parisian population against shortage. If from a political point of view this was the main role of mandatory storage, from an economic point of view it was a marginal one, because railway and waterway networks made it possible to supply Paris promptly and regularly from distant regions. The second role is more interesting. Stocks could be used by bakers to mitigate and/or postpone the effects of an increase in the price of flour. This is crucial to understand the subsequent decisions of the administration.

---

[44] *Journal d'agriculture pratique*, 1849-1856.

[45] *Journal d'agriculture pratique*, 1850, p. 640.

[46] A. Des Cilleuls, *Histoire de l'administration...*, tome 2, Honoré Champion, 1900, Paris 1900, p.177. The author did not quote the reference for this information.

[47] *Journal d'agriculture pratique*, 1854, tome 2, p. 255.

[48] See the decrees of the prefect 27 February 1858, 23 April 1858, 21 May 1858.

Figure 4 Transaction and volume stored at the Halle (1850-1856)

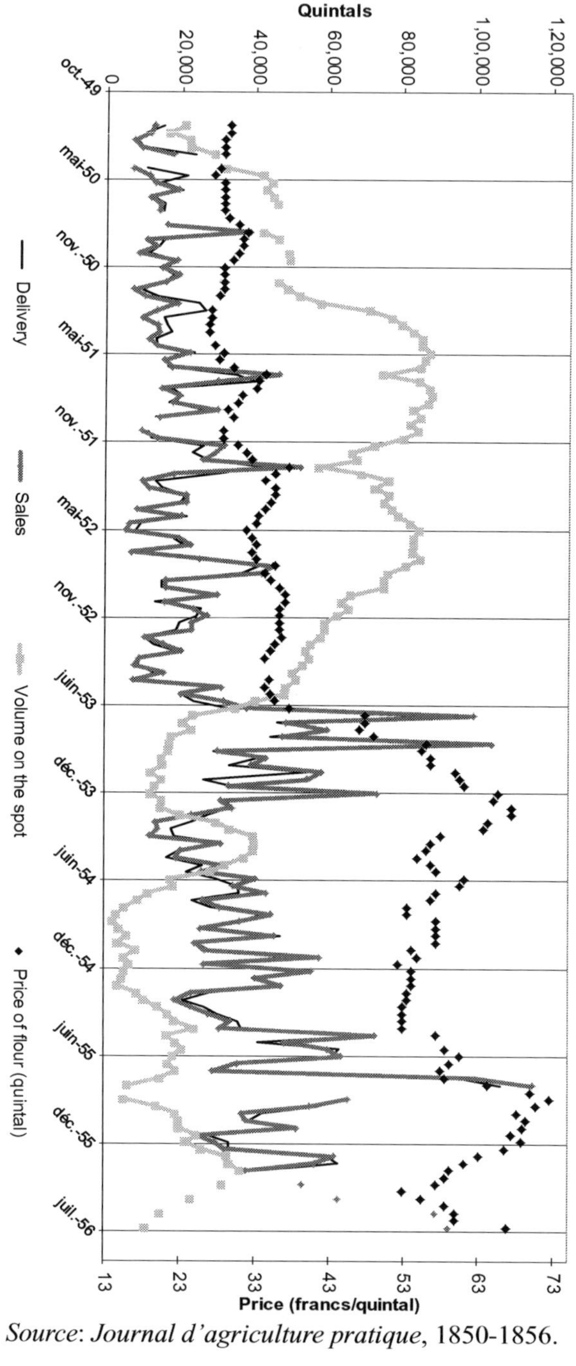

Source: *Journal d'agriculture pratique*, 1850-1856.

After the crises of 1853-1857, the price of grain fell down. Authorities extended the mandatory storage of flour to numerous provincial towns. Contrary to what one could expect, the true aim of this rule was not the constitution of a reserve stock in case of crises. A circular letter issued by the Ministry noted that the development of the mandatory stocks could assist agriculture during this period of low prices.[49] This rule aimed to support artificially the price of grain by obliging the millers to quickly produce a huge amount of flour. After a short moment of surprise, the markets of grain and flour returned to normal and the price of wheat did not increase. The decree had no effect on the price of grain even in the short run.

This last measure was not a last attempt to control the supply of French towns with flour and grain. It was an attempt to mitigate the effects of the price variability of grain and flour. It did not contradict the true movement towards market freedom symbolised by the periodical suspension of the sliding scale on imports and exports of grain from 1847 onward, and its final removal in 1860[50], the liberalisation of the baking industry in 1863, and the suppression of the *caisse de la boulangerie* after the fall of the Second Empire.[51] After 1863, in many towns the *taxe du pain* was the only rule which still remained until well into the twentieth century. This was not to control the supply of flour or wheat, but to limit the fluctuation of the price of bread. The liberalisation of the bread market was not then completed.

III. Conclusion

From the beginning of the nineteenth century to the fall of the Second Empire, the supply of Paris was an ongoing concern for the local and central authorities. From the Consulat to 1860, the mandatory storage of increasing quantities of flour was the main measure used by the authorities. Yet far from complying, bakers resisted this measure. Paradoxically, the period 1853-1857, when the price soared for almost 48 months and when therefore implementation of the rules would seem most important, was actually the period during which the authorities were less compelling. Moreover, it was during this period that new ideas were gradually introduced.

As proven by the very low level of stocks during the crises, and the postponement of the application of the decree of 1854, Paris never suffered from supply disruptions. More and more the supply of the city depended on the regularity of flows of flour from the Paris Basin and from Champagne, Lorraine, Normandy, and if necessary from abroad. The improvement of the road and waterways networks since the second part of the eighteenth century, and the building of a railway network radiating from Paris since the 1840s, contributed to the improvement of the supply and the enlargement of the grain catchment area of Paris. Still, this is only part of the story. To fully understand this phenomenon it is necessary to take in account other variables. The first one is the emergence in the Paris Region, but also in Lorraine and Champagne, of a milling industry able to provide quickly and regularly huge amounts of flour all year around. The second one, not less

[49] Imperial Decree of 16 November 1858. See also the circular letter sent by the Minister Rouher in *Journal d'agriculture pratique*, 1858, tome 2, p. 458 and following.
[50] See Ronsijn and Herment, 2016, pp. 818-819.
[51] See Horii, 1984.

important, is the implementation of close commercial and financial links between millers and bakers which allowed the bakers to finance their production.

This study allows us to reassess the evolution of the measures to supply Paris with flour. This evolution had its roots in the implementation of a range of commercial, technical and financial innovations. At the outset of the 1860s, these innovations allowed authorities to abandon the mandatory storage of flour. What is striking is the fact that the last form of mandatory storage was not implemented to reassure the population about the disruption of supply but to stabilize the price of wheat for farmers as well as bakers. This could appear as a continuation of the policy implemented in Paris during the 1853-1857 period of high prices. Despite four successive bad or very bad harvests, not only in the north of France but in a large part of Europe, there was not a subsistence crisis but only a period of high prices. At no moment the supply of Paris was threatened because the financial, commercial and technical infrastructure capable of conveying flour to Paris was available.

As Pierre-Louis Poyau has proven in a recent work, this range of measures did not protect Paris during the war against Prussia (Poyau, 2017). During the siege of Paris by the Prussian army, the city had to survive for four months on its own stocks. Bread consumption decreased in the course of the siege, and at the end the population was starving. The Imperial doctrine of the continuity of flows was defeated due to the encirclement of Paris. But more than the siege of Paris, the period 1853-1857 is the good indicator of the evolution of what Judith Miller has called "mastering the market". Indeed this does not mean that the government embraced the *laisser-faire* dogma, but accepted that market mechanisms could supply Paris regularly with flour. Yet from this point of view, it is not possible to split up financial, commercial, technical, agricultural, and administrative changes and choices of every stakeholder: railways companies, bakers, millers, and administration.

Printed sources

Annuaire de la boulangerie de Paris pour l'exercice 1850, Paris.

Blay, A. (1858) *Un mot sur l'opportunité d'admettre les farines fleur supérieure de M. Darblay jeune comme auxiliaires dans les Marchés de farines quatre marques*, Paris.

Des Cilleuls, A. (1900) *Histoire de l'administration parisienne au XIXe siècle*, Tome 1, Paris.

Enquête sur la boulangerie du département de la Seine, ou recueil de dépositions concernant les commerces du blé, de la farine et du pain, faites en 1859 (1859), Paris.

Jacque, L. (1871) *Ruines des greniers d'abondance après la Commune*, Paris.

Journal d'agriculture pratique, years 1845 to 1867.

Minard, Ch. (1855) *Carte figurative et approximative des tonnages des marchandises qui ont circulé en 1855 sur les voies d'eau et de fer de l'empire français*.

Quevy (d'Ouge), P. (1843) *Méthode nouvelle de comptabilité commerciale et spéciale des marchés à terme ou à livrer appliquée au commerce des grains et farines, à la meunerie, à la boulangerie et à la bourse. Contenant le nouveau tarif de taxe et les règles de cuisson.*

Thomas, A. (1841) *Mémoire sur les réserves des grains*, Paris.

Manuscript sources

Archives départementales de l'Essonne, J 78.
Archives départementales des Yvelines, 15 M 26.

Bibliography

Abad, R. (2002) *Le grand marché. L'approvisionnement alimentaire de Paris sous l'Ancien Régime*, Paris.

Barles, S. (2007) 'Feeding the city: food consumption and flow of nitrogen, Paris, 1801-1914', *Science of the Total Environment*, 375, 1-3, pp. 48-58.

Billen, G. et al. (2009) 'The food-print of Paris: Long-term reconstruction of the nitrogen flows imported into the city from its rural hinterland', *Regional Environmental Change*, 9, 1, pp. 13-24.

Billen, G. et al. (2012) 'Grain, meat and vegetables to feed Paris: Where did and do they come from? Localising Paris food supply areas from the eighteenth to the twenty-first century', *Regional Environmental Change*, 12, 2, pp. 325-335.

Billen, G., Garnier, J. and Barles, S. (2012) 'History of the urban environmental imprint: Introduction to a multidisciplinary approach to the long-term relationships between Western cities and their hinterland', *Regional Environmental Change*, 12, 2, pp. 249-253.

Bognon S. et al. (2018) 'Approvisionnement alimentaire parisien du XVIIIe au XXIe siècle: les flux et leur gouvernance. Récit d'une trajectoire Socioécologique', *Natures, Sciences et Société*, 17, 1, pp. 17-32.

Bourguinat, N. (2002) *Les grains du désordre. L'Etat face aux violences frumentaires dans la première moitié du XIXe siècle*, Paris.

Clout, H. (1980) *Agriculture in France on the Eve of the Railway Age*, London.

Caron F. (1997) *Histoire des chemins de fer en France. Tome 1 (1740-1883)*, Paris.

Farcy, J.-C. (1986) *Les Paysans Beaucerons au XIXe siècle* (2 tomes), Chartres.

Grantham, G. W. (1997) 'Espaces privilégiés: Productivité agraire et zones d'approvisionnement des villes dans l'Europe préindustrielle', *Annales. Histoire, Sciences Sociales*, 52, 3, pp. 695-725.

Grantham, G. W. (1989) 'Agricultural Supply During the Industrial Revolution: French Evidence and European Implications', *Journal of Economic history*, 49, 1, pp. 43-72.

Kaplan, S. L. (1988), *Les ventres de Paris. Pouvoir et approvisionnement dans la France d'Ancien Régime*, Paris.

Herment L. (2015) 'Land Use and Productivity: North of France 1750-2000', Thoen, E. and Soens, T. (eds) *Struggling with the Environment: Land Use and Productivity*, Rural economy and society in north-western Europe, 500-2000, Vol. 4, Turnhout, pp. 182-217.

Herment L. (2011) 'Les communautés rurales de Seine-et-Oise face à la crise frumentaire de 1853-1856', *Histoire et Mesure*, 26, 1, pp. 187-220.

Herment L. and Ronsijn W. (2015), 'Seasonal patterns in food markets in north-west Europe in the second quarter of the nineteenth century: the evidence of periodic markets in France, England, and Belgium, 1820 to 1850', *Agricultural History Review*, 63, 1, pp. 60-80.

Hubscher, R.-H. (1979-1980) *L'agriculture et la Société rurale dans le Pas-de-Calais du milieu du XIX*[e] *siècle à 1914* (2 vols), Abbeville.

Horii T. (1984) 'La crise alimentaire de 1853 à 1856 et la Caisse de la boulangerie de Paris', *Revue Historique*, 272, 2, pp. 375-401.

Le Noë, J. et al. (2018) 'Long-term socioecological trajectories of agro-food systems revealed by N and P flows in French regions from 1852 to 2014', *Agriculture, Ecosystems and Environment*, 265, pp. 132-143.

Miller J. (1998) *Mastering the Market: The State and the Grain Trade in Northern France, 1700-1860*, Cambridge.

Poyau P.-L. (2017) *Le pain pendant le siège de 1870-1871 et la commune de Paris. Approvisionnement et organisation de la répartition des denrées : une permanence de l'économie morale*, mémoire de Master, Sciences Po, Paris (sous la direction d'Alain Chatriot et Quentin Deluermoz).

Price R. (1983) *The Modernization of Rural France. Communications Networks and Agricultural Market Structures in Nineteenth-Century France*, London.

Ronsijn W. and Herment L. (2016) 'Les mercuriales du XIXe siècle. Le contrôle et la surveillance des prix et de l'offre de grains en France et en Belgique, 1789-1914', *Revue du Nord*, 98, 417, pp. 812-838.

Schwartz R. (2010) 'Rail Transport, Agrarian Crises, and the Restructuring of Agriculture: France and Great Britain Confront Globalization, 1860-1900', *Social Science History*, 34, 2, pp. 229-257.

Schwartz R., Gregory I. and Thévenin Th. (2011) 'Railways, Uneven Development, and Population Change in France and Great Britain 1850-1914', *Journal of Interdisciplinary History*, 42, 1, pp. 53-88.

Thevenin, Th., Schwartz R. and Sapet, L. (2013) 'Mapping the Distortions in Time and Space. The French Railway Network, 1830-1930', *Historical methods*, 46, 3, pp. 134-143.

7 Urban development and local food production. Ability and inability of feeding growing cities by urban agriculture in nineteenth-century industrialising Belgium

Pieter De Graef, University of Antwerp, Department of History

I. Introduction

In her thought-provoking book *The hungry city. How food shapes our lives*, Carolyn Steel makes us wonder at the amazing efforts it takes to feed a city the size of London, for whose inhabitants food for thirty million meals has to be produced, transported, sold, cooked and eaten every single day (Steel, 2008). This proves in itself the high degree of efficiency our food regime has reached by the specialisation and globalisation of the production and distribution of a number of key agricultural products (cf. Van Molle and Segers, 2013). Yet, our globalised food system has some pernicious environmental and social side-effects. The journey of food from farm to fork often takes on global dimensions, characterised by large 'food miles' and by production systems leading to soil fertility mining in peripheral regions and over-fertilisation in the core areas (Blake, Mellor and Crane, 2010: 409; Moore, 2000). Moreover, trade liberalisation and the run-down in price-supporting policies contribute to the problem of farmers being exposed to highly volatile prices of both input and output goods, which can severely affect the very survival of individual farms (cf. AMTF report, 2016). As a result, a growing strand of scholars and policy think tanks look for alternative approaches. In meeting local food demand by local food production, the potential of urban and peri-urban agriculture comes to the front as part of the solution. Home food production in backyard gardens can relieve the family budget of urban households and alternative revenue models (such as community-supported agriculture and direct marketing at the farm gate or at nearby farmers' markets) can help urban farmers to increase profit margins (and this both in the global south and north) (McClintock, 2010: 191; Taylor and Taylor Lovell, 2014: 285-305; Smith, Kostelecký and Jehlička, 2015: 223-332; Atkinson, 2013: 85-96; Parham, 2015). Beneficial social and environmental effects of urban agriculture are widely recognised, but it seems unrealistic to believe that urban food production will ever be sufficient to entirely feed all citizens (Mougeot, 2006: 6).[1] A lot of this contemporary literature on urban agriculture refers to the close link that existed between cities and food production in past societies, however without questioning its importance in reaching self-sufficiency (e.g. Castillo, 2003: 339-344).

As far as the provisioning of cities with food during the Ancien Régime up to the nineteenth century is concerned, a huge discrepancy exists between studies ascribing

[1] Though Robert Biel goes as far as to state that urban farming will be able to feed urban populations during a worldwide transition phase of mainstream agriculture towards organic farming (Biel, 2016).

Stocks, seasons and sales: Food supply, storage and markets in Europe and the New World, c. 1600-2000, ed. by Wouter Ronsijn, Niccolò Mignemi and Laurent Herment, CORN 17 (Turnhout, 2019), pp. 147-179.

 DOI: 10.1484/M.CORN-EB.5.118258

paramount importance to food supplied by countryside farming on the one hand and literature pointing to the contribution of urban agriculture in the relief of family budgets of urban dwellers and the delivery of fresh daily milk, fruits and vegetables on the other hand. Although recognising alternative, non-market food entitlements (to borrow the concept of Amartya Sen) based upon exchange relations (labour), property relations (rent payments in kind), or institutional arrangements (urban staple rights), most studies of the first strand of research stress the importance of market integration and long-distance food trade for the provisioning of cities and for urban development in general, at least since the late Middle Ages: agricultural production in the surrounding countryside was accompanied by import of foreign cereals and cattle to nourish urban populations (van Cruyningen and Thoen, 2012; Van Molle and Segers, 2013; Nützenadel and Trentmann, 2008; for sixteenth-century Antwerp, for instance, see Limberger, 2008).

Research on urban agriculture is far from integrated into these studies of the agro-food-chain. The reason is that historians focused on either the professional circuit of urban cultivators and horticulturalists (Broadway, 2013; Thomas, 1978; Beavington, 1975; Atkins, 2003; Gurvil, 2010) or the home food provisioning sector (Flavell, 2003; Burchardt, 2002), without accounting for the contribution of the total urban agricultural sector to the supply of cities. Commercial urban food production was often framed in a von Thünen-like specialisation model in which crop choice and livestock keeping was geared towards the production of quickly perishable vegetables and dairy. After all, closeness to the city centre would have given urban market gardeners and cow keepers preferential access to its markets (Atkins, 2003; O'Kelly and Bryan, 1996). Yet, most of these studies did not or could not reconstruct the precise rotation schemes, numbers of livestock, and the size of the holdings of these urban farmers (with the work of Clément Gurvil on early modern Paris as a noticeable exception), so that the specific organisation of commercial urban farming and its potential to feed citizens largely remains to be explored. With respect to home food provisioning, it is often argued that it could make a substantial contribution to the family budget, yet the amount of urban households having access to a backyard garden plot was difficult to estimate and hence received hardly any historiographical attention (except for some studies on English allotment gardening and urban commons, Burchardt, 2002; Flavell, 2003; French, 2000).

The fact that most of these studies focused on one particular city and did not oversee a broader urban network encompassing towns and cities of different size and morphology further explains why the overall share of urban farming in feeding cities could hardly be assessed and explained. Some authors, however, do render some insight into the capability of cities in feeding themselves. It is argued that small agro-towns or in German research the so-called *Ackerbürgerstädte* (Jäschke and Schrenk, 2003), which can be situated at the margins of the urban network, a substantial amount of town residents were involved in agricultural activities either as main occupation or as by-employment (on small towns in medieval England, Hilton, 1975: 76-94), resulting in fairly high levels of self-sufficiency at least in the case of some small Swedish towns in the eighteenth and nineteenth centuries (Björklund, 2010). The specific link between urban development and food provisioning of cities through urban food production remains largely to be scrutinised. This chapter aims to confront urban food demand with urban food production for a broad array of different types of towns and cities during a phase of urban growth, when more mouths to be fed can be seen as an opportunity for farming while constraints on urban open space only further aggravated the spatial limits within which urban agriculture had to be performed (Atkins, 2003: 133-144). Nineteenth-century Belgium, the first industrialising country on the Continent, characterised by a dense urban network of small, medium-sized and large cities, forms the ideal test case to reconstruct urban self-sufficiency levels.

Preliminary studies into Belgian agriculture and reconstructions of (urban) dietary patterns (Gadisseur, 1990; Goossens, 1992; Blomme, 1992; Segers, 2003) enable us to estimate the demand for agricultural products, such as cereals, potatoes, vegetables, milk, butter, beef and pork for each Belgian city.[2] The demand side will be confronted with the urban supply of food items, generated through urban agricultural production. A corpus of agricultural censuses (to which I shall further refer as "database") in combination with the aforementioned preliminary studies give the researcher the opportunity to map out the agricultural production of every Belgian city for a number of sample years along the nineteenth century. These censuses were compiled by order of the Belgian government and perhaps surprisingly also include urban territories. The most detailed of these censuses – the ones of 1846 and 1895, processed by the LOKSTAT program of Ghent University – inform the researcher on the cultivated acreage per type of crop (with garden crops as one of the categories), the number of different types of livestock, agricultural land prices and the population actively involved in agriculture as well as the size and property structures of all holdings, also when they were very small and only used for household consumption. The other agricultural censuses of the years 1866 and 1880 give less detail, but are equally informative on types of exploitation, livestock numbers and crop types (except for the 1880 census, which only details the latter variable).[3] The confrontation of food demand and supply for every Belgian city administratively labelled as such in the censuses will turn out that the size of a city, a proxy of urban economic development, as well as the urban shape (dense and compact cities versus open and diffuse settlement patterns) did indeed play a major role in the performance of urban food production, both in terms of commercial agricultural production and home food provisioning.

II. Urban food producers in towns and cities, a typology

The evaluation of the urban agricultural sector in this chapter takes a broad, yet well-delineated definition of "city" as the basis of analysis, namely every municipality legally described as a city at the time.[4] This includes small agro-towns as well as the main industrial and commercial hubs. According to the number of inhabitants, I distinguish six separate population size groups of cities, which are to be considered as proxies of urban development: very small towns with less than 3,700 inhabitants, small towns with 3,700

[2] Unfortunately, we cannot take into account inter and intra-urban differences in consumption patterns of food items in this macro-level study. After all, we lack sufficient preliminary studies to cover the broad urban network of Belgian towns and cities. However, the statistically significant differences in self-sufficiency levels between different groups of cities calculated in this study strongly support our conclusions.

[3] Historical Database of Local and Cadastral Statistics (LOKSTAT-POPPKAD), Ghent University, Quetelet Center for Quantitative Historical Research.

[4] Cf. the LOKSTAT-POPPKAD distinction between city and village.

up till 7,500 residents, middle-small cities with between 7,500 and 15,000 souls in their jurisdiction, middle-large cities in which 15,000 to 35,000 people live, large cities with 35,000 to 100,000 citizens and the largest cities counting over 100,000 inhabitants. These size groups are considered as fixed cut-off points for the entire research period (basically from 1846 until 1895), meaning that some cities shifted from one group to another in due course. Liège, for instance, grew from 75,961 inhabitants in 1846 and 99,129 inhabitants in 1866 to 123,131 and 157,760 inhabitants in 1880 and 1895 respectively and was hence analysed as part of the fifth size group in 1846 and 1866 and of the largest group of cities in 1880 and 1895 (cf. list of cities in annex 1).

In addition to the population numbers of cities, I also take into account the morphology of a city. On the basis of eighteenth-century (Ferraris) and nineteenth-century maps (including the so-called *Atlas des voiries vicinales* of 1841 and the cadastral maps of Popp compiled between 1842 and 1879),[5] I classified cities in two groups: (1) fragmented cities with a diffuse settlement pattern, characterised by streets gradually merging into the countryside (so-called *nevelsteden* such as Ronse); (2) cities with a compact and densely built-up inner core area (such as Mechelen).[6]

The pure juridical delineation of municipalities in the agricultural censuses means that a smaller or larger rural fringe was integrally part of the jurisdiction of cities, both of compact and fragmented ones. As the extent of the rural fringe self-evidently impacted on the agricultural production of cities, I subdivided towns and cities into five categories according to the size of their rural outskirts: towns/cities with a fringe of 0-6, 6-12, 12-18, 18-32, and larger than 32 square kilometres. Yet, this kind of categorisation should not be approached with analytical value in itself. After all, cities with small outskirts on their jurisdiction might equally have a large rural fringe (defined as an area economically oriented to or dependent on a city) expanding over neighbouring municipalities. So, differences in the data which can be related to the size of the rural fringe should be explained in terms of proximity or remoteness to the inner city (cf infra).[7]

A core issue in our research is to distinguish those cultivators who were professionally involved in agriculture and/or horticulture from those who were not. The first group includes all farming households who were able to commercialise at least a part of their agricultural produce: hence this group consists of both commercial city farmers with access to enough land to make a living from their agricultural activities and urban households who combined commercial food production with proto-industrial activities or retailing (cf. Vermoesen, 2015: 533-553; French, 2000: 171-199). Preliminary studies on rural farming guide us to take exploitations with a minimum size of 0.5 hectare as cut-off point from the second group of urban food producers (Ronsijn, 2014; Kint, 1989): home

[5] For Flemish cities, these maps can be consulted on www.geopunt.be; for Walloon cities, the 1841 *Atlas des voiries vicinales* can be consulted on http://geoportail.wallonie.be/walonmap.

[6] The inner city of the second type of cities was not seldom surrounded by city walls, before their demolition after the abolition of urban consumer taxes (so-called *octroi* taxes), Segers, 2001: 301; Ronsijn, 2014: 278.

[7] In the assumption of the centrality of the city core within the urban municipalities, the surface area groups of the rural fringe correspond to the following distances to the inner city (or the radius): 0-1.4 km, 1.4-2.0 km, 2.0-2.4 km, 2.4-3.2 km, and more than 3.2 km.

Table 1 Share of home food growing and commercial farming households for the total number of urban households, 1846 and 1895

City size groups	Home food growers		Commercial city farmers	
	Mean share (%)	*St.Dev.*	Mean share (%)	*St.Dev.*
		1846		
<3,700 inh.	42.53	*22.33*	19.29	*13.35*
3,700-7,500 inh.	25.93	*14.87*	17.64	*9.48*
7,500-15,000 inh.	17.71	*12.15*	17	*9.68*
15,000-35,000 inh.	4.72	*2.52*	7.46	*6.17*
35,000-100,000 inh.	2.29	*1.7*	2.15	*1.12*
>100,000 inh.	0.38	*0.4*	0.73	*0.91*
		1895		
<3,700 inh.	51.04	*17.23*	12.23	*7.35*
3,700-7,500 inh.	39.64	*16.71*	9.66	*10.33*
7,500-15,000 inh.	34.32	*18.59*	11.94	*10.18*
15,000-35,000 inh.	16.12	*15.25*	7.06	*5.29*
35,000-100,000 inh.	1.96	*1.85*	2.04	*2.08*
>100,000 inh.	1.68	*1.44*	0.55	*0.53*

Source: database.

food producing urban households for whom their tiny-scale farming was a complementary source of income. These two groups are not readily derivable from the agricultural censuses. I estimated the number of non-professional home food growers by distracting half of the professionally involved male agricultural labour force (assuming that one son was active as farmhand)[8] from the total number of exploitations (which also included the micro-holdings). The residual value then represents the (semi-)professional farming circuit.

From the confrontation of food producers with city size (table 1) we learn that the number of non-professional home food growers tended to decline as cities were larger: 40 to 50 per cent of urban households were involved in self-provisioning in the small agro-towns (most of them in Wallonia, such as Durbuy), between 20 and 40 per cent in small towns (such as Oudenaarde) and middle-small cities (such as Turnhout). 15,000 inhabitants seems to have been a cut-off point for the occurrence of self-provisioning urban households with shares of 4 to 16 per cent of households in the middle-large cities (such as Kortrijk) and only a fraction of urban populations (1 to 2 per cent of the households) having access to a home food garden in the two largest categories of cities. In the

8 On intra-familial labour division, see: Karel, Vanhaute and Paping, 2011: 192-201.

Table 2 Mean share of farm size groups for the total number of urban farm exploitations in the Belgian urban network, 1846 and 1895 compared

Farm size	1846	1895
0-0.5 ha	44.7	54.3
0.5-1 ha	11.3	10.5
1-5 ha	28.5	23.2
5-10 ha	7.4	6.4
10-30 ha	6.1	4.8
>30 ha	1.7	0.9

Source: database.

industrial hub of Ghent and the capital city of Brussels, for instance, a mere number of 147 out of 22,044 and 30 out of 30,550 households in 1846 and 556 out of 42,141 and 134 out of 55,993 households in 1895 respectively had access to a home food garden.

Commercial city farmers – both fulltime farmers and the ones combining commercial food production with other activities – made up around 10 to 20 per cent of urban households in small towns and cities up to 15,000 inhabitants. Again, the 15,000 limit is a cut-off point in that commercially involved city farmers made up approximately 7 per cent of urban households in the middle-large cities, whereas it represented a mere 2 per cent in the large cities (such as Mechelen and Leuven) and only a fraction of less than 1 per cent in cities exceeding 100,000 inhabitants. After the middle of the nineteenth century, whereas the percentages of the non-professional as well as the (semi-)professional farming circuit remained more or less stable in the cities with more than 35,000 residents, the proportions diverged in the small and middle-sized cities: in general the number of commercial farmers tended to decline, whereas the circuit of home food provisioning increased. This can be linked to a fragmentation process in which at least some commercially involved smallholding urban peasants – with their exploitations in the inner city or in the suburbs affected by urban building projects – were put out of commercial production and forced to move or to shift to home food production and to search for other core activities (table 2).

III. Consumption needs for cultivated crops, dairy and meat and their output figures

In order to reconstruct how well urban food production managed to meet food demand, I estimated the per capita consumption needs for wheat, rye and potatoes (Blomme, 1992: 78, 87), and for liquid milk and butter (Segers, 2003: 260) as well as for beef and pork (Segers, 2003: 259) (table 3). Unfortunately, differences in consumption levels and evolutions between cities and towns and between social groups within one city or town cannot be taken into account in this macro-level enquiry. Off-course, socio-economic differences between cities had an impact on living standards and eating habits of citizens

Table 3 Consumption of wheat, rye and potatoes in the second half of the nineteenth century

Period	Wheat (hl year^{-1})	Rye (hl year^{-1})	Potatoes (hl year^{-1})
1851-55	1.12	1.05	3.75
1877-1880	1.73	0.94	2.85
1891	2.3	0.74	2.41

Source: Blomme, 1992: 78, 87.

(e.g. recently once more highlighted in Beyers and Van Damme, 2016). The necessary abstraction of these inter and intra-urban differences however does not affect our main findings with respect to the relative position of small, medium-sized and large cities regarding their self-sufficiency levels of different food items.

Rye consumption and particularly potato consumption lessened in favour of wheat, as a result of a gradual rise in living standards and falling cereal prices as a result of cheap foreign imports in the final quarter of the century (Gadisseur, 1990: 671; Van den Eeckhout and Scholliers, 1983: 278-279; Segers, 2003: 258). For this reconstruction, I assume similar consumption levels and evolutions between cities (as has been argued for Ghent and Antwerp by Lis and Soly, 1977: 481), although regional variations and differences between cities of different size and socio-economic orientation are likely to have existed as demonstrated by Vandenbroeke for the early nineteenth century (1990: 120-122, 126-128; Scholliers, 1993: 25). The estimates of cereal consumption (table 3) seem to reflect an urban consumption pattern since wheat – i.e. the most popular bread grain in cities – took a prominent place in the food basket (de Vries, 1994: 200-202).[9] Beef and pork were the most popular meat products. Their consumption remained quite stable between 1846 and 1856, after which it increased during the 1860s up to the early 1870s, and further grew in the late 1880s and 1890s, when the gap between beef and pork consumption widened in favour of the latter kind of meat (table 4) (Segers, 2003: 259-262). The consumption of liquid milk was clearly on the rise in the second half of the nineteenth century, from 16 litres per head in the late 1840s to 29 litres in the 1880s up to more than 50 litres in the last decade of the century, whereas butter consumption remained quite stable between 7.5 and 8.5 kilograms per capita (table 4) (Segers, 2003: 260-262). Because domestic production of cheese turned out to be negligible, I did not take into account the increasing level of cheese consumption either. Reconstructions of vegetable consumption, although important for estimating the connection between local production and consumption of perishable horticultural produce in or close to cities, unfortunately turned out to be nearly impossible (Segers, 2003: 262).

For the assessment of total cereal and potato production on urban territories, I used five-year means of the standard crop yields estimated by Gadisseur (1990: 406, 407, 414, 415, 418, 419) for the various provinces, thereby inevitably neglecting potential

[9] The rather small difference for the years 1851-1855 might reflect the difficult harvest years in this period, cf. Scholliers, 1993.

Table 4 Consumption of dairy and meat in the nineteenth century

	Liquid milk (l year^{-1})	Butter (kg year^{-1})	Beef (kg year^{-1})	Pig meat (kg year^{-1})
1846	16	8.4	8.7	8
1866	21.5	7.5	9.8	10.3
1880	29.4	7.8	10.1	10.7
1895	54.1	8.5	9.5	16.9

Source: Segers, 2003: 259-262.

differences in yields between countryside farming and (peri-)urban agriculture (as has been observed in less densely urbanised regions, such as Prussia; Kopsidis and Wolf, 2012: 634-670) (annex 2).[10] These yield estimations were then multiplied by the acreage of these crops registered in the censuses. For potatoes, we took into account that a part of this crop was used as pig feed, namely 2 kilogrammes per pig per day (under the assumption that they were older than 2 months), 4 kilogrammes in 1866, and 6 kilogrammes in 1880 and 1895. These feed potatoes were distracted from the total potato output before calculating self-sufficiency of consumable potatoes (Segers and Dejongh, 2000: 10). In case of meat and dairy, we cannot but work with nation-wide estimations. Figures on yearly milk output per cow estimated by Goossens (1992: 148-150) and Blomme (1992: 139-140) were used to calculate total liquid milk output (by multiplying with the number of milking cows). Milk yields tended to increase from 1600 litres per cow per year in 1846 to 1912 litres in 1880 up to 2477 litres at the end of the century. The share of liquid milk used for butter production (85, 80, 75 per cent for 1846, 1880 and 1895 respectively) and animal feed (10 per cent for the entire research period)[11] (as estimated by Goossens and Blomme) enables me to assess the total output of consumable liquid milk and butter. The exact reconstruction of yearly beef and pork production was far more difficult, because of unclear slaughter coefficients. Martine Goossens (1992: 126-127) circumvented this problem by comparing the total amount of meat with the amount of animals, hence assessing meat yields per living animal.[12] To reconstruct beef and pork output, I multiplied the meat yields with the total number of animals as suggested by Goossens. Even though it is quite possible that the agricultural censuses somewhat underestimated agricultural surface areas and livestock numbers (especially in the case of the 1866 and 1880 ones) (Goossens, 1992: 56-59; Gadisseur, 1990), I believe that these data are to be preferred above arbitrary corrections. The general findings about self-sufficiency levels

[10] Except the 1846 potato harvests, which were based on the figures on "normal years" within the agricultural census, available through LOKSTAT.

[11] Though this level of 10 per cent of liquid milk as animal feed might be slightly overestimated for urban environments because milk would have been too expensive to use longer than necessary for raising calves.

[12] Meat yields per living animal (kilogrammes per animal): 1) Beef: 26.08 (1846), 27.01 (1866), 27.93 (1880), 37.86 (1895) 2) Pigs: 73.5 (1846), 97.69 (1866), 121.87 (1880), 121.87 (1895); Goossens, 1992: 126.

in this chapter prove to be sound as the main differences and similarities between cities of different size and shape are clearly shown. Possibly, the observed standard deviations and interquartile ranges are partly to be explained by these source limitations.

With respect to vegetable gardening, it is extremely difficult to reconstruct production figures as we lack information on types of vegetables within these gardens, the frequency of harvests as well as their yields per surface area.[13] Therefore, I take the observation of Gadisseur that a 0.03 hectare large garden plot was sufficient to provide a family of five members with enough produce for one year as a starting point to calculate self-sufficiency levels (Gadisseur, 1990: 540; similar estimations by Stanhill, 1977: 277). Blomme (1992: 149) assumes that commercial gardeners were able to reach substantially higher vegetable yields and more harvests than non-professional home food growers but I do not see the reasons why higher degrees of professionalism would make a great difference in a largely organically based production system where home food growers – like micro-holding rural peasants – had enough incentives to ease their family budget by meticulously taking care of their garden plots (on higher yields on micro-smallholdings, Thoen and Soens, 2015: 462). The combination of the city population with the number of households in the population censuses of 1846 and 1890[14] allows me to reconstruct the average size of a family, which I took into account as a weighting factor to estimate the self-sufficiency levels of the gardening sector.[15] Notice in this respect that I was not able to include urban demand for fresh vegetables, so that the calculated self-sufficiency levels are perhaps somewhat underestimated, since workers' households in cities like Antwerp, Ghent and Brussels had barely access to fresh vegetables in the middle of the nineteenth century as budgetary investigation had shown (Scholliers, 1993: 23-24).

IV. The (in)ability of cities to feed themselves

IV.1 Mean figures of urban agriculture for the total urban network

The general overview – dissociated from any city-specific features such as city size and the peri-urban surface area – reveals clear differences with regard to self-sufficiency between the high-yielding potato and vegetable crops on the one hand and the cereal crops on the other (table 5). Changing consumer patterns (a lessening share of potatoes in urban diets, compensated by a higher intake of cereals) together with a shift towards more potato cultivation (relatively speaking, cf. infra) explains the increasing capacity of urban agriculture for self-provisioning with respect to potato cultivation and the lowering

[13] It is, moreover, possible that a part of the gardens was devoted to potato cultivation. Unfortunately, we do not know the exact proportion of potatoes grown in vegetable gardens. This might imply that self-sufficiency levels for potatoes could have been somewhat higher than estimated in this chapter. Though, this does not affect the relative position of self-providing capacities of different urban environments.

[14] Processed by Historical Database of Local and Cadastral Statistics (LOKSTAT-POPPKAD), Ghent University, Quetelet Center for Quantitative Historical Research.

[15] Self-sufficiency level of urban vegetable gardens = number of hectares of garden plots divided by the weighting factor (i.e. 0.03 * (average number of family members/5)), divided by the number of households.

Table 5 Overall self-sufficiency of urban agriculture with respect to vegetables, potatoes, wheat and rye, liquid milk and butter, beef and pig meat during the nineteenth century

Crop	1846	1866	1880	1895
Vegetables	87.5	/	/	79.6
Potatoes	80.1	85.9	89.1	131.6
Wheat	50.6	56.4	32.1	16.1
Rye	48.8	46.5	40.8	56.5
Liquid milk	39.7	/	44.3	40.7
Butter	42.8	/	44.5	43.2
Beef	42.4	/	34	43.2
Pig meat	47.3	/	53.3	54.8

Source: database; Blomme, 1992: 78, 87, 139-140; Goossens, 1992: 126-127; Gadisseur, 1990: 406-407, 414-415, 418-419.

of it in the case of wheat. We should, however, not interpret this as the urban agricultural sector being irresponsive to evolutions in food demand, but rather see it in the light of responding to declining cereal prices (due to foreign imports) and the effects of shrinking amounts of urban agricultural land (cf. infra).

As far as dairy is concerned, urban agriculture at large seemed pretty much able to keep provisioning levels quite constant over time, even when demand for liquid milk increased sharply at the end of the century (Segers, 2003: 260-262). Increasing milk yields and the fact that less milk was processed into butter explains this stability in overall self-sufficiency of liquid milk. The higher milk yields sufficed to meet the stable per capita demand for butter of an increasing urban population in the course of the nineteenth century. With respect to beef and pork, no particular change in self-sufficiency levels can be noticed at the general level either. Especially the increasing demand for pork in the later end of the century could be met by the increase in the number of pigs kept (in accordance with general tendencies in the agricultural sector in the final quarter of the nineteenth century, cf. Blomme, 1992). It cannot be stressed enough that these are general overviews and averages of all cities taken together, hence hiding substantial differences among cities from our view. In what follows, differences in city size, shape and extent of peri-urban area shall reveal that the relevance of urban and peri-urban agriculture in meeting urban food demand heavily depended on those factors.

IV.2 The type of urban food producer

A broad range of city-specific factors had an impact on the performance of the urban agricultural sector as the correlations in table 6 demonstrate. First of all, we can see a connection between the type of food item and the type of urban food producer. In line of expectations, the self-sufficiency level of arable crops (wheat and rye) was clearly positively linked to the (semi-)professional farming circuit, whereas the correlation was generally higher between non-professional home food growers and self-sufficiency levels of vegetables and by and large also potatoes. This means that when more urban households had access to a garden plot for vegetables and/or potatoes, non-professional urban agriculture could substantially contribute to the aggregate supply of potatoes and vegetables. As far as livestock keeping (as represented by dairying and meat production) was concerned, it was generally more strongly linked to the (semi-)professional urban farming circuit. In case of pig keeping, however, correlations with home food provisioning were higher. Home food growing families were most probably also able to keep one or a few pigs on a diet based on kitchen refuse and garden crop residues (Atkins, 2003: 137-139). The strength of the correlation though subsided when 1846 is compared to 1895. Both in the case of potatoes and pig keeping, correlations shifted in favour of commercial farming. Even though the number of (semi-)professional urban farmers was on the decline at the end of the century (cf. supra), the remainder of them shifted businesses towards more livestock keeping (especially pigs) and potato growing, which perfectly corresponded with income strategies of countryside farmers (except for those in some parts of the highly fertile polder region and the Hesbaye) answering the challenges of falling cereal prices (Blomme, 1992: 207-208; Ronsijn, 2014: 265-277). Even against the background of declining numbers of (semi-)professionals, milk, butter, and beef production were increasingly correlated with the commercial circuit at the end of the century. Its correlation with the home food provisioning sector was quite substantial in the first half of the century before it lowered toward the 1890s. It is more difficult to explain this correlation between home food growers and keeping land-demanding cattle, except when a substantial number of non-commercial cow keepers had access to fodder or meadows outside the city centre, such as town commons (cf. widely observed for England, French, 2000; possibly also in the case of the small town of Oudenaarde with the Donkmeers as its town common)[16], private holdings or market purchase of fodder and hay (possibly in exchange for manure, De Graef, 2017: 48-50).

IV.3 Urban morphology

The relation of the urban form – either compact densely built-up cities or open cities with a dispersed settlement pattern – to the self-providing capacities of urban farming in general points to the obvious positive effects of the openness of cities, especially in the case of potato growing and livestock keeping. Table 6 makes clear that better access to land for growing potatoes and feeding livestock in cities with a diffuse settlement pattern in combination with the commercial food producing activities in these cities' peri-urban area resulted in higher self-sufficiency levels than in cities characterised by a densely built-up area in the inner city offering fewer possibilities to cultivate potatoes in backyard gardens or keep livestock. Yet, the correlations between urban shape and pig keeping were less strong than these for dairying and beef farming (table 6). This probably

[16] City Archives Oudenaarde, Modern Archive, 723.0-1 Donkmeers 1834.

Table 6 Correlations between self-sufficiency levels of potatoes, wheat, rye, vegetables, liquid milk, butter, beef and pig meat; N=86; '*': significant at the 0.05 level; '': significant at the 0.01 level**

	1846	1866	1880	1895
	Self-sufficiency of potatoes			
Self-sufficiency of wheat	not significant	0.245*	0.219*	0.239*
Self-sufficiency of rye	0.468**	0.559**	0.512**	0.562**
Self-sufficiency of liquid milk/butter	0.792**	/	0.732**	0.676**
Self-sufficiency of beef	0.791**	0.706**	0.700**	0.649**
Self-sufficiency of pig meat	0.747**	0.762**	0.837**	0.827**
City population	-0.341**	-0.340**	-0.338**	-0.331**
Peri-urban area (sq. km)	0.324**	0.422**	0.326**	0.460**
City size (class)	-0.402**	-0.410**	-0.450**	-0.490**
Peri-urban area (class)	0.447**	0.597**	0.479**	0.489**
Diffuse (i.e. 0) vs. Built-up (i.e. 1)	-0.291**	-0.364**	-0.408**	-0.400**
Home food growers (%)	0.603**	/	/	0.453**
Commercial farmers (%)	0.440**	/	/	0.728**
	Self-sufficiency of wheat			
Self-sufficiency of potatoes	not significant	0.245*	0.219*	0.239*
Self-sufficiency of rye	0.301**	0.346**	0.257*	0.384**
Self-sufficiency of liquid milk/butter	0.357**	/	0.478**	0.557**
Self-sufficiency of beef	0.265*	0.347**	0.389**	0.518**
Self-sufficiency of pig meat	not significant	not significant	not significant	not significant

Table 6 (Continued)

	1846	1866	1880	1895
		Self-sufficiency of wheat		
City population	-0.218*	-0.213*	-0.226*	not significant
Peri-urban area (sq. km)	not significant	not significant	0.223*	0.240*
City size (class)	not significant	-0.248*	-0.274*	-0.226*
Peri-urban area (class)	0.343**	0.384*	0.400**	0.328**
Diffuse (i.e. 0) vs. Built-up (i.e. 1)	not significant	not significant	not significant	not significant
Home food growers (%)	not significant	/	/	0.254*
Commercial farmers (%)	0.366**	/	/	0.366**
		Self-sufficiency of rye		
Self-sufficiency of potatoes	0.468**	0.559**	0.512**	0.562**
Self-sufficiency of wheat	0.301**	0.346**	0.257*	0.384**
Self-sufficiency of liquid milk/butter	0.433**	/	0.519**	0.684**
Self-sufficiency of beef	0.399**	0.611**	0.486**	0.632**
Self-sufficiency of pig meat	0.365**	0.520**	0.420**	0.607**
City population	-0.249*	-0.234*	not significant	-0.228*
Peri-urban area (sq. km)	0.401**	0.464**	0.455**	0.434**
City size (class)	not significant	not significant	not significant	-0.260*
Peri-urban area (class)	0.508**	0.570**	0.519**	0.443**
Diffuse (i.e. 0) vs. Built-up (i.e. 1)	not significant	not significant	not significant	not significant
Home food growers (%)	not significant	/	/	0.233*
Commercial farmers (%)	0.497**	/	/	0.652**

Table 6 (Continued)

	1846	1866	1880	1895
	Self-sufficiency of vegetables			
Self-sufficiency of potatoes	0.387**	/	/	0.364**
Self-sufficiency of wheat	not significant	/	/	0.345**
Self-sufficiency of rye	not significant	/	/	0.368**
Self-sufficiency of liquid milk/butter	0.478**	/	/	0.540**
Self-sufficiency of beef	0.487**	/	/	0.599**
Self-sufficiency of pig meat	0.573**	/	/	0.409**
City population	-0.359**	/	/	-0.394**
Peri-urban area (sq. km)	0.258*	/	/	not significant
City size (class)	-0.455**	/	/	-0.551**
Peri-urban area (class)	0.358**	/	/	0.254*
Diffuse (i.e. 0) vs. Built-up (i.e. 1)	not significant	/	/	not significant
Home food growers (%)	0.693**	/	/	0.669**
Commercial farmers (%)	0.473**	/	/	0.348**
	Self-sufficiency of liquid milk/butter			
Self-sufficiency of potatoes	0.792**	/	0.732**	0.676**
Self-sufficiency of wheat	0.357**	/	0.478**	0.557**
Self-sufficiency of rye	0.433**	/	0.519**	0.684**
Self-sufficiency of beef	0.953**	/	0.933**	0.930**
Self-sufficiency of pig meat	0.725**	/	0.767**	0.704**

Table 6 (Continued)

	1846	1866	1880	1895
	Self-sufficiency of liquid milk/butter			
City population	-0.417**	/	-0.384**	-0.366**
Peri-urban area (sq. km)	0.452**	/	0.468**	0.568**
City size (class)	-0.526**	/	-0.518**	-0.517**
Peri-urban area (class)	0.545**	/	0.588**	0.561**
Diffuse (i.e. 0) vs. Built-up (i.e. 1)	-0.441**	/	-0.419**	-0.369**
Home food growers (%)	0.663**	/	/	0.455**
Commercial farmers (%)	0.559**	/	/	0.735**
	Self-sufficiency of beef			
Self-sufficiency of potatoes	0.791**	0.706**	0.700**	0.649**
Self-sufficiency of wheat	0.265*	0.347**	0.389**	0.518**
Self-sufficiency of rye	0.399**	0.611**	0.486**	0.632**
Self-sufficiency of liquid milk/butter	0.953**	/	0.933**	0.930**
Self-sufficiency of pig meat	0.770**	0.653**	0.786**	0.641**
City population	-0.400**	-0.369**	-0.369**	-0.348**
Peri-urban area (sq. km)	0.477**	0.489**	0.490**	0.536**
City size (class)	-0.505**	-0.401**	-0.518**	-0.542**
Peri-urban area (class)	0.554**	0.612**	0.577**	0.528**
Diffuse (i.e. 0) vs. Built-up (i.e. 1)	-0.411**	-0.290**	-0.334**	-0.300**
Home food growers (%)	0.656**	/	/	0.458**
Commercial farmers (%)	0.535**	/	/	0.690**

Table 6 (Continued)

	1846	1866	1880	1895
	Self-sufficiency of pig meat			
Self-sufficiency of potatoes	0.747**	0.762**	0.837**	0.827**
Self-sufficiency of wheat	not significant	not significant	not significant	not significant
Self-sufficiency of rye	0.365**	0.520**	0.420**	0.607**
Self-sufficiency of liquid milk/butter	0.725**	/	0.767**	0.704**
Self-sufficiency of beef	0.770**	0.653**	0.786**	0.641**
City population	-0.324**	-0.315**	-0.301**	-0.296**
Peri-urban area (sq. km)	0.258*	0.245*	0.270*	0.390**
City size (class)	-0.454**	-0.438**	-0.474**	-0.481**
Peri-urban area (class)	0.395**	0.370**	0.409**	0.413**
Diffuse (i.e. 0) vs. Built-up (i.e. 1)	-0.264*	-0.271*	-0.237*	-0.282**
Home food growers (%)	0.711**	/	/	0.392**
Commercial farmers (%)	0.469**	/	/	0.701**

Source: database; Blomme, 1992: 78, 87; Goossens, 1992: 126-127; Gadisseur, 1990: 406-407, 414-415, 418-419.

points to the fact that it was easier to raise pigs within compact urban environments than it was for cattle (cf. Atkins, 2003: 137-139). Figures on self-sufficiency in vegetables, characterised by equally high-yielding capacities as potatoes and even multiple harvests per year, does however not correspond to the findings of potatoes, thus qualifying all too strong assumptions about the impact of urban morphology. Pure arable crops (wheat and rye) did not interact with the specific settlement patterns of cities because these cereal plots were likely to be located outside the inner city in the rural fringe (cf. observations of cereal cultivation in the *faubourgs* of sixteenth-century Paris by Gurvil, 2010: 424-430).

IV.4 The degree of urban development

The correlations indicate that degrees of self-sufficiency of all these food items heavily depended on the size of urban populations and hence on the degree of competition for land with the housing market and industrial/service sectors (Parham, 2015: 189). It is then no coincidence that high-yielding potatoes and vegetables perform better than pure arable crops. The table in annex 1a (and the p-values in annex 1b) shows clear cut-off points in the size of city populations for urban agriculture to be able to make a fundamental contribution in providing citizens with local food. These cut-off points greatly differed according to the type of crops. The production of wheat and rye on the territories of large cities (above 35,000 inhabitants) did barely add to aggregate supplies needed to feed these cities, and even in the case of potatoes, a self-providing level of 5 per cent was hard to reach in and near these cities (notice the contrast with the general figures in table 5) (annex 1). With vegetable gardens – of which we do not exactly know if potatoes were sometimes also included –higher levels of self-sufficiency were reached for large cities (up to 100,000 inhabitants), although figures decreased in the second half of the nineteenth century. Still a large market remained open to countryside deliveries. This stands in contrast to cities with less than 15,000 inhabitants, where fairly high levels of self-provisioning (70 to 80 per cent in case of both vegetables and potatoes) could be obtained.

It is nevertheless important to stress that urban (commercial) farmers devoted a greater share of their acreage to cereals than to higher-yielding potatoes or vegetables, even though the vicinity of large cities in particular entailed bid-rent competition with the housing market and industry and service sectors (Parham, 2015: 189). Urban development did play a role, however, in that the urban commercial farming sector in cities with less than 35,000 inhabitants devoted between 40 and 30 per cent of the arable land to cereals, whereas commercial farmers in cities of more than this amount of residents spent 20 to 30 per cent in 1846 and 10 to 20 per cent of the acreage in the final quarter of the century to cereal cultivation. Shares of potatoes and vegetables were lower, with the figures being higher in larger cities compared to small agro-towns. Proportions were lowest for the smallest (agro-) towns (i.e. 1 to 2 per cent of vegetables and 4 to 6 per cent of potatoes), increased to levels of 2 to 4 per cent of vegetables and 5 to 8 per cent of potatoes for groups of cities between 7,500 and 15,000 inhabitants, varied around 5 to 7 per cent of vegetables and 8 to 11 per cent of potatoes for the middle-large city size group, and further jumped to proportions of 11 to 25 per cent of vegetables and 9 to 16 per cent of potatoes in the case of cities counting more than 35,000 residents. Quite logically, these crops were more attractive in the vicinity of higher concentrations of people because of their high-yielding capacities, allowing commercial farmers to gain good harvests from a relative small acreage and home food growers to add to their family budget.

A case study for 1880 Oudenaarde, for which the individual census forms for each household with access to at least some amount of land were preserved, showed that self-provisioning households entirely devoted their backyard gardens to potatoes and vegetables. In accordance with what the evidence from our database on the general census data suggest for other cities, the group of commercially involved urban cultivators in Oudenaarde (most of them cultivating between 2 and 9 hectares of land) far from specialised in vegetable production (as one would think happened in line of von Thünen-like agricultural location theories), but devoted a more substantial share to cereals, complemented with fodder crops and grasslands. Even gardeners in Oudenaarde, the farm size of whom varied between 0.5 and 2 hectares and thus smaller than that of cultivators, dedicated a lot more of their acreage to vegetable and potato production but they did not fully specialise in horticultural production and still devoted 20 per cent of their acreage to cereals (De Graef and Ronsijn, 2017; Van Leuven, 1990: 94-95).

An explanation for the fact that the commercial urban farmers – even near large cities – did not abandon cereal cultivation altogether and did not specialise in vegetable and potato production has most probably to do with constraints of access to enough labour for these labour-intensive crops (as also suggested by Van Leuven, 1990: 90-93). At first sight, this seems contradictory as cities are pre-eminent suppliers of labour, given the demand for labour in urban industries and services. Agricultural wage formation in cities (cf. database), however, differed quite substantially from wage formation in urban construction works (Scholliers, 1991: 99, 106). In 1846, agricultural day labourers in or close to urban environments received on average 1.21 Belgian franc (BEF) per day compared to 1.51 BEF per day earned by construction workers, or a difference of 24.8 per cent. This wage differential between agriculture and construction works further increased to 52.3 per cent in 1895: agricultural day labourers got a daily payment of 2.14 BEF, whereas construction workers were paid 3.26 BEF. As such, it seems logical that commercial urban farmers at least kept a part of their acreage under cereals, even at the end of the nineteenth century. A continuing effort to provide for their own household needs might further add to the explanation.

Also in the case of dairying, beef and pork production, the degree of urban development played an important role in the performance of these branches of urban farming (annex 1). Clear cut-off points existed between small agro-towns and cities up to 15,000 souls, the former being able to provide more than half of the demand for liquid milk, butter, beef and pork, the latter between 35 and 45 per cent. The latter group of small towns and middle-small cities were significantly better able to provide themselves with dairy and meat than the group of middle-large cities with 15 to 35,000 urban dwellers, which could reach levels of self-sufficiency varying between 15 and 25 per cent (which is in accordance with observations of Atkins for English cities, 2003: 137-139). This group in its turn had to bring in less dairy and meat from the countryside than the large cities with 35 to 100,000 inhabitants and the largest ones with more than 100,000 inhabitants. The livestock-keeping households in cities of the category with 35 to 100,000 inhabitants were able to meet approximately 5 per cent of the dairy and meat demand, whereas their colleagues in the largest cities with over 100,000 dwellers could only supply the equivalent of approximately 2 per cent of the demand for dairy and meat.

IV.5 The friction of distance to the city centre

Looking at the impact of the size of the rural fringe (as proxy of the friction of distance to the city centre) on the levels of self-provisioning of urban farming, it becomes clear that this proxy indicator of the association of certain food items with longer allocation lines especially applies to cereals. Cereals relied on supplies from the surrounding countryside (annex 2a and 2b) and increasingly from foreign imports in the late nineteenth century as countryside farming shifted more and more from arable cultivation towards livestock keeping, potato and vegetable cultivation (O'Rourke, 1997: 775-801; Blomme, 1992: 290-292; Ronsijn 2014: 265-277; cf. import statistics in Degrève, 1982: 299-328). Cereal-cultivating urban farmers hence responded to international price developments in quite the same way as their colleagues in the countryside as shown by the decrease in cereal cultivation and increase in potato growing and pig keeping towards the end of the century (annex 1 and 2).

Yet, stressing the importance of countryside farming with respect to the provisioning of cities with bread grains and brewing/distilling grains should not lead us to underestimate the impact of the rural fringe on self-sufficiency levels of potatoes and vegetables. Next to the fact that small plots of potatoes and vegetables in and near cities substantially contributed to self-sufficiency levels for these food items,[17] the larger the size of the peri-urban area – or better the contribution of the commercial produce in a larger rural area around cities – the greater the chance that total supplies could be lifted above levels of self-provisioning (annex 2 comparing several sizes of peri-urban zones, which can be interpreted as the friction of distance to the city core). Though dairy and meat production in close proximity to city centres were able to meet 15 to 25 per cent of urban demand (epitomised in the dairy and meat production of cities at a distance less than 1.4 kilometre outside the city centre), commercial dairying and livestock farming in a wider area of more than 3.2 kilometres around the city centre helped to fill in more than 50 per cent of the needs for liquid milk, butter, beef and pork (annex 2).

V. Conclusion

This macro-level investigation into the self-providing capacities of urban agriculture for the broad urban network of Belgium during its age of industrialisation revealed that urban food production varied inversely with urban development (with city size taken as proxy). First of all, the size of cities largely determined the presence of both home food producing households and commercially involved urban farmers. The level of 15,000 inhabitants was thereby a major cut-off point as larger cities had seldom more than 10 per cent of their citizens belonging to either of these groups. The overall share of home food growers in the total city population as well as in relation to the total number of agricultural exploitations tended to increase throughout the nineteenth century, whereas the commercially involved city farmers decreased instead. This implies that the growth of the home food provisioning circuit at least partially needs to be considered as the consequence of the commercially oriented urban farmers running out of business and being forced to self-provisioning and to search for other core activities. The growth of self-provisioning cannot (only) be interpreted as a positive evolution towards more access to urban garden plots but at least in part as the downside of a fragmentation process, fuelled by urban growth.

Intertwined with the effect of urban development on holding size and number of exploitations (both commercial and non-commercial ones), the size of cities clearly affected the ability or inability to rely on intra-urban food supplies, ranging from arable crops and vegetables to dairy and meat. As argued by literature on German *Ackerbürgerstädte* (e.g. Jäschke and Schrenk, 2003), small medieval English towns (Hilton, 1975: 76-94) and small towns in eighteenth and nineteenth-century Sweden (Björklund, 2010), small agro-towns indeed maintained a stronger connection with agricultural production, resulting in higher levels of self-sufficiency than for larger cities. High-yielding crops, such as potatoes and vegetables,

[17] Although the food items generated by urban agriculture did not necessarily all had to end up on the urban market but might also have been distributed further away as transportation networks and food conservation techniques improved, cf. several contributions in Beyers and Van Damme, 2016.

resulted in a greater capability of reaching higher self-sufficiency levels than in the case of cereals. Urban agriculture in cities with more constraints on urban open space (hence the larger cities) devoted a higher share of its acreage to potatoes and vegetables, especially in the backyard gardens of home food provisioning households but also on the plots of smallholding urban cultivators and market gardeners. Though, cities with more than 35,000 inhabitants were not able to meet more than 10 per cent of the demand for potatoes and vegetables. In other words, access to market or backyard garden plots contributed to reaching higher self-sufficiency levels but had too little of an impact to be an alternative to countryside deliveries in order to meet the needs for potatoes and vegetables in a middle-sized to large city.

Cereal growing declined in importance as cities became larger, but that did not mean that the (semi-)professional circuit of urban farmers abandoned its cultivation altogether. Still a substantial share of arable land in peri-urban areas – up to 20 and 30 per cent in cities counting respectively more and less than 35,000 souls at the end of the nineteenth century – was sown with grain and this on both large exploitations and smallholdings. This runs against insights on agricultural location theories arguing that low transport costs in areas close to urban markets would trigger specialised cultivation of quickly perishable fruits and vegetables. Wage differentials between urban industries and agriculture, to the detriment of the latter, resulted in constraints on labour supply, which explains why more thorough specialisation in labour-intensive horticulture on holdings above 2 hectares did not take off in the course of the nineteenth century. Urban development also impacted upon the performance of urban dairy and meat production, again with small cities considerably better able to meet demand (up to 40 per cent) as compared to middle-large cities (up to 20 per cent), which in their turn performed better than the largest cities (less than 5 per cent).

Differences in urban shape generally point to positive effects on the performance of especially potato growing and livestock keeping for open cities with a dispersed settlement pattern characterised by streets gradually running out in the countryside, in which home food provisioning households most probably had more chances to access a backyard garden plot with room for a pigsty. The size of the rural fringe – a proxy of the friction of distance to the inner city – showed that vegetable, potato, dairy and meat production at close distance to city centres were able to contribute more to self-sufficiency levels of these food items than in the case of cereals, though it nevertheless indicated that deliveries from a larger peri-urban and rural perimeter were imperative for meeting the urban needs for these food items as well.

To sum up, nineteenth-century urban growth and development increased constraints on urban food production that made access to soil problematic for commercial urban farming households, many of whom saw the size of their holding shrink, sometimes to levels at which the search for other core income resources became inevitable (as such they swelled the ranks of home food provisioning households). In addition to the response of the agricultural sector at large to international price developments, it was this fragmentation process, more than market-driven specialisation, that increased the relative share of the remaining urban agricultural acreage devoted to high-yielding potato and vegetable crops or to keeping pigs and (milk) cows. These food items generated higher output and by consequence contributed to higher self-sufficiency capabilities of urban agriculture. In general, however, it can be stated that the inverse connection between urban agriculture and urban development meant that urban agriculture made a very poor contribution to feeding the largest cities, even in the case of these food items with high returns.

Annexe 1a **Self-sufficiency of urban agriculture according to the size of cities in the nineteenth-century Belgian urban network**

City size (inhabitants)			Wheat					Rye				
	N	Year	Min.	Max.	Med.	Mean	*St.Dev.*	Min.	Max.	Med.	Mean	*St.Dev.*
<3,700	24	1846	0	290.9	15.4	45.2	*66.1*	0	195.5	37.8	44.5	*42.7*
	22	1866	0	456	10.3	69.4	*116.9*	1.7	151.5	34.3	40.1	*32.7*
	21	1880	0	265.7	10.7	45.6	*66.3*	1	126.4	28.8	34.3	*30.6*
	19	1895	0.1	179.1	2.6	20.8	*41.3*	1.9	248.9	51.4	68.3	*59.4*
3,700-7,500	25	1846	1.1	421.5	53.9	77.8	*91.1*	4.4	213.2	33.5	34.1	*51.7*
	25	1866	0	282.6	49.5	69.7	*71.9*	0	229.2	31.8	54.9	*57.2*
	21	1880	0	117.6	12.7	29.5	*33.3*	0	217.4	23.8	43.5	*55.5*
	15	1895	0	83	2.9	18.4	*26.3*	0	398.4	25.7	67.3	*103.4*
7,500-15,000	21	1846	0.5	197.2	62	56.3	*47.4*	0	198.5	52.6	68.8	*56.9*
	21	1866	0.8	233.6	59.4	63.4	*58.8*	0.3	236.7	38.3	66.4	*66.7*
	23	1880	0.8	139	38	44.4	*39.3*	0.2	195.7	36	57.1	*57.6*
	28	1895	0.1	84.7	17.6	21.2	*21.3*	4.7	311	42.7	72.1	*77.4*
15-35,000	11	1846	1.2	28.4	10.4	12.2	*8.2*	0.2	113.4	16	26.2	*32.5*
	13	1866	0	57.8	12.6	18.8	*18.7*	0	147	13.5	26.5	*41.1*
	13	1880	0	36.4	9.2	12.1	*11.7*	0	171.8	13.3	41.4	*60.1*
	14	1895	0	39.3	7.1	8.4	*9.9*	0	124.5	21.4	35.9	*37.7*
35-100,000	3	1846	0.3	2.11	0.4	0.9	*1*	1.8	4.6	2.3	2.9	*1.5*
	2	1866	0	1.6	0.9	0.8	*1.2*	0	0.5	0.2	0.2	*0.3*
	4	1880	0	0.9	0.2	0.3	*0.4*	0	14.7	0.3	3.8	*7.2*
	6	1895	0	4.9	0	0.9	*2*	0	15.4	0.3	3.8	*6.3*
>100,000	2	1846	0.2	0.2	0.2	0.2	*0*	0.1	3.2	1.6	1.6	*2.1*
	3	1866	0.3	0.3	0.3	0.3	*0*	0.3	4.2	1.2	1.9	*2*
	4	1880	0	0.5	0	0.1	*0.2*	0	3.5	0.1	0.9	*1.7*
	4	1895	0	0.1	0	0	*0.1*	0	3.8	0.2	1	*1.8*

Annexe 1a (Continued)

City size (inhabitants)	Potatoes							Vegetables				
	N	Year	Min.	Max.	Med.	Mean	*St.Dev.*	Min.	Max.	Med.	Mean	*St.Dev.*
<3,700	24	1846	14.3	324.7	69.2	101.1	*84.2*	2.4	268.9	107.8	120.1	*64.5*
	22	1866	0.3	193.7	90.7	94.7	*56.4*	/	/	/	/	/
	21	1880	8.3	186.3	85.1	80.3	*50.1*	/	/	/	/	/
	19	1895	1	193.3	109.1	103.7	*58.1*	21.1	292.7	103.4	120.7	*63.4*
3,700-7,500	25	1846	3.2	134	58.5	60.8	*40.3*	4.1	192.5	93.9	88.6	*47.6*
	25	1866	0.3	140.2	52.7	61.2	*42.2*	/	/	/	/	/
	21	1880	7	122.6	44.4	56.1	*43.1*	/	/	/	/	/
	15	1895	2.1	133	64.2	61.6	*44.9*	10.9	167.2	65.7	85.8	*49.2*
7,500-15,000	21	1846	8.1	198.4	69.5	78.6	*45.6*	0	170.2	83.7	81.3	*46.1*
	21	1866	3.8	198.2	70.5	68.6	*46.1*	/	/	/	/	/
	23	1880	1.6	210.2	44.2	55.5	*47*	/	/	/	/	/
	28	1895	1.6	210.9	40	64.2	*64.3*	10.2	136.1	78.3	78.3	*33.3*
15-35,000	11	1846	2.9	65.4	25.6	32.2	*20.5*	5.5	104.8	48.9	52.6	*31*
	13	1866	2.9	133.5	43.5	49.8	*44.4*	/	/	/	/	/
	13	1880	3.8	149.2	45.8	51.8	*46.4*	/	/	/	/	/
	14	1895	0.1	138.6	66.4	64.5	*44.4*	26.5	151.1	54	66.1	*40.2*
35-100,000	3	1846	5	15.8	6.7	9.2	*5.8*	0.3	2.1	0.4	0.9	*1*
	2	1866	0	9.8	4.9	4.9	*4.9*	/	/	/	/	/
	4	1880	0.4	39.5	20	20	*27.6*	/	/	/	/	/
	6	1895	0.6	53.1	17	23.6	*26.9*	0	4.9	0	0.9	*2*
>100,000	2	1846	0.9	4	2.4	2.4	*2.2*	0.3	31.8	16	16	*22.2*
	3	1866	0.6	6.7	4	3.8	*3.1*	/	/	/	/	/
	4	1880	2.9	3.8	3.2	3.2	*0.8*	/	/	/	/	/
	4	1895	0.9	1.5	1.2	1.2	*0.4*	0.1	30.6	10.9	13.1	*12.9*

			Liquid milk					Butter				
<3,700	24	1846	8.7	131.6	57.5	59.7	*31.6*	9.4	142	62.1	64.5	*34.1*
	22	1866	/	/	/	/	/	/	/	/	/	/
	21	1880	6.9	156	72.3	69.6	*32.3*	6.9	156.6	72.5	69.8	*36.4*
	19	1895	16.3	132.6	56.2	60.2	*31*	17.3	140.7	59.6	63.8	*32.8*
3,700-7,500	25	1846	1.9	102.5	34.5	39.2	*26.7*	2.1	110.6	37.2	42.3	*28.8*
	25	1866	/	/	/	/	/	/	/	/	/	/
	21	1880	1.8	149.1	43.5	45.5	*35*	1.8	149.6	43.7	45.6	*35.1*
	15	1895	8.1	144.6	51.7	53.1	*37.8*	8.6	153.4	54.9	56.3	*40*
7,500-15,000	21	1846	4.8	69.9	39.2	36.7	*19.1*	5.2	75.4	42.3	39.6	*20.6*
	21	1866	/	/	/	/	/	/	/	/	/	/
	23	1880	4.7	125	42	45	*30.6*	4.8	125.4	42.2	45.3	*30.7*
	28	1895	8.4	127.3	33	41.7	*32.2*	9	135	35	44.2	*34.2*
15-35,000	11	1846	4	60.8	16.7	19	*15.9*	4.3	65.6	18	20.6	*17.2*
	13	1866	/	/	/	/	/	/	/	/	/	/
	13	1880	0.9	62.7	23.4	24.3	*19.7*	0.9	62.9	23.5	24.4	*19.8*
	14	1895	1	57.4	25.3	25.4	*16.1*	1.1	60.9	26.9	26.9	*17*
35-100,000	3	1846	2	4.6	4.6	3.7	*1.5*	2.2	4.9	4.9	4	*1.6*
	2	1866	/	/	/	/	/	/	/	/	/	/
	4	1880	2	17.9	4.4	7.2	*7.5*	2	17.9	4.4	7.2	*7.5*
	6	1895	0.6	10.7	4.6	5.3	*3.7*	0.7	11.4	4.9	5.7	*4*
>100,000	2	1846	1.8	3.9	2.8	2.8	*1.5*	2	4.2	3.1	3.1	*1.6*
	3	1866	/	/	/	/	/	/	/	/	/	/
	4	1880	1.5	3.6	2.2	2.4	*0.9*	1.5	3.6	2.3	2.4	*1*
	4	1895	0.7	3.1	2.3	2.1	*1.1*	0.8	3.3	2.5	2.3	*1.1*

Annexe 1a (Continued)

City size (inhabitants)			Beef					Pig meat				
	N	Year	Min.	Max.	Med.	Mean	*St.Dev.*	Min.	Max.	Med.	Mean	*St.Dev.*
<3,700	24	1846	10.5	166.3	57	64	*38.4*	5.1	232.9	51.6	79.5	*68.4*
	22	1866	3.7	63.1	30.7	30.5	*15.2*	2.1	243.5	71.6	91.7	*71.1*
	21	1880	3.5	137.3	59.8	55.6	*30.4*	1	266.1	81.6	101.3	*74.8*
	19	1895	15.1	187.3	55.9	72	*45.8*	4	298.3	77.6	99.7	*72.8*
3,700-7,500	25	1846	3.7	152.4	38.4	43.2	*33.5*	1.5	146.22	41.4	47	*36.4*
	25	1866	1.8	73.9	18.4	22.4	*16.8*	3.9	171.4	42	59	*52.3*
	21	1880	2.5	110.8	28.2	34.4	*26.6*	5.1	180.8	24.6	46	*49.8*
	15	1895	6.3	142.8	47.2	56.1	*42.5*	0.7	217.5	34.2	54.6	*60.4*
7,500-15,000	21	1846	3.1	73.9	40.4	39.1	*19.8*	0.4	125.4	24.3	38.7	*36*
	21	1866	1.1	88.2	22.9	26.7	*19.1*	6	194.9	28.1	52.9	*53.4*
	23	1880	2.8	116.9	27.2	34.7	*27.2*	1.2	176.7	33.1	54.3	*52.7*
	28	1895	6.6	129.7	32.4	40.2	*30.8*	2.7	213.9	40.7	59.3	*52.2*
15-35,000	11	1846	3.1	56.4	13.9	17.2	*15*	0.7	59.9	5.6	14.2	*17.4*
	13	1866	0.8	33.5	8.4	11.1	*10.9*	0.1	77.5	7.6	17.3	*22.7*
	13	1880	0.5	52.1	14.2	16.8	*15.2*	1.9	50.6	16	16	*14.2*
	14	1895	0.7	77	23.3	24.7	*19.1*	0.2	90.1	15.7	21.9	*23.3*
35-100,000	3	1846	1.9	4	3.4	3.1	*1.1*	1.8	6.6	3	3.8	*2.5*
	2	1866	1.2	1.3	1.2	1.2	*0.1*	4.6	4.9	4.7	4.7	*0.2*
	4	1880	0.9	10.3	2.4	4	*4.4*	0.6	19.1	2.2	6	*8.7*
	6	1895	0.4	8.2	3.8	4.1	*2.9*	0.1	13.6	2.8	4.3	*5*
>100,000	2	1846	1.1	3	2.1	2.1	*1.4*	0.2	4.2	2.2	2.2	*2.8*
	3	1866	0.9	2.5	1.9	1.8	*0.8*	0.4	4.1	3.6	2.7	*2*
	4	1880	0.7	2	1	1.2	*0.6*	0.2	3.9	1.5	1.7	*1.6*
	4	1895	0.4	2.5	1.4	1.4	*0.8*	0.2	3.7	1.9	1.9	*1.7*

Source: database; Blomme, 1992: 78, 87; Goossens, 1992: 126-127; Gadisseur, 1990: 406-407, 414-415, 418-419.

Annexe 1b p-values (Games-Howell PostHoc test) for different food items revealing statistically significant differences between cities in terms of population groups. 1) = Wheat; 2) = Rye; 3) = Potatoes; 4) = Vegetables; 5) = Milk & Butter; 6) = Beef; 7) = Pork

	<3,700 inhab.	**3,700-7,500 inhab.**	**7,500-15,000 inhab.**	**15,000-35,000 inhab.**	**35,000-100,000 inhab.**	**>100,000 inhab.**
<3,700 inhab.		3) 0.007; 5) 0,025; 6) 0.001; 7) 0.000	4) 0.006; 5) 0,001; 6) 0.001; 7) 0.000	1) 0.003; 3) 0.007; 4) 0.000; 5) 0.000; 6) 0.000; 7) 0.000	1) 0.000; 2) 0.000; 3) 0.000; 4) 0.000; 5) 0.000; 6) 0.000; 7) 0.000	1) 0.000; 2) 0.000; 3) 0.000; 4) 0.000; 5) 0.000; 6) 0.000; 7) 0.000
3,700-7,500 inhab.	3) 0.007; 5) 0,025; 6) 0.001; 7) 0.000			1) 0.000; 6) 0.000; 7) 0.000	1) 0.000; 2) 0.000; 3) 0.000; 4) 0.000; 6) 0.000; 7) 0.000	1) 0.000; 2) 0.000; 3) 0.000; 4) 0.000; 6) 0.000; 7) 0.000
7,500-15,000 inhab.	4) 0.006; 5) 0,001; 6) 0.001; 7) 0.000			1) 0.000; 2) 0.004	1) 0.000; 2) 0.000; 3) 0.000; 4) 0.000	1) 0.000; 2) 0.000; 3) 0.000; 4) 0.000
15,000-35,000 inhab.	1) 0.003; 3) 0,007; 4) 0.000; 5) 0.000; 6) 0.000; 7) 0.000	1) 0.000; 6) 0.000; 7) 0.000	1) 0.000; 2) 0.004		2) 0.000; 3) 0.000; 4) 0.009; 6) 0.000; 7) 0.001	2) 0.000; 3) 0.000; 4) 0.009; 6) 0.000
35,000-100,000 inhab.	1) 0.000; 2) 0.000; 3) 0.000; 4) 0.000; 5) 0.000; 6) 0.000; 7) 0.000	1) 0.000; 2) 0.000; 3)0.000; 4) 0.000; 6) 0.000; 7) 0.000	1) 0.000; 2) 0.000; 3)0.000; 4) 0.000	2) 0.000; 3) 0.000; 4) 0.009; 6) 0.000; 7) 0.001		1) 0.000
>100,000 inhab.	1) 0.000; 2) 0.000; 3) 0.000; 4) 0.000; 5) 0.000; 6) 0.000; 7) 0.000	1) 0.000; 2) 0.000; 3) 0.000; 4) 0.000; 6) 0.000; 7) 0.000	1) 0.000; 2) 0.000; 3) 0.000; 4) 0.000	2) 0.000; 3) 0.000; 4) 0.009; 6) 0.000	1) 0.000	

Source: database.

Annexe 2a Self-sufficiency of urban agriculture according to the size of the peri-urban area in the nineteenth-century Belgian urban network

Size of the peri-urban area			Wheat					Rye				
	N	Year	Min.	Max.	Med.	Mean	*St.Dev.*	Min.	Max.	Med.	Mean	*St.Dev.*
0-6 sq. km	18	1846	0	92.6	10.7	13.9	*21.7*	0	81.1	8.3	14.4	*20.7*
	18	1866	0	95.2	1.2	7.9	*22.1*	0	58.4	0.8	8.4	*17.6*
	18	1880	0	53.8	0.8	4.4	*12.5*	0	69.1	0.4	9	*18.4*
	19	1895	0	28.5	0.2	2.4	*6.4*	0	125.6	0.7	14.5	*31.6*
6-12 sq. km	17	1846	0.2	120.9	42.1	48.4	*44.2*	5.9	105	43.6	42.1	*28.3*
	17	1866	0.5	162.9	33.1	51.2	*53.2*	0.8	97.4	30.3	32	*25.6*
	17	1880	0.6	77.9	18.6	27.2	*27.5*	0	112	15.2	28.6	*29.1*
	16	1895	0	43.9	9.8	12.4	*13.1*	0.8	127.1	27.2	44.4	*44.2*
12-18 sq. km	18	1846	0	119.5	39	41.7	*38.6*	1.8	120.4	26.5	32	*31.2*
	18	1866	0	169.7	40.2	46.5	*48.6*	0.5	105.8	23.7	27.9	*25.6*
	18	1880	0	117.6	18.1	27.6	*32.2*	0.1	102.8	15.7	21.8	*23.7*
	18	1895	0	83	9.4	16.5	*22*	0.2	143.3	31.5	37.4	*34*
18-32 sq. km	18	1846	0.2	290.9	58	67.3	*73.1*	19	213.2	67.1	73	*56.3*
	18	1866	2.5	456	58.6	84.9	*107.3*	13.5	229.2	63.5	78.3	*62*
	18	1880	0.9	265.7	34	48.5	*61.1*	13.3	217.4	56.6	67.3	*59*
	19	1895	0	179.1	13.8	26.2	*40.2*	0.1	398.4	63	91.5	*100.5*
>32 sq. km	15	1846	1.1	421.5	32.5	87.8	*115.5*	10.9	198.5	67.5	88.9	*62.9*
	15	1866	0	318.4	57	98.2	*104.4*	8.5	236.7	94.1	92.8	*64.5*
	15	1880	1.1	164.4	41.6	56.6	*55*	6.6	195.7	72.6	83.6	*65.6*
	14	1895	0.8	84.7	12.5	25	*28.8*	0	311	85.9	104.3	*84.7*

			Potatoes					Vegetables				
0-6 sq. km	18	1846	0.9	193.3	16.4	32.5	*46.4*	0	268.9	29.9	50.8	*63.4*
	18	1866	0.3	63.4	7.5	15.1	*20.2*	/	/	/	/	/
	18	1880	0.4	145.2	13.1	36.4	*53.6*	/	/	/	/	/
	19	1895	0.6	184.3	10.1	38.7	*62.5*	0	175.1	36	41.8	*41.9*
6-12 sq. km	17	1846	16.7	231	56.5	65.9	*48.4*	13.9	199.9	96.4	84.4	*53*
	17	1866	3.8	128	36.8	50.2	*36.9*	/	/	/	/	/
	17	1880	3.8	115.8	37	45.1	*34.6*	/	/	/	/	/
	16	1895	0.1	135.4	37	51.1	*42.7*	17.9	292.7	84.9	96.3	*68.3*
12-18 sq. km	18	1846	4	286.4	46.4	58.3	*66*	5.5	215.8	86.3	89.7	*50.7*
	18	1866	4	158.4	40.8	63.4	*53.7*	/	/	/	/	/
	18	1880	2.6	151.5	44.4	50.1	*41.5*	/	/	/	/	/
	18	1895	0.9	138.1	57.5	68.6	*46.5*	13.6	167.2	88.5	88	*46.4*
18-32 sq. km	18	1846	17.1	136.7	70	74.4	*34.8*	22.1	201.2	101.8	107.8	*49.6*
	18	1866	32.5	193.7	71.9	83.1	*42.8*	/	/	/	/	/
	18	1880	7.7	186.3	75.5	81.7	*47.5*	/	/	/	/	/
	19	1895	1.5	193.3	88.1	87.5	*57.7*	8.2	220.1	93.1	88.1	*52.3*
>32 sq. km	15	1846	46.1	324.7	118	121.4	*70.2*	44.2	171	110.4	108.1	*40.2*
	15	1866	52.7	198.2	90.7	106.9	*43*	/	/	/	/	/
	15	1880	15.6	210.2	65.9	76.8	*52.3*	/	/	/	/	/
	14	1895	10.4	210.9	85.4	91.6	*69.3*	41.7	138.7	91.4	89.1	*32.5*

Annexe 2a (Continued)

Size of the peri-urban area			Liquid milk					Butter				
	N	Year	Min.	Max.	Med.	Mean	*St.Dev.*	Min.	Max.	Med.	Mean	*St.Dev.*
0-6 sq. km	18	1846	1.8	91.8	11.2	19.7	*24.2*	2	99.1	12.1	21.2	*26.1*
	18	1866	/	/	/	/	/	/	/	/	/	/
	18	1880	0.9	80.3	8.1	18.3	*24*	0.9	80.6	8.2	18.4	*24.1*
	19	1895	0.6	59.9	9.6	16.1	*16.1*	0.7	63.5	10.1	17.1	*17.1*
6-12 sq. km	17	1846	6.7	103.4	25.3	33.6	*25.3*	7.3	111.6	27.3	36.3	*27.3*
	17	1866	/	/	/	/	/	/	/	/	/	/
	17	1880	1.8	84.8	25.4	35.1	*25.8*	1.8	85.1	25.5	35.2	*25.9*
	16	1895	3.4	74.1	27.5	34.6	*23.5*	3.6	78.6	29.1	36.7	*25*
12-18 sq. km	18	1846	3.9	101.8	33.2	33	*24.6*	4.2	109.9	35.9	35.6	*26.6*
	18	1866	/	/	/	/	/	/	/	/	/	/
	18	1880	1.8	80.5	40	35.1	*23.2*	1.8	80.8	40.1	35.3	*23.3*
	18	1895	1.9	90.3	34	34.6	*22.3*	2	95.8	36	36.7	*23.7*
18-32 sq. km	18	1846	16.7	82.3	42.6	45.9	*20.1*	18	88.9	46	49.5	*21.7*
	18	1866	/	/	/	/	/	/	/	/	/	/
	18	1880	17.9	137.2	49.7	54.1	*32.4*	17.9	137.7	49.9	54.3	*32.5*
	19	1895	2.8	132.6	42	48.9	*36.7*	3	140.7	44.6	51.9	*39*
>32 sq. km	15	1846	29.2	131.6	62	71	*26.2*	31.6	142	67	76.6	*28.3*
	15	1866	/	/	/	/	/	/	/	/	/	/
	15	1880	36.9	156	73.1	85.1	*36.2*	37	156.6	73.4	85.4	*36.3*
	14	1895	35.8	144.6	68.6	77.9	*34.8*	38	153.4	72.8	82.7	*37*

			Beef					Pig meat				
0-6 sq. km	18	1846	1.1	98	9.9	18.9	*24.3*	0.2	178.9	9.7	23.3	*43*
	18	1866	0.8	39.1	4.6	8.7	*10.2*	0.1	243.5	8.6	33.7	*65.3*
	18	1880	0.5	73.5	5.6	12.9	*19.8*	0.2	200.8	5.4	28.6	*60.8*
	19	1895	0.4	64.7	9.4	14.9	*16.5*	0.1	195.6	6	28.6	*50.1*
6-12 sq. km	17	1846	5.8	108.7	35.3	36.9	*24.4*	4.4	135.4	27	37.5	*33.7*
	17	1866	2.6	45.6	15.1	19.1	*11.8*	4.3	130.7	29.6	42	*32.8*
	17	1880	2.5	63.9	25.9	28.5	*20.6*	6.3	108.7	22.9	35.3	*31.3*
	16	1895	2.3	131	25	40.2	*35.9*	4.2	91.2	28.5	36.1	*25.9*
12-18 sq. km	18	1846	3	102.5	27.2	33.4	*27.6*	0.7	232.9	12.7	38.7	*64.1*
	18	1866	1.3	47.2	16.9	17.3	*12.5*	1.9	201.7	10	42.2	*63*
	18	1880	0.8	66.1	25.4	26.2	*20.1*	1.3	200	14.7	40	*58.2*
	18	1895	1.2	102.9	29.9	34.7	*25.9*	2.3	154.8	12.6	42.9	*50.4*
18-32 sq. km	18	1846	13.9	78.6	46.2	45.7	*21.4*	4.6	177.4	39.5	56.6	*46.1*
	18	1866	8.4	57.7	25.3	28.1	*14.6*	7.7	171.4	44.7	71.1	*56.9*
	18	1880	10.3	85.8	35.1	37.8	*22.5*	9.8	180.8	39.1	65.6	*54.7*
	19	1895	1.6	143.7	42.1	49	*39.3*	0.8	298.3	42.6	73.6	*78.8*
>32 sq. km	15	1846	41	166.3	65.2	83.4	*37.5*	23.2	168.2	77.2	86.4	*40.6*
	15	1866	20.5	88.2	38	43.1	*18.4*	28.3	194.9	97.2	99	*51.6*
	15	1880	23.8	137.3	72	70.5	*32.1*	24.1	266.1	103.6	104.5	*67.3*
	14	1895	31.8	187.3	76.8	87.8	*43.2*	24.5	213.9	106.8	101.4	*54.8*

Source: database; Blomme, 1992: 78, 87; Goossens, 1992: 126-127; Gadisseur, 1990: 406-407, 414-415, 418-419.

Annexe 2b p-values (Games-Howell PostHoc test) for different food items revealing statistically significant differences between cities with a different size of peri-urban area (referred to in terms of the surface in square kilometres). 1) = Wheat; 2) = Rye; 3) = Potatoes; 4) = Milk & Butter; 5) = Beef; 6) = Pork; 7) Vegetables (anova with equal variances assumed, Bonferroni PostHoc test)

	0-6 sq. km	**6-12 sq. km**	**12-18 sq. km**	**18-32 sq. km**	**> 32 sq. km**
0-6 sq. km		1) 0.000; 2) 0.000; 3) 0.000; 4) 0.004; 5) 0.000; *7) 0.004*	1) 0.000; 2) 0.000; 3) 0.000; 4) 0.002; 5) 0.001; *7) 0.004*	1) 0.000; 2) 0.000; 3) 0.000; 4) 0.000; 5) 0.000; 6) 0.000; *7) 0.000*	1) 0.000; 2) 0.000; 3) 0.000; 4) 0.000; 5) 0.000; 6) 0.000; *7) 0.000*
6-12 sq. km	1) 0.000; 2) 0.000; 3) 0.000; 4) 0.004; 5) 0.000; *7) 0.004*			2) 0.000; 3) 0.039; 4) 0.043; 6) 0.003	2) 0.000; 3) 0.000; 4) 0.000; 5) 0.000; 6) 0.000
12-18 sq. km	1) 0.000; 2) 0.000; 3) 0.000; 4) 0.002; 5) 0.001; *7) 0.004*			4) 0.029; 5) 0.028	1) 0.045; 3) 0.001; 4) 0.000; 5) 0.000; 6) 0.000
18-32 sq. km	1) 0.000; 2) 0.000; 3) 0.000; 4) 0.000; 5) 0.000; 6) 0.000; *7) 0.000*	2) 0.000; 3) 0.039; 4) 0.043; 6) 0.003	4) 0.029; 5) 0.028		2) 0.000; 4) 0.000; 5) 0.000; 6) 0.018
> 32 sq. km	1) 0.000; 2) 0.000; 3) 0.000; 4) 0.000; 5) 0.000; 6) 0.000; *7) 0.000*	2) 0.000; 3) 0.000; 4) 0.000; 5) 0.000; 6) 0.000	1) 0.045; 3) 0.001; 4) 0.000; 5) 0.000; 6) 0.000	2) 0.000; 4) 0.000; 5) 0.000; 6) 0.018	

Source: database.

Bibliography

Agricultural Markets Task Force (2016) *Improving market outcomes. Enhancing the position of farmers in the supply chain*, Brussels.

Atkinson, A. (2013) 'Readjusting to reality. Urban and peri-urban agriculture to ease downward passage', *City*, 17, 1, pp. 85-96.

Atkins, P. J. (2003) 'Is it urban? The relationship between food production and urban space in Britain, 1800-1950', Hietala, M. and Vahtikari, T. (eds), *The landscape of food: the food relationship of town and country in modern times*, Helsinki, pp. 133-144.

Beavington, F. (1975) 'The development of market gardening in Bedfordshire 1799-1939', *Agricultural history review*, 13, pp. 23-47.

Beyers, L. and Van Damme, I. (eds) (2016) *Antwerpen à la carte. Eten en de stad, van de middeleeuwen tot vandaag*, Antwerp.

Biel, R. (2016) *Sustainable food systems. The role of the city*, London.

Björklund, A. (2010) *Historical urban agriculture. Food production and access to land in Swedish towns before 1900*, Stockholm.

Blake, M., Mellor, J. and Crane, L. (2010) 'Buying local food: shopping practices, place, and consumption networks in defining food as "local"', *Annals of the association of American geographers*, 100, 2, pp. 409-426.

Blomme, J. (1992) *The economic development of Belgian agriculture 1880-1980. A quantitative and qualitative analysis*, Brussels.

Broadway, J. (2013) 'Gloucester gardeners 1650-1763', *Trans. Bristol and Gloucestershire Archaeological Society*, 131, pp. 209-220.

Burchardt, J. (2002) *The allotment movement in England, 1793-1873*, Martlesham.

Castillo, G. (2003) 'Livelihoods and the city: an overview of the emergence of agriculture in urban spaces', *Progress in development studies,* 3, 4, pp. 339-344.

Eeckhout, P. Van den and Scholliers, P. (1983) 'De hoofdelijke voedselconsumptie in België, 1831-1939', *Tijdschrift voor sociale geschiedenis*, 31, pp. 273-301.

Flavell, N. (2003) 'Urban allotment gardens in the eighteenth century: the case of Sheffield', *Agricultural history review*, 51, 1, pp. 95-106.

French, H. (2000) 'Urban agriculture, commons and commoners in the seventeenth and eighteenth centuries: the case of Sudbury, Suffolk', *Agricultural history review*, 48, 2, pp. 171-199.

Gadisseur, J. (1990) *Le produit physique de la Belgique, 1830-1913. Présentation critique des données statistiques*, Brussels.

Goossens, M. (1992) *The economic development of Belgian agriculture: a regional perspective, 1812-1846*, Brussels.

Graef, P. De (2017) 'Food from country to city, waste from city to country: an environmental symbiosis? Fertiliser improvement in eighteenth-century Flanders', *Journal for the history of environment and society*, 2, pp. 25-61.

Graef, P. De and Ronsijn, W. (2017) 'From home food production to professional farming. A social continuum of urban agriculture: 19th-century Oudenaarde and Kortrijk, Belgium', paper presented at the *Rural History Conference*, Leuven.

Gurvil, C. (2010) *Les paysans de Paris du milieu du XVe au début du XVIIe siécle*, Paris.

Hilton, R. H. (1975) *The English peasantry in the later Middle Ages*, New York.

Jäschke, K. U. and Schrenk, C. (eds) (2003) *Ackerbürgertum und Stadtwirtschaft: zu Regionen und Perioden landwirtschaftlich bestimmten Städtewesens im Mittelalter*, Heilbronn.

Karel, E., Vanhaute, E. and Paping, R. (2011) 'The Low Countries, 1750-2000', in: Vanhaute, E., Devos, I. and Lambrecht, T. (eds) *Making a living: family, labour and income*, Rural economy and society in North-western Europe, 500-2000, Turnhout, pp. 185-207.

Kint, Ph. (1989) *Prometheus aangevuurd door Demeter. De economische ontwikkeling van de landbouw in Oost-Vlaanderen 1815-1850*, Amsterdam.

Kopsidis, M. and Wolf, N. (2012) 'Agricultural productivity across Prussia during the Industrial Revolution: a Thünen perspective', *The journal of economic history*, 72, 3, pp. 634-670.

Leuven, Eddy Van (1990) *Bijdrage tot de tuinbouwgeschiedenis: de Belgische groenteteelt, 1830-1914*, Aartrijke.

Limberger, M. (2008) *Sixteenth-century Antwerp and its rural surroundings. Social and economic changes in the hinterland of a commercial metropolis (ca. 1450-ca. 1570)*, Turnhout.

Lis, C. and Soly, H. (1977) 'Food consumption in Antwerp between 1807 and 1859: a contribution to the standard of living debate', *Economic history review*, 30, 3, pp. 460-486.

McClintock, N. (2010) 'Why farm the city? Theorizing urban agriculture through a lens of metabolic rift', *Journal of regions, economy and society*, 3, pp. 191-207.

Molle, L. Van and Segers, Y. (eds) (2013) *The agro-food market: production, distribution and consumption*, Rural economy and society in North-western Europe, 500-2000, Turnhout.

Moore, J. (2000) 'Environmental crises and the metabolic rift in world-historical perspective', *Organization and environment*, 13, 2, pp. 123-157.

Mougeot, L. (2006) *Growing better cities. Urban agriculture for sustainable development*, Ottawa.

Nützenadel, A. and Trentmann, F. (eds) (2008) *Food and globalization. Consumption, markets and politics in the modern world*, London/Oxford.

Parham, S. (2015) *Food and urbanism: the convivial city and a sustainable future*, New York.

O'Kelly, M. and Bryan, D. (1996) 'Agricultural location theory: von Thünen's contribution to economic geography', *Progress in Human Geography*, 20, 4, pp. 457-475.

Ronsijn, W. (2014) *Commerce and the countryside. The rural population's involvement in the commodity market in Flanders, 1750-1910*, Ghent.

Scholliers, P. (1991) 'Industrial wage differentials in nineteenth-century Belgium', in: Brenner, Y. S., Kaelble, H. and Thomas, M. (eds) *Income distribution in historical perspective*, Cambridge, pp. 96-116.

Scholliers, P. (1993) *Arm en rijk aan tafel. Tweehonderd jaar eetcultuur in België*, Berchem.

Segers, Y. (2001) 'Oysters and rye bread: polarising living standards in Flanders, 1800-1860', *European review of economic history*, 5, pp. 301-336.

Segers, Y. (2003) *Economische groei en levensstandaard. De ontwikkeling van de particuliere consumptie en het voedselverbruik in België, 1800-1913*, Leuven.

Segers, Y. and Dejongh, G. (2000) 'De hoofdelijke voedselconsumptie in België, 1830-1913. Reconstructie dataset en analyse', Segers, Y. et al. (eds) *Op weg naar een consumptiemaatschappij. Over het gebruik van voeding, kleding en luxegoederen in België en Nederland (19ᵈᵉ-20ˢᵗᵉ eeuw)*, Leuven.

Smith, J., Kostelecký, T. and Jehlička, P. (2015) 'Quietly does it: questioning assumptions about class, sustainability and consumption', *Geoforum*, 67, pp. 223-332.

Stanhill, G. (1977) 'An urban agro-ecosystem: the example of nineteenth-century Paris', *Agro-ecosystems*, 3, pp. 269-284.

Steel, C. (2008) *The hungry city. How food shapes our lives*, London.

Taylor, J. R. and Taylor Lovell, S. (2014) 'Urban home food gardens in the global north: research traditions and future directions', *Agriculture and human values*, 31, pp. 285-305.

Thoen, E. and Soens, T. (2015) 'Contextualizing 1500 years of agricultural productivity and land use in the North Sea area. Regionally divergent paths towards the world top', Thoen, E. and Soens, T. (eds) *Struggling with the environment: land use and productivity*, Rural economy and society in North-western Europe, 500-2000, Turnhout, pp. 455-499.

Thomas, J. H. (1978) 'Gardens, gardeners, nurserymen and seedsmen in Wiltshire 1700-1845', *Wiltshire archaeological and natural history magazine*, 91, pp. 113-127.

Vandenbroeke, C. (1990) 'La culture de la pomme de terre en Belgique (XVIIᵉ-XIXᵉ siècles)', *Plantes et cultures nouvelles. Douzièmes journées internationales d'histoire du centre culturel de l'Abbaye de Flaran*, pp. 115-129.

Vermoesen, R. (2015) 'Boerende stedelingen of verstedelijkte boeren. Een verkennend onderzoek naar *urban farming* in vroegmodern Antwerpen', *Tijdschrift voor geschiedenis*, 128, 4, pp. 533-553.

Vries, J. de (1994) 'The production and consumption of wheat in the Netherlands, with special reference to Zeeland in 1789', Diederiks, H., Lindblad, J. T. and de Vries, B. (eds) *Het platteland in een veranderende wereld. Boeren en het proces van modernisering*, Hilversum, pp. 199-219.

8 Between fearing shortage and stockpiling fresh fish: did the Venetian Republic have an environmental policy in the eighteenth century?*

Solène Rivoal, Aix-Marseille Université, CNRS, UMR 7303 TELEMMe, Birkbeck

This paper aims to study the legislative rhetoric developed by the Venetian Government and its concern about the potential shortage of fresh fish. In the early modern period, the inhabitants of Venice sustained themselves largely from the sea's natural resources, generally referred to in the sources as "*pesce*" (fish). This situation can be explained by the location of Venice on a lagoon. As a result, creating an efficient supply chain, from fishing to distribution, was a concern that greatly occupied the *Giustizia Vecchia*, the Venetian magistrates in charge of the city's trades and markets (Da Mosto, 1937: 191-193). Similar to grain in other cities, fish was a common food in Venice. For this reason, a fear of shortage prompted considerable reflection in the Venetian government.

Historians have been interested in studying political measures taken by governments to provide cities with grain (Kaplan, 1976; Vertecchi, 2009). In contrast, seafood has not attracted the same level of interest. Similarly, across disciplines fishing is often omitted in studies on agricultural environments and supplies, whether agronomy, geography or sociology (Fagan, 2018).[1] However, seafood has generated, and continues to generate, strong economic dynamics in the agri-food sectors[2] and must be taken into account from an economic, social, political and environmental point of view. In early modern Venice, authorities established policies to supply all urban inhabitants with seafood products, in order to ensure that city stalls were always supplied with high quality products at affordable prices.

* This work has been produced within the framework of the Unit of Excellence LabexMed – Social Sciences and Humanities at the heart of multidisciplinary research for the Mediterranean – which holds the following reference 10-LABX-0090. This publication has received funding from Excellence Initiative of Aix- Marseille University- A*MIDEX, a French "Investissements d'Avenir" programme.

[1] With regard to Venice, recent major studies which aimed to provide a global synthesis of all the political, economic, social and religious aspects of the Republic of Venice have rarely included information concerning fishing activities, fish consumption and fishing communities, despite its potential to provide insight onto Venetian society and the ways in which the Republic functioned. See, for example, the collection of Treccani encyclopedias, which published some twenty volumes entitled *Storia di Venezia* between 1995 and 2002: none of them mentioned these activities. Also see the first issue of *Archivio Veneto's* 6th collection (S. 6, 2011/1), which provides an overview of historical research on the Republic of Venice in the Middle Ages and the early modern period. Once again, nothing is written here about fishing.

[2] For the French case, see in particular Abad, 2002, especially chapter 1 in Book II, p. 398.

Stocks, seasons and sales: Food supply, storage and markets in Europe and the New World, c. 1600-2000, ed. by Wouter Ronsijn, Niccolò Mignemi and Laurent Herment, CORN 17 (Turnhout, 2019), pp. 181-192.

DOI: 10.1484/M.CORN-EB.5.118259

In the Venetian archives, legislative texts, especially documents produced by the Senate and the *Giustizia Vecchia*, reveal that fish supplies were a cause of concern throughout the medieval and early modern periods. In particular, the internal reports (*scritture*), written by the *Giustizia Vecchia* documenting the debates and internal reports within the Venetian Senate, show the importance of these supply policies. These sources give access to how Venetian authorities made laws. They also reveal the principles that influenced the city authorities' decision making. They illuminate how the magistrates frequently worried about possible fish shortages in the markets, as the term *penuria* appears repeatedly. Two types of shortage were feared by the *Giustizia Vecchia*:

- Firstly, they were afraid that too few fish would reach the markets for the city's inhabitants.
- Secondly, they feared that the primary source for the local supply of fish, the lagoon, would become depleted, thus causing a long-term shortage for the Venetian markets.

Even though fish supplies varied throughout the century, the city seems not to have experienced any real shortage that caused a disruption in supply. Thus, the challenge here is to study the social, environmental, and economic impact of these discourses about scarcity. This rhetoric existed throughout the early modern period. However, in the eighteenth century the fear of scarcity reshaped the economic and social system of Venice's fishing industry by linking production to distribution, and became a driving force behind the Venetian authorities' political thinking. In order to protect the lagoon's capacity to supply the markets, the Venetian authorities strengthened their control over local food resources: they took advantage of any tool at their disposal to implement far-reaching solutions (Rivoal, 2018).

These measures largely concerned fishing practices. In particular, they passed an increasingly complex set of laws concerning lagoon fishing: the lagoon was perceived by the magistrates as a *bona fide* warehouse, and thus they wanted full control over the existing stocks of fish in the lagoon.[3] Subsequently, by redefining the different areas within the lagoon, the *valli da pesca* (fish farming zones) were treated as storage areas for fresh fish, a move strongly favoured by the *Giustizia Vecchia* magistrates, perhaps to the detriment of protecting fishery resources.

I. Feeding the city with fish

No source from the eighteenth century (Venetian magistrates' archives, chronicles, gazettes, etc.) indicates that there was ever a lack of seafood in Venetian market stalls. Yet, the fear of scarcity was repeatedly vocalized by the magistrates who managed these activities. One of the main reasons for this concern is undoubtedly how important fresh fish was for the city's inhabitants. Indeed, all Venetian inhabitants consumed fresh fish. Some seafood products, such as sea bass and sea bream, were together referred to as

[3] Although these concepts (warehouse and storage) are borrowed from a vocabulary used to describe current practices, they will be used here as they can accommodate the concerns of eighteenth-century Venetian magistrates.

"white fish" and were primarily intended for the city's elites.[4] In contrast, "black fish" included the smallest fish such as mullet or red mullet, crustaceans, and also shellfish, and was considered by the magistrates to be a basic food consumed by a large number of the city's inhabitants (Rivoal, 2018). In the sources, the vocabulary used by the magistrates throughout the century reflected the important place of fresh fish in the daily diet. Thus, "the fresh fish that is so necessary for the *Dominante* (the city of Venice)" in 1707,[5] echoed the "such important traffic in this area" in 1713;[6] in 1748, it was necessary "to promote the abundance of this commodity for the convenience and benefit of this city in all possible ways" being "very important for the common benefit [...] [and the] people".[7] Again in 1748, it was mentioned that "a large portion of the fish caught by these companies consists of cheap fish (*menuaggia* and *pesce popolo*), so called because it is used to supply those living in poverty". In 1762, the magistrates once again wrote that fish was "a means of supporting poor families",[8] and in 1765 that fish was presented as "a commodity so necessary to sustain the population and the poor" and as a food "which must not be in short supply for the population, especially the poor, [with] this commodity being indispensable to their satisfaction".[9] Throughout the century, the rhetoric used by the magistrates in charge of controlling these foods focused above all on popular consumption, and exposes the concern felt by Venetian authorities about the potential lack of supplies of fish.

This is why the reduction in the lagoon's capacity was worrying. The two areas of production – i.e. the two fishing areas that supplied Venice with fresh fish – were the lagoon and, after new fishing techniques were increasingly used in the seventeenth century, the Adriatic Sea. Nevertheless, most black fish was caught in the Venetian lagoon around the city. For the magistrates, managing possible market shortages was directly linked to governing the fish "stock", understood as a permanent and readily available supply of fish in the lagoon for the city's consumption. This conception was expressly linked to the shape of the lagoon, which was presented as a restricted area and precisely demarcated by the Venetian magistrates. The organisation of this area was also entirely controlled by the Venetians who had developed and modified it continuously since the first human settlements.

---

4 Archivio di Stato di Venezia (henceforth ASVe), *Giustizia Vecchia* (henceforth GV), busta (henceforth b.) 5, registro (now reg.) 13., 29r to 31r.

5 ASVe, *Senato terra* (henceforth ST), filza (henceforth f.) 1366, fol. n.n., decree, 17th March 1707: "La vendita del pesce fresco tanto necessario per la presente Dominante".

6 ASVe, ST, f. 1461, fol. n.n., decree, 23th February 1713: " Nella materia de traffico tanto importante".

7 ASVe, ST, f. 2088, fol. n.n., decree, 5th February 1748: "L'oggetto importantissimo di promovere l'ubertà di questa Vittuaria a comodo e benefico della città per tutte le vie possibili [...] importantissimo per il comun benefizio [...] e benefizio del popolo".

8 ASVe, ST, f. 2367, fol. n.n., decree, 20th January 1762: "Un modo di sostenere le povere famiglie".

9 ASVe, ST, f. 2425, fol. n.n., decree, 9th January 1765: "Una vittuaria necessaria al mantenimento della popolazione e dei poveri [...] onde non manchi alla popolazione, principalmente alla povertà una vittuaria con indispensabile al loro contentamento".

As early as the fourteenth century, Venetian archives reveal concerns about the numbers of fish in the lagoon, which were supposedly becoming increasingly uncertain. Therefore, fish was understood as a resource that needed to be protected in order to prevent scarcity. From the Middle Ages to the early modern period, the city's consumption of fish and the number of fishermen operating in the lagoon put constant pressure on the reproductive capacities of the lagoon's fish. While these discourses about the fear of scarcity have been known from the Middle Ages (Zanetti, 1995, 289), sources from the end of the early modern period reveal theories about the cause of this decline. For Venetian authorities, the scarcity of available resources resulted from overfishing in the lagoon, meaning that any possible shortages were therefore man-made. The lagoon's fish was caught predominantly by men from a range of different communities.[10] These communities were defined as social groups consisting of all workers involved in the fish trade (fishermen, fishmongers and others sellers) grouped according to the territories they inhabited (Zago, 1982; Rivoal, 2015). Different types of fishermen lived in each community: those who fished primarily for fish offshore on boats in the Adriatic, and those who fished in the lagoon. The latter group was divided between the fishing activities of casting fixed nets, catching using movable nets thrown from small boats, and catching through the use of forks as fishermen walked through the swamps. In 1760, when new laws were introduced to regulate fishing activities, the *Giustizia Vecchia* wrote:

> Fishermen should show interest in this subject [scarcity], not only by obeying public laws, but also by virtue of the link that their particular interests have with this matter, for if they allowed this fish to grow, and if they caught it during the appropriate seasons, they would create a happy freedom and a universal benefit, the fulfilment of productive fishing, a real advantage for these same fishermen; but out of malice and greed, acting against the will of public organisations, against the common good and for their own usefulness, with an incorrigible and scandalous sense of personal right, some have taken the liberty to fish everywhere and at all times, using very dangerous equipment that is universally prohibited [...] which tends to render the resources of these lagoons, canals and waters sterile and poor.[11]

---

[10] At least five communities existed on the lagoon in the eighteenth century. Two of them were situated on the city's land, the *Nicolotti* based in the two parishes of San Nicolò dei Mendicoli and of San Angelo Raffaele, and the *Povegiotti* based between the parish of Sant' Agnese and the island of la Giudecca. The other three were divided between the most-populated islands: Murano, Burano and Chioggia.

[11] ASVe, *Compilazzione delle leggi* (now CL), Serie (now S.) 1, b. 302, fol. 538: "Sebbene nel grave argomento dove vano interessarsi da sè medesimi i Pescatori, non solo per quell'obbedienza, che devessi alle Pubbliche leggi, ma per quella conessione, che tiene con la materia il loro medesimo interesse poiché se il pesce si lasciasse crescere, e dalle sole opportune permesse stagioni li pescasse apporterebbe una gioconda ubertà a benefizio universale, e nella felicità delle Pesche copiose, un vero sensibile vantaggio a pescatori medesimi; tutta via la malizia, e d'ingordigia d'alcuni contro operando al voler delle pubbliche organizzazioni, ai riguardi del comun bene, ed a quelli dell'utilità propria, con dannoso corteggibile libertinaggio, con scandalo, e pessimo esempio si sono rilasciati a praticarne la Pesca in tutti i luoghi, in tutti in tempi con uso e d'invenzioni d'arti dannosissime, ed universalmente proibite, causando con ciò la totale distruzione del Pesce novello, che in gran parte perisce nell'atto della pesca, e d'esser tratto dal suo medio e rende sterile, e povera la Pescaggione di queste Lagune, Canali ed Acque dove dal Mare si ricovrà per alimentarsi e crescere".

This passage clearly demonstrates that, in the eyes of the magistrates, fishermen were the reason that the government did not achieve the benefits they desired: the sense of freedom, universal benefit, happiness and the common good (*comun bene*). The rhetoric used here evokes principles of a *politique annonaire* interwoven with a wish to control certain types of behaviour seen as harmful to a community (Thompson, 1975; Martinat, 2002). For example, the Republic of Venice also had a pricing policy for each species of fish according to its weight and quality.[12]

Thus, for the Venetian government, a reduction of resources in the lagoon that might lead to a market shortage was not a problem of natural cycle. Rather, it was the negative evolution of local production that was increasingly threatened. Subsequently, this enabled the authorities to put policies into place to protect this area.[13] Although restrictive measures existed as early as the Middle Ages, the *Giustizia Vecchia* used the fear of shortage in the eighteenth century as a driving force to introduce measures regarding supplies: they were not content simply with reducing fishing activities, but were looking for far-reaching solutions. These changes, which took place primarily between 1760 and 1781[14], were part of a reform movement instigated by Venetian patricians, some of whom wanted to review the city's economic and social organisation in the light of the new economic and political theories that were circulating throughout Europe at that time (Venturi, 1990: 12).

At the heart of these measures was a desire to know more about the Venetian seafood supply system. From the 1760s onwards, magistrates tried to collect data on fishing activities, ranging from the number of fishermen to the number of boats available for fishing in the lagoon and the Adriatic Sea. Magistrates also tried to collect data on fish markets and fish consumption in the city. Although these studies are no longer extant, they were repeatedly cited in Senate decrees during the second half of the eighteenth century, and some *scritture* retained traces of this policy. For instance, in 1765, the *Giustizia Vecchia* noted in a *scrittura* to the Senate that some Venetian inhabitants consumed two pounds of fish per head every week (Marangoni, 1974: 127).[15] In 1780, these same magistrates wrote another *scrittura* listing the number of large offshore fishing boats that were active,

---

[12] ASVe, Misc. Stampa, b. 112, fol. n.n., *terminazione*, 10th March 1706 for prices before 1707; ASVe, ST, f. 1856, fol. n.n., decree, 27th June 1737, for 1707 and 1737 prices; ASVe, CL, S.1, b. 302, fol. 112-114, for 1760 prices.

[13] See *La pesca nella laguna di Venezia. Antologia storica di testi sulla pesca nella laguna, sulla sua legislazione, sul popolo, la lingua e il lavoro dei pescatori sui pesci e sulla cucina*, Venice, Amministrazione della provincia di Venezia, 1981, p. 7.

[14] ASVe, CL, S. 1, b. 302, fol. 537-543: 4th September 1760; fol. 567-574: 30th July 1781.

[15] The author submitted a transcription of this document dated 23 August 1763. However, the original document has not been found in the archives and some doubts remain, such as the number of inhabitants concerned and the unit used in this text. Indeed, the pound (called *libbre*) can be *sottile* (about 300 grams) or *grossa* (about 480 grams). Similarly, Giovanni Marangoni, who transcribed this document, did not provide details on how this survey was constructed. This figure should therefore be treated with caution. However, a comparison with other large cities in the early modern period for which we have data (notably Paris, Marseille, Rome and Naples) reveals that consumption was high (Rivoal, 2018).

as well as the number of boats in the Venetian fishing community of San Nicolò, as a means of demonstrating that these same fishermen had capacity to supply fish to the city.[16]

Finally, these studies were used by the magistrates to take new measures concerning the supply of fish, arguing that the aim was to minimise the precariousness of lagoon resources and thus resolve the perceived problem of shortage.

II. Thinking the lagoon as a fish stock area

On the basis of this data, Venetian magistrates took various measures to protect the renewal of resources in the lagoon. The first measure was to encourage fishermen to build more boats suited to fishing in the Adriatic Sea rather than in the lagoon (Perini, 1989: 185-186). Incentives were often financial, with the bosses of fleets of boats gradually becoming exempt from taxes on fish entering the market. The second measure consisted of limiting fishing in the lagoon, as a means of safeguarding fish stocks.

During the eighteenth century, activities related to the fish trade were subject to an almost total legal overhaul: in the 1720s, in 1760 and in 1781.[17] In each case, the main motivation for this legislative reorganisation was the perceived decrease in supplies and the risk of shortage. The *Giustizia Vecchia* expressed this concern in the *scritture*, whilst at the same time sending new fishing orders for approval by the Senate.

For the authorities, the lagoon area, an area of well-defined swamps around Venice, needed to become a fishery warehouse regulated by the government in order to protect the threatened fish stock. There were very few opportunities to improve fresh fish stocks, the main reason being conservation. Once caught, fish had to be sold extremely quickly. Merchants sometimes kept their goods in wicker baskets immersed in the canals around the marketplaces.[18] However, this practice was not encouraged by the magistrates.[19] Thus, as there were no warehouses for storing fresh fish, one might consider that storage took place before fishing.

The stocks in the lagoon depended on one specific element: young fish (*pesce novello*, also known as *novellame*), which was fundamental to the renewal of resources. From the fifteenth century onwards, fishermen were closely monitored and their trade gradually controlled. However, from the second half of the eighteenth century onwards, the new fishing regulations focused on the *pesce novello*. In 1760, out of the twenty-four articles that existed, the new law included ten articles that specifically targeted the fishing of little fish. In the *incipit*, the justifications for a legislative change underscored the urgent need to preserve lagoon resources.[20] Subsequently, the magistrates stated that catching the youngest species before it had reached maturity had two harmful consequences. Firstly,

[16] ASVe, CL, S. 1, b. 302, fol. 577r.

[17] ASVe, CL, S. 1, b. 302, fol. 1085: 7th May 1726; fol. 537-543: 4th September 1760; fol. 567-574: 30th July 1781; fol. 1152: 30th January 1791.

[18] ASVe, *Inquisitorato alle Arti* (henceforth IA), b. 69, fasc. *bilanci*, fol. 68.

[19] Biblioteca Museo Correr (henceforth BMC), manoscritto (henceforth ms.), cl. IV, n° 98, *Mariegola dei compravendi pesce*, p. 130; ASVe, CL, S.1, b. 302, fol. 647, 1083.

[20] ASVe, CL, S. 1, b. 302, fol. 537r.

young fish that had been caught did not have sufficient time to reach their adult state, and therefore the quality of the catch and the quantity of food was insufficient. Secondly, this fish was essential for replenishing the lagoon, so if it was caught, it would not have time to reproduce.

Despite laws becoming more complex in 1760 and 1781, increasing yet again in the number of their articles, the limitations imposed on lagoon fishing remained constant and applied to three sections: to fishing times, to the places used by the fishermen, and finally to the objects and equipment used to fish.

With regard to fishing times, we know less about weekly cycles of fishing and more about annual cycles. The vast majority of regulations targeted the period between March and October, the breeding period for the fish.[21] During this time of year, fish, which was newly-born near the coast and at sea, entered the lagoon's waters which provided an environment favourable to their growth: the brackish waters were warmer and filled with vegetation barriers that both protected the young fish from predators and also enabled them to feed. This phenomenon was called *montata* or *montada* in the sources, and was known to fishermen and magistrates alike. *Montata* referred to the moment at which young fish came and replenished fish stocks in the heart of the lagoon (Zecchin, 1994: 17). There were many legislative limitations on the *montata*, which reinforced the idea that the lagoon was a vast storage space for fresh fish.

In terms of location, fishermen were increasingly limited as to where they could cast their nets or fish with forks. Indeed, access to the *barene* areas – land that was barely submerged and where small fish took refuge – was gradually banned by Venetian authorities between 1726 and 1781 (Bullo, 1940: 172). Other restrictions also concerned conflicts over the use of the lagoon: for instance, fishermen were prohibited from casting large nets in certain canals, so as not to hinder vessel circulation and Venetian port traffic.[22]

Finally, the third restriction concerned equipment, especially nets. The authorities' continual attention was in keeping with the state's desire to preserve the freedom of the youngest fish. Therefore, restrictions concerning the width of the mesh used for nets[23] were implemented, which determined that nets be large enough for young fish to swim through. This resulted in standardised nets. Each year, a commission composed of *fanti* (judicial guards), magistrates, and fishermen decided on the mesh size for the different nets. These decisions were adopted by establishing model nets, which were kept under lock and key at the *Giustizia Vecchia* headquarters.[24]

These measures were not new in the eighteenth century. Reference was made to restrictions on lagoon fishing in the fourteenth century, although the actual date of when these restrictions were implemented is unknown. However, at the end of the early modern period, and during the period under study, restrictions became increasingly detailed and complex for small-scale fishermen who used their fishing-boats in open marshes.

---

[21] ASVe, CL, S. 1, b. 302, fol. 540r.

[22] Biblioteca Querini Stampalia (henceforth BQS), ms., Ist. 12, *Compendio dei decreti et terminazioni più essentiali delle Acque* (1706): see "laguna" p. 81 to 103; and "valli" p. 116 to 119.

[23] ASVe, CL, S. 1, b. 302, fol. 543v.

[24] ASVe, CL, S.1, b. 302, fol. 539r.

Moreover, controls were strengthened. As from the Middle Ages, the *fanti* who worked for the *Giustizia Vecchia*, often accompanied by the leaders of fishing communities, patrolled the lagoon area to ensure that the standards set by the urban authorities were enforced. However, in 1781, the patricians of the Giustizia Vecchia decided to create a permanent patrol comprising four boats, each with six men, whose sole function was to track down fishing fraud in the lagoon.[25]

Judicial sources raise questions about the effective application of these published laws. Cases of prohibited fishing practices undertaken by the *Giustizia Vecchia* increased after the publication of the 1760 law. More importantly, each case involved several fishermen who were very often caught during the patrols in the lagoon. These sources show that while the fishermen's practices were not in keeping with the published laws, the magistrates were more concerned about implementing the regulations correctly.

Similarly, to limit pressure on resources of fish – pressure that the magistrates attributed to the fishermen – the *Giustizia Vecchia* encouraged them to fish at sea rather than in the lagoon. This solution was seen as doubly profitable. On the one hand, it limited the number of fishermen in the lagoon, thereby reducing the pressure on available stocks. On the other hand, the large boats that left for the open sea also helped to supply the Venetian markets, as these boats had much higher yields than the small lagoon boats. Throughout the eighteenth century, sardine fishing increased, especially in the Adriatic Sea. Schools of sardines were plentiful, and bountiful fishing made it possible to supply the city with cheap food. In terms of stocks and flow, the magistrates' logic was simple: all fresh fish which was caught in the northern Adriatic Sea were to be taken to Venice and sold in the Rialto market and therefore widely consumed across the city.

These measures demonstrate the extent to which authorities wished to limit fishermen's activities, in order to safeguard fishing because of authorities' fear of shortage. Some historians have described this as an environmental policy, as they consider that the Venetian authorities took an interest in the renewal of lagoon resources from very early on (Bevilacqua, 1996: 50, 79). A more in-depth analysis focusing on the different elements, especially fisheries in the lagoon, demonstrate that the policy which was in place in the eighteenth century seemed to challenge the idea on which the authorities based their early environmental concerns.

III. Was increasing lagoon stocks an ecological measure?

Throughout the eighteenth century, the lagoon was not uniformly regulated, and thus the space did not constitute a cohesive whole. Although *vagantiva* fishing – open fishing carried out in canals and open areas of public waters – was increasingly reduced, this was not the case for another activity linked to the fish trade: *valli da pesca* (fisheries).

Areas developed for fish farming had been documented since the early days of the lagoon's occupation. These structures were one of the productive spaces developed near the city (Zug Tucci, 1992: 491). Whereas in the Middle Ages the dominant activity was

[25] ASVe, GV, b. 22, reg. 16, p. 1v.

salt manufacturing (Hocquet, 1978 and 2012), in the eighteenth century the most important water facilities were those specifically designated for fishing (Caniato, 2009: 4-5). The fisheries occupied different bodies of water in which to breed fish and separate it according to their species, the most common being sea bream (Zanetti, 2009: 46-47). The vocabulary used in the sources described large fish storage areas: the fish was kept in a demarcated area, waiting to be used and transported elsewhere. Moreover, the sources refer to practices that were very different from the characteristics of fishing. For example, authorities used the expression "fields of water" (*campi d'acqua*), and the verb "to gather" (*raccogliere*) fish. Beyond the obvious connection with agricultural activities, which further reinforced the parallels that could be drawn between the *politiques annonaires* of grain, fisheries were also a means of limiting the risks and uncertainties associated with fishing. Indeed, whereas fishing on the high seas depended on maritime and meteorological conditions, and whereas open fishing in the lagoon was often limited in scope, fisheries provided a steadier albeit seasonal supply for markets.

Until the eighteenth century, the internal socio-economic functioning of fisheries was not well known: they were large properties owned largely by patricians and religious institutions not directly managed by Venetian authorities (Franzoi, Penzo, Pellizzato, 2002: 100). However, by the end of the early modern period, the *Giustizia Vecchia* gradually gained a greater right of scrutiny over the fisheries. For instance, this strengthening of control over the latter, the yields from the fish farming enclosures, as well as the boats that transported fish to the San Marco and Rialto markets, were all consistent with a favourable policy to further develop these structures. Thus, the fishermen who had been accustomed to unrestricted fishing now regularly complained about the expansion of the fisheries, saying that the fisheries worked to the detriment of the open waters of the lagoon.[26]

Nevertheless, the magistrates showed their favour for fisheries primarily through granting rights related to *pesce novello*. Indeed, the fisheries were successful thanks to the *montada* phenomenon, as mentioned above. In March, the fish enclosures were opened which allowed young fish to enter the swamps; the fish was then confined to this area. In spite of this, fish farmers throughout the eighteenth century complained that insufficient numbers of small fish entered the enclosures for yearly yields to be productive. Subsequently, the 1760 law mentioned above marked a turning point in the management of lagoon resources. Indeed, the 1760 law authorised the fisheries to rebuild their stocks by catching young fish outside their perimeter and then bringing it back to their enclosures until the fish reached maturity. This practice was tightly regulated but it was nevertheless legalised with the 1760 law, despite previously being strictly prohibited because this activity was thought to deplete the lagoon. This practice was managed through a system of licences issued to fishermen employed by fisheries who were authorised to catch only certain species of fish on very specific dates, determined by a system of drawing lots for the right to fish in the marshes. For instance, in the 1760 law permits for fishing for small sea bream were issued between 10 May and 19 June, and those for small sardines were issued between 10 June and 29 September.[27] Each registered fisherman's name was

---

[26] BMC, ms., cl. IV, n°112, *Mariegola della comunità di San Nicolò de mendicoli e dell'Angelo Raffael*, p. 163r.
[27] ASVe, CL, S. 1, b. 302, fol. 537r to 543v.

randomly associated with a particular area, a swamp (*palude*), through the drawing of lots in which each fisherman was able to set traps for several weeks.[28]

This supply policy favouring the fisheries can be explained by the fear of shortage felt by magistrates. Indeed, fisheries were seen as the most reliable means of obtaining a reasonable and sufficient supply of fish. Thus, the risks and unforeseen occurrences associated with fishing were less significant in this type of intensive farming system.

Moreover, this policy raises the issue of whether the Venetian government was implementing an environmental policy at that time.[29] On the one hand, although fishing for young fish in the lagoon was sanctioned throughout the early modern period and before, the 1760 law in fact made it legal for the first time. Nevertheless, this practice was criticised throughout much of the early modern period, as it was said to be responsible for the reduction in the number of species in the lagoon. In addition, transporting the young fish from the lagoon to the fisheries in containers caused significant losses, with many of the fish dying en route and thus further weakening the lagoon resources.[30] Nevertheless, in 1781, with a reappraisal of fishing regulations[31], these measures were not only maintained but also extended. Magistrates effectively decided to widen, in particular, the boundaries for catching young fish, thus reiterating the direction taken by Venetian authorities twenty years before, towards a policy of rationing fishing rather than protecting lagoon resources.

Despite these measures being taken to prevent shortage in food markets, the assumption is that they caused other types of shortages.

Firstly, the large fishery traders in the lagoon, generally the richest fishermen, and their employees were ultimately favoured to the detriment of independent fishermen, who were generally poorer. In fact, poor independent fishermen saw their stock of possible catches steadily decline. This situation created paradoxical pressures. On the one hand, the lagoon's productive fisheries were, at that time, focused on intensive fishing. On the other hand, the survival of the lagoon's fishermen depended on their ability to fish freely, and the extension of the fisheries went against this principle.

Secondly, small-scale fishermen became increasingly involved in this small-fish trade because the purchase of young fish was a much more lucrative activity than the sale of a few catches of larger fish on the markets. This new trade of lagoon fishing weakened the lagoon resources and sidetracked some fishermen from their primary function: that of supplying fish markets.

Finally, seafood from the fish farming zones was generally sold at the market at a higher price than fish caught in the lagoon. Subsequently, the consumption of white fish increased, but possibly to the detriment of cheaper species consumed more regularly by a large part of the population. The reduction of "black fish" was therefore likely caused by a general decrease in available fish in the open lagoon following the increased number of farmed fish, and also because many fishermen involved themselves in these activities, thereby fundamentally changing the supply mechanisms for the Venetian markets.

---

[28] Ibid.

[29] These assumptions have already been raised by Brian Payne, see Payne (2013: 29-43).

[30] ASVe, GV, b. 84, fasc. 120, 19r.

[31] ASVe, CL, S. 1, b. 302, fol. 567r to 572v.

IV. Conclusion

Even though the "shortages" in the markets, so feared by the magistrates, seemed to be a perpetual concern, it is necessary to examine the scarcity of lagoon resources over time. It is certain that, if the authorities raised this point as early as the Middle Ages, a decrease had undoubtedly been observed, but concern may also have been due to the increase in the number of fishermen, which went hand in hand with increases in the urban population. Historians of fishing working on a long-term basis with marine biologists have determined the date of overexploiting fishery resources, especially from the eighteenth century onwards, to when large-scale trawl nets radically changed the number of fish caught. Thus, there may still be doubts as to whether there was truly any resource depletion. Nevertheless, political rhetoric highlighting this eventuality seems to have been the driving force behind lagoon management policies that changed during the eighteenth century.

From the Middle Ages, the fear of market shortage led the *Giustizia Vecchia* increasingly to control lagoon fishing activities. Thus, until the end of the seventeenth century, fishing was controlled as a means of enabling numerous species of fish to reproduce and grow in numbers, and thus to preserve the fishery resources that supplied the markets. However, in the eighteenth century, at a time when economic and political knowledge was developing, magistrates chose to advocate fish farming in order to better predict fishing yields. The confidence placed in these intensive systems was based on the government's fear of shortage in the markets. Yet, this organisation led to other forms of shortfalls. Firstly, independent fishermen's activities in the lagoon seemed to become secondary. Secondly, this organisation challenges the image of Venice as a government which espoused an environmental policy. Instead, Venice's policies were designed to favour market returns rather than protecting lagoon resources, as the authorities allowed young fish to be farmed to supply the markets, which thus jeopardised the renewal of many species.

Bibliography

Abad, R. (2002) *Le Grand marché. L'approvisionnement alimentaire de Paris sous l'Ancien Régime*, Paris.

Bevilacqua, P. (1996) *Venise et l'eau*, Paris.

Bullo, G. (1940) *Le valli salse da pesca e la vallicoltura*, Venice.

Caniato, G., Turri, E. and Zanetti, M. (eds) (1995) *La Laguna di Venezia*, Verona.

Caniato G. et al. (2009) *Valli Veneziane. Natura, storia e tradizioni delle valli da pesca a Venezia e Caorle*, Venice.

Caniato, G. (1997) 'Il controllo delle acque', Benzoni, G. and Cozzi, G. (eds), *Storia di Venezia. Dalle origini alla caduta della Serenissima, vol. VII, la Venezia barocca*, Rome, pp. 479-508.

Fagan, B. (2018) *Fishing. How the Sea fed the Civilization*, New Haven and London.

Franzoi, P., Penzo, P., and Pellizzato, M. (2002) 'Vallicoltura e pesca del pesce novello', Pellizzato, M. (ed.), *Pesci, molluschi e crostacei della laguna di Venezia. Risorse ittiche e ambiente lagunare tra storia e innovazione*, Venice, pp. 99-117.

Marangoni, G. (1974) *Le Associazioni di mestiere nella repubblica veneta (vittuaria, farmacia, medicina)*, Venice.

Martinat, M. (1999) 'Les blés du pape: système annonaire et logiques économiques à Rome à l'époque moderne', *Annales, Histoire, Sciences sociales*, 54, 1, pp. 219-244.

Martinat, M. (2004) *Le juste marché. Le système annonaire romain aux XVI*[e] *et XVII*[e] *siècles*, Rome.

Martinat, M. (2004) 'L'annone romaine moderne entre contraintes morales et projet politique', Virlouvet, C. and Marin, B. (eds), *Nourrir les cités en Méditerranée, Antiquité-temps modernes*, Paris, Aix-en-Provence, Madrid, pp. 103-124.

Payne, B. (2013) 'Local Economic Stewards: The Historiography of the Fishermen's Role in Ressource conservation', *Environmental History*, 18, 1, pp. 29-43.

Perini, S. (1989) *Chioggia dal Settecento all'età della Restaurazione*, Padua.

Rivoal, S. (2015) 'Agir en être collectif. L'État, la communauté des *Nicolotti* et l'approvisionnement de Venise à l'époque moderne', *Tracés*, 29, pp. 65-84.

Rivoal, S. (2018) 'Gérer les ressources lagunaires. La pêche locale dans l'approvisionnement de Venise (XVIIIe siècle)', *Revue d'Histoire Maritime*, 24, pp. 97-112.

Thompson, E. P. (1975) *Whigs and Hunters: The Origin of the Black Act*, London.

Thompson, E. P. [(1975) 2015] *Les usages de la coutume, tradition et résistances populaires en Angleterre XVII*[e]*-XIX*[e] *siècle*, Paris.

Venturi, F. (1990) *Settecento Riformatore, vol. V: L'Italia dei Lumi, T. 2: La Repubblica di Venezia (1761-1797)*, Turin.

Zecchin, F. (ed.) (1994) *La Valle Millecampi: la valle Averto*, Padoue.

Zug Tucci, H., (1992) 'Pesca e caccia in Laguna', *Storia di Venezia dalle origini alla caduta della Serenissima, Vol. I, Origni-Età ducale*, Rome, pp. 490-514.

9 Preventing subsistence crises: the state and granaries of abundance in Old Regime France

Gérard Béaur, CNRS & EHESS, CRH, Paris, France

Translated by Judith Le Goff

Stocking grain from an over-abundant harvest for use in case of famine is not a new idea. From Neolithic times on, grain was stored in buried silos and the recent discovery of more than a hundred of these at Corent in the Massif Central confirms that this was a widespread practice in Iron Age Gaul (Poux, 2015).[1] In Egypt, the Pharaoh also stocked grain, in granaries this time, as a precaution against a possible failure of the harvest. It was the same in Ancient Rome with the public granaries of Domitian, then Galba, and those of Diocletian, which took in the corn from Sicily, Sardinia, Greece and Egypt. In the Middle Ages the Church built a great many tithe barns to store the grain it levied, which it was expected to redistribute if harvests failed. The tithe was thought to be a kind of insurance against bad crops and it has even been argued that the peasants generally accepted this type of levy as it guaranteed a reserve, managed by the ecclesiastical authorities, that was partly destined for their own survival (Arnoux, 2012). As we see, the initiative did not come only from individuals but from institutions, which took charge of this reserve that was intended to make up for any shortages in cereal production.

Such public reserves existed in the modern period in Italy, managed by the Abbondanza at Florence, the office of the Annona at Como (Sigaut, 1978: 37), the Wheat Office at Venice (Vertecchi, 2009) as well as the Annona at Rome (Revel, 1975), which used the Roman baths (*thermae*) converted into granaries under Pope Gregory XIII (1572-1585) and his sixteenth-century successors, as the population of the city boomed. Public reserves also existed in Germany, with the Kornhaüser at Nuremberg, for example (Beutler, 1979), and also in Switzerland, notably at Geneva (Piuz and Zumkeller, 1985; Weidmer, 1992). In France, this practice was not so widespread. We know that there was a granary of abundance at Besançon, founded in 1404, another at Strasbourg, the Kornspeicher, constructed in 1441, and a third at Nancy, from 1750 (Sigaut, 1978), but these were all created when the three towns were not yet part of the Kingdom of France.

In fact, it is striking to note that France was something of an exception. While in Italy, in Germany and in Switzerland all the towns, according to François Sigaut, maintained grain reserves under the control of the public authorities, this was not the case in France (Sigaut, 1978). Certainly, the monarchy, at an early stage, with the edicts of 1567 and 1577 regulating the trade and circulation of grain, had advised setting up storehouses of this sort (Persi Pivetti, 2014). But only a few towns were rich enough to respond to these injunctions. In Lyon the granary was not built until 1722-28, even though the *chambre d'abondance* had been founded in 1643 (Rambaud, 1911). The decision to build the granary at Marseille

[1] Each of these silos contained between 500 and 1,500 kg of grain. As the site is thought to contain a thousand of them, we can see how large these systems of storage were.

Stocks, seasons and sales: Food supply, storage and markets in Europe and the New World, c. 1600-2000, ed. by Wouter Ronsijn, Niccolò Mignemi and Laurent Herment, CORN 17 (Turnhout, 2019), pp. 193-210.

 DOI: 10.1484/M.CORN-EB.5.118260

was only taken after the shortages of 1679. Paris had no granaries, either because it was thought that its situation at the heart of a cereal growing area made them unnecessary, or because the king's requests were ignored. This was the case almost everywhere.

Why was there such reluctance to set up these stores, which, one would have thought, would have been an excellent tool for regulating the wheat market and protecting against shortages? The obstacles to creating them were technical and financial, but also economic and political.

I. Technical aspects

I.1 The risks

Although grain had long been stored in ditches dug in the soil and hermetically sealed, this practice had greatly declined since the Middle Ages. In the modern period it only continued in a few, mostly southern, regions: Quercy, Vivarais, Roussillon, Gascogne in France, but was more widespread in Spain, Italy and beyond (Sigaut, 1978). Even though there were very real risks, such as water infiltration, penetration by air, parasites and insects (Puig, 2011), and even though opening the ditch meant taking out and using all the grain if it was not to rot away quickly, this technique held clear advantages. Protected from the air, the wheat enclosed in these silos could be kept for many years with small loss, as long as the operation was carried out correctly (Sigaut, 1978). It is clear however that storing grain in granaries became the dominant method in France and elsewhere, and that the monarchy did not consider any other type of storage.

But storing grain in granaries also had many risks and limitations. Germination could render the grain inedible and even dangerous by encouraging bacteria, and heating, a great problem with wheat, made it smell stale (Sigaut, 1978: 57). Lastly, fermented grains could become "marronnés", that is, covered with a kind of skin and crawling with worms (Cerisier, 2004: 775). All these problems came from exposure to excessive temperatures and particularly too much damp. In fact, even when it was in the barn or in stacks for several months before threshing, grain quite frequently held too much moisture. This dampness resulted from the widespread practice of harvesting grain too early, before the wheat was completely ripe, in order to stop the grains from falling from the stalk (*égrainage*) and the resultant losses (Meuvret, 1977: 165).

Danger also came from creatures that enjoyed eating grain: birds, of course but also cats and martens. Rodents were a danger, as were mites, mildews, yeasts and bacteria and a fungal disease: the smut fungus (*carie du blé*). This caused the grains to become "niellés", light and hollow, without nutritional value (Michel, 2015: 31). Finally, we come to spiders and to insects, particularly the most feared of all: the wheat weevil, which delighted in damp grain (Michel, 2015: 99-100).

I.2 Precautions

In order to avoid germination, heating, and fermentation, bulk storage of grain in thick layers had to be avoided, even if it had been previously well cleaned. Generally, the depth of these layers was limited and carefully defined – but by criteria that varied from author to author: a maximum height of two *pieds* or two and a half *pieds* (60 to 75 cm approximately) according to Corinne Beutler (1979), but 18 *pouces* (about 50 cm) according to Jean Meuvret (1988: 17).[2] At Lille it was not to exceed 32 cm but a second layer of 16 cm could be added later as long as the total height remained less than 49 cm (Cerisier, 2004: 775). Finally, at Lyon, the total height could attain 71 to 96 cm (Nicolier, 2015). The important thing was that the mass of grain should not spill out and become difficult to shovel.

To prevent the stocks from absorbing more water, there were openings only in the north and east walls so that the air received by the grain would be cold and dry. There might possibly be ventilators to circulate the air; the windows were opened wide in daytime and dry weather and closed at night and in foggy or rainy weather; the grain was not stocked against the walls so that it would not absorb the damp emanating from the walls or entering through holes in the roof (Beutler, 1879: 74).

The windows of the granaries were not sealed, so that air could circulate, but they always had grills so as to prevent animals from entering. To keep away insects and rodents, particularly weevils, the scourge of the granaries, various products, some quite bizarre, but all smelly or repulsive, were placed around the heaps of grain – elder leaves, lavender oil, dry hay, garlic, vinegar, herring brine, wine lees, sheep fleece, and even wet canvas or old shoes – and it was recommended to treat the floor and walls with "washing liquid made of pepper, water and garlic, or of green walnuts, or of lime to which lavender oil had been added" (Michel, 2015: 22 and 99-100).

In any event, the floor was to be of wood or tiles: the walls were to be whitewashed and to be as smooth as possible so as not to harbour parasites. They were to be brushed to destroy caterpillars and butterflies. Finally, another reason for keeping the grain away from the walls was to keep it away from rat and mouse holes and to avoid impurities entering through the tiny gaps in the roof. Of course, traps were laid for rodents (Beutler, 1979; Meuvret, 1988: 17).[3]

I.3 Remedies

In order to remove all impurities and dust the new wheat had first of all to be sieved. This would make it keep much better. It was then necessary to get rid of any non-food grains, which might contaminate the whole stock. That required cleaning and riddling the wheat and, if necessary, drying it. Then it had to be heaped up again (Michel, 2015). All this was to be performed several times over (Meuvret, 1988: 18). This meant suffering a loss at each stage and employing a great deal of labour.

Then humidity, one of the main dangers, had to be reduced by passing air through the mass of grain so as to dry it. This was done by shovelling, another piece of heavy work; it brought the wheat into contact with the air, but required many workers. The grain was thrown a certain distance with a shovel, giving it a little sideways shake, so that it went from one end of the granary to the other and did not stay stuck together in a compact mass (Cerisier, 2004: 775). The wheat was shovelled once a week, or once every two weeks,

[2] Here, Meuvret quotes Duhamel du Monceau at length.
[3] This is again taken from Duhamel du Monceau.

depending on the level of humidity of the grain and according to its age, until, with time and numerous shovellings, it had sufficiently dried out (Sigaut, 1978: 52). In addition, the workers had to be careful not to do this in stormy weather, as the grain might absorb humidity from the atmosphere and it had to be done more frequently with new grain, because it was generally damper.

Shovelling also had other virtues. It made the grain less attractive to weevils by reducing the level of humidity and got rid of insect eggs, while the abrupt movements killed the weevils or made them fall to the ground (Sigaut, 1978: 54; Meuvret, 1988: 18). There were other, additional, ways of destroying weevils. One was to place dampened bundles of straw on the edge of the grain piles. The straw lured in the insects, which congregated there. Then all that had to be done was to throw the straw on the fire to get rid of them. Other methods were proposed, such as putting the grain in sacks, despite the extra cost, or heating in a kiln (*chaufournage*), which, unfortunately, only worked on limited amounts of grain (Michel, 2015: 148-150).

In the eighteenth century there was a raging battle over ovening (*étuvage*) a technique recommended by Duhamel du Monceau. Rising temperature was supposed to reduce humidity and kill the weevils, thus dispensing with the long and costly work of shovelling (Bourde, 1967: 937). An oven (*étuve*) was in fact built in Geneva in 1757 and another at Lyon in 1763 but the results of the experiments were disputed. At Lyon the experiment was abandoned by 1765 because the bread tasted bad and there were rats (Zeller, 1989); at Geneva, it was quickly noticed that there was a significant loss of volume and weight, which increased with use (Piuz and Zumkeller, 1985: 579-591). Parmentier concluded that the process was ineffective, that it allowed many weevils to survive, produced a kind of flour not white enough to suit urban customers, and that the cost of fuel was generally considered dissuasive (Sigaut, 1978: 46).

An alternative solution was proposed by which a flow of air was to be used to dry the grain and destroy the weevils. Unfortunately, the technical means of providing the necessary ventilation did not exist. But as a substitute, one might air the grain by making it descend from one granary to another through floor openings, and riddle it at the same time. This seems to have been done at Lyon (Gardes, 1983). The impurities were eliminated and the dampness of the grain was gradually reduced (Michel, 2015: 151-156). No doubt these labour-intensive processes would not have been needed if it had been stored on the same floor, but the movement of the grain did guarantee better conservation. Nevertheless, until the process could be mechanised and water power harnessed to the task, the frequent removal of grain to the upper granary on men's backs was extremely expensive.

II. Financial cost

The expenses involved were relatively high.

II.1 The building

First, it was necessary to have a sufficiently large building, preferably situated on a waterway so as to transport grain in good conditions, and not on land liable to flooding, for obvious reasons (Cerisier, 2004: 769). Thus, the granary of abundance in Lyon sat on the banks of the Saône, and that of Lille, near the Deûle. Of course existing storehouses could be used, as they were at Lyon before the building was erected at the beginning of the eighteenth century, but when they were scattered about it was harder to manage stocks, and if they were rented, the costs became prohibitive. When awaiting construction of the granary at Lille, several warehouses had to be rented in order to store about 6,000 hl of grain; that alone cost around 9,000 livres (Cerisier, 2004: 770)! The same happened at Lyon, before the granary was built in the 1720's.

Granaries were huge, as was noted above. The one at Lyon had a rectangular shape, 130 m in length by 18 m in width (Halitim-Dubois, 2012), with a capacity of about 4,278 m^2 of storage on three levels, theoretically capable of holding more than 16,000 tonnes of wheat (Zeller, 1989). In reality, it seems that at the outset it was designed to hold 30,000 *ânées* of grain, about 4,000 metric tonnes (or 5,000, if our calculations are right), but usually it contained something between 6,000 and 15,000 *ânées* (Nicolier, 2015) (or between 900 and 2,500 tonnes according to our calculations); so, once again by our calculation, it would have had no difficulty taking in the 1,300 tonnes stocked there in 1775 (Zeller, 1989).[4] Thus the granary was certainly oversized, as a single level was sufficient to hold that amount.

The Strasbourg granary held about 5,000 hl of grain (400 tonnes), in a storehouse measuring 130 m by 13 m (Cerisier, 2004: 769). At Lille the granary belonging to the local Artois estates, established in 1730, measured about 60 m by 18 m. It had five floors plus two other levels in the rafters and attic. In total it could hold 21,427 sacks in the whole store, or 2,000 tonnes, enough to feed about 10,000 inhabitants for a year (Cerisier, 2004: 769)! At Geneva, the reserves of the *Chambre de Blé* were the equivalent of about four months' worth of urban consumption in the seventeenth century (about 11,500 hl of wheat, or roughly 850 tonnes), and nearly nine months' worth in the 1780s (or about 46,000 hl / 3,500 tonnes) (Weidmer, 1992).

If available land could not be found, expropriations had to be carried out. This was the case at Lille, where the land cost 35,000 livres in the end. As to the expense of construction, after taking bids from the different guilds, the cost of the work amounted to 342,000 livres. The total expenditure thus came to 377,000 livres, a tidy sum to be sure, but not an exorbitant amount. It seems that the investment was much more costly at Lyon (Nicolier, 2015).

Clearly, though, technical requirements were such that the price of these buildings was quite high. The ground near rivers was unstable, so solid foundations had to be laid. At Lyon the use of cutstone to give the building solidity and good looks drove up the cost. Finally, there were also technical obstacles to be overcome: floors had to be made firm enough to take the weight of the grain and it proved all but impossible to divide up the storeys in a way that allowed the grain to be moved around and shovelled in the right conditions (Nicolier, 2015). The decision to build vaulted ceilings followed from these constraints, as did the limits on the number of bays and the reinforcement of 22 columns. And after that, the walls, which tended to go "out of plumb", had to be reinforced by buttresses in 1749 and 1763 (Nicolier, 2015)!

---

[4] It seems that according to the table and metrological equivalents indicated the granary really contained 8,000 and not 800 *ânées*. One *ânée* = 2.05 hl = 152,6 kg.

The decision to build and not to lease a building naturally avoided the cost of rent. However, it was calculated that as the annual repayment of the outlay could not exceed 2,000 livres a year, it would take 189 years to amortize the cost (Cerisier, 2004: 766)! The granary at Valenciennes was much cheaper; it cost around 200,000 livres, including the land. This avoided an annual rent of about 5,000 livres so the outlay could be amortized in only 40 years. The gap between these figures nonetheless makes one wonder (Cerisier, 2004: 788-779).

II.2 Labour

The next stage was to fill the granary by buying wheat on the market and storing the grain on the different floors. What did it cost to bring in grain? We know the amount for the temporary storehouse at Lille, used until the granary of abundance was completed (Cerisier, 2004: 770). The expenditure was 8,750 livres for every 10,000 sacks (1,000 tonnes) delivered, but the rent was 2,500 livres and the salary of the director, 750 livres. The real cost of the labour came to 5,500 livres, as follows:

4,375 livres for labour, ten workers to shift 10,000 sacks;

1,125 livres for 4,000 cloth sacks and a certain number of utensils: 6 measures, 6 flat shovels, 2 winnowing baskets, 3 baskets for putting the grain in sacks, 2 riddles and a set of scales.

We know that afterwards the grain was given regular shovelling. We can estimate its cost from the case of Strasbourg, where it took 6 workers to shift 50,000 sacks of grain in 15 days. This meant that the grain was shovelled 26 times during the year. At 7 livres a week per worker the total cost of labour would have been 2,184 livres, in addition to the cost of carrying and measuring. So, annually, it would have cost from 2,800 to 3,000 livres for this task, including the cost of the material used, but disregarding the living expenses paid to the inspector (Cerisier, 2004: 775).

II.3 Stock control

Naturally, the grain had first of all to be purchased, good quality wheat, well-cleaned, that would keep well. At Lille it was the *gros froment* of Artois, which was purchased at the Arras market, from well-known merchants, reputed to be competent and honest, at a reasonable rate, because prices there were generally low. It was usually best to buy between December and March, before prices rose in the springtime (Cerisier, 2004: 772). At Lyon it seems that buying was more likely to take place from August to September, as soon as the harvest was finished, when the prices were likely to be lowest, and that delivery took place from the end of October to the end of December, immediately after the threshing was over. It was then kept until May or June, the time when stocks were running out and when, in principle, the bakers were required to obtain grain from the granary (Nicolier, 2015). In principle, also, the granary was emptied (at least in part) to make room for the new grain.

Then the stocks had to be managed. It was claimed that wheat was kept up to 30 years in Prussia and Poland, 20 years at Strasbourg. Even better, at Basel and at Zurich the granaries were said to have contained wheat that was not just 20 to 40 years old, but even more than 100 years of age, and that the inhabitants of Basel even managed to sell it at a reasonable price, once they had cleaned it![5] In reality, 7 to 8 years was considered the maximum for good quality grain at Lille and in practice it was rarely kept beyond 3 years (Cerisier, 2004: 775). Everything depended on the quality of the grain. At first the grain that had been badly stocked and would keep least well would be got rid of when prices started to go up or when the grain began to spoil. For this, it was necessary to organise the rotation of stocks. Thus, in the storehouses of Flanders, the routine was to sell half of the stored grain and to replace it four months after the harvest (Cerisier, 2004: 761).

In order to make the best decisions the director had to be a good manager, and maintain contact with the merchants. Under him was a small staff, burdened with heavy responsibilities: the cashier who managed the funds, the concierge who kept the registers with the dates of entry and exit for the grain, the quantity, quality, price of purchase and sale, but also the expenditures on materials and the salaries of workers, porters and carters (Cerisier, 2004: 771).

The grain thus stocked was to be sold to artisans and the poor in case of need and subject to the decision of the intendant. What constituted a state of need? At what point should the grain be taken out and put on the market? The aldermen of Maubeuge pondered these questions. Should they feed small amounts of grain into the market, so as to slow down rising prices and not discourage merchants from supplying the market, or should they wait until the market was short of supplies before intervening to prevent shortages (Cerisier, 2004: 838)?

Then the price still had to be set. Selling above cost price would have gone against the principle behind intervention, which was to ease the common people's misery. Nor could they sell at too low a price, which would turn away the merchants or, worse, take a loss. The idea was to sell at the going price. But if the previous stocks were insufficient there was a double risk. Either they might pay a high price for the grain, hold off the sale, and be left with stocks that were worthless, sometimes sold off at a loss when a good harvest made prices tumble. Or they might intervene massively early on, at the risk of frightening consumers into buying, leaving themselves without reserves at the critical moment; or they might find themselves unable to sell the stored grain if the inhabitants refused to buy because they preferred wheat to rye, or wheat to rice. At that point stocks became unsalable or had to be unloaded at a loss when competing grain of better quality, or simply wheat, arrived and became affordable for the consumers. That was the problem: not to intervene too soon nor too late, not to sell too dear and not to sell too cheap, to buy enough but not too much.

II.4 The unattainable financial equilibrium

The aim was to make provisions at a low price and prevent prices from collapsing, and to sell as soon as prices rose, so as to slow down the rise. It follows logically that the granaries ought to have turned a profit. But was that really their aim? At Lyon this idea was liked but rejected on the grounds that it was necessary to accept a monetary loss for the sake of giving relief to the very large working population of the city. This reasoning was mainly followed in other urban centres, particularly industrial ones, as the aim was not to make money but to ward off the subsistence crises that drove poor families into poverty (Cerisier, 2004: 766).

---

5 Information from Anne-Lise Head-Konig.

Even if there had been a desire to make income and expenditure balance out, it is not certain that it could have been done. The magnitude of investment needed has already been emphasized. But there was also the question of the money needed to fill the granary of abundance. This meant getting access to credit, which had its cost. There were the occasional expenses for shovelling and all the operations needed to maintain the grain in storage. Shifting and riddling the grain resulted, on average, in a loss of 4 per cent and, in general, it was estimated that overall losses came to 7 per cent. With all these expenses it was hard to turn a profit. And the amounts involved were large, for two reasons. Leaving aside the situation of the countryside, a great many urban dwellers were in need when grain became dear. For instance, at Lille in 1740, it was estimated that 45 per cent of the adult population were poor (Cerisier, 2004: 835)! Hasty purchases to meet these shortages accelerated right in the middle of the crises, when the prices were at their highest, as was the case in Lille in 1740; in any event the granaries had to be replenished, for fear of lacking grain sooner or later.

What sort of balance sheet did these famine interventions generate? At Valenciennes, at the end of 1740, the books were balanced at 97,678 livres (Cerisier, 2004: 780). But as a general rule, building up stocks at short notice and having to put grain on the market at a lower price meant that either the provincial estates or town governments had to go into debt or the King had to provide relief. In 1775, Lyon had a reserve stock of 1,300 tonnes, quite inadequate for the needs of an urban population of 150,000 inhabitants, many of them workers who were falling into need. It is easy to see how stocks were quickly drawn down and why the aldermen (*jurats*) had to make emergency purchases at a high price. Unfortunately, wheat from Provence, bought at 49 livres per *ânée*, did not arrive until the summer, when prices had fallen to 34 livres 10 sols; the price continued to go through the floor in the following weeks and the grain eventually had to be sold off as low as 25 livres. To be sure, the previous stocks had been bought in 1773 at 35 livres, but replenishing them at 49 livres could only be justified by gambling on a sudden new peak in prices, which did not happen (Zeller, 1989). Turgot used the resulting shortfall, rather unscrupulously, to hasten the closure of the storehouse and thereby further his policy of liberalising the grain trade.

To be fair, the municipal storehouses in Flanders and Hainaut, which, prodded by the government, sometimes bought grain in great haste, were in the same situation. At Maubeuge, in the summer of 1740, the loss on supplies reached 8.79 per cent of the cost of wheat (*froment*) but it was greater in 1741 for rye, which became unsalable when wheat appeared on the market. The same year, the town of Bavay recorded a loss of more than 40 per cent. At Condé it was nearly 60 per cent. To be sure, the costs of the storehouses, as measured in labour, rent, waste and so forth, was very great and also weighed down their finances. For 111 sacks of wheat at Maubeuge, they came to 81 livres, under 2 per cent of the total, but for the rice and rye stored in the same year they were nearly 7 per cent. At Bavay, 823 livres were lost on 195 sacks of rye, or about 20 per cent of the cost. This went firstly on what the commission dealers spent for shipping, unloading, waste and so on (69 per cent of total losses), transport vehicles (21 per cent), and also shifting and measuring, unloading and guaranteeing the security and sale of the grain (Cerisier, 2004: 839-841).

The problem was that it usually took a long time to get rid of the grain, as only a bad harvest made it possible to empty the granaries. As long as the harvests were adequate and prices remained low it was not only useless but suicidal to sell off accumulated reserves, doubtless acquired at a higher price. However, scarcity, of its very nature, was unpredictable, both as to timing and extent. In such conditions, keeping grain imposed a double risk. One danger was that of selling it at a huge loss by buying before the market hit the floor, and selling at a lower price. The other was that of seeing it spoilt. If the grain was totally ruined the loss was irreparable; if only partially, the consumers tended to shy away from buying it, which came to the same thing. And of course, the risk increased as time went by.

It is symptomatic that the project for a public granary proposed by the town of Caen in 1758, for a cost of 90,000 livres, was put off until the end of the Seven Years' War and then abandoned, albeit on physiocratic grounds.

III. Political obstacles

III.1 The action of the monarchy

In principle, the government intervened heavily to regulate, oversee and control the market of a vital product (Miller, 1999; Kaplan, 1976). Replenishing the Paris market was the priority task, in order to prevent popular disturbances. Rather than managing granaries to provide for all eventualities, the government preferred to buy grain and distribute it secretly, or quietly put it on the market when grain supply problems arose, so as to avoid panic. It certainly seemed wiser for the state to buy on the market in times of scarcity, even to resell at a loss, rather than pay to build these storehouses as well as for the upkeep of depots, the salaries of workers and guards and the renewal of grain stocks. However, around 1750, the monarchy did manage to assemble considerable stocks to meet all eventualities; 15,000 hl in a dozen or so places around Paris. In 1764, the volume of grain stored there was multiplied by four, just before the wave of liberalism called this policy into question (Persi Pirvetti, 2014).

In fact, from the sixteenth century on, the monarchy had tried to establish a network of granaries of abundance to slow down price rises when grain was in short supply, and to prevent prices from collapsing when harvests were too abundant. There were frequent incentives to do so, provoking repeated and often unsuccessful attempts to carry out this policy. During the eighteenth century the monarchy tried harder, particularly after 1720, but continually ran into cost problems and strong political – and later ideological – resistance.

In general, the monarchy preferred to trust others to manage the stocks, particularly towns or other institutions. From 1577, it strongly "encouraged" provincial estates and town governments to set up such "granaries of abundance". This demand was frequently reiterated, particularly by Richelieu and Colbert (Persi Pivetti, 2014). It was echoed once again for Lille and the northern towns at the end of the 1720s. The obvious justification was the struggle against penury, to shield townsfolk from the worst effects of high prices, most notably at Lille in 1727. An equally important reason, but one that was not stressed so much, was the need to have stocks for the army in a frontier zone (Cerisier, 2004: 765-766).

Other solutions were tried for building up reserves, with a view to influencing markets by drawing on the "king's wheat" from these stocks. Rather than turning to municipalities and provincial estates, the state employed private actors to secure provisioning. Following the famine of 1725 and on the advice of the Paris Lieutenant General of Police, Hérault, religious communities were asked to help amass grain stocks to be held ready for use in case of shortage. Although 70 of them did create such reserves, most refused or found ways to avoid doing so. The same demands were repeated in 1736 but the amount of grain set aside remained notoriously insufficient (Miller, 1999: 55). In 1750, the Controller General of Finances turned to the General Entrepreneurs of Military Supplies (*entrepreneurs généraux des étapes*), whose function it was to supply the army, to construct a proper national network of granaries of abundance. These measures were a patent failure, as those concerned diverted the project to serve their own interests. In another attempt to set up granaries and reduce costs, a contract was signed in 1767 with the *Compagnie des blés du roi*, a private company run by the famous Malisset and a group of merchant associates; it was to amass and manage stocks, and although it existed for a very short time, it marked the beginning of the rise of the so-called "moulins et magasins de Corbeil", which were to play such a large role in provisioning Paris (Persi Pivetti, 2014).

III.2 The resistance of local authorities

It was inevitable that when it chose to lay this burden on town governments, the monarchy would provoke resistance. True, the aldermen (*jurats*) of Lyon argued in favour of building that town's granary of abundance (Nicolier, 2015) but the 1729 plan to build storehouses in four Flemish towns, Douai, Cambrai, Dunkerque and Condé, ran into immediate opposition.

These Flemish town authorities criticised the plan on three main points. They argued, in the first place, that the project was unnecessary or conceived on too vast a scale. Douai argued that it was already involved in building a granary at Lille. Cambrai maintained that it was at the centre of a cereal-producing region, so had no need for it. And, along with Dunkerque, it maintained that it did not have the necessary means.

Secondly, the means of financing imposed by the government, a municipal sales tax of one and a half farthings (*liards*) per tankard (*pot*) of beer for six and a half years, to be collected by the towns or by the estates, would weigh heavily on consumers, particularly the poorest of them, as beer was essentially a drink of the lower classes. The authorities at Douai were even more angered by the unfair profits made on the backs of consumers; they estimated that this tax, levied on 11,130 *tonneaux* (barrels) of beer would bring in 11,130 florins annually (nearly 14,000 livres), that is 72,345 florins over the entire period, or the equivalent of some 90,000 livres, while the outlay on the granaries would come to only 62,000 livres.

Thirdly, and most important, the towns pleaded that the measures proposed by the monarchy had been decreed unilaterally. Thus it was the defence of provincial privileges and the sovereignty of the estates in tax matters that crystallised opposition at Cambrai and Douai (Cerisier, 2004, 762-764). Ten years later, the construction of a new granary at Valenciennes was imposed, and it met with the same lack of enthusiasm. Once again it was decided to levy a tax on beer, for two years this time, and to farm out this duty. The amount collected went far beyond the amount spent on the storehouse so the surplus was put to various other purposes: maintaining hospices for beggars, quartering army officers and constructing a hospital for the poor in the city (Cerisier, 2004: 779).

III.3 The hostility of the actors

Consumers viewed any stocking of wheat with distrust; they saw it as a way of making prices rise by keeping grain off the market. They thought it encouraged speculation and suspected the administrators, if not the King himself, of encouraging price rises or, at least, of planning to keep bread prices high, and thereby penalising the poor. And indeed stocking grain, whether public or private, did have unintended effects. It contributed to a new wave of hostility against the monarchy, in the face of what was seen as speculation for the benefit of unscrupulous market manipulators. It contributed to making Louis XV very unpopular, to discrediting the monarchy and it opened the way to an accusation that continually resurfaced all through the eighteenth century and became significant during the Revolution: the "famine plot" or the "famine compact" (Kaplan, 1982). Thus, the Malisset company, which had the power of arbitraging and negotiating on the market, was accused of speculating. Although the initial contract was soon cancelled, the harm had been done. By association, the King was held guilty of signing a contract designed to starve the common people, thus confirming popular suspicion of a "famine plot".

On the other side, the merchants argued that stocking amounted to unfair competition. By flooding the market in times of food shortages, the government helped depress prices and reduce their profits. By preventing the law of supply and demand from operating, it dissuaded them from supplying the market, and was thereby, in the end, counter-productive. It was in fact the grain sellers who wrecked the plan to rely on granaries of abundance in the terrible crisis of 1709 and it was the producers and merchants who undermined the policy by holding back from supplying the market when the King put his wheat on sale at a knock-down price. They were not the only ones holding back. The bakers were totally hostile. At Lyon they even refused to take delivery of wheat from the municipal granary, claiming that it was of too poor a grade (Nicolier, 2015). Thus sellers, users and buyers of grain ultimately shared the same hostility to the policy of grain storage. But the monarchy also ran into resistance from those who denounced its excessive cost and emphasised its harmful effects.

In 1722 the Royal Society of Agriculture of Lyon organised a competition on the subject of granaries of abundance. The winning essays concluded that they were ineffective for several reasons: official incompetence, the laxity of municipal employees and bad purchasing policies, with grain bought in excessive quantities at excessive prices. They did not condemn the whole system but envisaged reforms that were hard to put in force: stable administration, rigorous management, avoiding intermediaries and buying good quality grain (Zeller, 1989).

Rather than bearing the cost of building and, above all, managing the granaries, rather than annoying the producers and sellers of grain and running the risk that they might desert the markets, many instead proposed leaving free trade to supply the market and relying on poor relief when the price of bread went too high.

III.4 The weight of ideology

Though the monarchy "encouraged" the creation of granaries in the first half of the eighteenth century, there was a lively debate between the partisans of free trade and those who, from the middle of the century on, favoured regulation (Kaplan, 1986). The first group wanted to free the grain market and end the time limits imposed by the monarchy on the conservation of grain. Up to then, the government had tried to combat speculative manipulation by farmers, who tended to supply the market according to their own interest and had no scruples about holding back grain in time of shortage, even if that meant weakening the market and blocking supplies. Free-traders argued that freedom to store grain would have beneficial effects. It would encourage farmers to lay in their grain after a good harvest and prevent prices from collapsing; the market could be supplied with these stocks if production failed. But, in return, freeing the grain market would mean that there would be no call on the state to regulate and that the responsibility of managing and supplying the market would fall on the farmers. The interventionists proposed quite the contrary policy: limit the freedom to stock grain so as to avoid the speculation that would result if the farmers kept back too much produce. They favoured ongoing control by the monarchy in order to regulate the market and guarantee the regular provisioning of consumers. Both sides agreed on the need to store grain but one wanted to leave complete freedom to the grain merchants and private initiative, while the other argued for protective control by the monarchy and for establishing public storehouses.

At first, the liberals prevailed over the interventionists. The victory of liberal ideas encouraged the practice of stocking grain but at the same time discouraged the monarchy from intervening. Granaries of abundance thus seemed to be condemned. Despite the mistakes made during the crisis of 1765-70, Turgot, who became controller general in 1774, set out to finish them off and his ministry saw the high-water mark of this policy. For example, he set out to discredit the conduct of the Lyon aldermen (*édiles*) in order to get rid of the city's storehouse (Zeller, 1989). But the debate was far from over, and his experiment came to an end with the riots of the Flour War (*Guerre des farines*) in May 1775. A return to regulation and the controlled grain trade were deemed necessary. Once again there was a call to set up public granaries, as with Malisset and the LeLeu brothers at the end of the Old Regime, and François de Neufchâteau who, in 1790, unsuccessfully proposed setting up a granary of abundance in every canton. During the radical Montagnard phase of the Revolution, the Comité des subsistances also expressed a desire to create a network of granaries, this time in the main towns of each District or in those with more than 3,000 inhabitants. This measure was intended to deal with the shortages then engulfing the young republic, but it did not achieve its aim. The victory of the liberals was, however, of brief duration, and it was left to the Empire to revive these stores, at a time when the spectre of shortage was fading and the circulation of grain was much freer (Persi Pivetti, 2014). It was Napoleon who created the Réserve in Paris, alongside the basin of the Arsenal (Hillairet, 1960; Faure, 2002: 150-151), while granaries were set up close to the city, at Corbeil, Meaux, Pontoise and Saint Denis (Berthelot-Cheneaux, 2015).

IV. Conclusion. The great rejection

As we have seen, the idea of creating these granaries recurred frequently in France over two centuries but they only came into being with difficulty, and briefly, if at all. Even when they were set up, they caused much disappointment. At Lille, the deliveries between 1728 and 1732 were on average about half of what had been planned (Cerisier, 2004: 772). As for the Lyon granary, it very quickly turned out to be oversized and several floors were given over to other uses. It disappeared in 1777 with a loss of 180,000 livres (Zeller, 1989), following hasty purchases at the height of the 1775 crisis (see above).

Why was there such reticence? Why were there so many failures? Why was there such distrust, even though the interventions of the public authorities often succeeded in mitigating the effect of shortages, particularly in the gaps before the new harvest? Had not the Geneva wheat chamber, created in 1628 and stocked with grains from quite far away, made it possible to avoid several important subsistence crises during the second half of the seventeenth century and the eighteenth century, even if it was expensive (Piuz and Mottu-Weber, 1990; Weidmer, 1992)? Had not the examples of Lyon, for over a century and a half, and of Strasbourg, for much longer, proven their success?

The first point to make is that during the early modern period granaries were primarily established in Protestant towns and, as we have mentioned before, tithe barns were intended to provide the same service as the granaries of abundance in towns that remained Catholic, for as long as they really took on that role. But is this explanation totally valid? On the one hand, it had long been the case that chapters and abbeys preferred to receive their tithes in cash, and so very often no longer could dispose of large stocks. This change no doubt explains the rapid failure of the attempt to make religious communities responsible for provisioning the population in time of grain shortage. On the other hand, the Italian example runs counter to this seductive but facile hypothesis. True, one might maintain that this was because of the traditional practice of keeping municipal grain reserves in the cities of the peninsula. But, Spain, just as Catholic as Italy, also experienced a version of the granaries of abundance, the *pósitos*, municipal reserves destined to blunt the effects of bad harvests, situated at Madrid (De Castro, 1987; Andrès Ucendo and Lanza Garcai, 2012) but also in ordinary villages (de Bourgoing, 1803: II, 51-52 and 163-164; de Rehfues, 1811: II, 6-7).

The arguments used by contemporaries to deny the utility of granaries were of three sorts, though they were closely interlinked. One: storage conditions were poor and the grain was frequently spoilt, which annoyed the consumers; two: the cost of building granaries and keeping grain stocks in them was prohibitive; three: it was hard, if not impossible, to anticipate future grain prices, which often left them liable to miscalculations.

True, these technical, financial, ideological and political obstacles were in no way specific to Old Regime France. But this statement needs nuancing.

First of all, the risk of damage to the grain and the ineffectiveness of the remedies was the same. The counter-measures described earlier were already used in Ancient Rome, which, in passing, shows that agronomists had not invented anything new. However, it is easier beyond a doubt to keep grain in dry countries like Spain or more continental ones such as Germany and Switzerland, than in a rainy one, where sheaves were still damp when they were brought in.

Secondly, there were the virulent attacks against the practice of public grain stocking which might explain why the French were so wary of engaging in such a policy. This objection would be more formidable if it were not the case that, after all, other countries had liberal ideas too, and more particularly, that the policy of freeing the grain trade was only a brief and rather late aberration. The difference with other countries goes much further back in time.

The principal argument against the granaries of abundance was, however, essentially financial. Over and over, it was repeated that they cost a great deal and that the cost of management was all the greater because it was hard, if not impossible, to predict outcomes. Was this cost prohibitive? Was it such a burden on the finances of the large towns? Was it not compensated for by a clear social benefit? Did it really paralyse the market? Taking everything into account, had not the mistaken calculations in Lyon come from the uncertainty surrounding the decisions of the aldermen and the impossibility of anticipating the size of future harvests? Could it not be argued that the enormous deficit of Lyon's granary of abundance resulted as much from the insufficiency of available stocks as from the erroneous calculations of the aldermen? This is all true, but towns which had maintained granaries for decades laboured under the same constraints and faced the same risks and expenditures. There must have been something else in play beyond purely financial calculations.

François Sigaut mentions the role of imports, which could have played a dissuasive role. He also argues that the blame should be put on the degree of autonomy enjoyed by the town authorities (Sigaut, 1978). The two arguments are somewhat elliptic and deserve careful examination.

France was not the only country to import grain in time of need. But once France was producing, in principle, a surplus, it became tempting, when production failed, to rely on emergency purchases brought in by sea. This was one of the reasons why a port like Bordeaux was less than enthusiastic about stocking grain. Of course, in case of armed conflict or a catastrophic harvest, it would be hard for it to carry out its role as redistribution hub for flour and grain to the Atlantic coast and the West Indies. So the Bordeaux councillors (*jurats*) and the intendant were particularly attentive to the state of the stocks and had no qualms about suspending exports when they thought prohibition was needed (Poussou, 2015a and 2015b). But it is quite certain that in peacetime and as long as the harvest was adequate, Bordeaux had no real supply problem. The towns had no intention of paying for storehouses, which they considered useless, unless a catastrophe was about to happen. In weighing the price to pay, the balance clearly tipped in favour of making emergency purchases rather than maintaining permanent stocks, no matter what happened to the poor as penury was approaching. After all, since the grain was drained from the countryside to the towns, the decision-makers, that is the urban oligarchies, were sheltered from need. As for the rural populations, who really cared, now that *jacqueries* no longer occurred? In 1693 and 1709, the poor politely died in silence. There, in times of crisis, even the rich were exposed to relative penury, not to mention the anger of the "populace".

The choices were obviously quite different for towns in the midst of regions with structural grain deficits and poor supply routes. Of course not all French towns were on the sea or had a port. Not all could rely on a great river for transport and/or be situated in the centre of a large-scale grain producing region, like Paris, which was normally provisioned from the Île de France, the Brie and the Beauce, or in a region near to breadbaskets like Lille, which was close to the Cambrésis. Similarly, it was not by chance that Cantabria, situated in northern Spain and easily provisioned by the sea, was one of the few regions where none of the renowned *pósitos* (public granaries) were to be found (de Rehfues, 1811: II, 6-7).

Naturally, in a crisis, turning to purchases from outside the country involved however rather forbidding obstacles. Grain would be in just as short supply in surrounding regions, so it would have to be brought in from countries that had a surplus but were not very close, from the Baltic or the Mediterranean (and also from Brittany, in the case of Bordeaux). This implied high prices and, above all, it took so long to send purchasing agents, conduct negotiations and ship the product that the crisis was sometimes over by the time the convoys arrived.

The second argument is equally valid, when spelled out. The towns were perfectly capable of putting up passive, or even open, resistance to the king's demands. Thus, there were also political reasons to oppose the call for granaries of abundance. It was the refusal of the urban oligarchies to bend to the orders of the central government and their desire to save what was left of their independent government which explains the persistent difficulties that public authorities experienced in creating these stocks. Municipal authorities suspected the state of trampling on their political prerogatives and levying taxes to their detriment. The government was thus faced with resolute opposition based on procrastination backed by a large array of arguments. The principal one was no mere pretext; it was, once again, the burden of financing the high cost of the operation. For though the monarchy strongly encouraged towns to acquire these marvellous granaries, it also left them to bear most of their costs. And those could be very heavy. We have looked at the situation in Lyon but the experience of Paris reinforces the point. The losses incurred by the state, or the city, in 1801, in 1812 and in 1815 ran into millions of francs (Thomas, 1841). Town governments could not fail to question the need for these expenses. The people of Lille had good reason to suspect that the government wanted to build stocks up for essentially military reasons.

In fact, when the monarchy was tempted to establish these granaries, it did so for two sound reasons. One was to ensure provisions for the armies by establishing what today would be called "strategic stocks". The other was to make up for a grain shortage that imperilled the food supply of the common people, thus provoking riots and uprisings, a danger of which the government was well aware. In other words, it was above all frontier towns and, even more, working class towns such as Lyon or Lille, which attracted attention, and particularly Paris, which became a near-obsession. The paradox is that although Lyon was given a granary very early on, and the monarchy so insisted on having one at Lille, the government built nothing for Paris. Here the problem of size was probably decisive. To shelter the 500,000 to 600,000 Paris consumers from need would have required an enormous building, complicated and highly costly to manage. It was not until the Second Empire that such a building emerged: the granary at the Arsenal, which was 350 metres long, 25 metres wide and 23 metres high (Hillairet, 1960; Faure, 2002). And other buildings would also be needed outside the urban area.

It is thus understandable that the town governments were reluctant to meet demands that did not concern them directly, to conform to the directives of a central power that was trampling on urban autonomy, to take on an expense that they thought did not fall to them. The division of political responsibilities added to the burden, and the financial weight led them to do – nothing. The situation was quite different in city-states, where most of the enthusiasm for public storehouses was to be found, as we have seen. The Spanish case is not even an exception to the rule as the *pósitos* came entirely under the municipal authorities. There were, so contemporaries said, more than 5,000 of them (5308?), mostly in Castile and Valencia. They were supplied directly by the peasants who gradually laid in their surpluses there, drawing out grain in time of shortage and who could borrow from them to feed themselves or to obtain seed (de Bourgoing, 1803: II, 51-52 and 163-164; de Rehfues, 1811: II, 6-7). *Pósitos* were collective institutions, usually established by pious foundations; they were storehouses on a human scale and therefore easier to manage and to put at the service of members of the community. Contemporaries however accused them of enriching the administrators at the expense of the people. In fact, they were diverted from their use but functioned more and more as credit agencies destined to make loans in the form of grain to peasants when there was a subsistence crisis (de Bourgoing, 1803: II, 164).

Thus the paucity of granaries of abundance in Old Regime France is not to be explained by the inconstancy of royal policy or by the opposition of the Physiocrats. Rather it was the combined result of callous economic calculations oblivious to the threat posed to poor folk by shifting bread prices, the superficially easy solution offered by the possibility of imports, and a clash of financial interests between an intrusive central power and jealously independent town governments.

Bibliography

Andrès Ucendo, J. I. and Lanza García, R. (2012) 'El Abasto de Pan en el Madrid del Siglo XVII', *Studia Historica: Historia Moderna*, 34, pp. 61-97.

Arnoux, M. (2012) *Le Temps des laboureurs. Travail, ordre social et croissance en Europe (XIe-XIVe siècle),* Paris.

Berthelot-Cheneaux, C. (2015) *L'Economie du blé dans le département de la Seine au XIXe siècle: permanences et mutations*, Thèse Université Paris IV.

Beutler, C. (1979) 'De l'approvisionnement en grains de quelques villes européennes au Moyen Age et à l'époque moderne', Beutler, C., Gast, M. and Sigaut, F. (eds), *Les Techniques de conservation des grains à long terme. Tome III, Leur rôle dans la dynamique des systèmes de cultures et des sociétés*, Paris, pp. 95-104.

Bourde, A. J. (1967) *Agronomie et agronomes au XVIIIe siècle*, Paris.

Bourgoing, J. F. de (1803) *Tableau de l'Espagne moderne*, Paris, t. II, 3e édition [Nouveau voyage en Espagne ou tableau actuel de la monarchie, 1789].

Cerisier, P. (2004) *Le Commerce des grains dans la France du Nord, fin XVIIe-1790 (Artois, Flandre, Hainaut, Cambrésis)*, Thèse Université Charles de Gaulle-Lille III.

De Castro, C. (1987) *El pan de Madrid, El abasto de las ciudades españolas del antiguo régimen*, Madrid.

Faure, J. (2002) *L'Arsenal de Paris, Histoires et chroniques*, Paris.

Gardes, G. (1983), 'Le Grenier à blé de Lyon dit de la "Grande abondance", 6 quai Saint Vincent', *Culture et création dans l'architecture provinciale de Louis XIV à Napoléon III*, Aix-en-Provence, pp. 75-85.

Halitim-Dubois, N. (2012) 'Le Grenier d'abondance', Privat-Savigny, M.-A. (ed.), *Lyon au XVIIIe, un siècle surprenant!*, Paris, Somogy, Lyon, pp. 49-51.

Hillairet, J. (1960) *Dictionnaire historique des rues de Paris*, Paris.

Kaplan, S. L. (1982) *Le Complot de famine, histoire d'une rumeur au XVIIIe siècle*, Paris.

Kaplan, S. L. (1976) *Bread, Politics and Political Economy in the Reign of Louis XV*, The Hague.

Kaplan, S. L. (1986) *Le Pain, le peuple et le roi*, Paris.

Meuvret, J. (1977) *Le Problème des subsistances à l'époque Louis XIV, I. La production des céréales dans la France du XVIIe et du XVIIIe siècle,* Paris.

Meuvret, J. (1988) *Le Problème des subsistances à l'époque Louis XIV, III. Le commerce des grains et la conjoncture*, Paris.

Michel, T. (2015) *La Conservation des grains en France au XVIIIe siècle: ruptures, continuités et limites*, Thèse EHESS.

Miller, J. A. (1999) *Mastering the Market. The State and the Grain Trade in Northern France, 1700-1860*, Cambridge.

Nicolier, A. (2015) 'Le Grenier d'abondance de Lyon, 6 quai Saint-Vincent (1722-1777)', HAL Id: halshs-01251873, https://halshs.archives-ouvertes.fr/halshs-01251873.

Persi Pivetti, V. (2014) 'Les Greniers publics. Approche comparative des réglementations à Rome et à Paris entre XVIIe et XVIIIe siècle', *Historia et ius, rivista di storia giuridica dell'età medievale e moderna* (www.historiaetius.eu), paper 12, pp. 1-13.

Piuz, A.-M. and Zumkeller, D. (1985) 'La Politique de stockage des grains à Genève au XVIIIe siècle', Gast, M. and Sigaut, F. (eds), *Les Techniques de conservation des grains à long terme*, Paris, pp. 579-595.

Poussou, J.-P. (2015a) 'Bordeaux, grand port de redistribution et de ravitaillement en farines et en grains des façades atlantiques européennes à l'époque de la guerre de sept ans (1751-1766)', Le Mao, C. and Meyzie, Ph. (eds), *L'approvisionnement des villes portuaires en Europe du XVIe siècle à nos jours*, Paris, pp. 129-165.

Poussou, J.-P. (2015b) 'Bordeaux et le commerce des farines au XVIIIe siècle', Catalogue de l'exposition des archives départementales de la Gironde *Au cœur des moulins*, Bordeaux, pp. 59-65.

Poux, M. (2015) 'Corent, découverte d'une importante batterie de silos enterrés de l'âge du fer', *Archéologia*, 536, pp. 22-25.

Puig, C. (2011) 'L'Apport de l'étude du stockage à notre connaissance de la conjoncture alimentaire autour de 1300 (Catalogne, Roussillon, Languedoc)', Bourin, M., Drendel, J. and Menant, F. (eds), *Les disettes dans la conjoncture de 1300 en Méditerranée occidentale*, Rome, pp. 159-177.

Rambaud, A. (1911) *La Chambre d'abondance de la ville de Lyon (1643-1777)*, Lyon, Thèse Université de Grenoble, Faculté de droit et des sciences économiques.

Rehfues, J. Ph. de (1811) *L'Espagne en 1808 ou Recherches sur l'état de l'administration, des Sciences, des Lettres, des Arts, du Commerce et des Manufactures, de l'Instruction publique, de la force Militaire de la Marine, de la Population de l'Espagne et du Caractère de ses habitants; faites dans un voyage à Madrid en l'année 1808*, Paris, t. II.

Revel, J. (1975) 'Les Privilèges d'une capitale: l'approvisionnement de Rome à l'époque moderne', *Mélanges de l'Ecole française de Rome. Moyen-Age, Temps Modernes*, 87, 2, pp. 461-493.

Sigaut, F. (1978) *Les Réserves de grains à long terme. Techniques de conservation et fonctions sociales dans l'histoire*, Paris.

Thomas, A. (1841) *Mémoire sur les réserves de grains*, Paris.

Vertecchi, G. (2009) *Il 'masser ai formenti in Terra Nova'. Il ruolo delle scorte granarie a Venezia nel XVIII secolo*, Rome.

Wiedmer, L. (1992) *Pain quotidien et pain de disette. Meuniers, boulangers et Etat nourricier à Genève (XVIIe-XVIIIe siècles)*, Geneva.

Zeller, O. (1989) 'Politique frumentaire et rapports sociaux à Lyon, 1772-1776', *Histoire, Economie et Société*, 8, 2, pp. 249-286.

10 Storage and financing of the French wheat market in the inter-war period

Alain Chatriot, CHSP, Sciences Po, Paris

Translated by Stephen W. Sawyer

The extent of the crisis in the wheat market in France during the interwar period and the measures taken to regulate it are fairly well known by now (Chatriot, 2016b). While these experiences are important to understand agricultural policies on the European scale, they were also new forms of state intervention just as they marked a change in grain storage policies. Grain storage policy was understood by the actors to play an important role in responding to the crisis of wheat prices in this period of overproduction. And yet, we still know relatively little about storage in spite of work done on grain silos in the realm of industrial archaeology. Our approach in this paper is to show how actors treated the problem of storage in this context and how the question became a central policy issue, especially its financial dimension.

Some of the players in the modern French wheat market are still unknown. Before the 1930s, grain storage was limited to small storage facilities since silo development was still to come (Loriette, 2008; Dorel-Fere, 2014). The world of grain dealers, traders and brokers in the first half of the twentieth century has not been studied in spite of the drastic changes that took place. A report from the National Economic Council in 1933 stated: "Until recently, the primary figures in the industry were traders who managed grain, collecting their wheat in the countryside on Michaelmas [September 29th, the usual date to pay the rent], which was then stocked and, along with the millers, delivered over several months. Their profits consisted in the difference between the 'farm' price at which they purchased and the 'trade' price at which they sold. Today, many transactions are done through brokers, the usual intermediaries between buyers and sellers. On the Paris market, certified brokers establish an official listing which converts the [real] prices of wheat sold under variable conditions into a price[-equivalent] of [a standard type of] available wheat, delivered in Paris and of a specified weight." (Delcasse d'Huc de Monsegou, 1933: 60).

Another report by the National Economic Council, which highlighted disagreements between players with divergent interests in the wheat market, concluded suggestively with the issue of market organization and storage by calling for a distribution policy. This policy should "first, discipline the market and strike a fair balance between production and consumption needs. To this end, it would improve the storage of crops, the periodicity of sales, the use of warrantage and agricultural credit, and in some detail the organization of futures markets, and in particular, the regulated wheat market at the Paris board of trade." (Brasart, 1931). To analyze these divergent projects and interests, the paper first presents the reorganization of the wheat producers' milieu, then explores the questions surrounding how storage was financed, and then the way in which the creation of the Wheat Board in 1936 proposed a solution to this problem. The story that emerges is a process of stacking laws and regulations by a state that had difficulty defining a coherent public policy in a context of economic and financial, as well as political, crisis.

Stocks, seasons and sales: Food supply, storage and markets in Europe and the New World, c. 1600-2000, ed. by Wouter Ronsijn, Niccolò Mignemi and Laurent Herment, CORN 17 (Turnhout, 2019), pp. 211-224.

 DOI: 10.1484/M.CORN-EB.5.118261

I. The new and contrasting world of cereal cooperatives

While the cooperative movement in agriculture was hardly new (Mignemi, 2017; Lefebvre, 1926), the number of agricultural cooperatives increased sharply during the interwar period. According to retrospective statistics published by the Ministry of Agriculture in 1946, there were 2200 agricultural cooperatives in 1908, 3800 in 1923 and 7420 in 1939 (Hirschfeld, 1957: 19). These cooperatives were concerned at once with crop financing (i.e. the question of finding funds to produce, harvest and store crops), with storage capacity through the construction of silos, and had an ambiguous relationship with the world of trade. It should also be noted that this was not merely a French phenomenon during this period (Seulesco, 1931).

The National Union of Agricultural Cooperatives for the Sale and Processing of Wheat (*UNCAVTB*) was created in early 1929 to actively pursue a policy of tax cover in close collaboration with the General Association of Wheat Producers (*AGPB*). Some observers clearly saw cooperatives as new full-fledged players on the market: "Cooperatives are currently an economic necessity. They will partially replace grain traders whose disappearance is one of the causes of the disorganization of the wheat trade. They will demonstrate their utility to the farmers and show them the benefits of the staggered sale of corn. They will be able to generate a more homogeneous product which will therefore have greater value. They will facilitate the relationship between agricultural credit and farmers. They will be able to obtain subsidies either to construct or develop silos and storage facilities or to keep the wheat of the farmers at a reduced premium in cooperative silos." (Fernagut, 1932: 86).

In September 1932, Minister of Agriculture Abel Gardey stated his ambition: "Storage, in order to avoid speculation brought on by the hasty offers of farmers after the harvest and in order to avoid putting a few million quintals of surplus – surplus that the consumption of the following year could absorb – onto the market that could offset prices. Credit to allow growers to wait and defend themselves against buyers at low prices. Organizing the rural profession – and I am aiming for cooperation – must, as you have no doubt understood, enable us to achieve this dual objective." – Talk on September 28th, 1932 in Verdun-sur-le-Doubs (Sirol, 1934: 347).

In 1932, an actor from the agricultural cooperatives gave an initial positive assessment: "The storage of wheat is of great interest from the point of view of our national economy; it appears to be an effective remedy for price instability. As a result, the public authorities have encouraged agricultural cooperatives to sell wheat, with a view to pushing them towards staggered sales." (Burgaud, 1932: 20)

In May 1933, an agricultural periodical provided an inventory of the situation: "The large agricultural groups soon recognized the usefulness of organizations whose purpose was to store wheat and stagger sales during the campaign, thus, thanks to their efforts, our major wheat-producing regions have for some three years been forming a number of storage and sales cooperatives, commonly known as 'cooperative silos.' As early as 1930-1931, about 20 cooperatives stocked 400,000 quintals of wheat. In 1931-1932 their number increased to 40, treating more than one million quintals. For the current campaign, the wheat that will pass through the storage cooperatives is estimated to be close to 5 million quintals." (Gibon, 1933: 291).

The growth of cooperatives in the field of cereals was therefore linked to the issue of storage and the financing of crops and it accompanied the development of silos, as Nicolas Loriette, an architectural historian who specializes in these constructions, makes clear. "The co-operatives benefited from favorable loans for the construction of the buildings as well as for the financing of the harvest. These benefits, together with the tax benefits provided for in the statutes of cooperatives, and in particular the tax exemptions on industrial and commercial profits and the production tax, truly allowed the movement to flourish." (Loriette, 2008: 53).

The very beginning of the 1930s was the period during which grain silos appeared in the French countryside (Du Fou, 1930). Loriette notes their specificity: "Built by state officials, partially financed by public funds and subject to some of the rules that govern the construction of public buildings, the silos are not entirely within the private domain. Consequently, the provision of grants in the early 1930s designated both a new kind of prime contractor, engineers of rural engineering, and a new category of sponsors, cooperatives" (Loriette, 2008: 66). He added that "the image of the silo undoubtedly played a role in its creation. A symbol of progress, success, strength of association, and new times; these aspects no doubt played in its favor." (Loriette, 2008: 60) For this period, he also noted the need to distinguish different situations: "1) Cooperatives stemming from agricultural unionism; 2) Cooperatives created by large farmers in a region or a village with a very local reach; 3) Cooperatives established for the construction of elevators; 4) Cooperatives created by the traders who benefitted from joining in cooperative structures through government incentives and fiscal advantages." (Loriette, 2008: 54).

The difference between these cooperatives was in fact their relationship to trade and the tensions related to it. A report from the Banque de France noted in 1934: "It must be recognized that, apart from the individualism of farmers, their dispersion and lack of cohesion, especially fiscal difficulties slowed the corporatist organization of the rural economy in France. These cooperative societies were, under the law of August 5, 1920, exempt from patent duties, and interest on the shares of their capital stock exempt from the tax on income (Article 31). But the silence of the same law on the impossibility of the turnover tax and the tax on industrial and commercial profits, the vagueness of Article 32 of the law of December 30 1928, which completed its position on these two points, cultivated a prudent reserve among farmers." (Picquet, 1934: 17-18).

The ambiguity of this fiscal situation became problematic: "Until 1925, the jurisprudence of the Conseil d'État [French Supreme Court for administrative law] exempted cooperatives from these two taxes because of their cooperative nature which prohibited them from making profits. But from that date forward, the Conseil d'État acted according to a different criterion. It investigated whether cooperatives were carrying out operations normally pursued in the context of agricultural operations. This was commonly called the 'industrialization' thesis. On this account most of the processing cooperatives and all the milling cooperatives became taxable. The UNCAVTB, in accord with the other unions (milk, beets, wine, etc.), studied [the implications of this decision for] the legal and fiscal status of cooperatives." (Fernagut, 1932: 138).

The development of the legal and fiscal status of agricultural cooperation gave rise to a "cooperative battle" between 1928 and 1935, in the terms of a juris doctor (Durand, 1936: 109-138). The agricultural and trade unionist specialist, Michel Augé-Laribé stated clearly on this matter: "The progress of this cooperative movement in agriculture is however slowed down by the hostility of the traders and by the bullying of the Ministry of Finance. This is where we see that successive governments have not had an agricultural policy. While the Ministry of Agriculture grants cooperatives based on the advice of rural engineers and advances by the Crédit Agricole (it is indeed the only practical interest that farmers can find to unite in cooperatives and they pay for it with restrictions on their freedom that no trader would accept), the Ministry of Finance does everything it can to prevent agricultural cooperatives from operating by claiming taxes that they are not legally entitled to and imposing fines on them that they could never pay." (Augé-Laribé, 1935: 1042).

In 1928, the debates on the budget initiated a government promise toward agricultural cooperation guaranteeing "a fiscal status intended to resolve a series of irritating questions and to put an end to the arbitrary practices of administration and jurisprudence," as one cooperative member put it (Nast, 1931: 3). The AGPB complained about this situation: "The tax administration does not understand the role of agricultural cooperatives. It sees in them only an immediate diminution of revenue without considering the development of agricultural production, and thus the general enrichment of the country, which is the consequence, proven by facts, of the development of the agricultural cooperative organization." (AGPB, 1929).

A commission was created in February 1929 to prepare a bill on the tax status of agricultural cooperatives (Durand, 1936: 111). But tensions between farmers, traders and taxation were compounded by the sluggishness of the parliament. A bill was proposed on June 26, 1930 but it did not satisfy the farmers… Proposals and a new bill then followed…but the end of the legislature at the beginning of 1932 left the text abandoned. During these years, press campaigns were carried out against agricultural cooperatives, for example, by *Le Matin* in 1933, which stated that "it wants fiscal equality and that those cooperatives, the majority of which are used to subsidize the parties of the extreme left, are subject to common fiscal law." (Noly, 1938: 39).

Another testimony of these tensions was given in a report by Pierre Lombrez entitled "Competition against free trade by agricultural cooperatives" presented at the congress of the French Federation of Grain Trade Unions in 1934. The attack was violent and primarily based on a comparison between different taxes that were paid. The conclusion was clear: "Farmers, on the whole, are paid by the state because of their profession, in the form of premiums, subsidies, etc. more than they give back. It is trade, in spite of the fact that it is overburdened with taxes, that subsidizes agriculture." The result was a demand that the government "limit the development of agricultural cooperatives that would cause the disappearance of trade." (Lombrez, 1934). The Secretary General of the Federation sent his report to the President of the Chamber of Commerce asking him to transform these wishes into deliberations and then transmit them on to the public authorities (Guignard, 1934).

But the reality was sometimes less simple: "The situation which resulted in the existence in many departments of pseudo-cooperatives created and directed by traders is extremely detrimental to the healthy and disinterested cooperative movement. The Committee drew the Minister's attention to this situation and requested him to strictly apply the terms of reference for cooperatives, which forbade them to be managed by grain traders, and that he would draw inspiration for his decisions from the opinions issued by the agricultural groups of the Departments, in particular by the Chambers of Agriculture." (*Du blé au pain*, 1934: 77) A local example in the Department of the Drôme, also opened the door to tensions and divisions within the cooperative world. The historian Martin Baptiste rightly notes: "Beyond the ideological oppositions, the local level can serve as a privileged observatory for the fierce competition that antagonistic cooperatives are engaged in on the same territory." (Baptiste, 2012: 168)

In March 1935, a High Council for Agricultural Cooperation was set up (Durand, 1936: 137). This new institution was preparing a project which finally culminated in the decree-law on August 8, 1935. More than a mere fiscal statute, this text was important for the regulation of agricultural cooperatives. Although some actors remained frustrated (Cramois, Labbé, 1937; Apchié, 1939), it confirmed the importance of these agricultural cooperatives for the organization of French agriculture more broadly.

II. The AGPB and the ambition to store crops

The AGPB developed in the mid-1920s as an alternative to the old forms of agricultural unionism (Chatriot, 2016a). The association was at the forefront of the fight against millers, traders and consumers. In 1930, the AGPB committed itself to the issue of crop financing: "The rational organization of the wheat market is now more than ever on the agenda. The alternation of the overwhelming harvest of 1929 and the deficit harvest of 1930 once again made it clear to producers how complex the problems of storage, conservation, financing and the staggered sale of wheat are and that they must be resolved." (AGPB, Office central du crédit agricole, 1930: 1). The AGPB encouraged cooperatives to take advantage of these new opportunities: "The General Association of Wheat Producers had always stated in principle that rational storage for the regularization of sales should be done *by the producers and for the producers*. Indeed, it would be of no interest to them if their buyers, during a period of massive supply and price collapse, could amass large quantities at low prices and then benefit from storing premiums and all eventual increases in value. This would be to attack the problem backwards and multiply the causes of speculative fluctuations which it is precisely necessary to make disappear. For this reason, the agricultural administration has the application of its special formula of 'storage markets and staggered sales' reserved for agricultural associations." (AGPB, Office central du crédit agricole, 1930: 17).

In this brochure, the AGPB emphasized the "future scope of the storage and maintenance premium system": "what we wanted and what we will get if the agricultural associations recognize their responsibility is *the beginning of a rational policy of market organization*. Everyone agrees that the foundation of this organization should be *the regular staggering of supply*. In the absence of a rational organization of the sale of wheat, producers, regardless of the legislative measures taken to help and protect them, will never be able to defend themselves; because they will not be able to take advantage of the measures in question. Their situation may be improved temporarily; but sooner or later, as a result of their dispersion, and their lack of cohesion, it will be their buyers, intermediaries and processors who will become the real beneficiaries; and producers will plunge once again." (AGPB, Office central du crédit agricole, 1930: 19) There was therefore one logical conclusion: "Past lessons thus already made it possible to affirm that there is no solution to the problem of financing the wheat market except on collective grounds. In this respect, the last crisis will have had the fortunate result of considerably strengthening the feeling of common interests among all the producers who are equally affected [...] The stored wheat becomes an instrument of credit." (AGPB, Office central du crédit agricole, 1930: 27)

This point was taken up again in the same direction by a new brochure in 1932: "The purpose of this study is to draw the attention of agricultural groups to the value of the storage markets; to encourage them not to hesitate before the necessary effort which will make it possible to orient definitively the policy of organizing the wheat market." (AGPB, UNCAVTB, 1932: 1).

The wheat cooperatives were privileged interlocutors in the processes of financing harvests, especially when it was a question of paying for storage in order not to impact the prices (Bourdin, 1937: 35-43; Alimanestianu, 1935). This storage was encouraged on the basis of the law of April 30, 1930 and codified through publication in the *Journal Officiel* with a list of successive specifications (JO, 1932: 6690-6693). In its first article, the law plans that the Minister for Agriculture is authorized, within the limits of a 30 million franc credit, to commit the necessary expenses to maintain a stock of safety of wheat and flours intended to assure the food supply of the population. It was not only a question of financing the carry-over and storage of grain but also the possible construction of state silos. A report by the Banque de France on this question stated: "When it is granted in France, the state's participation in the execution of these enterprises comes in the form of subsidies with lost funds of up to 33% of expenditures. These sums are taken from the credits made available to the rural engineers, which also intervened to provide technical assistance." (Picquet, 1934: 27).

III. How to finance storage?

The question of financing agriculture was often associated with two elements: the progressive development of agricultural credit (Gueslin, 1978; Gueslin, 1984) and the challenge of modernizing the world of French agriculture. To these questions must be added a more precise interrogation of the financing of cereal crops. Storage and the conditions that made it possible were indeed decisive in avoiding massive sell-offs that could on occasion lead to the collapse of prices. For wheat growers, the issue was crucial and they recalled regularly that "the problem of financing remains the key to organizing the wheat market." (AGPB, UNCAVTB, 1932: 54).

The agricultural warrant established by successive laws at the turn of the twentieth century was intended to be a solution to this problem, but soon proved to be an inadequate instrument (Baubeau, 2011; Gueslin, 1978: 182-193, 288-296). A document internal to the Banque de France summarized the situation: "The power given to farmers by the legislation of 1906 to allocate the movable products of their farms as guarantees to their loans, either by retaining custody or entrusting the deposit to a third party, hardly improved their situation; for, establishing the sole practical necessity of the constitution of a pledge, without dispossession imposed by the absence of stores or silos suitable for receiving the harvested crops, reducing the value of the security granted to the creditors, singularly restricted the scope of the new provisions." (Picquet, 1934: 16).

As noted by the historian André Gueslin, in the early 1930s agricultural credit officials were aware of this issue and explained in an internal report that "there is indeed a national interest in a country such as ours, where the cultivation of wheat plays a predominant role, in avoiding the hasty sales of farmers in need of advances, leading to an unjustified fall in prices and to speculation." (Report to the board of directors at the plenary commission of November 20th, 1932, quoted in Gueslin, 1984: 435). But the importance of these financing issues concerned different institutional actors: the Crédit Agricole as well as the Banque de France and the Treasury within the Finance Ministry.

In the summer of 1930, Minister of Agriculture Fernand David, with the support of the AGPB, sought the support of the Banque de France. At a meeting, the representative of the bank was reticent because with "the bank's assistance to a particular branch of national activity, such a commitment would constitute a precedent which would not fail to be recalled by agricultural, commercial or industrial sectors." The minister insisted, however, and concluded the interview by stating that "the Government and the world of agriculture would not understand if the Banque de France, whose interest is in harmony with France itself, refused to make an effort favoring national agriculture, which was experiencing such trying times." (ABF, 1069199520 1). The following year, the same debates resumed and the archives of the Banque de France revealed the many meetings requested by André Tardieu in order to move forward on this case. An agreement was reached between the bank and the credit institutions with a view to removing obstacles to the circulation of securities from cooperatives and agricultural unions.

An act of April 30, 1930 authorized the Minister of Agriculture "to incur the expenses necessary to maintain a stock of grain and flour security intended to ensure the food supply of the population" and this "within the limits of a credit of 30 million francs." A decree of May 31, 1930 supplemented the law's provisions by making use of military stewardship to guarantee past contracts concerning stocks. A decree of September 6, 1930 adapted storage to the results of the harvest. One jurist noted: "the great obstacle to such a procedure is obviously the limit of the financial possibilities of the nations that practice it." (Ménasseyre, 1934: 55).

A new decree of October 12, 1932 extended the domain of the law of April 30, 1930 and provided for storage with the producer himself. In a statement issued on October 6, the Minister of Agriculture stated: "It had become necessary to facilitate the market through a voluntarist measure that would be effective immediately. [...] It appeared that the most rational and least costly way to organize this postponement [of wheat sales] was to keep the wheat where it is, that is to say, with the producer himself." But as the jurist who quoted this circular noted: "the results were not achieved. As a whole, it can be said that this decree did not interest the country. Indeed, if it introduced a premium of 10 francs per quintal, it did not guarantee any basic selling price for the release of blocked wheat. Now, as the belief in decline was general, most farmers preferred, as always on such occasions, to limit their loss, by selling immediately." (Sirol, 1934: 286).

In November 1932, the Director General of the Deposit and Consignment Office wrote to the Minister of Finance stating that his institution agreed to make available to the Treasury a further advance of 300 million to facilitate the financing of the 1932 cereal harvest. But he pointed out that this advance "could have the consequence of reducing the sums likely to be advanced by the Treasury for the execution of the various programs of general interest and in particular for those of low-cost housing." (CAEF, B-0023039/2).

In response to a request from the Ministry of Agriculture, a note was prepared within the Ministry of Finance offering a rather severe account of the situation. Agriculture "envisages two solutions: a direct assistance from the treasury, or an intervention by the Banque de France. But in fact, it goes without saying that only this second solution may be examined, even if it cannot be actually pursued, considering that the situation of the treasury is such that it is absolutely impossible to subtract from these resources – or lack of resources – any amount whatsoever". As regards the intervention of the Banque de France, the note by the Department of Agriculture merely stated that "initially in any case, it does not seem impossible to reconcile the statutory rules of that institution with regard to a rediscount rate, with the financing of the necessary operation." On the contrary, there is an absolute incompatibility between the proposed measures and the traditional activity of the Institution of issuance." (CAEF, B-0023039/2).

The note goes on to explain that the Banque de France does not commit itself to medium-term credits. It then recalled the existence of warrants and comments: "it is clear that agriculture has had little recourse to the facilities at its disposal." The Minister of Finance then affirmed this perspective to his colleague and concluded with the "very serious reservations of principle that I have already made to you concerning the financing of the grain harvest, especially considering that we have prepared a more favorable and more stable price regime for the wheat farmers than that governing other crops, and that the draft also contains no provisions limiting the area planted. There is no doubt that the treasury is thus exposed to considerable risks if the next crop is still superabundant" (CAEF, B-0023039/2). The Act of January 26, 1933 finally provided for the financing of the 1932 harvest by the National Agricultural Credit Fund for an advance of up to 300 million for a maximum of one year. The funds were borrowed little by little by the Treasury and Deposit Office ("Caisse des depots et consignations"). A note from the early autumn of 1933 indicates that only 60 million had been mobilized for this purpose (CAEF, B-0000902/2).

The application of the law of July 10, 1933, which introduced the minimum price in terms of crop financing, was also quite complex. Article 24 provided for the creation of funds "in Treasury accounts" to capitalize on the proceeds of the different taxes envisaged by the law. Article 26 introduced a second account as well, also opened within the Treasury called a "special account," charged with collecting the proceeds of loans issued by the National Agricultural Credit Fund, which would have been necessary if taxes did not finance the measures. A memorandum for the Minister of Finance dated September 20, 1933, detailed the issues involved in the funding and contained a realist and somewhat worrisome reflection stressing that resources were limited to the milling tax alone. The text provided details on the loan with a ten-year amortization but above all stressed that "the net proceeds of this issue are not sufficient to enable the special account of Article 26 to maintain throughout the year 1934 an action equivalent to the one currently underway." (CAEF, B-0000902/2).

The role of the Banque de France was often questioned by farmers or their representatives. Thus in September 1933, a senator of the Somme, Edmond Cavillon, wrote to the President: "the Banque de France has a role to play in this matter. This role would consist in discounting the paper bearing three signatures and guaranteed by the very product that is deposited. The Banque de France would thus have the advantage of increasing its portfolio of discounted securities without the least amount of risk" (CAEF, B-0000902/2). In the same vein, the Minister of Agriculture wrote to his colleague in the Finance Ministry in September 1934 asking him to point out to the Governor of the Banque de France "how important it would be for the defense of the wheat market to intervene as actively as possible through the institution of issuance to facilitate the financing of this market. But the Banque de France remained very attentive to its prerogatives" (CAEF, B-0000902/2). In the parliamentary debate of December 1934, when the Socialist Vincent Auriol put forth an amendment, the bank immediately prepared a reply with the firm conclusion: "Such a transaction cannot be demanded of the Banque de France because it is contrary to the provisions and legal requirements of the laws and statutes that regulate the issuance of notes." (ABF, 1069199520 1) In August 1935, the Banque de France granted the government more money to finance the harvest in the context of the new collapse in prices. The national daily press treated the subject extensively.

In his study on agricultural credit, André Gueslin takes stock of these various forms of financing. He points out that the loans for agricultural credit were subscribed without difficulty (200 million francs on November 11, 1933, a new equivalent installment on August 28 1934, before two successive installments of one billion each in 1935) (Gueslin, 1984: 437-438). He proposed financial figures for the agricultural credit of the wheat crop of 105 million francs for 1931, 212 for 1932, 588 for 1933, 521 for 1934, and 420 for 1935 (Gueslin, 1984: 439). He considered that overall "the financial effort is insufficient." (Gueslin, 1984: 442). Some actors were more enthusiastic at the time, but an overall evaluation remains difficult (Daudé-Bancel, 1934). A note from the Ministry of Finance in September 1936 summarized the many measures which had been taken, in particular by making special credits available to the National Agricultural Credit Fund to enable it to realize the discounting of the effects created by wheat cooperatives (CAEF, B-0000902/2; Auboyneau, 1938).

IV. The creation of the Wheat Office: encouraging storage

Without returning in detail to the political adventures of the establishment of a National Interprofessional Board of Wheat in the summer of 1936 by the Popular Front government, during the parliamentary debates the issue of the organization of the market gave rise to many controversies (Chatriot, 2016b: 297-477). The Senate altered a specific point within the government's project by leaving room for grain traders in a system where, for the most part, a large place was given to the organizations of storage certified at the administrative level of the department.

The Chamber of Deputies had supported the project of the Minister of Agriculture George Monnet. During the second debate in the National Assembly, Renaud Jean, the President of the Agricultural Commission openly opposed the Senate's arbitration on the role of traders: "We believe that the question of the office must now be explored. If, as the Chamber desires, the traders are subordinate to cooperatives, the Office can succeed. If they are placed on an equal footing with cooperatives, or if they may be substituted for cooperatives [...] the office is doomed to failure" (JO, 1936b: 2271). Monnet then similarly stated: "the law of the minimum price of 1933 has sunk, precisely because traders have not respected the minimum price." (JO, 1936b: 2271).

But the Senate's offensive was victorious on this point. Moreover, it was accompanied by intense lobbying on the part of trade organizations and chambers of commerce. The senator from the Vienne, former Minister of Agriculture and member of a family of grain traders, Victor Boret defended them: "It is not because a few have committed mistakes that an entire corporation should be held responsible for a few individual failures [...] Traders of yesterday or small traders today, have always and everywhere been the best and most valuable auxiliaries of farmers and often their bankers." (JO, 1936a: 749).

Article 6 of the law that finally passed was the one that had been under extensive debate concerning the role of the traders. It was very detailed and clearly stated the protected role of the traders: "Without being able to claim the tax benefits and subsidies granted to wheat cooperatives, French patented grain traders – excluding millers and bakers – will be able to buy, store and deliver wheat under the same conditions and prices as the co-operatives as long as they have made a prior declaration to the departmental committee and remain under its control." (JO, 1936c: 8867).

The price of wheat constituted a different matter once the harvest could be stored more easily, at least partially. This point was also an element of differentiation between producers as noted by an analyst of agricultural issues in 1937: "storage is one of the cornerstones of the system. Large industrialists had accumulated extensive reserves when the prices were low, which allowed them to more effectively dominate the market. In the case of wheat, for example, the same manoeuver occurred every year: the release of part of the stock allows the mill to force lower prices during the harvest; a false campaign, cleverly maintained by the representatives of the trust, influences the market through the threat of further, more important drops; the small peasants who have no information other than that supplied by newspapers who work for large millers and importers, rush to sell their crops and thus contribute to the degradation of prices." (Braibant, 1937: 14).

Financing the harvest was therefore, at the same time, one of the great successes of the Office, as it finally offered price stability for producers and, at the same time, one of its Achilles' heels in the context of an abundant harvest.

Concerning the action of the cooperatives, the first general report on the action of the Office established that they ensured "the sale or use of 84.4% of the wheat sold during the 1936-1937 season. This is sufficient to express the importance of the action of these groups, on which the legislation had rightly intended to base the new organization" (Rapport, 1939: 866). In addition, cooperatives were encouraged to build storage centers and the office played a role in this scheme: "In order to coordinate these cooperatives' efforts, the Ministry of Agriculture proceeded to elaborate programs at the administrative scale of the department to build silos and wheat storage facilities. These programs, established by the chief engineers of rural engineering and the directors of the agricultural services, and submitted to the departmental committees for cereals, were then examined by a committee on silos set up within the Office. The Commission's proposals, submitted to the

Administrative Committee of the Office, constituted, after adoption, the definitive program of amenities. Outside the buildings provided for under this program, no new construction may be subsidized by the Ministry of Agriculture, a long-term loan for agricultural credit, or special Cooperatives having to bear depreciation charges on the capital invested in the construction or acquisition of their storage buildings." (Rapport, 1939: 869)

At the local level, and controlled by the departmental committees, the main role was that of the storage agencies, as emphasized in a report that stated: "The functioning of the wheat board is essentially based on the activity of the storage agencies: wheat co-operatives and grain traders registered in the departmental businesses" (Rapport, 1939: 851). At the time, a jurist noted this element by recalling the words of a parliamentarian: "Cooperatives have a very important task and although they do not have the character of bodies governed by public law, they constituted, as Senator Chauveau pointed out, 'the infrastructure of the agency.'" (Normand, 1938: 166). Conservative agricultural organizations were becoming increasingly aware of the Agency's interest in this context. By studying peasants in Britanny, Suzanne Berger has shown this fact very well: "The Office Central [of Landerneau], a very conservative association] protested the state role in price-fixing, but profited from the fact that the law required that all farmers stock their wheat in order to create a Coopérative du Blé which would provide storage facilities. [...] And the Office du Blé, creature of a Left government that Landerneau detested and feared, in fact gave the Office Central a near-monopoly of the wheat trade in Finistère." (Berger, 1972: 118).

If France was very concerned by the storage of wheat during 1930s it is not the only country in this case. The question was for example of importance in fascist Italy (Vaqueiro Pineiro, 2012). The question of storage is indeed at the same time at the heart of the regulation of the prices as condition to avoid too big fluctuations and too large price drops. But it is also central for certain authoritarian political regimes which dreamt about economic autarky and did not want to relive the shortages known during and at the end of World War I (Fernandez-Prieto, Pan-Montojo, Cabo, 2014).

In the French case, the situation was complicated by the transformations of the agricultural sector. The development of cooperatives (but which did not obey all the same logic), the birth of a trade unionism specialized for the cereal growers and the always delicate question of the financing accompanied political hesitations in choices to be made to regulate the market.

In the years that followed, the shortages due to the war and the Occupation reinforced the question of storage and the role of the Wheat Office, which became the unavoidable institution of supply management. Beyond its transformations, the Wheat Office, which became the Cereal Office, retained in the 1950s a leading role in the modernization of the sector. Professional organizations, the role of national financial structures, and technical changes were intertwined to make storage one of the key points of agricultural policies and regulation adopted in France during the 1930s. After initial difficulties, the Office of 1936 seems to have provided some stability. But multiple points merit further inquiry: little is known about the role of rural engineers in the construction of silos, the financial arrangements of cooperatives are not always clear even though they reveal changes in the professions, and the attitude of financial actors – the Banque de France and especially the Credit Agricole – needs further examination.

Bibliography

ABF (Archives de la Banque de France), 1069199520 1, Crédit agricole: concours de la Banque à l'agriculture: mobilisation du stockage du blé, 1930-1932, le marché du blé 1932-1934.

Alimanestianu, C. C. (1935) *Le Crédit Agricole dans ses rapports avec la Coopération*, Paris.

Apchié, M. (1939) 'Evolution récente de la coopération agricole en France', *Revue internationale d'agriculture*, pp. 429-440.

AGPB (Association générale des producteurs de blé) (1929) 'Le régime fiscal des coopératives agricoles de meunerie', *Bulletin de documentation*, 3 janvier.

AGPB, Office central du crédit agricole (1930) *La vente rationnelle et le financement de la récolte de blé*, Paris.

AGPB, UNCAVTB (Union nationale des coopératives agricoles de vente et de transformation du blé) (1932) *L'organisation du stockage et le financement de la récolte de blé*, Paris.

Auboyneau, J. (1938) *L'organisation du crédit à l'agriculture*, rapport au Conseil national économique, Melun.

Augé-Laribé, M. (1935) 'Nos agriculteurs devant la crise', *La Revue des Vivants*, juillet, pp. 1038-1046.

Baptiste, M. (2012) 'Vers l'Office national interprofessionnel du blé: le projet de la Fédération drômoise des coopératives céréalières (1935-1936)', Chatriot, A., Leblanc, E. and Lynch, E. (eds), *Organiser les marchés agricoles. Le temps des fondateurs, des années 1930 aux années 1950*, Paris, pp. 165-181.

Baubeau, P. (2011) 'Le warrant agricole (1880-1914): objet interstitiel ou bricolage juridique?', Levratto, N. and Stanziani, A. (eds), *Le capitalisme au futur antérieur. Crédit et spéculation en France, fin XVIII*e *- début XX*e *siècles*, Bruxelles, pp. 171-198.

Berger, S. (1972) *Peasants against Politics. Rural Organization in Brittany 1911-1967*, Cambridge, MA.

Bourdin, F. (1937) *Le Crédit agricole et la crise*, Paris.

Braibant, M. (1937) *La tragédie paysanne*, Paris.

Brasart, C. (1931) 'La politique du blé', rapport présenté devant le Conseil national économique, *Journal officiel de la République française, Annexes administratives*, 28 juillet.

Burgaud, J. (1932) 'La vente coopérative des céréales', *Du blé au pain*, n°2, mai-juin, pp. 20-24.

CAEF (Centre des archives économiques et financières), B-0000902/1 Direction du mouvement général des fonds: crédit agricole, marché du blé 1933-1937.

CAEF, B-0000902/2, Direction du mouvement général des fonds: crédit agricole, marché du blé 1929-1942.

Chatriot, A. (2016) 'Le rôle des organisations agricoles françaises dans la politique économique au XXe siècle. L'exemple de l'AGPB (1924-1940)', Fraboulet, D., Margairaz, M. and Vernus P. (eds), *Réguler l'économie. L'apport des organisations patronales. Europe XIX*e*-XX*e *siècles*, Rennes, pp. 281-291.

Chatriot, A. (2016) *La politique du blé. Crises et régulations d'un marché dans la France de l'entre-deux-guerres*, Paris.

Cramois, A. and Labbé, R. (1937) *Le mouvement coopératif agricole et ses possibilités de développement*, Melun.

Daudé-Bancel, A. (1934) 'Les crédits agricoles en France à court terme, à moyen terme et à long terme', *Revue des études coopératives*, n° 53, octobre-décembre, pp. 47-59.

Delcasse d'Huc de Monsegou, J. (1933) *Les répartitions des denrées alimentaires, rapport présenté au Conseil national économique*, Paris.

Dorel-Feré, G. (ed.) (2014) *Les silos, un patrimoine à inventer (colloques, 2011)*, Chambéry.

Du blé au pain, n°5, septembre-octobre 1934, p. 77.

Du Fou, A. (1930) 'La conservation des grains et le financement de la récolte française', "Le Blé", *L'Europe nouvelle*, n° 666, 15 novembre, pp. 1671-1674.

Durand, A. (1936) *Le statut juridique et fiscal des coopératives agricoles de production, de transformation et de vente*, Paris.

Fernagut, B. (1932) *Le redressement agricole par l'association professionnelle. L'exemple des producteurs de blé*, Paris.

Fernandez-Prieto, L., Pan-Montojo, J. and Cabo, M. (eds) (2014) *Agriculture in the Age of Fascism. Authoritarian Technocracy and Rural Modernization, 1922-1945*, Rural History in Europe: 13, Turnhout.

Gibon, J. de (1933) 'Les coopératives de stockage et de vente de blé', *L'Agriculture nouvelle*, 13 mai, pp. 291-292.

Gueslin, A. (1978) *Les origines du crédit agricole (1840-1914)*, Nancy.

Gueslin, A. (1984) *Histoire des crédits agricoles*, 2 vol., Paris.

Guignard, A. 'Lettre du 17 mai 1934 au président de la chambre de commerce', Archives départementales de Paris, Chambre de commerce et d'industrie de Paris, 2ETP/2/2/13 13.

Hirschfeld, A. (1957) *La coopération agricole en France*, Paris.

JO, *Journal officiel de la République française, Lois et décrets*, 21 juin 1932.

JO, *Journal officiel de la République française, Débats parlementaires, Sénat*, séance du 21 juillet 1936.

JO, *Journal officiel de la République française, Débats parlementaires, Chambre des députés*, séance du 30 juillet 1936.

JO, *Journal officiel de la République française, Lois et décrets*, 18 août 1936, pp. 8866-8871.

Lefebvre, G. (1926) *Etude de la coopération agricole dans le département de l'Eure, coopératives d'Evreux et du Neubourg*, Paris.

Lombrez, P. 'Rapport du 25 avril 1934', Archives départementales de Paris, Chambre de commerce et d'industrie de Paris, 2ETP/2/2/13 13.

Loriette, N. (2008) *Les édifices de stockage des céréales dans les grands départements céréaliers français: 1929-1969*, thèse de doctorat d'histoire de l'art, sous la direction de J.-Y. Andrieux, Université de Rennes 2.

Ménasseyre, R. (1934) *Politique du blé. La Loi du 10 Juillet 1933 et son Application*, Toul.

Mignemi, N. (2017) *Coopératives et mondes agricoles. France et Italie (1880-1950)*, Rennes.

Nast, A. (1931) *Les Coopératives agricoles devant l'impôt. A propos d'une brochure de M. Compeyrot*, Paris.

Noly, P.-J. (1938) *Le rôle des coopératives agricoles des producteurs de blé*, Paris.

Normand, A. (1938) *Une expérience d'économie dirigée en agriculture: l'Office du blé*, Grenoble.

Picquet, J. (1934) 'La nouvelle organisation financière du marché français du blé', thèse de l'inspection des Finances, Archives de la Banque de France (ABF), 1000198801 17.

Rapport sur le fonctionnement de l'Office national interprofessionnel du blé pendant la campagne 1936-1937, Journal officiel de la République française, Annexes administratives, 4 juillet 1939, pp. 849-875.

Seulesco, G. (1931) *Coopératives et ententes agricoles pour la vente du blé*, Paris.

Sirol, J. (1934) *Les problèmes français du blé*, Paris.

Vaqueiro Pineiro, M. (2012) 'Wheat-storage in Fascist Italy: evolution and policies', Lorenzetti, L., Barbot, M. and Mocarelli, L. (eds), *Property rights and their violations. Expropriations and confiscations, 16th-20th century, La propriété violée. Expropriations et confiscations, XVIe-XXe siècles*, Bern, pp. 263-280.